Published under the auspices of

The African Studies Center
University of California, Los Angeles
and of the
Center for International and Strategic Affairs (CISA)
University of California, Los Angeles

A list of other publications of the African Studies Center
and the Center for International and Strategic Affairs
appears at the back of this book.

African Crisis Areas and U.S. Foreign Policy

Map 1.   African Crisis Areas

African Crisis Areas and U.S. Foreign Policy

EDITED BY

Gerald J. Bender
James S. Coleman
Richard L. Sklar

UNIVERSITY OF CALIFORNIA PRESS

Berkeley · Los Angeles · London

University of California Press
Berkeley and Los Angeles, California

University of California Press, Ltd.
London, England

© 1985 by
The Regents of the University of California

Printed in the United States of America

1 2 3 4 5 6 7 8 9

Library of Congress Cataloguing-in-Publication Data
Main entry under title:

African crisis areas and U.S. foreign policy.

  Bibliography: p.
  Includes index.
    1. Africa—Foreign relations—United States—Ad-
dresses, essays, lectures.   2. United States—
Foreign relations—Africa—Addresses, essays, lectures.
3. Africa—Foreign relations—1960–   —Addresses,
essays, lectures.   4. Africa—Politics and governments—1960–   —Addresses, essays, lectures.
5. Africa—Economic conditions—1960–   —Addresses, essays, lectures.   I. Bender, Gerald J.
II. Coleman, James Smoot.   III. Sklar, Richard L.
DT38.7.A39   1986   327.7306   85-8579
ISBN 0-520-05548-9 (alk. paper)

Dedicated to
Nthato Motlana
and
Rupert Emerson

Contents

CONTENTS

List of Maps and Tables

Preface

The critical analysis of crisis areas in Africa has a compelling rationale for students of international relations. Bipolarity in the global balance of power, involving nuclear stalemate and mutual deterrence, tends to reduce the probability that general war will result from conflicts between the industrial powers themselves. However, in the Third World, conflicts between states often result in warfare. Inevitably, such conflicts engage the partisan interests of strategic planners in the Soviet Union and the United States, and the superpowers may become deeply committed to their embattled clients, as in the Horn of Africa; or each superpower may seek to enhance its own influence and to limit the influence of its rival, as in southern Africa. Such confrontations, or crises, inevitably serve to polarize thought, discussion, and policy perspectives into so-called globalist and regionalist camps.

Critics of American foreign policy toward Africa (and other Third World regions) often allege that its formulation is far too powerfully influenced by official American perceptions (and misperceptions) of Soviet intentions and capabilities. The disposition to subordinate American policies to narrowly defined imperatives of anticommunism and anti-Sovietism, they argue, betrays an insensitivity to the discrepancy between African and American priorities, and this distorts American foreign policy to the long-term disadvantage of the United States. Their critique is amply documented in this volume, which also does justice, the editors believe, to the counterarguments and concerns of American strategic planners of globalist persuasion, who stress the primacy of the bipolar East-West dimension. By presenting the so-called Africanist case fully and objectively, but without prejudice to the reasonable claims of strategic thinkers, this volume attempts to bridge the gap between scholarship and policy that occasions so much distress today.

Many of the papers in this volume were first prepared for a conference sponsored by the African Studies Center and the Center for International and

Strategic Affairs at the University of California, Los Angeles. This book has been dedicated to Dr. Nthato Motlana, a citizen of the Republic of South Africa, who unfortunately could not attend the conference because he was denied a passport by the government of the Republic of South Africa; and to Professor Rupert Emerson—teacher, friend, exemplar.

The editors wish to thank Professor Michael D. Intriligator, Director of the Center for International and Strategic Affairs, and Professor Michael F. Lofchie, Director of the African Studies Center, for their encouragement and support. A special word of appreciation is due to Ms. Gerri Page for her resourceful management of the conference. This project could not have been undertaken or completed without external support; the editors are especially grateful to the Ford Foundation and to the University of California Institute of Global Conflict and Cooperation for timely and generous grants.

The manuscript was prepared for publication by members of the staff of the UCLA Office of International Studies and Overseas Programs. The editors are especially grateful to Ms. Nona Arguelles for typing the manuscript and to Ms. Monica Dunahee for preparing the maps.

An acknowledgment cannot do justice to the contribution of Ms. Norma Farquhar, who edited all of the papers, arranged meetings of the editors, and served as liaison with the University of California Press. Her editorial and literary skills, complemented by her wise judgments, perseverance, and impeccable tact, have been indispensable to seeing this book through to publication.

On the 20th of April, 1985, less than a month after Coleman, Sklar, and Bender had given the University of California Press the final manuscript of this book, James Smoot Coleman died of a sudden heart attack. His co-editors wish to express their admiration and respect for a superb scholar and teacher whose impact on the fields of Africana and political science will be permanent. We were deeply influenced by his classic study *Nigeria: Background to Nationalism* early in our respective careers as students of African politics. Sklar followed him in Nigerian studies; Bender turned to the study of Portuguese-speaking Africa at his suggestion.

Jim taught most effectively by asking pertinent questions. That approach informed the conference from which this book resulted. Good questions, he believed, are more important than good answers. Jim had a rare ability to comfortably shift his relationship with former students from that of professor/teacher to that of colleague/friend. He was an instinctive egalitarian: if his students or colleagues felt themselves to be on a lesser plane, it was never because of anything Jim said or did but because they could not help but hold him in awe. Over the years we have benefited so much from him that we can only hope that we managed to return a modicum of what we gained. We are proud to have our names appear with his as co-editors of this, his last, book.

G. J. B., R. L. S.

Introduction

JAMES S. COLEMAN and RICHARD L. SKLAR

AFRICAN CRISIS AREAS

The Concept of Crisis

The term *crisis* is laden with so many meanings and has such varied usages, both in common parlance and in a wide spectrum of disciplines ranging from medicine and psychology to the social sciences, that the need for clarity of communication might well rule it out as an organizing rubric for a collective effort such as ours. Even in the specialized field of international relations, several different competing conceptions are current (e.g., Bell 1971; Brecher 1980; George 1983; Hermann 1969 and 1972; Holsti 1979; McClelland 1961; Robinson 1968 and 1972; Snyder 1976; and Snyder and Diesing 1977). It is, as Robinson (1968, 510) notes, "a lay term in search of a scholarly meaning." Its connotative richness, however, endows it with an enduring utility; if the word did not exist, it would have to be invented. But it must be given an explicit conceptualization for the immediate purpose at hand.

Our special concept of crisis as applied to contemporary Africa refers to a situation of acute tension and/or armed conflict generated and precipitated by local indigenous factors, interacting with external influences, which threaten to engage, or actually have engaged, the involvement of the United States and the Soviet Union either directly, or indirectly through their surrogates. A *crisis area* is a geographical area of the continent, either within one or among two or more states, which is in these terms either crisis-prone or the actual locus of an existent crisis. The crux of the concept is caught by Gorman (1981, 5) in his phrase "the internationalization of a local hot spot." This narrower stipulation of meaning excludes, for example, both the Nigerian civil war (1966–69) and the Uganda-Tanzanian border war of 1978. However, given our comparative concern with the conditions under which local conflicts escalate and become internationalized, those that escape a cold war engagement are theoretically as interesting as those which do not.

1

The disciplined focus upon political crisis, domestic or international, has a persuasive rationale. Three aspects warrant special mention: their centrality as clarifying revealers of a holistic perspective, their potential for theory building in international relations, and their sometimes positive consequences. Numerous scholars of differing disciplines and persuasions have stressed the very special quality of crises as holistic revealers. Snyder and Diesing (1977, 3–4) argued, for example, that:

> Lying as they do at the nexus between peace and war, crises reveal most clearly and intensely the distinguishing characteristics of international politics. . . . In a crisis the expectation [of potential war] is dramatically elevated and its behavioral effects stand starkly revealed. Related core elements, such as power configurations, interests, images, and alignments tend to be more sharply clarified, to be activated and focused on a single well-defined issue. . . . A crisis distills many of the elements that make up the essence of politics in the international system. It is a "moment of truth" when the latent product of all these central elements becomes manifest in decision and action.

A crisis focus enables the analyst to study the nexuses and interactions between the domestic and international political systems (Gorman 1981, 5), thus helping to bridge the bifurcation in the discipline between the comparativist and the international relations specialist. Verhaegen (1974, 190), well known for his intensive case studies of rebellions, stressed the special insight into the overall structure of society they revealed by studying them in their totality. For Balandier (1971, 484ff) and Ilunga (1965, 331ff), crises are moments of truth (*minutes de vérité*) or vantages (*champs privilégiés d'observation*) or revealers (*révélateurs*), the study of which enables the social scientist to achieve a comprehensive awareness and global perspective of total power configurations and the operative network of fundamental relationships. And, in a related vein, for Richard Nixon crises were "mountaintop experiences" in which he discovered "all the latent strengths he never knew he had" and often "performed at his best" (Holsti 1979, 99).

Scholars specializing in international crises have lamented the lack of cumulation of knowledge concerning crises and the consequential dearth of theorizing about them (Bell 1971, 4; George 1979, 43; Hermann 1969, 409; Holsti 1979, 100; Robinson 1972, 20–29; Rosenau 1968, 197ff). Many appear to share Waltz's (1975, 1) lament about the state of the subject: "Nothing seems to accumulate, not even criticism." As inherently unique and complex historical configurations, international crises have tended to be regarded as nonreplicative case histories properly the province of the diplomatic historian, and not of the generalizing or policy-oriented social scientist. During the past decade, however, the critics have led a major effort to introduce a more emphatically self-conscious theoretical orientation. As Snyder and Diesing (1977, 3) have argued, "progress toward a general theory of international politics will proceed fastest . . . by focusing empirical research initially on phenomena that lie at the center of the field. . . . crises admirably meet this criterion of centrality."

Two influences have converged to advance efforts aimed at a more pronounced theoretical orientation in international crisis analysis. One has been the increasingly manifest need imperatively expressed by academic specialists, as well as decision makers in this field, for more policy-relevant theory— or at least some more systematic extraction of "lessons learned" from past crisis experiences—for more effective crisis prevention and management (George 1983, 365–398). As Robert McNamara declared in the aftermath of the Cuban missile crisis: "There is no longer any such thing as strategy, only crisis management" (Bell 1971, 2).

The other development has been the growing persuasion among some social scientists that even when dealing only with unique cases the quest for theory—or at least for probabilistic generalizations—is feasible, minimally, under two conditions: (1) if the seemingly unique international crises are disaggregated into types and more systematically compared and analyzed as members of a class of phenomena (George 1979, 45), and (2) if explanations for such crises are sought and expressed in general-variable, rather than in idiosyncratic, terms (Eckstein 1975, 92ff; George 1979, 46–47). Given the underdeveloped state of comparative studies of the foreign policies and international relations of Africa in general, and of African crises in particular, there exists no reservoir of experience and data upon which the present volume can build to make a significant contribution to a deeper theoretical understanding of these phenomena. However, the studies contained in this volume do focus upon a defined "class" of phenomena—the cold war internationalization of local African conflicts—the collective juxtaposition and analysis of which we hope will contribute to the cumulation of insight upon which firmer generalizations can be developed in the future.

A third reason for focusing upon crises is, paradoxically, the need for a deeper and more abiding appreciation of their potential for exerting or having certain constructive or generally positive effects (Robinson 1972, 32–34). It is important to dispel the conventional but erroneous negative image of a crisis as something that is undesirable, dangerous, and fraught with destructive violence, if not disaster. In keeping with its Greek derivation, the term *crisis* connotes a decision or turning point, the outcome of which can be for the better or for the worse. To be sure, experience has shown that there are undeniably negative potentialities in international crises. The psychology of a crisis situation can trigger a *conflict spiral*, a dynamic of uncontrollable escalation in which "the first party misperceives the intent of the second party which then acts upon the misperception that further confirms the original misperception of the first party," finally culminating in violence (Robinson 1972, 32). Also, under the pressure of crisis situations, key decision makers are compelled to act on less information than usual, on "gut" feelings, value preferences, and behavioral dispositions, and on perceptions regarding the intentions and alternatives of adversaries that tend to be simplistic (Holsti 1979, 107–111). And because adversaries in crises are operating under similar limiting and distorting conditions, the predictability of their responses is markedly reduced. The exhilarating atmosphere of Nixon's mountaintop does not necessarily ensure greater prudence, restraint, or rationality.

Yet, as George (1983, 1) has pointed out, the word *crisis* in the Chinese language is composed of two characters meaning "threat" and "opportunity," and both of these dimensions were experienced by U.S. and Soviet leaders during the Cuban missile crisis, following which there was a manifest improvement in U.S.–Soviet relations. In industrial conciliation, the concept "crisis into settlement" underscores the "inevitable and positive functions of negotiation conflict" (Robinson 1972, 34–35). In psychoanalytic theories such as those of Erikson (1968, 63) a crisis can be a turning point even for worse, but "worse can ultimately lead to better" through the confluence of the constructive energies of the individual and society. Also, while unremitting crisis pressure may not be conducive to prudence or rationality, exposure to multiple crises can have a positive educative function: "participants gain experience in ways of coping with the environment and adversaries . . . [and] uncertainty is reduced. Thus, repeated exposure to acute crises may reduce the probabilities of an outbreak of general war" (Holsti 1979, 103).

If ideological dispositions allow, lessons can also be learned. George (1983, 9) observes that "if U.S. policy in Angola suffered because it lacked sensitivity to the local and regional political terrain, the United States learned its lesson there and was able to deal much more effectively with the . . . transition from white rule to the creation of Zimbabwe." Crises can, as well, be early warning signs of disaster, illuminating the location of the powder kegs and how they can be avoided. And, paradoxically, as Zartman (1983, 352–353) notes, "conflict resolution plays on perceptions of an intolerable situation, pointing out that things 'can't go on like this,'" thereby leaving open the possibility of preventive diplomacy bringing about a shift from a "winning mentality to a composing mentality on the part of both parties." Thus, while crises should obviously not be courted, if they inexorably emerge, the turning point need not always be for the worse.

Crises in Africa

The studies in this volume explore conflicts between and within African countries which have been internationalized to extra-African levels of involvement. Two main types of such conflict can be identified. The first type is deeply rooted in a country's national history and persists for a long period of time despite great variation in the identity and impact of external actors. The struggles in southern Africa and the Horn of Africa correspond to this type. A second type of conflict involving extra-African antagonists arises from local causes that are relatively evanescent and coincidental. Such causes, to be sure, are stern political realities; they sometimes entail poignant instances of human suffering, as in Uganda during recent years, or deadly political disputes, as in Chad. Yet the local issues which give rise to this type of international conflict do not involve tensions between non-African external powers and would probably subside within a short time were it not for the conflicting interests and policies of the latter. In such cases, external opportunism is the main threat to peace and security. In this symposium, examples of this type are represented by the divergent cases of Zaire, the Western Sahara, and Chad. Conflicts of this kind are chronic in a continent that is militarily vulnerable and splintered into more than fifty sovereign states.

The deep-seated conflicts in southern Africa and the Horn are consequences of imperial rule in those regions. In southern Africa, settlers of European origin acquired regional dominion by means of warfare, occupation, and treaty during the seventeenth, eighteenth, and nineteenth centuries. Ultimately, the British Empire in South Africa gave way to the present-day Republic of South Africa, founded upon principles of white supremacy and the equality of two official languages—Afrikaans and English. Until 1974, the white supremacist republic, with its formidable economic and military power, was ringed by a broad belt of buffer states under European or white settler control. Within that subcontinental system of states, resourceful nationalist insurgents managed to combat their oppressors, but the region as a whole was securely within the Western sphere of influence and Western hegemony was virtually uncontested by the communist powers.

This condition was suddenly transformed by the Portuguese revolution of 1974, itself a direct consequence of the burdens of empire and costs of war in Africa. Espousing Marxist-Leninist principles, the newly independent governments of Angola and Mozambique aligned themselves with the Soviet Union and its allies in world politics. In due course, the armed African liberation movement also prevailed in Zimbabwe. Genuinely nonaligned with any of the extracontinental power blocs, Zimbabwe has joined Angola and Mozambique in active, but as yet nonviolent, confrontation with the minority regime in South Africa. No longer do the Western powers hold hegemonic sway over this important region of Africa. The Soviet Union and its allies have established a credible communist presence in the region and contest the claim to hegemony by the Western powers with increasing fervor and effect.

In the war-torn Horn of Africa, nationalistic conflicts are an outgrowth of the history of Ethiopian imperial expansion under Christian (Amharic and Tigrean) potentates and of Muslim (mainly Oromo and Somali) resistance. These conflicts rend the revolutionary regime in Ethiopia and convulse that country's northern, secessionist province of Eritrea. Eastern Ethiopia—the Ogaden—is a battleground defended by Ethiopians with Cuban and Soviet support against the forces of irredentist Somalia. For nearly three years, from the Ethiopian revolution of 1974 to Somalia's 1977 offensive in the Ogaden, Moscow attempted to maintain supportive relationships with all three avowedly Marxist-Leninist leadership groups—in Mogadishu, Addis Ababa, and the secessionist province of Eritrea. Compelled to choose, the Soviet Union cast its lot with Ethiopia. Somalia then became a de facto ally of the United States. More recently, Ethiopia's own flexibility in foreign relations, including evidence of a disposition to resume normal relations with the Western powers, has grown in direct proportion to its military success in the war zones. The regime's inclination to maintain Ethiopia's traditionally friendly relationship with Israel is yet another indication that historical affinities (or antagonisms) between peoples normally survive ideological earthquakes.

In Part III of this symposium, we examine two "crisis areas" of the second type—i.e., areas the problems of which cannot be attributed to primarily historic tensions between nations and peoples. The first of these involves the Republic of Zaire, a deeply troubled nation from the day of its birth as the Democratic Republic of the Congo in 1960. Since its establishment in 1965, the regime of President Mobutu Sese Seko has enjoyed Western, especially American, support as a redoubtable opponent of Communist expansion and Soviet influence in Africa. On two occasions, in 1977 and 1978, Belgium, France, Morocco, and the United States provided emergency military support for Zaire, which could not, by itself, cope with an invasion of Zairian dissidents based in neighboring Angola. Zaire's chronic insolvency, marginally effective government, and vengeful, revolutionary exiles add up to a permanent crisis for the regime and its foreign, particularly American, protectors.

The two remaining crises of circumstantial, rather than long historical, provenance, which have elicited firm responses from the United States, are, like Mobutu's rule in Zaire, related to American fears of Soviet and Communist expansion. Three successive American administrations have chosen to back Morocco's claim to the former Spanish colony of Western Sahara in opposition to an independence movement sponsored by Algeria. Similarly, in Chad, the United States has taken sides in a strictly local conflict to oppose the actions of Libya and the ambitions of its "leader," Colonel Moammar Qadhafi. To that end, the United States joined with the Sudan, Egypt, and Saudi Arabia in 1982 to equip an anti-Libyan army headed by Hissène Habré, which then seized the capital, Ndjamena, and drove the army of the Libyan-supported government to the far north. As might have been expected, the Libyan-backed forces regrouped and counterattacked. Their campaign of 1983, powered by Libyan armor, elicited American, French, and Zairian military assistance for the suddenly overmatched victors of the previous year. In Western parlance, the Habré government had become "legitimate," despite the inconvenient fact that its Libyan-backed opposition was probably more broadly based among the sectional factions which structure Chadian politics.

As a practical matter, the historical origins of African conflicts do not seriously affect the processes whereby they become "crises" in the eyes of American leaders. A single factor appears to account for the transition from African conflict to "crisis" for the United States. Invariably, the essence of a crisis is the perception by American policymakers of a potential gain for the Soviet Union or world communism which could be prevented by resolute American action. Once discovered, crises are nurtured to maturity by guardians of the anticommunist faith.

THE INTERNATIONALIZATION OF CRISES

Integral to our concept of a crisis, as we have already mentioned, is its internationalization through engulfment in or penetration by East-West cold war rivalry. Although there are powerful internal dynamics of escalation inherent in the interactions of adversaries in any crisis, the escalation of a local crisis to the level of cold war engulfment is significantly furthered by at least three generic push-and-pull forces and influences in the external environment of the crisis: (1) the overall structure and ethos of the prevailing international system; (2) the perceptions and motivational assumptions of the two superpowers regarding each other in their global competition for parity, which psychologically each interprets to be primacy; and (3) the penetrability of the African crisis by external powers. These broad contextual features in the external environment of crises operate, separately or in combination, to promote crisis internationalization, quite independently of the motives and interests of the local adversaries.

The Structure and Ethos of the International System

At the core of the international-system perspective is the balance-of-power theory which postulates that the structure of the international system (i.e., its multipolarity or bipolarity) explains—indeed, it determines—the international behavior of states (East 1978, 143; Waltz 1975, 117; Morgenthau 1978, 348ff). The implicit structural determinism in the balance-of-power theory has ensured its continuing controversiality (e.g., Rosecrance 1981, 691ff), but this is not the place to enter into that debate. We should, however, extract from this widely accepted theory—if for no other reason than to test it—the crux of the explanation it purports to offer for the internationalization of crises in contemporary Africa. The argument, in brief, is that the unstable pre–World War II multipolar balance that failed was transformed after 1945 into a far more stable bipolar one (Waltz 1964, 881ff) in which the U.S. and USSR are globally dominant; that a broader equilibrium was established as a result of the mutually tolerated progressive consolidation of a bipolar two-bloc alliance structure in the "central international system" of the north

(Osgood 1981, 2); that despite a discernible movement toward greater flexibility and a "new multipolarity" throughout the 1970s and early 1980s (e.g.,
China's emergence as a nuclear power, the loosening of the Western alliance,
and strains in the Eastern bloc), the contemporary structure remains essentially bipolar in military terms (Snyder and Diesing 1977, 462–463); that the
emergence of a nuclear stalemate between the two superpowers has rendered
war in the central international system no longer a plausible option; and that
there has been a consequent gravitation of U.S.–Soviet competition to low-
risk targets of opportunity presented by regional crises in the vulnerable and
penetrable south, particularly in Africa. As Gupta (quoted in Ayoob 1980,
242) puts it:

> The very stability of the global power balance and the determination of the
> Great Powers to avoid a confrontation makes them prone to seek lower levels of
> conflict and less dangerous ways of conducting their rivalries, which, in effect,
> means a concerted attempt to confine their conflicts to problems that impinge
> on them less directly and to localize them in such areas as are far removed from
> the areas where their vital interests are involved. To fight out their battles in the
> Third World is one way of ensuring that their own worlds are not touched by
> their conflicts and that they retain a great measure of option to escalate and de-
> escalate their conflicts according to the need of their relationships.

From this structural determinist perspective, the strong disposition of the
superpowers to intervene, penetrate, and manipulate crises in the periphery
is not an old-fashioned imperialistic impulse but a function of the bipolarity
of the system.

A similar gravitation of dominant powers to lower risk peripheral areas
also characterized the heroic period of great-power multipolar stability between 1870 and 1914. During that period, however, the opportunity existed
for the dominant world powers to obtain compensatory territorial satisfac-
tions, mainly through colonial expansion in Africa, thereby obviating the
danger of general war in the then central international system of Europe. During those four decades the "great issues of world politics were connected with
African names, such as Egypt, Tunis, Morocco, the Congo, South Africa. . . .
[Conflicts in Europe were avoided or postponed because there was] so much
political no-man's land with which to compensate one's self and allow others
to do the same. There was always the possibility of compromise without com-
promising one's vital interest" (Morgenthau 1978, 357).

Despite the apparent similarity in the international systems of the two periods (1870–1914 and our contemporary era), the differences in structure and
ethos between the two are fundamental. The European balance-of-power system, with its highly developed mechanisms for regulating rivalries and obviating crises, was well defined and well organized; however, few of the modalities employed in that earlier period (Lauren 1983, 31–64) offer the possibility
of adaptation for crisis prevention in the contemporary situation. Explicit

big-power agreements on spheres of influence, occupation, and ownership, such as characterized the Berlin Act of 1884, are, for example, no longer even conceivable. The then common practice of collective decision making by the great powers to settle regional conflicts would, if done by today's superpowers, "trigger fears of a superpower condominium" (George 1983, 6). The Basic Principles Agreement signed by Nixon and Brezhnev in May 1972 was explicitly aimed at crisis prevention in third areas as part of the overall policy of detente; however, ambiguities and flaws in that agreement failed to limit in any way U.S.-Soviet strivings for influence and primacy in third areas, and particularly in Africa since 1975. The psychology of flexibility, bargaining, sidestepping, and unlimited shareout of the earlier epoch has been replaced by one of zero-sum assumptions and omnipresent confrontation at the periphery. The former preoccupation with crisis prevention through an orchestrated use of a wide range of modalities serving that purpose has given way to an obsessive concern with total mutual preclusion and a seeming indisposition or incapacity to moderate or control the dynamics of crisis escalation.

Perceptions and Motivational Assumptions of the Superpowers

Even brief analysis of the many sources of U.S. and Soviet policies and behavior are beyond the scope of this essay; the individual case studies will illuminate their diversity and complexity in distinctive contexts. Here we are concerned with only one generic dimension, namely, the effect of perceptions and motivational assumptions of the superpowers upon the internationalization of African crises. Analysts differ on the effects of misperception in conflict causation and crisis escalation. Cottam (1977, 7) argues that historians "will record the Soviet-American Cold War as one that rested predominantly on motivational attribution rather than on conflicting objectives"; and Ayoob (1980, 241) states flatly that "in international relations, perceptions, whether they do or do not coincide with reality, are infinitely more important than reality itself." Stein (1982, 505ff), however, suggests that misperception does not always affect foreign policy choices and outcomes, is often irrelevant to the cause and escalation of crisis and war, has effects in only a limited set of circumstances, and "can lead to cooperation as well as to conflict" (e.g., Soviet misperception facilitated de-escalation of the Cuban crisis). The logic of Stein's analysis notwithstanding, the importance of perception and motivational assumptions in U.S.–Soviet competition in African crises remains compelling. The Angolan crisis of 1975, for example, demonstrated dramatically "how easy it is for the United States and the USSR to stumble into confrontations as a result of misperceptions, miscalculations, poor intelligence and analysis, faulty signaling, and bad judgment" (George 1983, 9).

Ever since the cold war and the policy of Soviet containment were formally acknowledged by Kennan in 1947 (X 1947, 576ff), there has been, within a broad spectrum, a fairly stable set of American perceptions of Soviet motivation and behavior. They range from one extreme, which sees the Politburo as "relentlessly carrying out a master plan for world domination," to the other extreme, which perceives the USSR as "only an ordinary great power trying to offset its internal weaknesses and its external encirclement by defensive measures, which the United States provokes by emotional and messianic overreactions" (Osgood 1981, 7ff). Between the extremes are, to put it simplistically, a "globalist" perspective, exemplified by the realpolitik African policies of Kissinger, Brzezinski, and Reagan, and a "regionalist" perspective exemplified best by the policies of the Andrew Young wing of the Carter administration. For nearly four decades the common denominator of all perceptions except that of the extreme left has been and remains "containment."

This is all well known; less commonly probed are the more fundamental differences in perspective, of which these perceptions and the motivational assumptions associated with them are surface expressions. Jervis (1981, 59) reminds us that "differences in interpretation of specific Soviet actions are rooted in difference in basic views about Soviet motives and intentions, but it is hard to tell where the views come from. Personality characteristics such as a generalized predisposition to perceive situations as conflictful may play a large role. Some dimensions of liberalism and conservatism may be present. There may be differences in styles of analysis and approach." Hough (n.d., 53) answers Jervis's query about the deeper origins of differing perceptions by attributing them to "fundamental assumptions about human nature." At the extremes, those with a perception that there is a Soviet master plan for world domination have a Manichean image of the world divided between the forces of good and evil; others with a more conservative and pessimistic view of human nature lack that crusading sense of moral purity which treats adversaries as untouchables. The fact that policy options in crisis situations are derived from—possibly limited by—perceptions and assumptions about the motivation of an adversary which are not mainly based upon logic or rational analysis, but upon more deep-seated idiosyncratic conceptions of human nature or highly personal psychological orientations is "psychologically painful," but "a possibility we must consider" (Jervis 1981, 57, 59).

Perceptions and assumptions about the motives of adversaries, it is argued, tend to be unreflective, visceral, and, as Cottam (1977, 15ff) argues, deterministic. "Ask almost any scholar what is possible and desirable with respect to Vietnam or the Middle East [or the Horn, Chad, Angola, or Namibia, one could add] . . . and he is likely to give an unqualified answer—one that derives from moral judgment, assumes motivation, and simplifies causation" (Rosenau 1968, 198). And such gut perceptions are even more pronounced in crises. In situations of high stress, Holsti (1979, 108–109) argues, "tolerance for ambiguity is reduced," information that is unpleasant or contrary to one's visceral preferences and expectations tends to be suppressed, and responses are made "in terms of personal predispositions." Yet, he (Holsti 1979, 110) prudently cautions that these suggestive propositions should be tested by specific evidence from actual crises, which is, of course, what this volume of focused comparisons is all about.

A second caution, we suggest, is to be mindful both of the need to distinguish rhetoric from practice and of the fact that fundamental changes in perception can and do occur. In practice, for example, the allegedly doctrinaire globalist Reagan administration has not pursued "unmitigated globalist policies in Africa"; indeed, apart from the issue of the Cubans in Angola, it "has tempered its globalism with a sensitivity to the realities and complexities of local and regional conflict" (Bienen 1983, 68–69). Similarly, after the Soviet invasion of Afghanistan, globalism was fully embraced by the previously regionalist Carter administration. As Jervis (1981, 59) warns us, our knowledge about the sources of beliefs and perceptions is still very limited.

Penetrability of Africa's Crisis Areas

The internationalization of Africa's crisis areas is a function of the disposition and capacity of the United States and the Soviet Union to penetrate them. The ever-present compulsion of each superpower to intervene in a crisis situation in order to preclude the other, if this is perceived as necessary, is, as we have seen, strongly encouraged, if not dictated, by the bipolar structure of the international system. We have also noted the phenomenon of a seemingly self-energizing dynamic of crisis escalation resulting in the incremental engulfment of the superpowers in crises. Other theories hold that superpower intervention is a calculated self-serving policy designed to sell, test, and perfect their respective weapons systems, or to perpetuate a dependency relationship (Ayoob 1980, 242). There is no lack of theories about the disposition of the superpowers to become engaged, even against their will and intent. And they have adequately demonstrated that they have the capacity to project their military power if they decide to do so.

Penetration is relatively unconstrained because the mechanisms for controlling the escalation potential of superpower competition are weak and ineffective. Tacit norms exerting restraint tend to be area-specific, and for Africa they have not yet emerged. The principal reason, it is argued, is because neither superpower has high stakes in Africa and both are therefore paradoxically disinclined to clarify their interests and intentions. This reluctance is explained by the imperative of preclusion—there is a mutual resistance "to define and delimit their interests—lest they 'give away' such areas or encourage the other side to proceed in efforts to consolidate or increase its influence by allowing it to assume that such efforts will not risk a strong response" (George 1983, 387). This common determination to maintain fluidity and uncertainty, however, can only operate to heighten misperception and miscommunication, and consequently to further the disposition of each to intervene in a crisis that seems to be evolving in a direction perceived to be to its strategic disadvantage.

The penetrability of Africa's crises is also a function of the vulnerability and receptivity of the African adversaries involved. The comparative weakness, dependence, and vulnerability of the new states of postcolonial Africa are commonly accepted. Most of them are more juridical than empirical entities; both their formation and their persistence are due mainly to external factors which have "frozen them in their inherited colonial jurisdictions" (Jackson and Rosberg 1982, 21ff). Despite a few encouraging successes in conciliations, the OAU, like all regional organizations, has not been a serious factor in the maintenance of regional order. Nor has an African regional balance of power yet emerged—as in East Asia or intermittently in the Middle East—to perform that function (Rosecrance 1981, 695). Moreover, when crises erupt, although preventive diplomacy has occasionally succeeded (e.g., post–Shaba II and the Zimbabwe settlement), in most instances adversaries regard continued low-level conflict (Namibia, Western Sahara, Chad, the Horn) as preferable to possible political compromise (Zartman 1983, 350, 358). The critical factor in their vulnerability, however, has been the impulsion to seek outside allies to augment their power. One recent study of six African crises concluded that "in every case parties have looked abroad for the power to win when their domestic sources of power have proven to be insufficient. The escalation in the search for borrowed power is a familiar one: arms, technicians, advisers, and finally troops" (Zartman 1983, 362). Thus, the internationalization and penetrability of Africa's crises have been as much the result of African invitation as of external intrusion.

Despite superpower willingness, however contingent, and African readiness, however reluctant and conditional, jointly to risk the hazards of internationalizing a local crisis, one overpowering certitude is that in the postcolonial world of the 1980s the liaison is bound to be ephemeral and probably alienating. The concept of "power vacuum" as applied to Africa, or any other part of the Third World, is totally anachronistic (Hansen 1982, 14ff; Kitchen 1982, 169; Feinberg 1983, 14ff). Power is relative; overwhelmingly superior military power is, in the long run, no match for the socially mobilized power of peoples fiercely determined to preserve their independence and to right historic wrongs. The vastly increased impotence and humiliation of the superpowers in the Third World has aptly been called "the Second Imperial Requiem" by Galbraith (1982, 29ff): "The U.S. is not on a collision course with the Soviets in third countries—unless, in error, we will it so. The commitment to independence is imposing withdrawal on us both. . . . The age of imperialism, both old and new, is over." Seizing "targets of opportunity" in the presumed "power vacuums" of Africa's crisis areas, or taking countermeasures to preclude such seizures, can only lead, at worst, to the quagmires of Vietnam and Afghanistan, or at best, to the costly maintenance of a presence which ineluctably becomes intolerable, even if invited.

AFRICAN CRISIS AREAS AND
AMERICAN FOREIGN POLICY

After the Second World War, the antifascist coalition of liberal and communist powers divided on the great question of reform versus revolution as the path to progress. Constrained by its capitalist and liberal traditions, the United States viewed the prospect of social revolution anywhere in the world with varying degrees of suspicion and hostility, depending upon the perceived extent of communist leadership and socialist inspiration. Unlike social revolutions, which are justified with reference to class exploitation, anticolonial revolutions could be and indeed were reconciled with the American vision of a global economy under American leadership. Hence, the wartime and immediate postwar American administrations insisted, contrary to British opinion, that the declaration by Winston Churchill and Franklin Roosevelt in the Atlantic Charter of 1941, on the "right of all peoples to choose the form of government under which they will live," must apply to all colonies as well as the territories then occupied by the Axis powers. This attitude on the part of the United States was appreciated and commended by leading African nationalists of that era (Azikiwe 1943; Awolowo 1947).

Invariably, constitutional and peaceful transitions to independence in Africa and other colonial regions were approved by the United States, while revolutionary struggles against various imperial overlords were viewed with disfavor. Political leaders, publicists, and many American intellectuals propagated the idea that Marxism-Leninism was, first and foremost, a weapon with which communist powers menaced the so-called free world. The American public at large has never appreciated the more fundamental significance of Marxism-Leninism—that it is the leading, if not the sole important theory of social revolution for the nonindustrial societies of our time. Failing to comprehend the relationship of Marxism-Leninism to revolutionary action, American leaders and conformist intellectuals have espoused the fallacious notion of exported revolutions—the myth that revolutionary movements were/are produced by sinister persons in Moscow, Peking, or Havana rather than by local circumstances in downtrodden societies.

The fallacious idea of exported revolutions cannot survive exposure to the light of history. Recent African history does not reveal a single instance of revolutionary action which is not the unmistakable product of local circumstances and initiatives. Since 1950, social revolutions in Africa have resulted in a dozen instances of sustained warfare: the rural Kikuyu, or Mau Mau, rebellion in Kenya (1952–58); the Algerian revolution (1954–62); the rebellion against the government of Cameroon (before and after independence, 1955–61); the Angolan revolution (1960–75); the armed struggle for Eritrean independence (1961 to date); the revolution against Portuguese rule in Guinea-Bissau (1962–74); the preparation and gradual escalation of armed struggle against the government of South Africa (1962 to date); the rebellions in the Democratic Republic of the Congo (later Zaire; 1964–67); the armed struggle against Portuguese rule in Mozambique (1964–74); the armed struggle against South African rule in Namibia (1966 to date); the armed struggle in Zimbabwe (1966–80); the campaign for independence of the Western Sahara (1973 to date). Not a single one of these revolutionary wars was fomented by an external power.

The attitude of the United States toward insurgency in Africa has not been uniformly negative; however, the exceptional cases are themselves revealing. Highly influential Americans, including policymakers, have been sympathetic to revolutionaries who disdain doctrinaire socialist or communist principles. Hence Kenyan nationalism was strongly supported in the United States despite the notoriety of Mau Mau violence (Murphy 1976, 106–107). Where nationalist movements have been divided between pro- and anticommunist factions, as in Angola and Mozambique, the United States has supported the antis and opposed the pros (Bender 1978; Stockwell 1978; Isaacman and Davis 1978, 37). Occasionally, the United States has been sympathetic to nationalist revolutionaries despite their socialist orientations. For example, the Algerian liberation movement earned great respect in the United States and, with the election of John F. Kennedy in 1960, presidential support (Nielsen 1969, 268–270; Wallerstein 1975, 17). Similarly, the Zimbabwean revolutionaries were admired and dealt with in a positive spirit by the administration of President Jimmy Carter (Clough 1982, 27–56).

The Kenyan, Algerian, and Zimbabwean revolutions draw attention to a determinant of American policy that should not be minimized, namely public opinion. Each of these insurgencies made a deep impression upon "attentive publics"[1] in the United States. The South African revolutionary movement has also appealed to a large and ever-growing segment of American opinion despite the stridently anti-American and pro-Soviet stance of the African National Congress (ANC),[2] by far the leading representative of the South African revolution in international political affairs. The ANC's virtual demand for American enmity is offset in the United States by the paramount importance of racial equality as an American political value. The heterogeneity of the movement within South Africa against apartheid, carried on by militant trade unionists, church-related activists, and others, ensures the continued growth in the United States of a broad and powerful support movement for South African black liberation despite dogmatic anti-Americanism on the part of the ANC.

A memorable instance of sympathetic neutrality on the part of the United States toward an insurgent movement in Africa can be found in chronicles of

---

1. The term *attentive public* was introduced by Almond (1960, xxii, 138, and 241).

2. For unmistakable evidence, see the ANC's official quarterly journal, *Sechaba;* for a corroborative observation by authors who are partisan to the ANC, see Saul and Gelb (1981, 137).

the Nigerian civil war of 1967 to 1970 (Stremlau 1977, 280–294). While the United States did formally support the cause of Nigerian unity and refuse to recognize the secessionist Republic of Biafra, it still displeased the Lagos government by imposing an arms embargo on the sale of military equipment to either side. Furthermore, millions of Americans were distressed by the terrible toll of children who succumbed to starvation in the beleaguered yet defiant Biafran enclave. Nigerian officials deeply resented the food aid and financial support provided by the American government to a pro-Biafran interdenominational relief consortium, known as Joint Church Aid (Wiseberg 1973). In short, congressional and public sentiment prevented the adoption of a strictly realistic (i.e., profederal) posture by the United States despite the unwavering official American commitment to a united Nigeria.

Evidently, the potential for imagination and inconsistency in the African policy of the United States should not be minimized. Despite a normal preference for reformist, as opposed to revolutionary, regimes within stable national boundaries, American officials and the public at large remain susceptible to the effects of value-laden appeals that arise from profound stirrings of the national conscience. These cultural imperatives of foreign policy include respect for the principle of racial equality and moral support for the proverbial "war" against poverty and deprivation on a world scale. Time and again, they clash with the realistic imperatives of more narrowly conceived national interests.

Salient Determinants of Policy Formation

The Cultural Dimension.   The United States is a multicultural society. Many millions of Americans harbor sentimental attachments to ancestral lands and real or imagined "kith and kin" abroad. In a democratic society, foreign policy is regularly responsive to domestic political pressures. However, the door of American diplomacy rarely opened for Afro-American claims or claimants before the 1970s, when the newly established congressional Black Caucus convened successive meetings attended by intellectuals and the representatives of organized groups, leading to the formation, in 1977, of Transafrica, Inc., which would seek to influence American policies toward Africa and the Caribbean (Jackson 1982, 123–126, 148). With the appointment in 1977 of a leading participant in this process, namely Congressman Andrew Young, Jr. (D-Ga.), as ambassador to the United Nations, the long-sought Afro-American role in foreign policy, with particular regard for the concerns of Third World peoples, attained symbolic recognition.

The cultural determinants of American policy toward Africa are both particularistic and universal or society-wide. While black American affinity for the ancestral continent and other communities in the black diaspora is certainly the prime particularistic determinant, it is difficult to assess the relative importance of those cultural determinants that are society-wide. Were we to undertake a systematic inventory, it would be necessary to weigh various contradictory predispositions, for example, interracial respect versus insensitivity toward the values of blacks and other racial minorities in the United States; the positive orientation of many Americans toward other cultures versus a parochial tendency toward ethnocentrism; a growing appreciation of global interdependence versus traditional isolationism, and so on. All such society-wide values and attitudes are conditioned by the fact that most Americans—indeed all but a relatively few—are either ignorant of African realities or badly misinformed. Few American newspapers publish reports from black Africa on a regular basis; few American correspondents are equipped to transmit realistic interpretations. A personal reflection on the performance of one leading American newspaper which does publish news and features from Africa on a regular basis may be revealing. It maintains two resident correspondents in sub-Saharan Africa, one in white-ruled South Africa, with responsibility for the entire southern African region; the other in Kenya with responsibility for the rest of sub-Saharan Africa, including Nigeria! A former foreign news editor for that newspaper seriously doubted the value of African area training for correspondents on the ground that specialists were inclined to minimize the significance of factors which were, to his mind, fundamental, particularly "tribalism."

In addition to the low level of public knowledge about Africa, Americans are confused by the multiplicity of its sovereign states, fifty-one in all. Editors, commentators, and newscasters clutch at explanatory straws and rest content with superficial expositions of complex and weighty matters. As Martin Staniland (1982) has observed, American policymakers and publicists routinely resort to "simple analogies" to compensate for their superficial knowledge of the cultural and historical backgrounds to African issues. Two such analogies—the legendary American revolution and "the shadow of Vietnam"—have been overworked by those who conduct and interpret American diplomacy toward Africa. As Staniland observes, analogical reasoning is not wrong per se: "We need to simplify, to compare, and to draw on past experience" (1982, 26). However, the tendency to perceive Kinshasa as *Saigon noire* is greater among Americans than Europeans. Furthermore, most American intellectuals, unlike their European counterparts, read local or regional newspapers; they do not digest the daily news coverage of a premier national newspaper. Yet Americans, unlike Europeans, also have a continental mentality which is not consonant with the political fragmentation of a cultural region into many sovereign states. Americans may even be inclined to equate political fragmentation with backwardness. As in the case of Central America and the Caribbean region, discourse relating to African issues in the United States is hindered by the public's incomprehension of the political heterogeneity of Africa. Hence the constant resort to racial stereotyping, an American cultural pathology, in commentaries and deliberations relating to Africa.

Perceived National Interests. American relations with Africa have been influenced to a very great extent by a relatively few material interests. A pithy statement by Senator John Tower (R-Tex.), chairman of the Senate Armed Services Committee, during the Chadian crisis of 1983, captured the sentiment of many self-styled realists.

> Africa is a source of raw materials for this country, and it is a potential market. We do not have altruistic reasons for being there. It has been identified as an area of vital interest to the United States.(*Los Angeles Times,* August 8, 1983)

In other "realistic" assessments, Africa has been styled "strategic space" with reference to its geopolitical significance for the industrial powers. Southern Africa, by itself, has been tendentiously "characterized as the 'Persian Gulf of minerals'" (see Jackson 1982, 170). These and similarly instrumental characterizations obviously minimize the importance of Africa to Africans while they maximize and exaggerate the uses of Africa to the West.

Let us examine the case for tough-minded realism with an equally severe partiality for the national interest. At present, Africa's impact on the American economy is modest by comparison with that of other major regions of the world. Thus, in 1982, imports from Africa amounted to 7.3 percent of the value of all U.S. imports (U.S. Department of Commerce 1983, S–17). Oil from Nigeria accounted for most of that item; about 10 percent of the value of American imports from Africa corresponds to the purchase of strategic minerals—chromium, manganese, the platinum group, and vanadium—from South Africa. To be sure, the United States would be inconvenienced by the loss of access to either Nigerian oil or South African minerals. On this ground, certain analysts perceive a significant national interest in unimpaired trade with South Africa and the maintenance of good relations with its government (Crocker 1980–81, 346); others, however, emphasize the availability of alternative sources of supply and dispute the alleged linkage between access to strategic minerals and political support of South Africa (Bienen 1983, 72–73). The judicious national Study Commission on U.S. Policy Toward Southern Africa, sponsored by the Rockefeller Foundation and chaired by the president of the Ford Foundation, cited the long-term need for strategic minerals from South Africa as a reason for American disengagement from the white supremacist regime (Study Commission . . . 1981, 412).

American exports to Africa in 1982 accounted for 4.8 percent of U.S. exports worldwide; exports to South Africa alone accounted for just 1 percent (U.S. Department of Commerce 1983, S–16). At the end of 1981, the value of U.S. direct investments in Africa stood at $6.9 billion, which was 3 percent of all U.S. foreign investments; that for South Africa amounted to $2.6 billion, or slightly more than 1 percent of U.S. investment abroad (Whichard 1982, 22). American investments in South Africa are concentrated in high-technology sectors, including the computer and electronics industry, petroleum processing, and the production of motor vehicles. While these holdings are very profitable—the rate of return for U.S. investments in South Africa currently exceeds 18 percent—they rarely represent more than 1 percent of the assets of the corporations concerned. As Bertolin (1978, 53) has observed, investments in South Africa "are not vital to the health of the [American] national economy."

The military aspect of American strategic planning is focused on the Soviet Union as the prime adversarial referent. However, actions which may be taken to counteract or prevent the extension of Soviet military power might also affect local African interests in ways which would be detrimental to the political interests of the United States. For example, South Africa commands the attention of naval strategists in the United States because of its proximity to crucial sea lanes which traverse the Atlantic and Indian oceans. Despite growing pressure from military support groups in the United States to accept South Africa's invitation to use the naval station at Simonstown, successive American administrations have thus far refused to bite because the political costs of extensive military collaboration with South Africa would be too high (Bissell 1982, 66–69; Bowman 1982).

A notorious instance of costly preoccupation with Soviet aims in Africa involves the tortuous negotiation for South African withdrawal from Namibia. The most intractable issue of that negotiation has been South Africa's insistence upon the withdrawal of Cuban troops from Angola in return for its agreement to an internationally supervised election that would probably be won by its great adversary—SWAPO. Unlike its predecessor, the Reagan administration is unequivocally identified with the South African position on this issue (Legum 1982, A16–17, 31). The effect of this position is to taint the United States with imputed sympathy for South Africa's desire to control Namibia, either directly or through Namibians who would be utterly dependent upon Pretoria's protection. A further effect is the perpetuation of a border war that involves continuous South African military operations in southern Angola. This, in turn, ensures the continued presence of Cuban combat forces in Angola to protect the central and northern regions of that country; the Cubans have not as yet commenced operations against South African units in the southern sector.

What perceived national interest does the Reagan administration serve by its linkage of South African withdrawal from Namibia to the presence of Cubans in Angola? That policy frustrates an avowed American commitment to the negotiation of a settlement based on free elections in Namibia. It perpetuates the Cuban troop presence in Angola (the Angolan government has said that Cuban troops will be withdrawn when the South African army leaves

Namibia). It flaunts a demand upon the state of Angola which offends Africans of all political persuasions because it reflects contempt for the sovereign prerogatives of a government with which all countries save the United States and South Africa have, or are prepared to have, normal relations. It prevents the normalization of relations between Angola and the United States to the consternation of American businessmen and the detriment of American influence with many other African countries, from socialist Mozambique to capitalist Nigeria. For many analysts who are sympathetic to American aspirations worldwide, the rationale for this policy is difficult to fathom.

Neither the United States nor the Soviet Union can escape from the dilemmas of choice between military objectives prompted by their mutual adversarial relationship and policies which would be responsive to local expectations in Africa. Neither one has escaped political damage as a result of the audacious deployment of 38,000–40,000 Cuban troops in Africa, particularly in Angola and Ethiopia (Gonzalez 1980). While the United States is widely criticized in Africa for its compulsive insensitivity toward the beleaguered government of Angola, the Soviet Union has harvested resentment in many quarters, particularly Somalia and the other Muslim countries which nearly encircle Ethiopia. Paradoxically, Ethiopia's most reliable allies in its own region are capitalist Kenya and (denials to the contrary notwithstanding) Israel, both firm supporters of the United States against the Soviet Union in global politics. What, one wonders, is the long-range Soviet gain from partisanship, rather than mediation, in the Horn? And what lasting benefit will the United States realize from its partisan posture in the Angolan, Namibian, or Chadian conflicts? The costs of regarding Africa as a strategic space for military maneuvers against the Soviet Union have been dispassionately assessed by Ravenhill and Rothchild (1982–83, 116).

> By stressing military solutions to political problems, the Reagan orientation has tended to pay insufficient attention to the complexities of politics on the continent. In particular, it has underestimated the strength of African states' commitment to non-alignment, to the ending of racism in southern Africa, and to an improvement of international economic relations. At the same time, it has overestimated the extent to which African states share its perceptions of the seriousness and centrality of the Soviet "threat" and has overreacted against those states which do not share its priorities. In doing so, it quickly lost the goodwill that the previous administration built up. The importance of these good relations to the ultimate realization of American aspirations in Africa has been underrated.

Crisis Management

Properly understood, national interests are subjective determinations formulated with reference to the shared values of a national entity. Crisis areas, we contend, are also defined with reference to subjective criteria, including perceived threats to national interests. In formulating policies for crisis areas, national leaders and their advisers should be aware that it is rarely, if ever, necessary to choose between combat and capitulation. Crisis areas can be used constructively to clarify national interests and deepen the meaning of their underlying values. It would be logical for global powers to adopt constructive approaches toward crisis areas in Africa rather than confrontational policies for which Africans have little empathy and which are fated, in any case, to produce unanticipated outcomes.

If predictability is a criterion for policy selection, the confrontational approach to crisis management in Africa is not a rational choice for the United States. Each of the fifty-one sovereign states is motivated by self-defined goals which intersect with those of other African states in complex patterns of action. The impact of multiple sovereignty and self-regarding nationalism upon the best-laid plans of intrusive outsiders is often devastating. However cautious or decisive they may be, intruders are doomed to miscalculate and stumble into traps which they do not anticipate and cannot avert. For example, the United States erred in assuming that Hissène Habré's seizure of Ndjamena in 1982 would cook Colonel Qadhafi's goose in Chad. When, a year later, Libyan-backed forces counterattacked to seize northern Chad, the United States gestured furiously: U.S. warships approached the Libyan coast and two AWACS radar-surveillance aircraft were stationed in Sudan. Shortly thereafter, the United States was put on notice by opponents of Libyan expansion, including Nigeria, Senegal, and France, that a negotiated settlement would be preferable to a crusade against Qadhafi on Habré's behalf. Obviously relieved by the French government's decision to defend southern Chad against the threat of Libyan conquest, Washington backed away from the concealed pitfalls of further miscalculation through precipitous intervention.

The Chadian incident may herald a positive turn away from the stridently confrontational temper of President Reagan's foreign policy during the tenure of Alexander Haig as secretary of state. His successor, George P. Shultz, is also outspoken, but evidently disposed to negotiate disputes in crisis areas with a view toward the conservation, rather than expenditure, of political and economic assets. As such, he is a more formidable obstacle to reckless anticommunism in the Reagan administration than his constantly embattled predecessor could ever have become. Under Shultz, it may be possible for Dr. Chester A. Crocker, assistant secretary of state for African affairs and a knowledgeable, if unsentimental, Africanist scholar, to pursue the course of compromise as a constructive art.

By falling into step with Africa's healthy penchant for political and social experimentation, the United States could maximize the advantages of its own example of constitutional government in the marketplace of political ideas. In recent years it has become apparent that dictatorial and statist strategies of development do not achieve their economic goals in small or medium-sized Third World countries. Time and again, attempts to impose "socialism" coercively by means of a dogmatic dictatorship have resulted in economic stagnation, mock socialism, and disillusionment. As a matter of necessity, the African nations are searching for new forms of social and political organization based upon amalgams of indigenous and universal values. During the present era of culturally assertive nation-building and self-directed social discovery, paternalism in the form of attempts to export democracy to Africa is as repulsive to Africans as is paternalism in the form of attempts to export revolution. External powers (and here we particularly address the United States) would be well advised to learn that democracy in Africa, like revolution, can hardly be other than an indigenous product.

With respect to influencing political movements in Africa, as elsewhere, the Soviet Union and the United States have distinctive strengths and weaknesses. Despite its loss of favor with many avowed socialists and revolutionaries in all parts of the world for sundry reasons, including disillusionment with the evolution of Soviet society and the "hegemonic" or ultranationalist thrust of Soviet foreign policies, Moscow remains a mecca for revolutionaries who are dedicated to the overthrow of capitalist orders. So long as Africa contains egregious objects of socialist scorn, such as the capitalist and racialist oligarchy in South Africa and dictatorships which facilitate the accumulation of personal wealth by officials and parasites of the regime, the Soviet Union will command admiring attention among many African intellectuals. For its part, the United States and other industrial powers which practice constitutional democracy at home are widely reputed to exploit the poor countries of the world as a condition of their own prosperity. Nonetheless, developmental imperatives in Africa compel respect for the institution of entrepreneurship and for the type of political environment which enables it to flourish. Pragmatists in Africa, as elsewhere, are disposed to value free inquiry and freedom of political association. Hence in several African countries, the spirit of political freedom has materialized in self-determined forms of constitutional and liberal democracy. While it would be jejune to either expect or desire tension-free relations between democracies in Africa and the United States, clusters of complementary political values could make it easier for the United States to adopt constructive rather than confrontational approaches to conflicts in African crisis areas.

When governments based upon democratic principles counsel the United States to treat revolutionary movements and forces which are friendly to the Soviet Union with consideration and restraint, the United States would be wise to weigh the benefits of deference to that opinion against the perceived need for confrontation. As Ravenhill and Rothchild (1982–83, 119, 123) have observed, anti-Soviet confrontational policies often result in estrangement of the United States from democratically inclined governments in Africa, while the rightist autocrats are happy to embrace a belligerent Uncle Sam. It may be instructive to recall that in 1976, while the United States schemed, ineptly and in vain, to topple the MPLA government in Angola, Nigeria, then ruled by military officers who were presiding over the restoration of constitutional government, refused to receive the American secretary of state. Then, as now, the closest American relationships in Africa were with the Mobutist dictatorship in Zaire and the monarchical autocracy in Morocco. Each of those relationships was founded upon rapport with an exalted personality rather than mutual respect for each other's systems of political values. Then, as now, it was surprisingly difficult for the American government to establish and maintain good working relationships with governments in Africa that were founded upon democratic principles. The American penchant for rightist autocrats in Africa offends common sense. What if the dictator in Zaire were to be displaced by an officer who had been trained, and positively influenced, by the North Korean military advisers who have served there intermittently? What if a suddenly ascendant Zairois soldier were to turn against his quondam patrons, in the manner of Idi Amin?

We ponder such questions, not for their alarmist implications, but for the light they shed on American policies toward Africa. Crisis areas are images of conflict situations in the eyes and minds of policymakers. African crisis areas test the mettle of a lordly and conservative nation for pragmatic and compassionate leadership in the formulation of its foreign policy in this revolutionary age.

REFERENCES

Almond, Gabriel. 1960. *The American People and Foreign Policy.* New York: Praeger.

Awolowo, Obafemi. 1947. *Path to Nigerian Freedom.* London: Faber.

Ayoob, Mohammed, ed. 1980. *Conflict and Intervention in the Third World.* London: Croom Helm.

Azikiwe, Nnamdi. 1943. *Political Blueprint of Nigeria.* Lagos: African Book Company.

Balandier, G. 1971. *Sociologie actuelle de l'Afrique noire.* 3d ed. Paris: Presses Universitaires de France.

Bell, Coral. 1971. *The Conventions of Crisis: A Study in Diplomatic Management.* London: Oxford University Press.

Bender, Gerald. 1978. "Kissinger in Angola: Anatomy of Failure," pp. 65–153 in René Lemarchand, ed. *American Policy in Southern Africa: The Stakes and the Stance.* Washington, D.C.: University Press of America.

Bertolin, Gordon. 1978. "U.S. Economic Interests in Africa: Investment, Trade, and Raw Materials," pp. 21–59 in Jennifer Seymour Whitaker, ed. *Africa and the United States: Vital Interests.* New York: New York University Press.

Bienen, Henry. 1983. "The United States and Sub-Saharan Africa," pp. 66–85 in John P. Lewis and Valeriana Kallab, eds. *U.S. Foreign Policy and the Third World: Agenda 1983.* New York: Praeger.

Bissell, Richard E. 1982. *South Africa and the United States: The Erosion of an Influence Relationship.* New York: Praeger.

Bowman, Larry W. 1982. "The Strategic Importance of South Africa to the United States: An Appraisal and Policy Analysis." *African Affairs* 81, no. 323 (April): 159–191.

Brecher, Michael. 1980. *Decisions in Crisis*. Berkeley and Los Angeles: University of California Press.

Clough, Michael. 1982. "From Rhodesia to Zimbabwe," pp. 1–60 in Michael Clough, ed. *Changing Realities in Southern Africa*. Berkeley, California: Institute of International Studies.

Cottam, Richard W. 1977. *Foreign Policy Motivation: A General Theory and a Case Study*. Pittsburgh: University of Pittsburgh Press.

Crocker, Chester A. 1980–81. "South Africa: Strategy for Change." *Foreign Affairs* 59, no. 2 (Winter):323–351.

East, Maurice. 1978. "The International System Perspective and Foreign Policy," in Maurice A. East et al., eds. *Why Nations Act*. Beverly Hills: Sage Publications.

Eckstein, Harry. 1975. "Case Study and Theory in Political Science," pp. 79–138 in Fred I. Greenstein and Nelson W. Polsby, eds. *Handbook of Political Science*, vol. 7. Reading, Mass.: Addison-Wesley.

Erikson, Erik H. 1968. "Identity, Psychosocial," pp. 61–65 in *International Encyclopedia of the Social Sciences*, vol. 7. New York: Free Press.

Feinberg, Richard E. 1983. *The Intemperate Zone: The Third World Challenge to U.S. Foreign Policy*. New York: Norton.

Galbraith, John Kenneth. 1982. "The Second Imperial Requiem." *The Harvard Magazine* (September-October):29–33.

George, Alexander L. 1979. "Case Studies and Theory Development: The Method of Structured, Focused Comparison," pp. 43–68 in Paul Gordon Lauren, ed. *Diplomacy: New Approaches in History, Theory, and Policy*. New York: Free Press.

————. 1983. *Managing U.S.–Soviet Rivalry: Problems of Crisis Prevention*. Boulder, Col.: Westview Press.

Gonzalez, Edward. 1980. "Cuba, the Soviet Union, and Africa," pp. 145–167 in David E. Albright, ed. *Communism in Africa*. Bloomington: Indiana University Press.

Gorman, Robert F. 1981. *Political Conflict on the Horn of Africa*. New York: Praeger.

Hansen, Roger D. 1982. "National Security in the 1980s: A Reappraisal," pp. 3–48 in Overseas Development Council, *U.S. Foreign Policy in the Third World: Agenda 1982*. New York: Praeger.

Hermann, Charles F. 1969. "International Crisis as a Situational Variable," pp. 409–421 in James Rosenau, ed. *International Politics and Foreign Policy*. New York: Free Press.

————, ed. 1972. *International Crises: Insights from Behavioral Research*. New York: Free Press.

Holsti, Ole R. 1979. "Theories of Crisis Decision Making," pp. 99–136 in Paul Gordon Lauren, ed. *Diplomacy*. New York: Free Press.

Hough, Jerry F. n.d. "The Politics of Africa: Changing Soviet Views." Photocopy of typescript.

Ilunga, Kabongo. 1965. "Crise politique: concept et application à l'Afrique," in *Cahiers économiques et sociaux* 3, no. 3 (October):321–338.

Isaacman, Allen, and Jennifer Davis. 1978. "US Policy Toward Mozambique, 1946–1979: 'The Defense of Colonialism and Regional Stability,'" pp. 17–62 in René Lemarchand, ed. *American Policy in Southern Africa: The Stakes and the Stance.* Washington, D.C.: University Press of America.

Jackson, Henry F. 1982. *From the Congo to Soweto: U.S. Foreign Policy Toward Africa Since 1960.* New York: William Morrow.

Jackson, Robert H., and Carl G. Rosberg. 1982. *Personal Rule in Black Africa.* Berkeley and Los Angeles: University of California Press.

Jervis, Robert. 1981. "Beliefs about Soviet Behavior," pp. 55–59 in Robert E. Osgood, *Containment, Soviet Behavior, and Grand Strategy.* Berkeley, Calif.: Institute of International Studies.

Kitchen, Helen. 1982. "Six Misconceptions of Africa." *The Washington Quarterly* (Autumn):167–174.

Lauren, Paul Gordon. 1983. "Crisis Prevention in Nineteenth-Century Diplomacy," pp. 31–64 in Alexander L. George, ed. *Managing U.S.–Soviet Rivalry: Problems of Crisis Prevention.* Boulder, Col.: Westview Press.

Legum, Colin. 1982. "The Southern African Crisis," pp. A3–A62 in Colin Legum, ed. *Africa Contemporary Record: Annual Survey and Documents, 1981–1982.* New York: Africana Publishing Company.

Los Angeles Times. 1983. August 8.

McClelland, C. A. 1961. "The Acute International Crisis." *World Politics* 14 (October):182–204.

Morgenthau, Hans J. 1978. *Politics Among Nations: The Struggle for Power and Peace.* New York: Knopf.

Murphy, E. Jefferson. 1976. *Creative Philanthropy: Carnegie Corporation and Africa, 1953–1973.* New York: Columbia University Teachers College Press.

Nielsen, Waldemar A. 1969. *The Great Powers and Africa.* New York: Praeger.

Osgood, Robert E. 1981. *Containment, Soviet Behavior, and Grand Strategy.* Berkeley, Calif.: Institute of International Studies.

Ravenhill, John, and Donald Rothchild. 1982–83. "Reagan's African Policy, A New Unilateralism." *International Journal* 38, no. 1 (Winter): 107–127.

Robinson, James A. 1968. "Crisis," pp. 510–514 in *International Encyclopedia of the Social Sciences.* New York: Free Press.

_____. 1972. "Crisis: An Appraisal of Concepts and Theories," pp. 20–35 in Charles F. Hermann, ed. *International Crises: Insights from Behavioral Research.* New York: Free Press.

Rosecrance, Richard. 1981. "International Theory Revisited." *International Organization* 35, no. 4 (Autumn):691–714.

Rosenau, James N. 1968. "Moral Fervor, Systematic Analysis, and Scientific Consciousness in Foreign Policy Research," pp. 197–238 in Austin Ranney, ed. *Political Science and Public Policy.* Chicago: Markham Publishing Co.

Saul, John S., and Stephen Gelb. 1981. *The Crisis in South Africa: Class Defense, Class Revolution.* New York: Monthly Review Press.

Snyder, Glenn H. 1976. "Conflict and Crisis in the International System," pp. 682–720 in James N. Rosenau, Kenneth W. Thompson, and Gavin Boyd, eds. *World Politics.* New York: Free Press.

Snyder, Glenn H., and Paul Diesing. 1977. *Conflict Among Nations.* Princeton: Princeton University Press.

Staniland, Martin. 1982. *Africa, the American Intelligentsia, and the Shadow of Vietnam*. ACIS Working Paper no. 35. Los Angeles: Center for International and Strategic Affairs, University of California.

Stein, Arthur A. 1982. "When Misperception Matters." *World Politics* 34, no. 4 (July): 505–526.

Stockwell, John. 1978. *In Search of Enemies: A CIA Story*. New York: Norton.

Stremlau, John J. 1977. *The International Politics of the Nigerian Civil War, 1967–1970*. Princeton: Princeton University Press.

Study Commission on U.S. Policy Toward Southern Africa. 1981. *South Africa: Time Running Out*. Berkeley and Los Angeles: University of California Press.

United States Department of Commerce. 1983. "Foreign Trade of the United States." *Survey of Current Business* 63, no. 6 (June):S section.

Verhaegen, Benoit. 1974. *Introduction à l'histoire immédiat*. Gembloux: Duculot.

Wallerstein, Immanuel. 1975. "Africa, the United States, and the World Economy: The Historical Bases of American Policy," pp. 11–37 in Frederick S. Arkhurst, ed. *U.S. Policy Toward Africa*. New York: Praeger.

Waltz, Kenneth N. 1964. "The Stability of a Bipolar World," *Daedalus* 93, no. 3 (Summer):881–909.

———. 1975. "Theory of International Relations," pp. 1–85 in Fred I. Greenstein and Nelson W. Polsby, eds. *Handbook of Political Science*, vol. 8, Reading, Mass.: Addison-Wesley.

Whichard, Obie G. 1982. "U.S. Direct Investment Abroad in 1981." *Survey of Current Business* 62, no. 8 (August):11–29. U.S. Department of Commerce.

Wiseberg, Laurie S. 1973. "Humanitarian Intervention: Lessons from the Nigerian Civil War." Paper presented at the Annual Meeting of the American Political Science Association, New Orleans.

X. [George F. Kennan.] 1947. "The Sources of Soviet Conduct." *Foreign Affairs* 25, no. 4 (July):566–583.

Zartman, I. William. 1976. "Africa," pp. 569–594 in James N. Rosenau, Kenneth W. Thompson, and Gavin Boyd, eds. *World Politics*. New York: Free Press.

———. 1983. "The Strategy of Preventive Diplomacy in Third World Conflicts," pp. 341–364 in Alexander L. George, ed. *Managing U.S.–Soviet Rivalry: Problems of Crisis Prevention*. Boulder, Col.: Westview Press.

PART I

Southern Africa

Map 2.   Southern Africa

South Africa has been the primary source of racial and military destabilization for more than a quarter of a century in the region of southern Africa (Angola, Mozambique, Zimbabwe, Botswana, Swaziland, Lesotho, Namibia, and the Republic itself). Apartheid, South Africa's infamous system of racial separation, has provoked violence within the republic and across its borders since it was imposed nearly four decades ago. Although the nations of the world continue to condemn this unique and abhorrent attempt to organize a modern political and economic order along racial lines, the precious metals reposited within the republic have protected it from total isolation.

South Africa's minerals have attracted massive investment from many foreign powers, but the country has been especially important to three world empires: the Dutch, the British, and in recent times, the informal American empire. Given the prominence of American economic and political interests in South Africa (which have increased considerably under the Reagan administration's policy of "constructive engagement"), many diplomats, scholars, journalists, participants, and partisans, from left to right, look to the United States to promote change in the system.

That Washington possesses the means or leverage to engender fundamental change in South Africa is taken as an article of faith by many; as a result, their questions tend to center on the American *will* to effectuate that change. They conclude that the absence of fundamental change in South Africa is proof, ipso facto, that the United States lacks the will to produce the desired change. At the same time, others scoff at the notion that the United States has the leverage or power to end the apartheid system. They point to South Africa's considerable military strength and economic self-sufficiency to buttress their position. These contrasting views, along with other competing perspectives on how to move Pretoria away from apartheid, are analyzed in Part I.

South Africa's racism and minerals are not the only factors which have attracted outside attention. Pretoria's claim that it represents the front line for the West against the encroachment of communism in Africa has appealed to many foreign politicians from Ronald Reagan and Jesse Helms to Franz Josef Strauss. A contrary perspective, also discussed in these chapters, is that South Africa's very policies invite the presence of communist powers in southern Africa.

The debate over South Africa's role as a positive or negative force for attracting the presence of the Soviet Union, Cuba, and other communist countries to southern Africa took on new prominence with the Angolan civil war of 1975 to 1976. The issue of who did what first has degenerated into a hen and egg question: Did Pretoria's invasion of Angola in late 1975 bring the Cubans to Africa, or did the Cuban presence in Angola propel South Africa to invade? Did Pretoria teach Havana a lesson in Angola or was it the other way around? One undebatable result of the Cubans' arrival in Angola, however, was to attract American attention to Africa. By Henry Kissinger's own admission, the Nixon and Ford administrations (and Kissinger himself) had essentially ignored Africa for most of the previous seven years.

Kissinger spent much of his last year as secretary of state working on southern African matters. He succeeded in garnering Ian Smith's cooperation to proceed toward independence in Rhodesia. The Carter administration plunged into the southern African imbroglio with a fervor hitherto unknown in the annals of American relations with the African continent. The Anglo-American plan for Rhodesia and the efforts to unlock South Africa's illegal hold on Namibia were major foci of American foreign policy from 1977 to 1980. The Carter administration worked closely on the Namibian question with the Western Contact Group, comprised of the United States, Great Britain, France, Canada, and Germany (those Western countries which were members of the U.N. Security Council in the late 1970s). A high point was reached when South Africa and the South West Africa People's Organization (SWAPO) accepted the United Nations plan for Namibian independence (U.N. Security Council Resolution 435) in 1978.

An acceptable formula for moving South Africa toward implementation of the Security Council resolution was a goal shared by both the Carter and Reagan administrations. Their approaches to achieving this goal, frequently characterized as sticks (Carter) versus carrots (Reagan), engendered considerable, mostly polemical, debate. The issues of those debates are thoroughly covered in the chapters found in Part I. Irrespective of the debate, however, the fact remains that neither sticks nor carrots have yet persuaded Pretoria to fulfill its agreement since, thus far, it does not perceive Namibian independence, as formulated by the U.N. resolution, to be in its best political and military interests.

During the Reagan administration, South Africa has pursued Jekyll and Hyde policies toward its neighbors in southern Africa. On the one hand, militarily and economically Pretoria attempted to destabilize most of the black-ruled nations in the region. On the other hand, it concluded diplomatic and military accords with Mozambique (Nkomati Accord) and Angola (Lusaka Accord) in early 1984, actions considered by most to be unthinkable less than a year before they were signed.

South Africa's direct and indirect military attacks against those neighbors harboring either members of SWAPO or the African National Congress (ANC) have been especially costly to Angola and Mozambique. Angolan president Jose Eduardo dos Santos estimated that the cost to the Angolan infrastructure of South African attacks between 1975 and 1983 amounted to more than $10 billion. President Machel of Mozambique maintains that regional instability and the drop in trade with South Africa have cost Mozambique $4.2 billion during the past decade which, he noted, is enough to pay Mozambique's fuel bill for the next twenty years.

These attacks came during historically unprecedented droughts and, later, floods, which further devastated the shaky economies of all countries in the region. In addition there has been considerable government mismanagement, if not nonmanagement, especially in Angola and Mozambique. Both states demonstrate that it is not possible for a government to direct a centrally controlled economy when it lacks qualified personnel. The combination of these factors resulted in poor servicing of the rural areas, leaving a large segment of the peasantry to fend for itself under the most arduous circumstances. It appears that this neglect assisted opposition movements, such as the National Union for the Total Independence of Angola (UNITA) and the Mozambican National Resistance (MNR) in Mozambique, in spreading their insurgencies in the countryside.

The dramatically increased activities in the region of opposition movements armed by South Africa are often directed at economic targets, greatly exacerbating the misery of the rural populations. UNITA and the MNR, for example, have mined and ambushed roads used to transport agricultural goods to market or points of distribution. The International Red Cross has estimated the levels of malnutrition and starvation in Mozambique and southern Angola to be as bad, if not worse, than those found in Biafra during the Nigerian civil war.

Undoubtedly the economic and military damage that South Africa has inflicted on its neighbors played a crucial role in convincing major actors in the region to reach political and military accommodations with South Africa in 1984. Pretoria signed the historic Nkomati Accord with Mozambique in early 1984, followed by the Lusaka Accord with Luanda for a disengagement of South African forces from Angola. Washington hailed these accords as victories for the Reagan administration's policy of constructive engagement. But for constructive engagement to succeed, Angola must be convinced that it can guarantee its own security against South Africa without the Cuban troops. Luanda's ultimate decision on the Cubans will depend heavily on South Africa's respect of the Nkomati Accord in Mozambique.

In these 1984 agreements the South African government went further toward accommodation with its neighbors and proclaimed enemies than any previous South African regime. Nevertheless, by the end of the Reagan administration's first four years, it was still not clear whether Pretoria was ready to implement the 1978 U.N. Resolution 435 on Namibia. Nor was it clear whether it was Dr. Jekyll or Mr. Hyde who inspired South Africa's regional policies.

1

United States Policy toward South Africa: Is One Possible?

WILLIAM J. FOLTZ

Since at least the Eisenhower administration, the United States policy toward South Africa has been assailed from both right and left. While critics have disagreed fundamentally over what policy ought to be, they have usually agreed that the policy in force has not succeeded in advancing their version of America's true interests or in removing threats to peace and to cherished social and political values in South Africa itself. Expectations that new administrations in Washington would fundamentally change relations with Pretoria have not long survived each new president's first years in office.

This paper seeks to explain why U.S. policy toward South Africa has evolved as it has over recent years. It will do so principally by looking at the way American interests and events in South Africa are taken into account by the U.S. foreign policy process. From the same perspective the paper will try to assess the possibilities for significant change in the content and goals of America's South Africa policy.

American Interests in South Africa

It is no simple task to present a list of U.S. interests in South Africa. It is even more difficult to rank specific interests in terms of any consensual view of an overriding "national interest" (Foltz 1981). What follows here is a list of prudent concerns which any U.S. administration must bear in mind.

Economic Interests. In aggregate terms, American economic interests in South Africa are small and have remained remarkably stable. Since the end of World War II, South Africa has accounted annually for about 1 percent of U.S. foreign trade and between 1 and 2 percent of U.S. direct investment overseas. These investments have yielded substantial rates of profit for some U.S. corporations, though smaller than profits elsewhere in Africa (Seidman 1978,

181–182). In almost every case South African holdings represent a small part of a U.S. corporation's activity. U.S. investment and exports have been limited by the relatively small size of the South African market, itself a function of the poverty of the South African majority and of South Africa's limited ability to sell its industrial production outside its borders.

Aggregate trade and investment figures alone, however, overlook the special nature of much of this production. South Africa is a major source of key minerals for the U.S. and other Western economies. As the South African government unceasingly points out, for many minerals the principal alternative supplier is the Soviet Union or a country under Soviet control. This fortuitous conjunction raises the specter of a massive "resource war," often discussed in extravagant terms:

> In view of the dependence of the West on supplies of strategic minerals from South Africa . . . should a Soviet puppet regime ever be installed in Pretoria, the international scenario would assume apocalyptic proportions for the West. (South Africa, Dept. of Foreign Affairs and Information 1982)

Yet such scenarios erroneously assume that the present South African regime is the only alternative to Soviet control over those resources and ignore technological innovation, which over the last two decades has continually changed the mix of materials required by modern industry (Goeller and Weinberg 1976; Broad 1980).

This said, no one disputes the importance, both present and future, of South African mineral production to the United States and its allies. When such dependence is placed in a broad national policy context, however, the key issues are reliable access to and orderly marketing of mineral production, and diversified sources of supply to keep prices low. Ownership of production facilities is a side issue. Given the importance of continued access to South African minerals, prudent U.S. policymakers will also be concerned that policies toward South Africa do not jeopardize the supply of resources from other sources: inter alia, oil from Nigeria, Libya, Algeria, Angola, and Cameroon; manganese from Gabon; cobalt from Zaire and Zambia; and chromium and nickel from Zimbabwe.

Military Security Interests.   The southern tip of Africa has been of strategic importance to Western shipping for several centuries. At present, up to 65 percent of Western Europe's and 28 percent of U.S. oil imports pass around the Cape (Bowman 1982, 161). Since modern shipping does not require intermediate ports of call to take on coal, avoiding threatening presence at any one of the restricted passageways along the Cape route is far more important to the West than control of land near these passageways. Besides the Cape of Good Hope, these restricted passageways include the Strait of Hormuz (the only passage narrow enough to permit a blockade); the Mozambique Channel (and the alternative Madagascar–Mascarene Passage, practicable for weather reasons only eight months of the year); the Cape Verde Passage; and the Canary–Cape Bojador Passage. Except for the Strait of Hormuz, which can be interdicted by sortie from land bases in the USSR, attack on the other passageways would require massive deployment of naval and air resources. These would have to be forward based, either in Africa or on one of the islands in the Indian or the Atlantic Ocean.

Since the West cannot hope to acquire direct control of all the promising basing sites along the oil routes, it has an overriding interest in preventing the Soviet Union from acquiring even one. This is more a political than a military task. Governments throughout the area have made it clear that they view foreign military bases as threats to domestic tranquillity and to their continuation in power. They are likely to yield to Soviet importuning only in extreme circumstances. Given the state of relations between Pretoria and its neighbors in southern Africa and the Indian Ocean islands, most of these regimes would feel under enormous pressure should the United States—or any NATO power—conclude a major military agreement with South Africa, a fortiori were it to acquire a significant military installation. This move would likely attract a major Soviet base in the region, in Maputo or Nacala, Luanda, or even the real strategic prize, Diego Suarez.

New Western military bases in South Africa would make sense only as part of a massive Western military expansion—far in excess of anything the Reagan administration has budgeted—that deliberately sought to disperse Soviet air and naval assets and to force that government into even greater levels of military expenditure. Such a strategy is attractive to some "naval hawks," mostly *retired* admirals, but is discounted, even ridiculed, by Department of Defense planners who otherwise are not reticent about expanding American military power (Moorer and Cottrell 1980; Hanks 1981; Bowman 1982).

While the establishment of Western bases in South Africa is not on anyone's current agenda, Pretoria has sought greater military cooperation with the United States. South Africans have vigorously promoted seaward defense, and in expansive moments they have spoken of forming a NATO equivalent with Argentina and Brazil that would protect shipping routes in the South Atlantic. The idea has had its supporters in the U.S. military (Bowman 1982, 175–177). Indeed, during the 1980 election campaign some advisers to Ronald Reagan (who have since not been given government positions) actively promoted the idea (Hoge 1980). For the moment at least, any such plans have been shelved. The Falklands War removed the possibility of Argentina's playing a role, while Brazil has shown little interest in any alliance that might jeopardize its access to Angolan and Nigerian oil. South Africa, meanwhile, lost the bulk of its blue-water navy with the accidental sinking of the cruiser *President Kruger* in 1982. Finally, the cost of blue-water patrols capable of interdicting or deterring a major power has escalated well beyond the power of even South Africa's ample military budget. Recognizing this, the South African navy has converted itself to a "small-ship" force concentrating on coastal patrol. Such patrol capability may serve the temporary interests of the United States and has the virtue of requiring no direct American participation or subsidy.

Strategic intelligence also links South Africans and U.S. defense interests. The centerpiece of South Africa's activities is Project Avokaat, a sea and air surveillance system covering large areas of the South Atlantic and Indian oceans. The system's capabilities are reportedly impressive and may provide a rationale for some continuing contacts between U.S. and South African intelligence services. U.S. satellites, however, provide essentially the same information, so at best the South African system serves only as a backup. Furthermore, the arrest in late 1982 of a South African naval officer as a Soviet spy suggests that its worth has been compromised.

Finally, since 1948 South Africa has sought to be a regional peacekeeper and a "bulwark against Communism" in Africa. For over two and a half decades the United States rebuffed these attempts (Lake 1974, 50–52). In 1975, however, South Africa found what it took to be its chance to render invaluable service to the United States by intervening militarily against the Soviet-backed MPLA in the Angolan civil war. It is not known what, if any, assurances Henry Kissinger gave South Africa about American support for the intervention. It is clear, however, that then Defense Minister P. W. Botha felt betrayed when the United States failed to support a decisive thrust against Luanda (Stockwell 1978; Bender 1981). The South African connection proved damaging when its discovery deprived the National Front for the Liberation of Angola (FNLA) and the National Union for the Total Independence of Angola (UNITA) of African diplomatic support. Rather than proving an effective regional surrogate for U.S. military force, South Africa was a liability that reduced U.S. freedom of maneuver and legitimized the continued presence of Cuban and Soviet forces.

South Africa remains, however, the primary military power in southern Africa (Jaster 1980, 1983). Its technological capacity to produce atomic weapons and tactical delivery systems ensures that its military power will be taken seriously (Adelman and Knight 1979). As other regionally dominant pariah states have found, however, such military power has limited utility. It can punish and harass neighbors and can throw their political and economic systems into turmoil, but it cannot build productive relations or stabilize the region. This poses problems for a power like the United States that has a stake in regional stability. It also confers upon South Africa the opportunity to manipulate the United States. Pretoria can sow disruption in the region under the calculation that this should deter local opponents.

International Political Interests.   These may be arbitrarily divided into *world order* issues involving the structure of international society, and *third-party* issues in which America's dealings with South Africa affect its relations with other countries. Under either heading, South Africa has regularly complicated America's pursuit of larger foreign policy goals.

The most pressing world order issue is South Africa's control over Namibia. As this control is maintained in defiance of rulings by the International Court of Justice and the Security Council, it calls into question the effectiveness of institutions that have been instruments of U.S. foreign policy (Dugard 1973; Rotberg 1983). It also provides effective diplomatic cover for Soviet involvement in southern African affairs. Since at least 1977, when the Western Contact Group[1] began its search for a settlement, the United States and its closest allies have exerted an unprecedented amount of diplomatic energy in the frustrating search for a solution (McHenry 1979). American abandonment of the Contact Group initiative without strong action to replace it would be a major diplomatic setback, and would harm U.S. relations with the other members of the Contact Group and U.S. influence within the United Nations.

South Africa's nuclear capabilities pose a chronic world order issue for the United States. South Africa continually refuses to sign the Nuclear Nonproliferation Treaty or otherwise permit international inspection of its key nuclear operations, including the uranium enrichment facilities at Pelindaba. While no one disputes South Africa's technological capacity to produce nuclear weapons, some fear that an actual detonation would weaken worldwide restraints on proliferation.

Both these world order concerns have enmeshed the United States in complex dealings with the South African government. The Namibian issue has required the West to negotiate steadily with Pretoria and thus to moderate punitive actions designed to influence South Africa's domestic policies (Barratt 1982). Similarly, during the Carter administration proposals by State Department Africanists to end all forms of nuclear cooperation with South Africa were vigorously opposed by "liberals" in the Arms Control and Disarmament Agency and other regional bureaus. They insisted that this action risked inciting a South African nuclear explosion, thus undermining their nonproliferation efforts. As Betts (1979) has pointed out, South Africa's nuclear efforts make the most sense as a "diplomatic bomb" restraining Western actions and are not justified by military necessity.

South Africa presents a moral issue that even the most cynical policy cannot ignore, if only because third parties insist on taking it into account. Like other countries, the United States pays a political price for dealing openly with the Pretoria regime. The closer the third party is to South Africa—in space or political concern—the more significant the price. In Europe and most of the Third

---

1. See the introduction to this section, p. 30.

World, U.S. relations with South Africa play only a minor role in shaping the local images of an American administration. In contrast to this, in black Africa, American policy toward South Africa deeply colors the views of the administration in Washington and the country that elected it. The impact of such attitudes on U.S. relations with black Africa or with a particular African country, however, is difficult to assess. Overall, it is likely that under almost all circumstances, policy toward South Africa has been only a minor factor shaping the decisions of African countries that are of great interest to the United States. The same has been true for the Soviet Union, whose degree of influence with African states is only marginally affected by its systematic opposition to the South African regime (Nolutshungu 1982).

A crude thought experiment illustrates this. If the United States were to sever all ties with Pretoria—a move Washington perceives as costly—would the United States find compensatory gains elsewhere on the continent? Would Qadhafi recognize Israel? Would Nyerere even stop lecturing the world about declining terms of trade? The absurdity of the questions stems from the reality that all nations compartmentalize decisions; there is a limit to trade-offs between issues. Furthermore, in the short run the United States wants little that Africans can easily give, and Africans cannot sacrifice their highly ranked domestic goals for distant issues, even those about which they care passionately.

The situation is different when what the United States wants from an African government is directly linked to American–South African relations, as in the Rhodesian negotiations. The Carter administration correctly understood that bringing the nationalist movements fighting the white Rhodesian regime to the bargaining table required the active cooperation of the leaders of the neighboring black-ruled states on which the movements relied for military and diplomatic support. Those leaders would cooperate only if they believed that the United States was not committed to perpetuating white supremacy in the region. Thus, U.S. pressure on South Africa to dismantle apartheid demonstrated American bona fides to reassure African leaders that cooperation was worth the risk. Such cases may not be common. The Reagan administration appears to have calculated—correctly or not—that the relevant African states are so locked into the Namibia process that the United States can afford to subordinate demonstrations of support for African goals to a perceived necessity to reassure the South African government of American understanding for its problems. Linkage, thus, works both ways.

Yet the price of subordinating black African goals may not always be low. The constraints so painfully felt by African states in the current world recession may not always be present; change in the oil market could again make Nigerian good will seem of national interest. Thus, a prudent U.S. policy would avoid provocative displays of enthusiasm for Pretoria's actions that would bring African leaders who wish to cooperate with the United States under unbearable pressure from their peers or citizenry. While even the dimmest American policymakers should understand such a basic principle of statecraft, divining the threshold of "provocation" is more difficult. The formal position on relations with South Africa endorsed by the black African position, expressed most simply in the *Lusaka Manifesto*, holds that "South Africa should be excluded from the United Nations.... It should be ostracized by the world community." Whatever the merits of systematic ostracism, it lies so far outside the realm of relevant policy discourse in Washington that formal African statements insisting on it are discounted as empty rhetoric. Without clear and relevant guidance from African leaders themselves, long-term policy will rely even more than usual on past practice and on extra-African consideration.

Domestic Political Interests. The symbolic connection between relations with South Africa and domestic American politics is something no administration can avoid. Even though fine details may be lost or misperceived, the general tenor of U.S. policy toward South Africa will be interpreted with reference to America's own racial issues. To see how this occurs, and the limits to its impact, it is necessary to step back and see how a peripheral concern like South Africa enters American politics through the public's perception.

Most Americans perceive South Africa only dimly; their information on the country is shaky and their opinions not firmly anchored (Foltz 1979b; Barron and Immerwahr 1979; Baker et al. 1979a). Nevertheless, in the aggregate, American public opinion on South Africa has shown considerable consistency over the past several years, as well as a trend toward disapproval of apartheid when the issue is forcefully brought to mind. For example, Table 1–1 summarizes the responses to a Harris survey, which asked a nationwide sample the following leading question in 1977 and 1981:

> The government of South Africa, run by the whites, has closed down the leading black newspapers, and has put many of the moderate black leaders in jail. As you know, they have a system called apartheid, under which the white minority runs the country and the black majority is kept separate and given fewer rights. Do you think the system of apartheid in South Africa is justified or not?

Such a question, of course, is only indirectly related to U.S. foreign policy. The consequences Americans will draw from their attitudes toward apartheid depend on the context of the policy decision. The 1981 Harris poll asked respondents to agree or disagree with some statements on what U.S. policy should be. As Table 1–2 demonstrates, when the statements related to racial or human rights themes, a positive concern for such rights showed through. When moral principles were put in conflict with more tangible interests, policy changed, as shown in Table 1–3. In a manner consistent with all other such polls, the Harris respondents' attitudes and policy preferences were strongly influenced by their general political ideology. Asked whether they thought the "Reagan administration was right to take a more friendly ap-

TABLE 1–1   American Public Opinion on Apartheid (percent)

	1977	1981
Apartheid is justified	12%	11%
Apartheid is not justified	63	74
Not sure	26	15

SOURCE: *The Harris Survey* Release no. 86 (October 26, 1981).

TABLE 1–2   American Attitudes toward South Africa:
Racial Issues (percent)

	Agree	Disagree	Not Sure
The whites in South Africa have a right to run their government, and it's about time we stood up for the rights of white people abroad.	36%	54%	10%
It is immoral for the United States to support a government that oppresses blacks.	62	30	8

SOURCE: *The Harris Survey* Release no. 86 (October 26, 1981).

TABLE 1–3   American Attitudes toward South Africa:
Strategic Issues (percent)

	Agree	Disagree	Not Sure
The United States should support the South African government because they are an ally of ours in opposing Russian Communism.	54%	35%	11%
South Africa contains many important resources, such as minerals, that are vital to our national security, so we must stay on good terms with the white South African government.	54	38	8

SOURCE: *The Harris Survey* Release no. 86 (October 26, 1981).

proach to the South African government than had the Carter administration," 58 percent of the conservatives agreed, 52 percent of the liberals *disagreed.*

The opinions of Americans in elite positions, particularly of those professionally involved in international affairs, reflect those of the populace as a whole, but are more consistent and more clearly related to political ideology. The most extensive study of American elite opinion on African issues found that a single ideological dimension underlies Council on Foreign Relations members' views of U.S. African policy (Foltz 1979b:3–6). On only two out of forty-five questions asked did responses fail to correlate significantly with four different measures of ideology. As one would expect, foreign affairs elites are more consistent on points of principle involving relations with South Africa; however, they are less willing than ordinary Americans to give verbal approval to backing up these principles with governmental action (see Table 1–4).

The opinions of black Americans reflect those of the nation as a whole on most issues of relations with South Africa, although blacks are marginally more willing than other Americans to endorse various forms of governmental action against South Africa (Baker et al. 1979a; 1979b). Perhaps the most important difference between black and white opinion is that blacks consistently accord Africa a higher importance than whites in their views of the world. However, the dominant concern is directed more toward the immediate general welfare of black Africans than toward radical political change. In this sense, much of black American opinion (like much white American opinion) is prepolitical. This welfare orientation seems to have been the dominant factor accounting for a national sample of blacks supporting *more* vigorously than whites the proposal to lift sanctions against the Muzorewa/Smith regime in Rhodesia/Zimbabwe in June 1979 (Department of State 1979).

The salience of South African issues is even greater for black American elites.

> For American black leaders, policy toward South Africa is . . . a litmus test of
> domestic racial attitudes, and our relations with South Africa are regarded as a
> mirror image of those attitudes. Thus the goal is to reaffirm our fundamental
> commitment to racial equality through our policy toward South Africa. (Baker
> et al. 1979b)

Despite the intensity of the commitment, its policy implications are not clear. Thus, while many black elites endorse economic sanctions against South Africa, others, like Vernon Jordan and Leon Sullivan, prefer to promote American corporate practices that will immediately improve the welfare of black South Africans.

This said, the American black community remains the only population group for which South Africa is steadily a salient issue. At a minimum, contin-

TABLE 1-4   U.S. Pressure on South Africa (percent)

		Sample	Favor	Oppose	Not Sure
a.	Should the United States and other Western nations pressure South Africa to give the blacks there greater freedom and political participation?	Public Elite	46% 83	26% 10	28% 7
b. 1.	Should the United States get its companies in South Africa to put pressure on the South African government?	Public Elite	46 70	28 24	26 6
2.	Prevent all *new* business investment in South Africa?	Public Elite	42 16	33 74	25 9
3.	End all U.S. trade with South Africa?	Public Elite	24 2	51 92	25 6
4.	Force all U.S. businesses now in South Africa to close their operations there?	Public Elite	21 1	51 94	28 5
5.	Cut off shipments of military supplies and replacement parts for South Africa?	Public Elite	51 49	24 37	25 14
6.	Persuade its allies to join us in refusing to send military supplies and replacement parts to South Africa?	Public Elite	48 45	26 41	26 14
7.	Send military supplies to nearby black nations in Africa?	Public Elite	13 8	65 75	22 17
8.	Help build up military pressures in Africa on South Africa?	Public Elite	12 5	64 86	24 9
9.	Urge blacks inside South Africa to engage in guerrilla warfare against the white government?	Public Elite	4 2	76 93	20 5
10.	Start a limited military action against South Africa?	Public Elite	7 0.5	73 99	20 1

NOTE: "Public" sample is national sample of Americans polled by Louis Harris Associates in November 1977. "Elite" responses are from 1,800 Council on Foreign Relations members polled in February 1979.

SOURCE: Foltz 1979b:20

uing black interest guarantees that South Africa cannot be "just another country," and the major policy initiatives toward South Africa will be interpreted as symbols of an administration's attitude toward racial justice in America. If black public opinion cannot give clear foreign policy guidance, at least it points out the direction in which policy should head and sets limits to backsliding. That is about as much of a role as public opinion can be expected to play in the formation of any foreign policy.

From Interests to Policies

While many distinctions can be made between governmental structures and their different policy approaches, it suffices for our purposes to lump them into two: Congress, which amalgamates and expresses different domestic interests, and the foreign affairs bureaucracy, which semiconsciously articulates concerns deriving from the need for long-term relations with foreign governments.

Congress. On southern African issues Congress reflects the general tendencies of American public opinion, with all their uncertainties and confusions. The principal difference between public attitudes and congressional voting on southern African policy issues, is that in Congress general political ideology has a much stronger and more systematic influence (Converse 1964). Obscure or unfamiliar issues enhance this tendency. Ideology provides a handy interpretive guide to these issues and the member of Congress whose voting lead one should follow. The strength of the association between ideology and direction of voting is startling. Using the 1978 Americans for Constitutional Action rating of senators as an index of domestic issue liberalism/conservatism and looking at the 62 senators who achieve either strongly conservative scores (80–100) or strongly liberal scores (0–20), all but 3 voted in the predicted direction on at least two-thirds of a possible ten southern African issues during the Carter administration. When a similar measure is used for House voting during the same period, only 3 out of 228 congressmen do not vote in the predicted direction at least two-thirds of the time on nine possible southern African issues. With only minor exceptions, constituency pressures from corporate interests do not appear to exercise an important influence on congressmen's voting on southern African issues independently of ideology. One-third of the Senate and one-half of the House fall in the ideological middle ground, and their votes on southern African issues are more difficult to predict. For most of them, the specific context of a policy issue is often decisive. If it is perceived as a cold war issue, or to a lesser extent as a narrow economic one, middle-of-the-road congressmen tend to favor the South African government. If the issue is perceived primarily as reflecting racial or, to a slightly lesser degree, political repression, their vote is likely to be in the opposite direction. The House has been marginally more "liberal" than the Senate with regard to southern Africa, largely because the Black Caucus has reinforced other members' definition of southern African issues as matters of "racial justice."

As with the public at large, Congress provides no substantial or consistent backing for heroic measures in favor of or against South Africa. The reactions of both Congress and the public depend on the way South African issues are defined. Above all, the tendency of Congress is shaped by the ideological distribution of those who sit in it, which is a matter over which the American people have some control.

The Foreign Affairs Bureaucracy. Two contrasting, and firmly rooted, bureaucratic perspectives, the regionalist and the globalist, must be taken into account by any administration formulating and executing policy toward South Africa (Foltz 1979a; 1980). While other differences separate the two perspectives, the key dividing line is the relevance of the East-West issue to Africa. Whereas regionalists consider the cold war competition secondary to black nationalism as a force in Africa, globalists view Africa primarily through the lens of the U.S.–USSR struggle. Although the regionalists have affinities with liberal ideology, and the globalists with its conservative counterpart, the fit is far from perfect. Neither perspective sees itself as ideological or seriously interested in African ideologies, neither concerns itself centrally with human rights as such, and neither is particularly concerned with expanding American corporate interests. Alliances with congressional supporters are thus easily strained.

Neither perspective offers clear policy guidance on dealing with apartheid. For most globalists, it is a marginal, if occasionally a troubling, issue. Their concerns typically are short-run worries about Soviet direction of the African National Congress (ANC) and about episodes of violence for which both Pretoria and the black opposition may be blamed. The regionalists' concern with black nationalism provides few clues to daily action in a situation where that historic force remains far from the reins of power. The regionalists are more in their element on peripheral southern African matters; Namibia's independence is a priority, as is the development of stable, black-ruled regimes in southern Africa.

The actions of the South African government further complicate policy formulation and execution. Both globalists and regionalists know that many of Pretoria's actions benefit Soviet interests in the region; both groups were upset by South Africa's 1981 raid on the ANC headquarters in Mozambique that triggered a prompt visit to Maputo by two Soviet warships. Furthermore, both groups have learned how difficult it is to influence the South African government (Olivier 1982). Thus the task confronting any U.S. administration seeking to influence events in South and southern Africa is a daunting one.

Is an Effective Policy Possible?

Confronted with these complexities under a series of administrations, the U.S. government has sought to avoid paying any substantial and immediate economic or strategic price for doing so (Study Commission 1981:340–362). That stance has been epitomized by regular public expressions of "abhorrence" of apartheid and by the repetition of the delicately phrased statement: "The U.S. government neither encourages nor discourages trade and investment in South Africa." The distance and concern manifested have varied with the ideological orientation of the administration in power, and, to a lesser degree, that of Congress. Periodic outrages, such as Sharpeville, Soweto, and the murder of Steve Biko also have increased the distance, which typically is only partially decreased in the interim.

The Carter and the Reagan administrations are the first two that have deployed substantial diplomatic resources to deal with South Africa on either Namibia or domestic South African racial issues. The two administrations differed strikingly (in American political terms at least) in ideology and in the style and background of their African diplomatic teams. The Carter team was oriented toward black Africa, and black African concerns shaped the way it dealt with South Africa. The Reagan team, headed by a specialist in white Africa, has treated South Africa as the preeminent regional power whose regime's interests must be accommodated if negotiations are to succeed.

The Carter administration emphasized increasing the distance between the United States and the South African government and on publicly employing symbolic deprivations. It lacked the domestic and the international backing for applying more serious pressures. Primacy was given to the Rhodesian and Namibian negotiations, though to facilitate those negotiations "progress" was demanded from the South African government on domestic racial matters as well. The Carter administration did not emphasize globalist concerns about the relationship of southern African issues to East-West conflict, although it could have made a good case that its largely "regionalist" policy did blunt Soviet pressures in southern Africa. When the global East-West rivalry intensified, conflicting signals emerged from Washington (Brzezinski 1983, 139–145; Vance 1983, 84–92). As pressures on the administration increased, attention to southern Africa wandered and support for costly initiative evaporated.

The Reagan administration's policy of "constructive engagement" has lessened, though not eliminated, the symbolic distance that the United States has taken from the Pretoria regime; many symbolic and a few substantive barriers to normal relations have been removed. Assistant Secretary of State Crocker repeatedly has put the defense of white interests in South Africa on a par with the defense of black interests, and he has sought to treat the South African government on a par with the governments of black states in the region (e.g., Crocker 1981). Crocker and his associates know that they pay a price for such an "understanding" approach to Pretoria, but argue that it must be paid to achieve a Namibian settlement and, in the longer run, to encourage the emergence of a South Africa that can exist peacefully and fruitfully with its neighbors.

The South African government has not, however, been more responsive to symbolic incentives and quiet pleading than to earlier symbolic deprivations and public harangues. The Reagan administration has been even less successful than the Carter administration in conveying a consistent message to Pretoria. President Reagan himself has undercut his words of concern with statements that South Africans have interpreted as assurances of support for their policies (e.g., CBS News 1981). Moreover, Reagan has been unwilling to protect his principal agents from attacks emanating from the outer reaches of his own party. Thus, Crocker and company have had to build their own alliances with the globalist parts of the bureaucracy and congressional conservatives by promising payoffs in policy areas of central concern to those groups. This domestic political imperative is behind the "practical," if unofficial, linkage of Cuban withdrawal from Angola with the Namibia negotiations. Pretoria has seized on this domestic American concern to hamstring the negotiations, and while increasing its military adventures in neighboring countries, to identify America's "engagement" as public license for unrestrained intercourse. As awareness of Pretoria's actions spreads, and as Namibian settlement recedes even further, congressional opposition has increased and added to policy confusion.

The preceding discussion has not sought to spell out what U.S. policy ought to be toward South Africa, but to clarify the enduring domestic and international constraints on that policy. Nevertheless, it suggests three basic requirements that have to be met if any U.S. administration is to influence the pace and direction of change within South Africa.

1. A strong, sustained, and public presidential commitment to influencing change within South Africa, endorsed, at least in its general outlines, by Congress. This in turn requires a domestic political payoff, or else initial enthusiasm will flag. Since southern African issues are peripheral to most Americans most of the time, it is unlikely that the payoff can take any form other than ardent support of black voters. In the absence of an equivalent conservative group for whom South Africa has sustained salience, a Reagan-type administration is unlikely to have the political backing to carry out a sustained, forceful policy.

2. A policy approach that integrates South African concerns with issues central to large numbers of Americans. This approach must be articulated in moral and/or political terms capable of mobilizing ideological support, and in strategic terms capable of reassuring Americans that economic and security interests are being advanced. This requires that the East-West dimension of southern African policy be dealt with explicitly, calmly, and logically by

tying policy to a strategy for blocking, preempting, or rolling back Soviet influence. It is not enough to declare, as did President Carter, an end to "an inordinate fear of Communism"; rather, an administration must use the American electorate's "ordinate" fear to its policy advantage.

3. Strong, unambiguous, and persistent policy guidance from within South Africa itself. As the colonial powers eventually discovered, effective policy requires *interlocuteurs valables,* responsible African spokesmen commanding significant political support. A strongly reformist white government in South Africa could play such a role initially; alas, no such government seems imminent. Thus, the voice must be that of one or more black leaders within South Africa who can command broad support from blacks and a few whites within South Africa and also the endorsement of respected leaders of black-ruled southern African states. If such a voice were to speak the language of nationalism, rather than international revolution, it might be heard in Washington and provide a stimulus for far more heroic measures than Congress or American public opinion has yet contemplated. New episodes of heavy-handed repression by the South African government would likely amplify rather than muffle the voice. Unfortunately, while further repressive episodes are quite likely, the emergence of a clear voice still seems far off (Foltz 1982).

Meeting these three conditions under the best of circumstances will not be easy, and the best of circumstances may take a long time to develop. For the foreseeable future, U.S. policy is likely to stay within the familiar parameters of symbolic distance coupled with problem management. If this is the case, prudence dictates that policy should attempt to keep immediate domestic and international political costs low, to do as little harm as possible to long-run U.S. interests in Africa, and to attempt quietly to facilitate the emergence of the *interlocuteurs valables* within South Africa who will be essential when the United States can no longer afford merely symbolic policies.

REFERENCES

Adelman, Kenneth L., and Albion W. Knight. 1979. "Can South Africa Go Nuclear?" *Obris* 23, no. 3 (Fall): 633–647

Baker, James E., J. D. O'Flaherty, and J. de St. Jorre. 1979a. *Public Opinion Poll on American Attitudes toward South Africa.* New York: Carnegie Endowment for International Peace.

————. 1979b. "The American Consensus on South Africa." *Worldview* 22, no. 10 (October):12–16.

Barratt, John. 1982. "The Namibian Dilemma: Factors Preventing a Settlement." Johannesburg: South African Institute of International Relations, Occasional Paper, September.

Barron, Deborah D., and J. Immerwahr. 1979. "The Public Views South Africa: Pathways through a Gathering Storm." *Public Opinion* (January/February):54–59.

Bender, Gerald. 1981. "Kissinger in Angola: Anatomy of Failure," pp. 63–144 in René Lemarchand, ed. *American Policy in Southern Africa: The Stakes and the Stance.* 2d ed. Washington, D.C.: University Press of America.

Betts, Richard K. 1979. "A Diplomatic Bomb for South Africa?" *International Security* 4, no. 2 (Fall):91–115.

Bowman, Larry W. 1982. "The Strategic Importance of South Africa to the United States: An Appraisal and Policy Analysis." *African Affairs* 81, no. 323 (April): 159–191.

Broad, William J. 1980. "Resource Wars: The Lure of South Africa." *Science* 210, no. 5 (December):1099–1100.

Brzezinski, Zbigniew. 1983. *Power and Principle: Memoirs of the National Security Advisor 1977–1981.* New York: Farrar Straus Giroux.

CBS News Special Report. 1981. "A Conversation with the President." March 3.

Converse, Philip. 1964. "The Nature of Belief Systems in Mass Publics," pp. 206–261 in David E. Apter, ed. *Ideology and Discontent.* New York: Free Press.

Crocker, Chester A. 1981. "Assistant Secretary Crocker's Speech to the American Legion, Honolulu, August 29, 1981." U.S. Department of State Press Release.

Department of State. 1979. AF/P Briefing Memorandum, July 9.

Dugard, John. 1973. *The South West Africa/Namibia Dispute.* Berkeley: University of California Press.

Eastern Province Herald. 1981. "Carter Diplomacy Over—US Officials." May 14.

Foltz, William J. 1979a. "La Politique des Etats-Unis face aux problèmes de l'Afrique australe." *Politique Etrangère* 44, no. 1 (Fall):109–126.

———. 1979b. *Elite Opinion on United States Policy Toward Africa.* New York: Council on Foreign Relations.

———. 1980. "United States Policy in Southern Africa: What Next?" in *Südafrika: Internationale Lösungsstrategien und innerer Wandel.* Friedrich Ebert Stiftung, Analysen aus der Abteilung Entwicklungsländerforschung, no. 85/86 (October):62–93.

———. 1981. "U.S. National Interests in Africa," pp. 93–103 in Prosser Gifford, ed. *The National Interests of the United States in Foreign Policy.* Washington: University Press of America for the Woodrow Wilson International Center for Scholars.

———. 1982. "South Africa: What Kind of Change?" *Africa Notes.* Georgetown University, Center for Strategic and International Studies, November.

Goeller, H.E., and A.M. Weinberg. 1976. "The Age of Substitutability." *Science* 191, no. 4227 (20 February):683–689.

Hanks, Robert J. 1981. *The Cape Route: Imperiled Western Lifeline.* Cambridge, Mass.: Institute for Foreign Policy Analysis.

Hoge, Warren. 1980. "Reagan Aides, in South America, Say He Would Not Favor Dictators." *New York Times,* September 22.

Jaster, Robert S. 1980. *South Africa's Narrowing Security Options. Adelphi Papers* no. 159. London: International Institute for Strategic Studies.

———. 1983. *A Regional Security Role for Africa's Front-Line States. Adelphi Papers* no. 180. London: International Institute for Strategic Studies.

Lake, Anthony. 1974. "Caution and Concern: The Making of American Policy Toward South Africa, 1946–1971." Ph.D. dissertation, Princeton University.

McHenry, Donald F. 1979. Testimony in *The Current Situation in Namibia,* Hearing before the Subcommittee on Africa, Committee on Foreign Affairs, House of Representatives, May 7.

Moorer, Adm. Thomas H., and A. J. Cottrell. 1980. "The Search for U.S. Bases in the Indian Ocean: A Last Chance." *Strategic Review* 8 (Spring):30–32.

Nolutshungu, Sam C. 1982. "African Interests and Soviet Power: The Local Context of Soviet Policy." *Soviet Studies* 34, no. 3 (July):397–417.

Olivier, Gerrit C. 1982. "South Africa's Response to Shifting Nuances in United States Foreign Policy." *Africa Insight* 12, no. 2:85–88.

Rotberg, Robert I., ed. 1983. *Namibia: Political and Economic Prospects.* Lexington, Mass.: D. C. Heath.

Seidman, Ann, and Neva Seidman. 1978. *South Africa and U.S. Multinational Corporations.* Westport, Conn.: Lawrence Hill.

South Africa, Department of Foreign Affairs and Information. 1982. *Vital Role of South Africa's Minerals.* Pretoria.

Stockwell, John. 1978. *In Search of Enemies: A CIA Story.* New York: Norton.

Study Commission on U.S. Policy Toward Southern Africa. 1981. *South Africa: Time Running Out.* Berkeley: University of California Press.

Vance, Cyrus. 1983. *Hard Choices: Critical Years in America's Foreign Policy.* New York: Simon and Schuster.

2

South African Policy and United States Options in Southern Africa

SAM C. NOLUTSHUNGU

On the question of South Africa, Western policy has, for nearly four decades, been dominated by two beliefs: that the white minority regime is not only staunchly pro-West, but that it is, in a deeper economic and racial sense, a Western regime, an integral part of the West; and that there are important and growing economic and military interests to be maintained and advanced in South Africa which the West collectively cannot renounce without some inconvenience to itself. In a Manichean vision of good states and bad, friends and foes, there has appeared to be little room for a somewhat more complicated reality—one that could be greatly troubling (and not only in southern Africa) in the years to come, namely, the phenomenon of dangerous friends, menacing not only to enemies and less valued friends but also to the Western countries themselves because of their ability to entangle others in their troubles, to widen and escalate limited conflicts to unmanageable and ruinous proportions. In considering South Africa's strategic responses to its deepening crisis, its potential as a dangerous friend will be underlined.

Western Perceptions of South Africa

Traditionally, international concern about South Africa has focused on its internal racial policies rather than on the means it uses outside its borders to preserve its distinctive internal order. While the United Nations over the last decade has dealt with a series of complaints from the republic's neighbors, South African external policy has always seemed to Western governments far less in need of international attention and corrective action and, generally, free of the odium pertaining to its domestic political arrangements. Characteristically, South Africa has been viewed as the object, the *victim*, one might say, of the outrage—real or imagined, justified or spurious—of other states, blacks, non-Westerners, and communists. If the West has felt challenged to "do something" about South Africa, Pretoria, in Western eyes, has always appeared in a predominantly defensive attitude, occasionally tempted, it might be conceded, to be too forceful in its own defense and altogether too unyielding, but essentially not disposed to disrupt the international status quo or to frustrate Western purposes unduly. Opposition to Pretoria has, therefore, always been a more or less reluctant concession to the demands of others, and only occasionally has South Africa seemed likely to become, even in a remote and by no means inevitable future, an insupportable burden to the West.

Critics of Western policy toward South Africa have pointed to the danger of alienating black Africa and the Third World if the West failed to support critical international action against the regime. The cost of supporting Pretoria would mount as these countries became more important markets and sources of raw materials while all the time losing patience with the West over South Africa and increasingly looking elsewhere for support against their sworn enemy (Study Commission 1981).

The credibility of this argument has varied with the change of governments in Western countries between conservative and liberal, and with the ups and downs of politics on the African continent. The emergence of Nigeria as an important oil exporter, and also as a growing market for Western merchandise, pointed to the need to please the black Africans. The advent of the nationalist military regime of Generals Murtala Mohammed and Olusegun Obasanjo in the mid-1970s, with its militant anti-apartheid policy, reinforced this view. Marxist victories in Angola and Mozambique, and more ambiguously in Zimbabwe, seemed to clinch the argument.

In the 1980s, with the Soviet Union attracting attention elsewhere on the globe, the revolutionary tide in southern Africa fading from press headlines, and African states, including Nigeria, experiencing their worst economic difficulties since independence, a shift in perspective seems to have occurred. "Moderate" leaders and idiosyncratic right-wing dictatorships seem to predominate and are certainly not disposed to upset their relations with the West over South Africa. As African states file abjectly in hopes of Western economic relief—often military aid to preserve their governments in power— the threat of African retaliation against the West seems overzealously farsighted and even fanciful.

Evidence has always abounded in support of a contrary view, that most of the black-ruled African states would not, and in many cases could not, do much more than complain or rage impotently, dependent as they were on the West and lacking the means themselves to do anything to South Africa. In any event, there has always been an alternative to meeting African demands, namely, pressuring the African states to accommodate South Africa in exchange for whatever ambiguous, piecemeal reforms South Africa might be persuaded to make out of consideration for the West and in its own good time—an evolutionary time (Nolutshungu 1980). A combination of weakness on the part of the African states and toughness on the part of the West, as at present, renders that option all the more attractive.

Such Western official perceptions have come under searching scrutiny and powerful criticism within the West, and it would serve no purpose here to repeat all the familiar arguments. It might be useful, however, to look at recent developments in southern Africa and particularly at South Africa's own external posture to present the view that such Western perceptions are substantially in error, and, more important, to suggest that there may be room for a reappraisal of Western policies, especially with respect to South Africa's external policies, even within the conventional self-conceptions of the West and its own interests.

Fundamental to the argument which follows is the fact that South African policies are utterly self-regarding and do not arise out of any larger commitment (such as the defense of the West), other than very parochial defense of a very local interest of South African whites in their own continued mastery over blacks. In hard accounting terms, it is extremely difficult to show that the West has benefited politically or strategically from its relationship with South Africa—beyond the normal gains from trade and investment that have accrued with equal ease from trade with other members of the international economic system and which would, therefore, have been obtained even if quite different attitudes had prevailed in the West on the matter of opposing the apartheid regime.

In at least two important situations in recent years—Angola and Zimbabwe—it is possible to demonstrate that South Africa effectively undermined Western policies, or made Western ends much more difficult of attainment, and, more importantly, greatly increased the potential for ruinous international conflict for all concerned. Contrary to British purposes and United Nations Security Council policy (and there have been very few explicit policies indeed in the history of that world body), South Africa sustained the rebel regime in Rhodesia with arms and men as well as money. In doing so they made a peaceful resolution of this dispute impossible, and if at length British interests did not fare too badly in Zimbabwe, it was in spite of, not because of, South Africa. As an intermediary between the rebel regime and London, and as a force for moderation on Smith, South Africa was much less than an honest broker, as Whitehall well knew. If in this respect it may have rendered some service to the cause of ending the rebellion, that was more than outweighed by its prolongation of the conflict.

South Africa's military intervention in Angola may have been encouraged by Washington, yet it was because Pretoria was involved that the West failed to gain support for its side in the civil war among the more influential African states. Indeed, had South Africa not been involved militarily, the Soviet Union and Cuba might well have followed a different policy, at least with regard to the extent of their own military involvement. Moreover, had South Africa stayed out of Angola after the civil war instead of effectively occupying Angolan territory and sustaining UNITA, a Cuban withdrawal might have been possible and a more consensual resolution of the many-sided political conflicts of the country might have had more chance of success. Civil wars have been fought before in Africa, but in most other cases they have been brought to a close by the natural limits of the expendable resources of the contending sides.

In entangling itself in Angola, from which it has carried on its war against Namibian nationalists, South Africa has rendered the resolution of the Angolan problem infinitely more intractable, exalting it from a basic question of decolonization to an elemental conflict between East and West, or what often appears to be the same thing, a campaign by a succession of American presidents against the leader of a Caribbean island on the other side of the Atlantic. To be sure, Americans have had their own reasons for aiding this transformation of the Angolan and Namibian conflicts, but they have had to work on a terrain chosen by South Africa, and increasingly in subordination to the latter's own aims. Ideology and global interests apart, it cannot, surely, be argued that even the most hawkish cold-war enthusiasts might not have preferred an easier struggle with a clearer definition of specifically American— and, indeed, Angolan and Namibian—aims without the millstone of apartheid round their necks. The United States can point to no tangible success in either Angola or Namibia. Moreover, American policy options—including the option of *learning* to deal with an ideologically more differentiated context in Africa while supporting the preferred African attitude of nonalignment—have clearly been significantly narrowed by these developments.

Insofar as these South African policies can be said to be serviceable to Western interests they are so only according to a very particular definition of those interests shared in the West by a small and diminishing minority among those who think seriously and knowledgeably about international affairs. In narrowing the options, such policies preclude the effective representation of significant sections of Western public opinion which prefer a more pacific way of doing things and one that does not involve a deepening entanglement in the conflicts that white South Africa has created for itself, but which could easily be transformed into an East-West confrontation of global significance.

South Africa's Strategies for Preserving
White Supremacy

Since the Second World War, South Africa has conceived of the defense of white minority rule in terms of a double strategy, directed at both its internal environment and the rest of the world, particularly the West and Africa. The methods of dealing with these two contexts and the relative emphases of successive administrations have differed. Roughly, until the early 1960s the internal political landscape received the greatest attention, though the international context was by no means ignored. Since the emergence of independent

African states and the deepening of the conflict between black and white in southern Africa, and, particularly, the development of armed liberation struggles, the external relations of the regime have received increasingly urgent attention. Part of the concern was to neutralize the political and military dangers that might arise, but part of it was also to ensure a continued flow to South Africa of Western investments as well as trade, to maintain markets in Africa, and particularly to sustain and consolidate the system of economic dependence of neighboring African states on South Africa to ensure markets for South African industry, labor for its mines and farms, and custom for its communication services. In addition, South Africa would benefit from being both the conduit and the center of Western economic activity in the region if the investor countries could be persuaded that their activities in the rest of southern Africa must radiate from their South African interests since, as Pretoria indefatigably argued, no realistic policy of development of any kind could succeed in any of these countries independently of South Africa. To achieve a dominant economic role, and to acquire a focal military and political role in the international affairs of all of Africa are aims that have been pursued consistently and assiduously.

In the decade or so following the Second World War, South African governments, seeing the dangers that might follow from decolonization, sought increased influence on imperial policies in Africa. The National Party, from the moment it took power in 1948, struggled to halt or slow down the decolonization of the continent and conceived of defense arrangements in which Pretoria would have an important role within the imperial order. It foresaw two kinds of danger that might arise to support blacks and their demands within the republic: (1) agitation and subversion by black Africans from the new African states recently freed from colonialism, and (2) growth in the influence of unfriendly powers (e.g., the Soviet Union, India, and the United States) as well as of the United Nations. External security was essential if South Africa was to carry through the process of building apartheid and, given its own limited capabilities, South Africa relied entirely, and not in vain, on the major European imperial powers to maintain favorable conditions in Africa, to give support at the United Nations, and to guarantee its security from Soviet interference. The latter was considered a real possibility even in the 1950s. South Africa's only contribution to Western defense was its limited participation in the Korean War. Britain, it is true, continued to enjoy treaty rights over the naval base in Simonstown and Pretoria did propose a South Atlantic Treaty Organization, which never materialized.

In the 1960s, as opposition to apartheid mounted within South Africa, attempts were made, hesitantly and with many reservations, to work out a diplomatic modus vivendi with the emerging states, a policy pursued with some vigor by the Vorster government in the late 1960s and 1970s. At the same time, despite the Pretoria government's pretense of legalism in international affairs, it commenced to violate the sovereignty of neighboring African countries by kidnaping its opponents. The Congo crisis in the early 1960s launched a period of more or less clandestine South African military participation on the side of right-wing elements in African conflicts. Under Vorster's "outward-looking" policy, espionage, intimidation, and military incursions into the territory of such countries as Zambia were undertaken. In addition to aiding the settler rebellion in Rhodesia, South Africa did all it could to help to uphold the Portuguese colonial presence in Angola and Mozambique— mainly through the investment funds which its state corporations provided for huge projects of "colonial development" in those territories. In sum, its interventions in other African states and territories were not limited to retaliation for or prevention of armed incursions into its own territory; rather it reflected a calculated policy of subversion and open dictatorial interference.

A natural complement of this policy was the development of an expensive military capability designed to achieve effective self-defense against any conventional attack that might come from an African source not backed by a superpower and to uphold South African prestige, for as the international anti-apartheid campaigns gathered strength, South Africa sought to maintain business confidence and to preserve its generally favorable standing among Western governments. It endeavored to prove that it could take care of itself, contribute significantly, if need be, to Western defense, contain "communist subversion" in the region, and provide the framework for an expansion of Western economic power and ideological predominance in that part of Africa.

So long as business in South Africa was profitable, the blacks and other opponents effectively contained, life for white immigrants, visitors, and businessmen agreeable and spacious, Western leaders had little difficulty in accepting South Africa's pretensions to power status in Africa. To a Western world still deeply racialist in its own right, Africans in the African-ruled independent states seemed, by contrast, ignorant, weak, and miserable. Where such wretchedness might portend future revolution, U.S. policy, as late as 1974, was based upon an all but unshakable belief that the national liberation movements could not prevail against the white regimes.

South African military leaders have long believed that the "communist menace" should be met as far away from the country's borders as possible. Though this belief now appears to be questioned by some military chiefs, it nevertheless remains dominant, serving as a cover for nondefensive motives of hegemonism and interventionism with respect to less powerful states to the north. As South Africa's military strength mounted in the late 1960s and 1970s it was increasingly attracted to the idea of imitating Israel's strategy of seeking a decisive military superiority in its region, freely entering neighboring countries in hot pursuit of "terrorists," and undertaking punitive military raids while all the time strengthening its arms and arms production. Military and nuclear collaboration with Israel began and grew immensely as Israel became increasingly isolated in Africa after the October War of 1973.

Until the mid–1970s South African attacks on neighboring countries were restrained by a number of factors. First, the armed establishment of South Africa was still small and the regime itself was more concerned with internal repression. This emphasis reflected the predilections of the then prime minister and the structure of power within the ruling party, in which the Bureau of State Security and the Special Branch of the police enjoyed a very privileged status. Second, while they lasted, the white regimes in Rhodesia and the Portuguese colonies served as buffers. Third, Vorster was still convinced that he could win over most of the newly independent black states to cooperate with South Africa through the use of economic incentives, as well as a controlled use of intimidatory force. Fourth, within South Africa itself black resistance seemed to be controllable. However, in the latter part of the decade the situation changed: revolutionaries acceded to power in neighboring countries, domestic tranquillity within South Africa was shattered, and South Africa's leaders, for various reasons, were unable to produce a clear or convincing formula for restoring permanent order and security. With the Cuban and Soviet involvement in Angola, that communist threat so long advertised and almost wished for had, in South African eyes, acquired a certain urgency.

Partly as a result of these new circumstances, but partly also for reasons internal to South Africa and its ruling National Party, important divisions within the ruling bloc surfaced. This led to the ascent of a military—indeed, militaristic—faction led by P. W. Botha, the long-serving minister of defense, who succeeded Vorster as prime minister in 1978. Botha's rise signified an increasingly important role for the military in decision making and in the suppression of popular unrest, amounting to a kind of "creeping coup." Botha adopted a dual strategy, in his parlance a "total strategy," which included vigorous military activity across the country's borders and an attempt to "win the hearts and minds" of the population at home by a series of superficial reforms. It is the strategic opportunities seen and seized by South Africa, far more than the evident dangers to the survival of white rule, which require attention, precisely because they go far beyond the task of merely passively defending the "South African way of life." Before this is examined more fully, it is necessary to review the positions of the powers with whom South Africa has been most concerned.

American and Western Policies and the South African Vortex

Western policies of opposition to South Africa have emerged mainly as a series of reluctant concessions to black African demands and to opposition within the West itself to collaboration with the apartheid regime. For years, Western countries insisted that apartheid was a domestic affair of the republic, and Britain in particular claimed that it had vital strategic interests in South Africa, notably the Simonstown naval base and the Cape sea route. It was the British government which first propounded the view that only by maintaining friendly cooperation with Pretoria could the West hope to influence its leaders away from their universally condemned racial policies. The image of South Africa as a friendly state to Britain was exaggerated to such an extent that successive British governments looked to Pretoria to exert pressure on the Ian Smith government in Rhodesia in support of British aims and did nothing about South Africa's resolute defiance of U.N. Security Council sanctions requested by Britain itself. At the same time there was a long struggle to maintain arms sales to South Africa in the face of demands from other members of the British Commonwealth for a total ban of arms sales. Indeed, South Africa and its ally and affine in Rhodesia ensured that racial division and bitterness would be a lasting feature of the Commonwealth by providing racist groups in Britain with a cause to champion, reinforcing antiblack (antiimmigrant) sentiment. As other markets in Africa became more important (particularly Nigeria), arms sales to South Africa were curbed at length, and Britain's own domestic economic and social problems were mounting, South Africa all but dropped out of the political debate in Britain except as regards sporting relations. Cooperation with South Africa in business continued apace, limited only by Britain's own declining ability to trade. As far as Rhodesia was concerned, the South African contribution to peaceful change was minimal and more than counterbalanced by the aid it gave to Ian Smith's rebel regime. Where Britain's policy after the transfer of power has been to try to preserve British influence and to foster pro-Western development in Zimbabwe, South Africa's activities toward the Mugabe government have shown little responsiveness to such concerns.

From the Second World War until the Carter administration, the United States took virtually no initiative in southern Africa, content at first to rely on the European imperial powers to maintain Western supremacy there. Only when this policy failed in the Congo did the United States take a direct interest, initiating an association with Zaire which has proved to be immensely functional to the white regimes in the area. The Portuguese in Angola, for example, benefited from the exclusion by Zaire of the Popular Movement for the Liberation of Angola (MPLA) in favor of its rival, the National Front for the Liberation of Angola (FNLA) led by a relative of the Zairian dictator, Mobutu, on a retainer from the CIA. Similarly, after the collapse of Portuguese rule in Angola, Zaire, backed by the United States, effectively cooperated with South Africa in a joint unsuccessful effort to prevent the MPLA from gaining control over the central government of independent Angola.

On the Rhodesian problem the United States followed Britain's lead. An exception was the Byrd Amendment, an explicit authorization from the U.S. government which permitted American firms to import chrome from Rhodesia in violation of a U.N. embargo. However, as later transpired, the British government itself permitted an oil company in which it was a majority shareholder to violate its own sanctions against Rhodesia.

Also, as regards relations with South Africa, the United States employed the same rationale as Britain; "constructive engagement" is little more than an elaborate restatement of British Prime Minister Macmillan's propaganda of the early 1960s. If South Africa was aiding settler rebellion and colonial repression, neither of these phenomena upset any important American objective. On the contrary, there was a certain sympathy with Portugal, a trusty NATO ally, and even with white Rhodesians in some circles—as the choice of the Tar Baby Option[1] and the passing of the Byrd Amendment both demonstrated. America, rich and predominantly white, naturally backed those who were also rich and white in a world created by imperialism in which race and class were not only the instruments of Western dominance but also the deepest sources of Western anxieties for the future. Until the mid–1970s there was no reason for urgency in doing anything about South Africa, or its regional position, beyond making the absolute minimum of concessions to African states (and critical Americans) who had to be kept in good humor.

This situation began to change when black movements in southern Africa demonstrated their capacity to seize power. If they were aided by communist arms, it was still ominous that for the first time Africans had shown a capacity to use Soviet aid decisively, undeterred by all the Western hostility to such a collaboration. After Vietnam such victories were bound to have a profound psychological impact on Americans and Africans alike. They seemed to point to a fundamental change in international relations and to underline a certain American impuissance in the face of this transformation in the world distribution of power. After the fall of Portugal's dictatorship, all that remained of the inter-imperial order in Africa were Britain's failing powers in Rhodesia, and a framework of postcolonial dependencies, largely sustained by coercion and dictatorship, politically unreliable, and under the domination of European powers that were losing popular support at home for forceful policies in Africa.

An ineffectual American intervention in Angola (contrasted with the successful, Soviet-Cuban one), the succession of crises in Zaire's Shaba province, and treaties of friendship signed between the Soviet Union and Angola and Mozambique all portended danger. Britain kept its head down and sought to get out of its Rhodesian entanglement with all convenient speed; France rapidly played down the ties of political cooperation with South Africa built up over the preceding decade, while at the same time strengthening its military ties with francophone governments in Africa and steadily improving its commercial position in Nigeria (Luckham 1982). While Western European governments decried the perceived expansion of Soviet influence in Africa, it was left to the United States, a comparative stranger in Africa, to reestablish clear Western superiority in Africa.

---

1. "Tar Baby" was the name given to the second of five options in a once secret 1969 National Security Study Memorandum (#39) which Henry Kissinger recommended and President Nixon accepted, emphasizing "communication" with the white dominated regimes of southern Africa, and including relaxation of sanctions, which for chrome importation from then Rhodesia was actually realized via the Byrd Amendment (Lake 1976).

Kissinger went to southern Africa expressly to address the Rhodesian problem and with some hope of "fixing" the South African problem as well. On South Africa Kissinger said and did nothing worthwhile, and his attempts to end the Rhodesian dispute ended in failure (Oudes 1976 and 1978; Keesings 1976). It then seemed all the more important to achieve peaceful transitions to majority rule to forestall communist-backed revolutions, which, given the public mood in the United States after Vietnam, Chile, and Watergate, might be difficult to counter by intervention. The successor government of President Carter, dominated by that mood and pledged to uphold human rights everywhere, proclaimed its unequivocal support for one-man-one-vote in South Africa and for an end to South African rule in Namibia. Yet it opposed coercive measures against South Africa, particularly rejecting any idea of economic divestment by American companies in South Africa. But there was a certain improvement of relations with African countries which opened the possibility of further collaboration on this and other issues. For the first time ever, Pretoria faced the possibility of a real and progressive deterioration of its relations with Washington and the repudiation of its self-imposed role as regional defender of Western interests. While it would serve no purpose here to speculate whether Carter's policy ever would have had any success in changing South Africa itself, it is clear that from the start his policy was never as radical as it sounded.

While the U.S. ambassador to the United Nations, Andrew Young, won approval among Africans for his personal willingness to accept the fait accompli of the MPLA's victory in Angola and a degree of peaceful coexistence with Moscow in Africa, the progress of Carter's presidency demonstrated that no American administration could afford to even seem to accept any Soviet achievement of any kind anywhere in the world; nor could any policy be freed from that obsessive preoccupation with the Kremlin. Carter continued to make an issue of the Cuban presence in Angola and withheld recognition of the Luanda government. After the Shaba crises, Carter himself led the hue and cry against Soviet subversion in Zaire, blaming the Cubans for Mobutu's difficulties in Shaba. The United States came within an ace of intervening to save that notorious dictatorship (*Africa Contemporary Record* 1978–79; *Africa Research Bulletin* 1978). When it became clear that South Africa was developing an offensive nuclear capability, Washington took no clear position on the issue even though the U.S. embassy was supplied with the means to spy on the project—a camera fitted to the embassy's private plane (*Africa Research Bulletin* 1979). It was clear that so long as the United States hoped to be "constructively engaged" in South Africa there was precious little that it could do to make South Africa more accommodating to its view. Toward the end of Carter's period of office, policy toward South Africa had lost its sense of urgency—and conviction—but by then the black civil rights leader who had refurbished the American image in black Africa, particularly in Nigeria, had been forced out of the administration.

If South African government leaders found the Carter government somewhat awkward to deal with, having been taken aback by its initially forthright denunciation of what they stood for, it did not take long for them to conclude that they had little to fear from Carter's displeasure. They indicated as much not only when they ejected the United States representative for spying and made a public issue of it, but, more dramatically, when they launched a raid on the South West Africa People's Organization (SWAPO) in Angola in 1978 when many believed that a negotiated settlement of the Namibian conflict was in sight. After a change of government, South Africa's military policy became more bold. As the toll of dead and maimed civilians and refugees in neighboring states visited with South African air attacks steadily mounted, the notion of a Western moralizing influence on Pretoria lost all relevance. On the contrary, it seemed to distract attention from the increasingly dangerous acts of external aggression committed by South Africa in favor of interminable ruminations about how to make American participation in the racist economy more humanitarian and so to civilize South African rulers—something the United States had always failed to accomplish with lesser dictatorships nearer home and more abjectly dependent on the United States, even in the routine matter of internal repression. Yet, in foreign relations, American anticommunist campaigns in southern Africa helped rather than hindered South Africa's evolving strategy.

If no dramatic solutions were possible internally; if, as the African response to South Africa's effort in Angola had shown, dialogue had achieved no clear success; and if, moreover, the blacks within South Africa were becoming more militant, then South Africa could only play to its own best advantage. In this way revolution might be forestalled and, equally important, confidence within the white polity might be reestablished. International assessment of the regime's viability would be positive if it seemed that reform was taking place within South Africa and that externally South Africa was willing and able to take care of itself. For its part, South Africa played the Soviet threat for all it was worth. In its last days, the Rhodesian regime with its attacks on Angola and Mozambique seemed even to be seeking to provoke a Cuban involvement that might win the rebel state more sympathy in the West.

The manner of Rhodesia's transformation into Zimbabwe did not please South Africa, which had placed great hopes on a "moderate" alternative being returned to power. Optimism about such a solution in Namibia faded, and South Africa resorted to stalling the Contact Group (Canada, France, Great Britain, the United States, and West Germany) while maintaining military pressure on Angola. With Rhodesia's fall, the isolation of the republic became more evident, and whatever existed by way of a dialogue with black African neighbors all but disappeared. South Africa continued to cling to its idea of a constellation of southern African states to complement its Bantustans, to assert its regional superiority, to defuse the threat of subversion, and to create more scope for its own economic expansion. Military intimidation began to be accompanied by attacks on economic targets, like the Zimbabwe-Mozambique oil pipeline, and by acts of sabotage committed by South African—backed expatriates. In a similar way, the attacks on southern Angola disrupted economic reconstruction and were, in part, intended to make the Benguela railway inoperable as an alternative outlet for Zambian (and at the margin, Zimbabwean) exports. There was a clear South African interest in accomplishing two ends: to keep up the sense of international crisis in southern Africa, and to resist and disrupt attempts by the neighboring states to reduce their dependence on the South African economy and its communication links. In this regard, Zimbabwe, the most industrial and agriculturally the most productive neighboring country, was crucial. If it could be coerced out of an autonomous path of development, particularly one based on closer cooperation with the Southern African Development Coordination Conference (SADCC) members, then the threat to South Africa's economic hegemony (and its attendant economic attractiveness to Western interests) would be defused.

Since Zimbabwe's independence, and particularly since the election of President Reagan, with his far more sympathetic policy toward South Africa, the pressure on neighboring states has been intensified. South Africa has had more opportunity to link its own self-regarding strategies with warding off threats to Western global interests by the "Soviet menace" in southern Africa. The Reagan administration from the outset was less worried about South Africa than about the need to undo the damage done by the Soviets and the Cubans and by Western "lack of resolve." It was, for example, far more concerned with prizing the Cubans out of Angola than with obtaining a speedy, internationally acceptable solution to the Namibian problem. South Africa seized the opportunity to step up its own destabilization of Angola and Mozambique and to make the Cuban issue central to its own negotiating position on Namibia, a linkage which black African states and most members of the Contact Group—and the United Nations—rejected.

The U.S. government was motivated by its ideology and the interests it set out to serve. It is not the aim here to examine that ideology or to evaluate the ways the interests have been interpreted. One point only has to be made, namely that U.S. policy has adopted the South African view of the dangers and the way to cope with them. Between Pretoria's globalist interpretation of its situation and Washington's own perspective on southern Africa there are differences mainly of detail, not of substance. This undoubtedly arises out of a shared anticommunism encapsulating all manner of right-wing capitalist anxieties. South Africa's task is made easy so long as American power enables the United States to refuse to distinguish between global strategic advantages that are necessary and those that are merely desirable. Most states see no prospect of a Soviet "takeover" of southern Africa and are, by and large, constrained to accommodate themselves to the course that the internal history of the region may take. It is not America's needs but its sense of its own power that makes the difference.

U.S. policy also fails to recognize the very specific nature of South African purposes. South Africa's commitment to the West does not extend beyond the defense of its own relatively privileged position in Western capitalism and, specifically, that of its own ruling class. Beyond that, Pretoria will shoulder no responsibilities and will make no concessions to the West, but will defend its system of white minority rule and its regional dominance in southern Africa even if the heavens fall. Now, given that there is a substantial American and Western stake in the South African economy, given also that there is a common interest between the South African ruling class and that of the United States in securing capitalism in southern Africa, and given further that with regard to the Soviet Union itself there is an identity of sentiment, it is nevertheless still sensible to believe that the United States can, if it wishes, take the longer and broader view. While there may be, for all one knows, irresistible psychological and ideological attractions for some Americans in aligning themselves with the racist regime, there are no decisive rational, material grounds for the view that American and South African policies cannot be uncoupled to American advantage.

One option which has not been adequately explored by a U.S. government is that of determining American interests and policy in the rest of the region independently of those of South Africa, i.e., pursuing an autonomous U.S. policy. Instead of linkage, which subordinates U.S. policy toward the other states in southern Africa to its role in the republic, the United States could, if it wished, examine the possibility of developing stronger economic and political relations with the rest of the region. It could support the efforts of the SADCC countries at regional integration and development, and act positively to discourage South African military attacks on them. In the long run, the potential for economic development in southern Africa is great, and dependence on South Africa merely retards it. As future economic partners, these countries are not without attraction to the United States, given their resources, territorial extent, and population strength. Indeed, U.S. and South African interests in this regard could be competitive and even in conflict rather than complementary. That scenario is based, however, on the optimistic assumption that the United States would be able to accommodate itself to the efforts of southern African states to develop autonomously under economic philosophies appropriate to their own circumstances and needs and to cooperate with radical nationalist and socialist oriented countries. Yet, even the United States must increasingly learn to live with the world as it finds it.

Politically, there is every advantage to be gained in furthering nonalignment in southern Africa. There is precious little that the black states can add to the strength of either the United States or the Soviet Union in the global military balance, and yet, pressed into it, they could add to instability and ruinous conflict. South African pressure makes nonalignment an increasingly unattractive option for at least some of those states. It seems unavoidable that the long-term effect of that pressure will be the increasing militarization of those states and the disruption of orderly, peaceful internal development. It is difficult to see what advantage there would be for the United States in such a turn of events. For white minority rule in South Africa, by contrast, that would be a fitting end game that might delay the inevitable.

Vigorous support of the independence of neighboring African states is one area where U.S. policy could be both autonomous and effective. It could also have more effect on South Africa's own internal development than any of the policies so far directed specifically to that end. The claim that the Western countries (first Britain, now the United States) are able to influence South Africa's racial policies by cooperating with Pretoria is mostly cant. It also conceals a depressing reality: that Western influence on South Africa's racial policies has been minimal with regard to either their internal or external dimensions. Even the "reforms" announced after Soweto and the defeats in Angola are superficial and are still totally racist in conception, necessitating a very high degree of continued repression to even seem to work. If that is all that has been achieved after nearly four decades of cooperating with the apartheid regime then there is not much to be said for reform-by-cooperation. By contrast, South Africa, for its part, has been able to commit the Western powers to its diplomatic and economic support, and to a steady entanglement via its defense and intelligence establishments with the very instruments and symbols of apartheid's survival. That is no mean achievement for a small country whose political system is universally condemned. Such discrepancies force the Western powers to assume a conspiratorial manner in their dealings with South Africa—as in the silences over its nuclear efforts, as well as half-truths over the U.S. role in South Africa's war in Angola—which is profoundly antidemocratic and prevents clear consideration of the issues. What is to be feared as South Africa's total strategy unfolds is not only that the Western powers may do too little to change white domination, or that they will support the wrong kinds of "change," but that South Africa may succeed in entangling them in its own adventures outside its borders. It is also to be feared that those Western governments (or government agencies) may be tempted to encourage South Africa to take measures which they are themselves prevented from taking by their own domestic opinion. South Africa's insistence on linkage between the settlement of the Namibian dispute and the question of Cuban troops in Angola (originally an American policy), suggests that this possibility is a very real one indeed.

From discrete acts of collusion in Angola and Mozambique, and from numberless minor acts of cooperation in the areas of intelligence and defense on a day-to-day basis may grow a commitment that may eventually be impossible to renounce, and all the more so since South African policy will do all it can to give substance to that commonly feared and watched-for "Soviet threat," for example, by forcing the radical neighboring states to arm themselves with the aid of the Soviet Union and its allies. For South Africa to be an Israel, privileged with categorical U.S. support, and for southern Africa to be its Middle East, all that Pretoria needs now is for an important alliance of black states to emerge backed by Soviet arms. Then South Africa may hope for an unlimited American guarantee, not of perpetual peace, but of long survival through perpetual war. It must still be possible for the United States to prevent such a development.[2] Policies of cooperation and support, rather than dictation and intimidation, toward the neighboring African states and the liberation movement are the only real means of avoiding the predictable catastrophe. Such means require the complement of American disengagement from South Africa, and most particularly, the absolute cessation of military cooperation at all levels and of financial assistance, both direct and through multilateral institutions, which merely enables the republic to maintain its high level of military expenditure and costly system of internal repression.

REFERENCES

Africa Research Bulletin. 1978. Political, Social and Cultural Series, May 1–31: 4855–4862.
_____. 1979. Political, Social and Cultural Series, April 1–30: 5249–5250.
Africa Contemporary Record. 1978–79. "Zaire." B571–B579.
Keesings Contemporary Archives. 1976. 27943B, 2777A.
Lake, Anthony. 1976. *The "Tar Baby" Option: American Policy Toward Southern Rhodesia.* New York: Columbia University Press.
Luckham, Robin. 1982. "French Militarism in Africa." *Review of African Political Economy,* no. 24:55–84.
Marcum, John A. 1978. *The Angolan Revolution.* Vol. 2, *Exile Politics and Guerrilla Warfare (1972–1976).* Cambridge, Mass.: M.I.T. Press.
Nolutshungu, Sam C. 1980. "External Intervention in South Africa," pp. 173–195 in A. Yansane, ed. *Decolonization and Dependency Problems of Development of African Societies.* Westport, Conn.: Greenwood Press.
Oudes, Bruce. 1976. "The United States' Year in Africa: Postscript to the Nixon Years." *Africa Contemporary Record* VIII, 1975–76:A118–A126.
_____. 1978. "The United States' Year in Africa—Reinventing the Wheel." *Africa Contemporary Record* X,1977–78:A66–A81.
Stockwell, John. 1978. *In Search of Enemies: a CIA Story.* New York: Norton.
Study Commission on U.S. Policy toward Southern Africa. 1981. *South Africa: Time Running Out.* Berkeley: University of California Press.

2. If, as seems to be the case, the dominant interests in the United States are incapable of such a change of outlook, the American public at large, despite its currently low level of involvement with southern Africa, may yet be moved to opposition against a political position that is impossible to defend on any clear rational or moral grounds, but which may yet impose great burdens on U.S. citizens and on race relations in their own country.

3

Creating New Political Realities: Pretoria's Drive for Regional Hegemony

ROBERT M. PRICE

On March 16, 1984, the president of Mozambique and the prime minister of South Africa met on the banks of a river that separates their two countries and, amid much pomp and ceremony, signed the Nkomati Accord. The document signed by the two leaders pledged each government "to refrain from interfering in the internal affairs of the other" and committed them to active mutual cooperation in the elimination from each other's territory of political groups that would "plan or prepare to commit acts of violence . . . against the territorial integrity or political independence of the other, or may threaten the security of its inhabitants." The Nkomati Accord represented the second security pact to be signed between the white minority government of the Republic of South Africa and a Marxist-oriented African state in southern Africa. Exactly one month to the day prior to the ceremonies at Nkomati, and with much less pomp and publicity, the governments of South Africa and Angola, meeting in Lusaka, Zambia, signed a cease-fire agreement. South Africa pledged to withdraw its military forces from Angolan territory (where they had been operating for several years), and Angola agreed to prevent the South West Africa People's Organization (SWAPO) from using its territory for attacks into South African–controlled Namibia.

On the surface these accords between South Africa and her neighbors would appear to represent the establishment of normal interstate relations between countries occupying the same geographic region; they would seem to indicate a breakthrough toward peace and a commitment to nonhostile modes of interaction. This is certainly the manner in which President Machel and Prime Minister Botha portrayed the Nkomati Accord, and it is also the way in which the southern African accords have been viewed in the United States, by observers across the political spectrum.

But, while it might appear normal for neighbors to exist in a state of non-aggression, the southern African agreements can also be viewed as anomalous. Until Lusaka and Nkomati, African states had not granted that South Africa had any legitimate security interests with respect to the political movements that sought an end to racial rule. They had viewed the military as well as the political actions of these movements as acts of liberation, not aggression. What accounts for this situation, in which African governments militantly opposed to white minority rule, and with long-standing ties to the political and armed opposition within South Africa and Namibia, were willing to sign a pact of nonaggression and cooperation with the white minority government in Pretoria?

An answer to this question requires looking beyond the surface meaning of the accords. Like any other negotiated settlement between opponents or competitors, nonaggression pacts are reflective of an existing balance of power between contending parties. Thus the Nkomati and Lusaka accords are a political barometer. Just as a barometer indicates the relationship between high and low pressure in the atmosphere and on that basis indicates future weather trends, the accords indicate the power relationship between southern African states and suggest related future political developments. Put another way, they are a concrete manifestation of an emergent relationship of power between the Republic of South Africa and its African-ruled neighboring states. This essay seeks to explain that relationship and to comprehend both how it has developed and its implications for the future.

The underlying perspective which informs this analysis sees the southern African region as an area whose long-time political order had been torn asunder by the collapse of the Portuguese empire and which is undergoing the crystallization of a new political order. The view adopted here is that this recrystallization is, moreover, the result of a purposive regional foreign policy employed by the Republic of South Africa in response to the changed circumstances it faced with the end of Portuguese colonialism. Much of this essay will be devoted to an analysis of that policy or strategy.

Pretoria's Regional Context

In order to comprehend South Africa's southern Africa strategy it is necessary to place that strategy within the regional context out of which it developed, and to be clear about the specific goals toward which it is directed. Since the end of the Second World War, the leaders of South Africa's white minority government have perceived their internal security (their ability to maintain white political supremacy in the face of a potentially politicized black majority) to be intimately intertwined with South Africa's international situation. Their greatest concern has been the possibility that the forces of African nationalism, moving southward throughout sub–Saharan Africa in the 1950s and 1960s, would eventually link up with the forces of black opposition within the Republic of South Africa. They have also long been concerned that the relations between the emergent new states of black Africa and the powerful industrial countries of Europe and North America would put in jeopardy

South Africa's good relations with the latter. Until the mid–1970s, however, these concerns remained in the realm of hypothetical contingencies. South Africa was buffered from the political forces of African nationalism by the European-ruled territories that surrounded it; domestic policies of apartheid and repression had by 1970 produced a state of political quiescence among South Africa's own black population, and the ANC had been driven into exile and ineffectiveness; and, given the above, the significance of South Africa's strategic minerals and the attractiveness of its profit potential enabled the republic to maintain its status as an important partner for Western trade and investment.

The coup in Portugal in 1974 changed all of this. Its aftermath had a profound impact on the political landscape of southern Africa, shattering the geopolitical basis upon which Pretoria had rested its security since the Second World War. Four developments in the wake of the Portuguese coup were especially troublesome from Pretoria's vantage point: (1) The pro–South African white regimes on the Republic's borders were rapidly replaced by three African-ruled states that were militantly opposed to white rule in Pretoria. (And there was the prospect that a fourth such state could emerge in an independent Namibia.) (2) These political changes in Mozambique, Angola, and Rhodesia reverberated domestically within the republic. Active black opposition to the apartheid system was stimulated—as manifested in the Soweto Rebellion of 1976—and the fortunes of the ANC were revived. (3) The political conflicts that gave birth to Angola, Mozambique, and Zimbabwe were accompanied by the introduction into southern Africa of new extraregional actors—Cuba and the Soviet Union—who were viewed by Pretoria as hostile. And (4) the volatile mix of regional change and domestic political tensions within the republic led the countries of North America and Western Europe to distance themselves politically from Pretoria, and raised questions about the latter's continued access to international trade, capital, and technology.

Not surprisingly, faced with this changed situation, the South Africans began to mold their foreign policy to take account of the new regional realities. Although perhaps initially only a series of ad hoc maneuvers, these policy adjustments emerged by the early 1980s as a comprehensive strategy for southern Africa. The fundamental goal of this strategy has been to create a new political reality in southern Africa—one more in tune with the perceived security needs of the white government in Pretoria. More specifically, South Africa seeks to fashion regional policy so as to blunt the international threat to white rule in the republic; a threat which Pretoria sees as emanating from three sources:

1. *"Liberation movements" based in neighboring states.* Since they will not in the near future have the capability to defeat Pretoria's defense force, South African insurgent groups, or liberation movements, which are provided with military training, material support, and territorial sanctuaries by

neighboring states in southern Africa, represent little immediate threat to the survival of white political power. However, their ability to carry out acts of sabotage against symbols of governmental power, isolated white farming communities, transportation infrastructure, and urban industrial and commercial targets is real and has grown over the last ten years. Even if it were unlikely that externally supported domestic insurgents could ever come to power through guerrilla warfare, the expanding capacity of such groups to wreak havoc on what has been an essentially placid white South African society is a major security preoccupation of Pretoria.

2. *A conventional military threat from abroad.* Pretoria's perception of a conventional military threat focuses primarily on the black African states of southern Africa. As the contemporary military organizations of black African states, singly or in combination, are no match for the South African military forces, Pretoria's neighbors cannot be considered an immediate threat. Nonetheless, South African security and foreign policy planners have to be concerned with the future day when economically strong and politically viable African states might develop the capability to launch a credible attack on the white redoubt to their south.

3. *International economic pressure.* South Africa is an export dependent country, and it relies upon access to Western capital and technology for industrial growth and development. The Afrikaner government, ever concerned over what it terms "pressurizing" South Africa on its domestic policies, is very sensitive to the economic leverage available to Western countries as a consequence of this dependence (Price 1980, 313–318; Price 1982, 80–82). Pretoria must concern itself with the possibility of trade embargoes and boycotts, as well as with blocked access to technology, capital markets, and direct foreign investment. These are not just hypothetical contingencies. The international economic threat became a reality in the wake of the Soweto Rebellion of 1976. South Africa found that the terms of its access to international capital and technology had severely deteriorated. Under pressure from both governments and domestic political lobbies, multinational corporations and international banks became less ready than they previously had been to do business with South Africa.[1] Access to goods embodying advanced technologies was also hampered, as the United States and other governments expanded their definition of products with potential military usage whose export was prohibited. Although the rapid increase in the price of gold and changes in the governments of Western countries had, by 1980, reduced the international economic pressure on South Africa, Pretoria has recognized that the potential for economic threat to white rule continues, and has acted

1. Within six months of Soweto, South Africa's capital flow switched from positive to negative. The capital account swung from a net inflow of R528 million in the last half of 1976 to a net outflow of R810 million in 1977. In 1978, the capital account registered an even larger deficit of R1,370 million (*Barclay's* 1979; *Africa Research Bulletin* 1977, 4402).

accordingly. In part, Prime Minister Botha's effort to reform apartheid is directed at foreign audiences, as domestic policy is used to render South Africa's internal system less odious to the international community. But foreign policy, as well as domestic policy, is concerned with blunting the international economic threat to white rule. This should be seen as one constant goal of South Africa's overall southern African strategy.

Under Prime Minister Botha, Pretoria's response to the altered regional reality, and the specific external threats embodied in it, has been to fashion a strategy composed of three distinct, although interconnected, policy dimensions. Each dimension involves its own strategic objective, and together they cover Pretoria's perceived long-, medium-, and short-term security needs. For the achievement of each objective reliance has been placed on a specific set of policies, although policy having primary significance with respect to one objective has had secondary or spillover benefits with respect to one or both of the other strategic goals. To comprehend Pretoria's new southern African strategy it is useful to analyze the three policy dimensions separately so that the goal of each can be specified and the interconnections between dimensions can be revealed.

Long-Term Objective–A Constellation of Southern African States

As already noted, prior to the mid–1970s, South Africa could count on a cordon sanitaire of primarily European-controlled territories acting as a buffer between itself and the forces of African nationalism external to the republic. With the collapse of that cordon, as a result of the demise of Portuguese colonialism and the end of minority rule in Rhodesia, South Africa was in need of an alternative mode of protecting itself from the potential politico-military threat to its north. The idea of a constellation of southern African states, introduced by P. W. Botha shortly after he assumed the prime ministership in 1978, represents Pretoria's response to this new need.

Although Pretoria has not spelled out the specifics of the constellation concept, the essence of the idea is the creation of a formal grouping of states in southern Africa based upon South Africa's primacy in the region with respect to economic strength, transportation infrastructure, and port development.[2] In Pretoria's thinking, the constellation would ideally include, in addition to itself as sponsor, patron, and protector, the African states of Mozambique, Zimbabwe, Malawi, Swaziland, Lesotho, Botswana, Zambia, Zaire, Angola, and independent Namibia, *along with* those South African homelands that have "achieved" independent status (at present Transkei, Ciskei, Bophu-

---

2. That South Africa can serve as the focal point for a southern African grouping of states based primarily on economic considerations is an idea that has been around for many years. Botha's constellation proposal thus represents the resurrection of an old idea to serve changed circumstances.

thatswana, and Venda). To be effective for Pretoria's purposes, the constellation need not be as inclusive as this, but it must at a minimum include several neighboring African-controlled states *and* the "former" South African homelands. The formal institutionalization of even a minimal grouping of this type would represent a major breakthrough for Pretoria in respect to a number of its international problems. At least four significant gains can be recognized:

1. A constellation of southern African states would lock Pretoria's neighbors even more firmly into the South African economic system. This would increase Pretoria's leverage over neighboring African states, and thus constrain these states from aiding South African liberation movements and/or preparing militarily for an assault on the republic.

2. A constellation of southern African states would entail, at a minimum, the indirect recognition, by at least some black African states, of the independence and sovereignty of the South African homelands-cum-states. Thus, for the first time South Africa's policy of separate development would achieve some international legitimacy. With some African countries recognizing the sovereignty of the homelands, the way would be opened for diplomatic recognition by major Western powers. It is important to note that the Botha regime, while proclaiming a commitment to end apartheid, has been steadfast in its commitment to the policy of separate development, whereby all black South Africans (with the possible exception of some long-time urban dwellers) would cease to be members of the South African nation-state. Thus, the creation of a constellation of southern African states would be a significant move toward gaining that which has eluded South Africa's Nationalist government for the past twenty-five years—some international acceptance of apartheid's grand political design.

3. The establishment of a constellation of southern African states would split the countries of tropical Africa on the issue of relations with Pretoria, making it more difficult to coordinate support for black liberation movements, and undermining efforts to establish an all-African military opposition to the white republic.

4. The above three "gains" would be the basis for a fourth achievement—the creation of an international environment conducive to rapprochement between South Africa and the West, and on Pretoria's terms. With the African states split over the issue of South Africa, Western countries and their international firms would find themselves under less pressure to demonstrate opposition to minority rule in the republic.

When Prime Minister Botha launched his idea of a constellation of southern African states the situation looked promising from Pretoria's vantage point. It appeared that in Rhodesia an internal settlement would produce a conservative African-led government, heavily dependent upon its own white minority and on the white regime to the south. With such a success in Rhodesia a similar future could be envisioned in Namibia. These new African states, along with South Africa and its independent homelands, could then constitute the initial constellation. Economic pressure could easily be applied to Lesotho and Swaziland, enclosed as they are within South Africa's borders, to extend the grouping to them. Events in the region after 1979—the victory of Robert Mugabe and his ZANU party in Rhodesia, and the related international pressure for a similar result involving SWAPO in Namibia—rendered the environment much less conducive, indeed hostile, to the constellation idea.

Noting the changed political realities in the region, observers have generally assumed that Pretoria had scaled down its goal to that of a limited constellation, including only South Africa and its "independent" homelands (Geldenhuys 1982, 152). In my view, however, neither the evidence nor the logic of South Africa's actions suggests such a conclusion. In the spring of 1981 South African Foreign Minister Pik Botha, in a conversation with U.S. Assistant Secretary of State Chester Crocker, described his country's view of southern Africa's future as "involving a confederation of states, each independent, but linked by a centralizing secretariat" (Crocker 1981a, 50). And, after the signing of the Nkomati Accord with Mozambique in 1984, South African officials and media reemphasized the constellation idea. More significant than these statements of intent, however, were the concrete actions taken by Pretoria to move the constellation notion from concept to reality. During 1982 Pretoria initiated the institutional foundation for a constellation by forming the Southern African Development Bank (SADB) and the Multilateral Development Council (MDC). Although the initial members of these parallel economic institutions are South Africa and the four "independent" homelands, the new bank's chief executive officer stressed that the bank "will be open to membership of any independent country in southern Africa." A similar point was made about the MDC when, at its inaugural meeting in Pretoria, its creation was described as "a milestone in the confederation idea in southern Africa." In a related move, Pretoria has pushed for a revision of the seventy-two-year-old Southern African Customs Union (SACU), which consists of South Africa, Botswana, Lesotho, and Swaziland. Apparently, Pretoria wishes to see SACU funds channeled to the member African states through the newly created SADB and also to have the homelands governments receive customs revenues through the SACU mechanism (*Africa Confidential*, July 20, 1983, 6–7). If these moves are successful, South Africa will have succeeded in integrating SACU, with its membership of sovereign African states, into the newly created institutional web of Pretoria's incipient constellation.

At the same time that it moves ahead to establish the institutional framework for a constellation of southern African states, Pretoria has focused its main effort at creating the political realities that would bring African membership into such institutions. A major instrument for this political engineering has been a campaign of military destabilization directed by Pretoria against its neighboring states. To date the main targets of these efforts have been the "Marxist" successors to Portuguese colonialism, Angola and Mozambique, but there are indications that Zimbabwe may become a venue for destabilization as well.

In Angola, Pretoria has constructed its destabilization exercise on a combination of the legacy of Angola's 1975–76 civil war and its own Namibian counterinsurgency effort. Although by 1976 the Angolan civil war had produced a Popular Movement for the Liberation of Angola (MPLA) government in Luanda, the rival National Union for the Total Independence of Angola (UNITA) movement managed to retain an organizational remnant as well as a base of political support among the Ovimbundu people of southern Angola. These constituted a foundation from which the military struggle with Luanda could be continued. These also presented an entry point for Pretoria to influence political and power relationships within Angola, as South Africa came to the assistance of the hardpressed UNITA insurgents with military supplies, logistical support, and the backing in the field of its own armed forces. Frequent incursions into Angola by the South African military began in 1977 and grew in size and scope, so that by 1981 they involved air strikes, sizable ground forces, penetrations of as much as 200 miles inside Angolan territory, and the actual occupation of parts of southern Angola (Jenkins 1983, 20–21). The South African military actions are said by Pretoria to be directed at SWAPO military units that use Angolan sanctuaries for operations within neighboring Namibia. While Pretoria's anti-SWAPO purpose is not in doubt, its military operations within Angola have served other purposes as well. There exists considerable evidence that these military actions have been used to simultaneously assist UNITA. Pretoria's attacks have apparently been coordinated with the UNITA forces of Jonas Savimbi, and towns and villages that have been taken by the South African military have been turned over to UNITA to administer (*West Africa*, February 9, 1981, 266–269; March 9, 1981, 492–493; September 14, 1981, 2090–2091).

Since its near extinction in 1976 the fortunes of UNITA have risen dramatically. Estimates in the spring of 1983 place the number of fighters under its command at 40,000 and suggest that it controls fully one-third of Angolan territory and operates with relative ease in an additional one-third (Bridgland 1983; Girardet 1983; Jenkins 1983, 21). One need not deny the indigenous contributions to UNITA's renewal in order to acknowledge the crucial role played by Pretoria in providing the movement with the military means to effectively challenge the MPLA's rule.

In Mozambique, South Africa's main destabilization effort takes place through its support, if not outright sponsorship and control, of the Resistencia Nacional Moçambicana (MNR). Originally composed of former African and European members of the Portuguese colonial army and secret police, in recent years the MNR has been able to recruit defectors from the government's security agencies as well as take advantage of the political disaffection which Mozambique's economic disarray has produced (Jenkins 1983, 23). By 1982, MNR was able to place the Front for the Liberation of Mozambique

(FRELIMO) government under increasing military pressure, and by the summer of that year was operating in seven of Mozambique's eleven provinces, as well as in the environs of the capital, Maputo, and the main port, Beira (*Africa Confidential*, July 21, 1982, 1–6). Considerable evidence exists that there is close liaison between MNR and the South African military and intelligence services; that South Africa supplied the anti-FRELIMO guerrillas by both sea and air; that South African instructors inside Mozambique have trained MNR cadres in weapons use, communications, and sabotage; and that MNR leaders moved between Mozambique and South Africa for consultations.

While Angola and Mozambique have been the main targets of South African destabilization efforts, there are indications that Zimbabwe could become the arena for such activities as well. To begin with, the conditions for Pretoria's entree have been prepared by the dynamics of Zimbabwe's domestic politics. Zimbabwean government actions that are perceived by the Zimbabwe African People's Union (ZAPU), the main opposition political party, as intended to emasculate or even eliminate it, have combined with a brutal campaign of political repression in Matabeleland, the ZAPU stronghold, to create circumstances strikingly similar to those upon which destabilization in Angola was constructed. That is, there now exists in Zimbabwe a dissident political movement which possesses a military arm, which has a very strong regional-ethnic base of support, and which finds that military assistance for its struggle to survive can be found only in Pretoria. There are already indications that Pretoria may be planning to involve itself in Zimbabwe's political problems. It is reported that the South Africans are providing military training for Ndebele refugees from Zimbabwe at the Pafuri and Spencer camps in northern Transvaal (Jenkins 1983, 26). An Ndebele language radio station, Radio Truth, which attacks the Zimbabwe government of Robert Mugabe, broadcasts into Matabeleland from the Transvaal (Jenkins 1983, 26). There is also clear evidence of South African military activity within Zimbabwe. In August of 1982, the Zimbabwean army engaged a military unit that had apparently infiltrated across Zimbabwe's southern border. In the fire fight that ensued, three white soldiers of the invading force, veterans of the erstwhile Rhodesian army, were killed by the Zimbabweans. South Africa, at first, denied involvement with the incident. Later, it admitted that the three dead soldiers were indeed members of the South African military, but claimed they were part of a "rogue unit" operating on its own. Given the disciplined nature of the South African army, and the capabilities of its military intelligence, knowledgeable observers viewed with extreme skepticism Pretoria's claim that it lacked all knowledge of and complicity in the incident (*New York Times*, August 23, 1982, 3).

As will be seen later, South Africa's destabilization campaign serves multiple purposes. However, its primary goal can be seen as the collapse of radical anti–South African governments and their replacement by regimes that are clients of Pretoria. Should the MNR and UNITA come to exercise significant power in the governments of Mozambique and Angola, should Robert Mugabe's government be replaced with one beholden to South Africa, then a new political reality more conducive to South Africa's long-term strategic objective will have been created. The way will have been cleared for the establishment of the constellation of southern African states; a major barrier to each of Pretoria's perceived external threats will have been erected.

One virtue of the destabilization policy, from Pretoria's vantage point, is that the achievement of its objective does not necessarily require military victory by the dissident movements that South Africa supports. Military destabilization forces African countries to direct large amounts of scarce government revenue and energy to the military threat posed by the Pretoria-supported insurgents, or by the South African military itself. Angola, for example, allocates fully 50 percent of its foreign exchange to the military (*Africa Confidential*, August 25, 1982). Given the economic situation of most states of southern Africa, the diversion of scarce resources to military uses jeopardizes, if not devastates, efforts at economic development. This, in turn, has the virtue of indirectly producing popular dissatisfaction with existing governments. If economic hardship translates into political disaffection, radical anti–South African regimes might be replaced without having to be actually defeated by dissident insurgents.[3]

For Pretoria, the attractiveness of the destabilization policy goes beyond its primary contribution to South Africa's long-term strategic objective of creating a constellation of states. Aspects of the policy dovetail with other of Pretoria's regional policies, so as to make a contribution to South Africa's medium- and short-term strategic objectives as well.

Medium-Term Objective–The "Neutralization" of Neighboring States

The idea of creating a constellation of states has such a powerful attraction to Pretoria because it provides a counter to all three of its perceived external threats. The idea's drawback, however, lies in the difficulty of bringing it to fruition. At best the governmental transformations, which the destabilization program is designed to achieve, will take time to materialize; at worst, even if such transformations occur, there is no guarantee that successor regimes, once installed, will be willing to cooperate with Pretoria to the extent it desires. Thus South Africa has a need for other policies that can respond to threats in the interim, in the period before the political realities conducive to a constellation have been created. Consequently, in the medium term, Pretoria seeks to prevent the existing regimes in her neighboring states from adopting

3. The translation of economic hardship into active political opposition is, of course, not automatic, and may require more political acumen than the Pretoria-backed movements possess. Nevertheless, economic problems can be seen to have played a part in providing some popular support to UNITA in Angola and MNR in Mozambique (*Africa Confidential*, April 8 and August 25, 1982).

policies that are directed toward ending white rule in the republic. In particular, it seeks to deny the support of these regimes to the African National Congress (ANC), the most significant of the South African liberation movements. But more generally, Pretoria also seeks to put an end to diplomatic efforts by her neighbors which are designed to isolate South Africa and to bring international pressure to bear upon her. In other words, Pretoria seeks to render her neighbors neutral in respect to efforts that would foster and direct change within the South African system. Whereas destabilization seeks this goal through replacing regimes deemed hostile, neutralization attempts to achieve it by altering the policy of existing regimes.

The strategic objective of neutralization is pursued through two policies— "forward defense" and economic leverage. Forward defense involves South African military strikes across international borders and against ANC targets located within neighboring states. The first of these occurred in January of 1981. South African commandos raided a suburb of Mozambique's capital city, Maputo, attacking three houses in which ANC cadre were living, and killing twelve people. A spokesman for the South African Defense Forces said the attack followed information that Maputo "is used as a springboard for terror against South Africa" (Sun [Baltimore], January 31, 1981). In December of 1982 South African soldiers crossed into Lesotho. They entered Maseru, the capital city, searching private houses for South African exiles associated with the ANC. Some two dozen homes were fired upon and forty-four people killed (New York Times, December 11, 1982). In a statement after the raid, a South African military spokesman said the Lesotho-based ANC members were "planning to carry out deeds of terror" in South Africa and that "a ᴄumber of well-trained terrorists moved from other southern African states to Lesotho during the past month to execute these plans" (Sun [Baltimore], December 10, 1982). Then in May of 1983 Pretoria launched its second attack on Maputo, the capital of Mozambique. This time jet fighters strafed houses and a factory. By Mozambique's account nineteen people were killed and nearly two hundred were wounded. (Pretoria claimed that "at least 40" ANC exiles were killed [New York Times, June 6, 1983]). The air attack was announced as a reprisal for the ANC bombing of military offices in Pretoria two days previously.

South African spokesmen have made clear that these efforts at what has here been termed "forward defense" were intended to do more than make the ANC pay for its acts of sabotage within South Africa. After the May 1983 air raid on the Maputo suburb, Pretoria explicitly tied the action to a general regional strategy designed to bar the ANC from neighboring states. Commenting on the cross-border attacks against the ANC, General Constand Viljoen, chief of the South African Defense Force, explained: "If we deny them bases in all our neighboring states, either through the cooperation of the states themselves, which we hope will be possible, or by means of military actions against their bases, . . . it makes it almost impossible for them" (New

York Times, June 6, 1983). Pretoria, moreover, leaves little doubt that it sees the cross-border raids against the ANC as providing the necessary incentive for the cooperation by neighboring states that General Viljoen alluded to in the above quote. South African Foreign Minister Pik Botha thus declared that countries which gave "terrorists" access should expect retaliation—"Terrorism," he stated, "has a boomerang effect—it hits back to those who allow it" (*South African Digest,* May 27, 1983, 3). Although targeted on South African exiles associated with the ANC, the cross-border raids exact a heavy political price within the African states. By revealing them as defenseless in the face of foreign military attack and as unable to protect their own citizens (citizens of both Lesotho and Mozambique have been killed in South African attacks), Pretoria's anti-ANC raids have the effect of undermining the credibility of neighboring governments. Pretoria hopes that in order to avoid such political cost neighboring African governments will themselves bar their territory to the ANC, and cooperate with South African intelligence in monitoring the activity of South African exiles within their borders. "If the population in neighboring states realized the potential danger of ANC bases and to their residential areas [from South African attack]," wrote the editor of the Afrikaans-language daily, *Beeld* (June 10, 1983), "and if their leaders looked after their own interests, realism, neighborliness and eventually peace would stand a chance in the sub-continent." Of course, if neighboring governments fail to act "in their own self interest," then forward defense, by undermining their credibility, has a secondary pay-off in the area of destabilization.

In pursuing its objective of neutralization, Pretoria speaks specifically in terms of barring ANC "terrorists" and "bases." But the meaning it attaches to these terms is quite broad. Thus in describing what South Africa considered inappropriate ANC activities within neighboring states, Pik Botha included recruitment, planning, routing, and advance identification of targets and methods of infiltration. Making reference to such activity he warned: "My point is that a government can hardly be unaware of large-scale operations including those elements and if they are aware of it, they should do something about it or accept the consequences" (*South African Digest,* June 24, 1983, 3). In what would appear to be a follow-up to this and similar warnings, Pretoria sent Zimbabwe a diplomatic note a month after the Maputo air raid. In it Pretoria made it plain that it expects the Mugabe government not only to deny bases to the ANC, but also to see that it does not "allow members of the ANC to operate from its territory," or "cross its territory . . . en route to or from South Africa" (*South African Digest,* June 24, 1983, 3).

In summary, through its policy of forward defense Pretoria has sought to use military attacks, and the threat thereof, to directly disrupt ANC operations, and, more importantly, to force neighboring states to eliminate the ANC's organizational activity from their territories.[4]

4. The "retaliatory" attacks upon the ANC also serve domestic political purposes for the ruling National Party. They show the government's white constituency that it is not standing idle

In seeking to neutralize its neighbors Pretoria supplements forward defense with economic leverage. The economic component of the neutralization effort is rooted in the integrated southern African regional economy, within which South Africa represents the core and dominant unit. The economic interrelationship between South Africa and its neighbors is such as to create crucial dependencies of the latter on the former (Grundy 1982, 167–177; Burgess 1981, 12). The effect of this asymmetric economic interdependence is to provide South Africa with political leverage over its neighbors, allowing it to discourage policy deemed hostile to the republic. A clear example occurred during 1981, when in a variety of actions South Africa put the economic squeeze on Zimbabwe. First Pretoria threatened to terminate a trade agreement that provided significant benefits to the Zimbabwean economy (preferential customs duties for Zimbabwean exports to South Africa, as well as guaranteed quotas for some products). Next, it threatened to send home the approximately 40,000 Zimbabweans who work in South Africa. Then it precipitated a transport crisis and squeezed Zimbabwe's supply of essential fuel by withdrawing a large number of locomotives, freight trucks, and tanker cars that were on loan to Zimbabwe's railroad. Although the South African government claimed these actions were dictated by its own domestic needs, the foreign policy purposes in respect to neutralization of neighboring states were in fact quite clear. *The Citizen,* a South African newspaper with close ties to official Pretoria, spelled out the appropriate message:

> If Zimbabwe hadn't been so hostile to South Africa, attacking it in international forums, reducing our diplomatic mission to that of a trade consulate, and announcing that it would give full political and moral support to the "liberation" forces which intend to attack this country in growing numbers, South Africa might have been disposed to go out of its way to help Mr. Mugabe to overcome his transport crisis. . . . Indeed, what is happening in Zimbabwe is only a foretaste, on a small scale, of what might happen. (*South African Digest,* September 9, 1981, 23)

In the spring of 1983 Lesotho became the target of another instance of "neutralization through economic leverage." After a car bomb exploded in the South African city of Bloemfontein, located near the Lesotho border, Pretoria retaliated by imposing strict searches on the cross-border road traffic between landlocked Lesotho and South Africa. The result was such immense congestion that Lesotho's tourism and commerce were temporarily crippled. Lesotho responded by seeking discussions with Pretoria on their "mutual problems." Reviewing the situation, the editor of *Beeld* (June 10, 1983),

---

in the face of ANC sabotage and "terrorism." Public opinion polls show that the policy of retaliation is very popular with the electorate—eighty-one percent of all whites approved of attacks on "terrorist bases" across international borders, in an opinion survey following the Lesotho raid (*New York Times,* December 11, 1982).

commented that "the message [of border delays] was understood, perhaps better even than the earlier Maseru raid. . . . The two countries undertook not to allow any elements into their country who plan, advocate or are involved in subversion."

The policy of using economic leverage to neutralize neighbors is supported by aspects of Pretoria's program of military destabilization. A secondary effect of that program has been to prevent the type of economic integration among the black states of southern Africa that would reduce their individual dependence on South Africa, and thus nullify Pretoria's economic leverage. The effort recently initiated by the black states of the region to create an economic grouping—Southern African Development Coordination Conference (SADCC)—founded upon an integrated transportation network independent of that of South Africa is viewed as a threat by Pretoria (Clough and Ravenhill 1982, 161–186). Significantly, the existing west-to-east rail and motor roads, which link the black states with each other rather than to South Africa, have received particular attention from the Pretoria-supported insurgents in Angola and Mozambique. In Angola, a primary "military" target of UNITA's has been the Benguela railroad which, if operational, would provide both Zaire and Zambia with routes to the sea other than those that pass through South Africa. The success of UNITA in its operations against the railroad has maintained the vital dependence of both Zambia and Zaire on Pretoria. The MNR's tactics in Mozambique have been undertaken to cut all motor roads and rail lines, as well as vital bridges, that link Zimbabwe to the Mozambique ports of Beira and Maputo (*Africa Confidential,* July 21, 1982, 4). In this manner, landlocked Zimbabwe is kept completely dependent upon South Africa for its only viable outlet to the sea. In addition the oil pipeline between Zimbabwe and Mozambique ports has been frequently sabotaged, forcing Zimbabwe to rely on South African assistance for its vital fuel supplies (*Christian Science Monitor,* November 26, 1982).

The discussion of Pretoria's long- and medium-term strategic objectives has shown how South Africa's regional policies interact and support each other. The policies of forward defense and economic leverage, whose main objective is the neutralization of neighboring states, have the secondary effect of undermining the credibility and economic viability of existing regimes and thus contributing to the destabilization of these states. Destabilization, the primary objective of which is to alter the political character of neighboring states, has the secondary effect of maintaining and increasing Pretoria's economic leverage. The policies complement each other while being directed at different primary objectives.

It might be argued that the forward defense and destabilization policies of Pretoria actually work against South Africa's own declared interests because one of their consequences is the increased reliance of neighboring states on the Soviet Union and Cuba. With Pretoria posing a military threat to its neighbors, the latter are likely to turn for assistance to whomever will provide it, and that translates into an increased political and military role in southern Africa for the Soviets and their allies. Since Pretoria is well aware of this logic, one can ask, How can the policies described here be related to its declared priority of ridding southern Africa of Soviet presence and influence? The answer to this question lies in looking beyond declared policy—what leaders say—to the relationship between South Africa's objective international situation and the logic of the policy it is following. If this is done, it will be seen that what serves Pretoria's interests is the maintenance, not the removal, of the Soviet/Cuban presence. Indeed, that, I would argue, is the third and short-term objective in South Africa's overall strategy for southern Africa.

Short-Term Objective: Maintain Soviet/Cuban
Presence in Southern Africa

A major concern of Pretoria's, as was discussed earlier, is to obtain Western acquiescence in white minority rule, and concomitantly to avoid "pressurization" for change in South Africa's domestic sociopolitical system. Ultimately, I have argued, it is Pretoria's hope to achieve security vis-à-vis Western pressurization through the establishment of a constellation of southern African states. But bringing forth such an arrangement is a long-term proposition. In the meantime it seeks, through neutralization, to dissuade its African neighbors from using their diplomatic influence to rally Western countries against white South Africa. However, the short-term repercussions of the means Pretoria uses to achieve these ends could be extremely counterproductive. For Pretoria's military and economic actions in the region could lead to a Western perception of South Africa as an aggressor state and as a threat to regional peace. Should such a perception develop, then pressure from the Western industrial countries against South Africa would be likely to escalate; the third external threat against Pretoria, international economic pressure, would be intensified.

The dilemma faced by the white regime in Pretoria is how to resolve the contradiction between its domestic and external efforts to repress the black liberation movements, on the one hand, and its need to avoid pressure from the Western industrial countries, on the other. In the short term, Pretoria seeks to resolve this contradiction and escape its dilemma by recourse to the Soviet/Cuban presence in southern Africa. The "Soviet/Cuban threat" is Pretoria's best guarantee against hostile actions by the West. This is especially true in regard to the United States, which, because of its economic size, military power, and historical position as leader of the Western alliance, is regarded as particularly important to South Africa's policymakers. Thus, South African spokesmen make much of the supposed strategic importance of their country with respect to the protection of sea lanes and access to essential minerals. And they present Pretoria's conflict with the ANC as part of a global struggle against Soviet expansion and domination. Note, for example, the commentary of the official South African Broadcasting Company following the May 1983 raid on the ANC in Mozambique:

> The ANC is a self-declared revolutionary movement dedicated to the . . . imposition of a communist order on the Soviet pattern. The evidence of its control by the Soviet Union . . . is conclusive. As an instrument of the Kremlin its aims are . . . to achieve strategic dominance for the Soviets in Southern Africa. . . . The Palestine Liberation Organisation is a terrorist movement similar to the ANC in its operations and its affiliation with Moscow. There is close liaison between the two movements. . . . The ANC like the PLO is not amenable to debate. . . . The only answer . . . is to stop them. (*South African Digest,* June 3, 1983, 20)

Presenting the southern African conflict as part of a global struggle, rather than as merely a regional matter, is important for Pretoria. For the existence of strategic Western interests in South Africa is, *in itself,* of little policy relevance. What makes these interests more than simply an academic matter is the perception that they are under threat. In this respect, the political and military presence of the Soviet Union and its allies in southern Africa is crucial. It raises the issue, or at least the perception, of a threat and thus complicates immensely the relationship of Western countries to the southern African regional conflict. Pretoria needs the presence of the Soviet Union in its region; without it the salience of South Africa to the West is rendered marginal at best.

Of course, should the Soviet Union use its presence in southern Africa to attack the republic, this dimension of South African strategy would seriously backfire. But, despite its rhetoric about the "total communist onslaught," Pretoria must recognize that it has little to fear in terms of a direct Soviet military attack. The USSR has sent military advisers, but not combat troops, to southern Africa, and the Cuban troops in Angola have, since 1976, shown little inclination to engage the South African military. The real threat to Pretoria is in the training and material support provided by the USSR to the liberation movements and to neighboring states. Pretoria's response to this is its destabilization and forward defense policies. These have the ironic "virtue" of both countering the Soviet "threat" and maintaining the Soviet "presence." If destabilization should achieve its ultimate objective, and anti–South African governments should be replaced by ones beholden to Pretoria, then the stage would be set for a constellation of states. At that point the Soviet presence would be reduced, since one could expect the new regimes to demand Soviet/Cuban withdrawal. At that point, too, South Africa would no longer need the Soviet presence, since that presence is really a stop-gap for what the constellation is intended to accomplish in respect to deflecting the hostility of Western powers.[5]

5. Although a Soviet presence in southern Africa is crucial to South Africa's strategy, Pretoria does not, of course, require that this presence be manifest through 19,000 Cuban troops in An-

Nkomati and Beyond

The signing of the Nkomati Accord and, to a lesser extent, the Lusaka Agreement, represents the first fruits of Pretoria's new strategy for southern Africa. Through a combination of destabilization, direct military force, and economic leverage Pretoria has been able to force the governments of Mozambique and Angola to draw a distinction between their own national interests and the interests of the ANC and SWAPO.[6] In doing so it has taken a significant stride toward recreating in southern Africa a political order in tune with its security requirements. What the accords have made manifest is Pretoria's drive to be recognized by regional states as a hegemonic power. If carried forward, active hegemony would replace the erstwhile buffer of white-ruled states as the geopolitical basis for Pretoria's security.

What are the implications of South Africa's initial success in its drive for hegemony? A prognosis for the medium-term future can be developed if one places Nkomati within the logic and goal-structure of the overall southern African strategy being pursued by Pretoria. In addition, the interpretations of the agreements emanating from South Africa in the weeks after signing at Nkomati and Lusaka can be used as signposts to future directions.

Neutralization of the African National Congress. The most direct and immediate meaning of the Nkomati Accord is that it represents the achievement, with respect to Mozambique, of Pretoria's medium-term strategic objective—the elimination of the ANC presence in neighboring states. The terms of the accord are strikingly similar to the demands made by South African spokesmen in June of 1983, when they were defending their "forward defense" attacks (see page 75). The activities prohibited are defined so broadly as to essentially make any presence of the ANC within Mozambique a violation of the accord. Nkomati not only bans ANC military personnel, units, and bases from Mozambique's territory, but also prohibits the shelter, accommodation, or transit of any individual or organization engaged in planning or preparing for armed actions in South Africa. It also prohibits the use of Mozambique territory for "acts of propaganda that incite acts of terrorism and civil war within South Africa" ("Full Text of SA, Mozambique Accord," *South African Digest,* March 23, 1984).

Since the legal, official, and public position of the South African government is that the ANC is a terrorist organization and anyone connected with it

---

gola. A substantial reduction in Cuban troop strength would be consistent with South Africa's overall strategy. At the same time such a reduction ought not be considered as high a priority as Pretoria publicly proclaims.

6. Pretoria's success was aided by nature. During 1983–84 Mozambique has experienced the worst drought in a century. Thus the ravages of nature have been added to the damage emanating from Pretoria's policies, to produce the situation of desperation out of which the Nkomati Accords were born.

is planning, preparing, propagating, or committing acts of violence, it seems clear that the South African government will interpret Nkomati as calling for a complete break between Maputo and the ANC. While the Mozambique government has drawn a distinction between the ANC's military and political activity, and publicly holds that it continues to support the ANC diplomatically and morally, Pretoria makes no such distinction. Given the imbalance in power that led to the accord, one can confidently expect that it will be Pretoria's definition that will become operational.

In the months following Nkomati, Mozambique is likely to find itself under continuing pressure to fully live up to Pretoria's understanding of their accord. Within two weeks of the Nkomati signing, the Afrikaans media was pointedly suggesting to President Machel that a pledge by his government to continue moral and diplomatic support for the ANC represented a contradiction to his praise for the Accord of Nkomati. Thus *Beeld* (April 10, 1984), a newspaper that usually reflects official thinking in Pretoria, noted these "apparent contradictions" and pointedly reminded Machel of the South African understanding:

> The question arises as to whether *support of any* kind lent to a terrorist organization can be reconciled with an accord which has as its objective the combating of ANC acts of terrorism. (emphasis added)

Immediately following the signing at Nkomati the operational implications of the accord became manifest. Mozambique security police launched armed raids on the homes of ANC personnel in Maputo, arrests were made, and hundreds of South African political refugees fled from Mozambique into neighboring Swaziland. This was a significant blow to the ANC's organizational and logistical infrastructure in southern Africa, since Mozambique was the only remaining country bordering South Africa that was still relatively open to the ANC's military wing. Pretoria's use of military power and/ or economic leverage had already, by mid–1983, led to a clamp-down on ANC activities in Lesotho, Swaziland, and Zimbabwe. The first two expelled numerous South African refugees with ANC connections in summer 1983. Ironically many of these moved to Mozambique (*Africa Confidential,* July 6, 1983; Jenkins 1983, 23).

In effect, with the implementation of Nkomati by Mozambique, South Africa has achieved the de facto neutralization of neighboring states in respect to the ANC military threat. In the months ahead one can expect South Africa to move to extend this achievement in two respects. First, it will seek to make de jure what has been accomplished de facto, by pushing to sign security agreements similar to the Mozambique Accord with other southern African states. Indeed, within only two weeks of Nkomati this process had begun.

In early April 1984 the governments of Swaziland and South Africa announced from Pretoria that they had two years previously signed a security agreement identical in its principles to the Mozambique–South Africa Accord (*South African Digest,* April 6, 1984, 3). And one week later the South African Minister of Foreign Affairs met with the president of Malawi to discuss Nkomati and "the political and economic situation in Southern Africa" (*South African Digest,* April 20, 1984, 3). It is highly likely that Botswana and Zimbabwe, and particularly the latter, will now come under intense pressure from South Africa to accept Nkomati-style accords. Pretoria's thinking and intentions are probably closely reflected in the following scarcely veiled warning which appeared as an editorial in the Afrikaans newspaper *Beeld* (April 18, 1984):

> Mr. Robert Mugabe finds himself ... on the same road as President Samora Machel of Mozambique during his first years as head of government. [He] does not nearly approach the realism which is necessary in Southern Africa. *True, Mr. Mugabe has not given the ANC their bases from which to operate, but he has also not shown that he can handle the economic and security requirements of the sub-continent.* ... he does not find it necessary to conclude a peace agreement with South Africa, although he must realise that this is the one factor which could lead to the opening up of all kinds of possibilities for his country. ... Only when Mr. Mugabe acknowledges that he must normalise relations with South Africa ... will ... the economic content of Zimbabwe's "freedom" be given substance.
>
> If Mr. Mugabe is a true realist, he will not permit this lesson to take so long and be so expensive in his country as it was for Mozambique. ... In his fifth year of rule, is Mr. Mugabe to continue turning his back on the Nkomati Accord, or is he prepared to make a second start? (emphasis added)

The significance of the above passage lies not only in the hints it offers of future South African policy in respect to Zimbabwe. It also provides clear evidence that in the thinking of those with close ties to official Pretoria the security accords are directed at something beyond the elimination of ANC military bases.

As Pretoria pushes ahead with the signing of security agreements, it can be expected to pressure its neighbors not only to end their political, moral, and diplomatic support for the ANC, but also to cease their militant verbal opposition to apartheid. Pretoria's purpose, predictable within its overall southern African strategy, is to reduce the diplomatic cost of white supremacy by limiting the extent to which African countries mobilize world opinion against South Africa in international forums.

South Africa's Diplomatic Breakthrough. As discussed earlier, a major concern of Pretoria's is its pariah status internationally, and the insecurity and instability that status imparts to its foreign economic relations. South Africa's international isolation is, however, a political concern as well as an economic one, for as long as policymakers in Pretoria must concern themselves with threats of trade sanctions, disinvestment, credit squeezes, embargoes, and the like, their options for dealing with domestic political opposition are constrained. Coercive measures against political opponents, or outbreaks of mass unrest like that which occurred in Soweto in 1976, which in turn call forth regime repression, can become the triggers for international economic pressure. In other words, for the white supremacist regime, international outcast status creates a contradiction between the domestic political requirements of maintaining white political power, on the one hand, and international access to the economic and technological resources required for a healthy and growing South African economy, on the other. The Botha government's southern African strategy is directed, as has been shown, to dissolving this contradiction. As they are a product of that strategy, it can be expected the Nkomati and Lusaka agreements will be purposively utilized by Pretoria as a platform from which South Africa's return to international acceptability can be launched. They are, according to the South African *Sunday Times* (March 18, 1984), "the beginning of a new road which could, if followed . . . yet lead South Africa back into Africa and through Africa back into the world." In this manner the exercise of regional hegemony becomes the basis not only for neutralizing African neighbors but simultaneously for securing Pretoria's economic and diplomatic relations with Western Europe and North America.

Two aspects of the Nkomati and Lusaka agreements are vital to the pursuit of Pretoria's international agenda—the fact that they involve radical and "pro-liberation" African states and that they require the African partners to cooperate actively with the security forces of South Africa in the repression of the ANC. Nkomati and Lusaka represent a sharp break with the Africa-wide consensus on the need to impose diplomatic ostracism on South Africa. While the agreements are in effect it is likely that the Organization of African Unity (OAU) will find it difficult to maintain its unified and clear stand in support of South African "liberation" movements and on the need for international pressure against the apartheid regime. And with African states divided on how to appropriately deal with Pretoria, the way will be open for non-African countries to improve their relations with South Africa. This effect would likely not have been nearly as profound had security agreements been signed initially with African countries that carry on an extensive sub rosa relationship with Pretoria and are perceived as heavily influenced by its geopolitical and economic dominance.[7] But the involvement in the security arrangements of two African countries that have been among the most ideologically and practically opposed to the apartheid regime imparts a kind of

7. In all likelihood the South Africans did not publicly announce their security pact with Swaziland until after Nkomati because they recognized that such a deal with the Swazis would have been internationally received as an unfortunate action by a conservative African state already heavily involved with Pretoria. As such, a Swazi-Pretoria pact coming first might well have made more difficult the extension of such pacts to other countries and would have reduced the striking symbolic impact of the Nkomati Accord with Mozambique.

symbolic legitimation to dealing and working with Pretoria. The fact that the security accords require Angola and Mozambique to actively cooperate with the South African security apparatus in the repression of their erstwhile allies, the liberation movements, provides a striking and substantive exclamation point to this symbolic message. The establishment of joint monitoring commissions to oversee the implementation of the security agreements, and the actual use of armed force by Mozambique and Angola against the ANC and SWAPO in the days immediately after Nkomati, represent an important advance for Pretoria in the fulfillment of its international goals.

The international benefits of Nkomati and Lusaka in respect to a breakout from South Africa's diplomatic isolation were not long in arriving. Exactly one month after the signing of the Mozambique–South African Accord, Prime Minister Botha was invited for official visits to Portugal, West Germany, and Great Britain. By the time of his European trip in June of 1984 his itinerary had expanded to eight countries, with Switzerland, Belgium, France, Austria, and Italy joining the original three. The trip was the first official visit of a South African prime minister to Europe in twenty years, and the most extensive since the National Party, the organizational architect of apartheid, came to power some thirty-six years ago. "The fruits from the Nkomati Accord are beginning to ripen," announced one South African newspaper. "Within a few weeks Pretoria's diplomatic offensive will move into top gear with the Prime Minister's scheduled tour of a number of European countries. . . . A completely new . . . game is under way. . . . And with so many new teams in the league it should be clear to all but the most dense of overseas observers that there is just no place on the field for purveyors of sanctions, boycotts and disinvestment" (*Natal Mercury,* May 5, 1984).

The Constellation of Southern African States.   With the signing of the Nkomati and Lusaka agreements, what becomes of Pretoria's long-term strategic goal—the formation of a constellation of states in southern Africa? It might be thought that the Nkomati Accord would undermine the pursuit of this goal since it requires Pretoria to cut off its military assistance to the MNR, and thus to abandon the destabilization policy that has been the main instrument for achieving a constellation. Nkomati, however, requires not the abandonment of the constellation but rather a shift in the means to achieve it. Indeed, in the wake of Nkomati the constellation idea has experienced a revival in official statements and in National Party–connected media. Significantly, in his speech at the Nkomati signing ceremonies, Prime Minister Botha remarked that the accord provided a foundation for "a vision of the nations of Southern Africa meeting each other in every field of human endeavor: a true constellation of states" (*South African Digest,* March 16, 1984, 5 , 17). Echoing the prime minister, *Die Transvaler* (March 19, 1984) commented: "The realisation of the South African ideal of a constellation of states will depend to a great extent on the success with which the agreement can be carried out."

With Nkomati the effort to create a constellation will likely shift from a military-political (destabilization) "track" to an economic one. In negotiations leading up to Nkomati, as well as in the statements that followed it, Pretoria held out the promise of South African economic assistance for Mozambique—especially in the areas of trade and investment—should political-security differences be resolved. Similar blandishments are being made to other southern African states in an effort to have them follow the Mozambique lead. And by May of 1984 the first substantive step in the economic follow-up to Nkomati was taken, as an agreement was signed for South African purchase of electricity from Mozambique. This agreement will likely be followed by other economic accords providing for increased involvement of South Africa in the Mozambique economy. Increases in South African supplies of foodstuffs and expanded tourism are likely to be followed by preferential trade agreements and even some direct investment. Should these developments take place, as now seems probable, and should they be replicated with other southern African states, three significant implications would follow: first, South Africa's already considerable economic role in the region, and within its constituent countries, would be enlarged. Consequently, its leverage over the foreign and diplomatic policies of regional states will be enhanced. Second, by further intermeshing the South African economic system with the economies of its neighbors a halt will have been placed to the SADCC effort at reorienting the southern African economies away from the white republic. And third, the further economic integration of the region will make the application of economic sanctions by South Africa's Western trading partners more difficult. As one African newspaper explained:

> The new alliances in Southern Africa will have a valuable spinoff benefit in the international arena by making the prospect of economic sanctions against South Africa—ever present for two decades—more remote. Pro-sanctions people ... have always been careless of the hurt which would be inflicted upon the poorest communities by punitive economic measures.... Now they'll have to contemplate the starvation of our neighbors as well. (*Sunday Times,* March 18, 1984)

The Nkomati economic follow-up will also lay the basis for the formal institutionalization of a constellation of southern African states. Once new economic relations between South Africa and its neighbors are ongoing it will be possible for Pretoria to insist that some of these transactions be carried on through the Southern African Development Bank, the Multilateral Development Council, or through new agencies with similar features. These institutions were created in 1982 by Pretoria as the institutional foundation for its constellation, and they hold special significance because the erstwhile and now "independent" homelands hold membership in them. If the immediate economic benefits derived from the South African connection make it impossible for the southern African states to resist the pressure to join these institutions Pretoria will have advanced toward securing its long-term strategic objective. A formal constellation will have begun to take shape. And most important, by their membership black African states will have granted de facto diplomatic recognition to the homeland states. A first important step will have been taken toward that which has eluded Pretoria for twenty-five years, the international legitimation of apartheid's grand design.

This discussion of the ramifications of Nkomati represents extrapolation from a situation that is just unfolding at the time of writing. That the post-Nkomati relationship between Pretoria and its neighbors will develop as extensively is far from certain. The extrapolations have been introduced here in order to show first how the Nkomati Accord, and to a lesser extent the Lusaka agreement (1984), reflect the strategy pursued by Pretoria since the late 1970s; and second how the accords themselves can play a central role in furthering South Africa's strategic aims in the region.

Can the South African Agreements Last?

The discussion so far has proceeded on the assumption that the accords entered into by South Africa and Mozambique would hold for a period of time. This is, however, by no means a certainty. The forces working against them are substantial. In each of the countries involved the accords have domestic political opponents. Within South Africa the right wing of the Afrikaner community finds it ideologically difficult to accept the agreements with governments they consider Marxist agents of the Soviet Union, and objects to abandoning those they consider allies—the MNR and UNITA. Perhaps more significant, the segments of the South African military and intelligence services that have been involved in the destabilization campaign are likely to be unhappy with Nkomati and Lusaka, preferring to push destabilization to its conclusion and installing UNITA and the MNR as governments in Angola and Mozambique, respectively (*Frontline*, April 1984, 11). As a result Pretoria may not, despite the accords, entirely sever its military support for UNITA and the MNR. In such circumstances the value of the agreements to Angola and Mozambique would be substantially depreciated.

Even if Pretoria, Angola, and Mozambique do fully implement the military aspects of their agreements, there would still exist in the field four relatively well-supplied and independent armed forces—those of SWAPO, UNITA, MNR, and ANC. They are certain to carry on their armed struggle for some time whatever governments decide. This will put considerable strain on the agreements. With a continuation of armed conflict the value of the agreements will not only be diminished in the eyes of officials, but political leaders will likely come under constituency pressure to abrogate accords that do not appear to be achieving their stated purpose. Those factions that oppose the agreements on ideological or principled grounds will be able to make a strong case for their position.

In respect to Mozambique, the longevity of its accord with South Africa will probably depend upon the extent to which short-term economic benefits are seen to flow from its relationship to Pretoria. Given the desperation of its economic situation, the Machel government might well accept some level of continued South African support for MNR rather than abrogate Nkomati and thus sacrifice economic benefits. For Mozambique the South African economic connection may act as a narcotic—withdrawal carries a high price. Consequently, if Pretoria delivers some real economic resources to Maputo the Nkomati Accord may last despite the considerable political forces working against its survival. In contrast, the Lusaka agreement is likely a more precarious undertaking since the economic benefits Angola derives from a South African connection will be less needed and less extensive, and therefore less relevant to decisions made in Luanda. Nkomati is, however, more central to the pursuit of Pretoria's southern African strategy.

Conclusion

This chapter has sought to draw out the underlying logical connections among South Africa's bilateral, regional, and international policies. I have suggested that the central dynamic of southern African affairs in the past decade has been the conscious effort of Pretoria to remake to its own advantage the regional political landscape, which has been torn up after the collapse of Portuguese colonialism in 1975. Military force and economic leverage were used by South Africa in order to obtain from its neighbors recognition as the hegemonic power in the region. The "nonaggression" pacts signed by Mozambique and Swaziland, and likely to be entered into by others as well, have as their specific focus the ANC and other armed political groups operating in southern Africa. But the larger meaning of these pacts lies in the symbolic and practical recognition they grant to Pretoria's hegemonic role. As symbols, the southern African accords are not merely passive signs, or reflections, of relative power between states. Rather, they become instruments in the continued unfolding of Pretoria's drive to alter regional political realities so as to gain better security domestically and internationally for white supremacy.

REFERENCES

Africa Confidential. April 8, 1982; July 21, 1982:1–6 ("Mozambique: Havoc in the Bush"); August 4, 1982: 5–7 ("Mozambique II: Havoc in the Bush"); August 25, 1982; July 6, 1983.
Africa Research Bulletin. (Economic Financial and Technical Series). 1977. August 15–September 14: 4402.
Barclay's. 1979. *Barclay's Country Report, South Africa,* May 3.
Beeld. June 10, 1983; April 10, 1984; April 18, 1984.

Bridgland, Fred. 1983. "What if the Angolan Rebels Win?" *Washington Post*, May 29.

Burgess, Julian. 1981. "Stranglehold in Southern Africa." *African Business* 38 (October):12–13.

Christian Science Monitor. 1982. November 26.

Clough, Michael, and John Ravenhill. 1982. "Regional Cooperation in Southern Africa," pp. 161–186 in Michael Clough and John Ravenhill, eds. *Changing Realities in Southern Africa.* Berkeley, Calif.: Institute of International Studies.

Crocker, Chester A. 1981a. "Memorandum of Conversation, April 15/16, 1981." *CounterSpy* (August–October): 50–53.

———. 1981b. "Scope Paper, May 14, 1981." Reprinted in *CounterSpy* (August–October):54–57.

Frontline. 1984. April.

Geldenhuys, Deon. 1982. "South Africa's Regional Policy," pp. 123–160 in Michael Clough and John Ravenhill, eds., *Changing Realities in Southern Africa.* Berkeley, Calif.: Institute of International Studies.

Girardet, Edward. 1983. "Angola's UNITA: Guerrillas . . . or Shadow Government?" *Christian Science Monitor.* June 1.

Grundy, Kenneth W. 1982. "South Africa in the Political Economy of Southern Africa," pp. 148–178 in Gwendolen M. Carter and Patrick O'Meara, eds. *International Politics in Southern Africa.* Bloomington: Indiana University Press.

Jenkens, Simon. 1983. "Destabilization in Southern Africa." *The Economist* (July 16): 19–28.

Johnstone, Frederick A. 1970. "White Prosperity and White Supremacy in South Africa Today." *African Affairs* 67, no. 275 (April): 124–140.

Natal Mercury. 1984. May 5.

New York Times. August 23, 1982; December 11, 1982; June 6, 1983.

Price, Robert M. 1980. "Apartheid and White Supremacy: The Meaning of Government-Led Reform," pp. 297–332 in Robert M. Price and Carl G. Rosberg, eds. *The Apartheid Regime.* Berkeley, Calif.: Institute of International Studies.

———. 1982. "U.S. Policy Toward Southern Africa," pp. 45–88 in Gwendolen M. Carter and Patrick O'Meara, eds. *International Politics in Southern Africa.* Bloomington: Indiana University Press.

South African Digest. September 9, 1981; May 27, 1983; June 3, 1983; June 24, 1983; March 16, 1984; March 23, 1984; April 6, 1984; April 20, 1984.

Sun (Baltimore). January 31, 1981; December 10, 1982.

Sunday Times (Johannesburg). 1984. March 18.

Transvaler. 1984. March 19.

West Africa. 1981. February 9; March 9; September 14.

4

Congressional Initiatives on South Africa

ANNE FORRESTER HOLLOWAY

Given the high correlation between the salience of an issue in the Congress and the size of the domestic constituency on the issue, it is important to identify the size and significance of the "Africa constituency" in the United States. This constituency can be characterized as comprising individuals and organizations in the United States who avidly monitor and petition government entities regarding African issues and developments. Until recently, its political orientation has been largely liberal to progressive in tone. If, as some argue (e.g., William Foltz, in this volume, pages 32ff.), Africa is peripheral to U.S. foreign policy, this suggests that the Africa constituency in the United States is small and lacking in influence and power.

It would be naive not to acknowledge that the Africa constituency is indeed small; but it is not without influence and, in selected cases, power. What follows is a brief analysis of that constituency with special focus on its complexity and role regarding South Africa.

In keeping with the lack of widespread public attention paid to African issues, congressional representatives do not have much acquaintance with such issues. Nor is the American electorate encouraged to voice opinions on African issues at the ballot box. By and large, U.S. citizens are not well informed on Africa, and their elected representatives reflect that absence of knowledge and perspective.

Thus, the presence of the Africa constituency inside the Congress and in nongovernmental organizations and other advocacy groups is not always easily discernible. It is unlikely, for example, that the citizens of Michigan's Third District were fully aware they were electing to the Congress an Africanist (Howard Wolpe, Democrat) who would become chairman of the Foreign Affairs Subcommittee on Africa.

The congressional Africa constituency is comprised of overlapping caucuses whose members share concerns on many foreign policy matters. Groups such as the Congressional Black Caucus, Arms Control and Foreign Policy Caucus, the Ad Hoc Monitoring Group on Southern Africa, and the Foreign Affairs Committee selectively coalesce to address specific African issues and to adopt policy responses to African events.

Nongovernmental organizations are often more active on specific African issues but share the congressional groups' narrow base of appeal to larger public constituencies. Groups such as TRANSAFRICA, the Washington Office on Africa, and the American Committee on Africa over the years have sustained a strong advocacy concerning apartheid in South Africa and the regional crisis it has engendered. Thus far, however, these groups have not been powerful enough to move U.S. public policy on South Africa toward a more critical stage of intervention and radical change in American relations with that country.

Two reasons can be offered to explain the Africa constituency's lack of success. Its failure, in part, lies in the reactive nature of the Congress, which is crisis-oriented on both foreign and domestic policy. The peoples' elected representatives will not act unless a situation is so critical that it impinges on U.S. interests in a harmful way, which in turn prompts the citizenry to appeal for congressional action.

Until recently, developments in southern Africa have not been perceived by the general American public as interfering with its civic well-being. If the larger public interest does not force a congressional reaction, then the executive branch looks to coopt legislative support for its traditional "crisis-management" policy response. The Reagan administration since 1981 has taken this approach regarding South Africa and implemented it as a policy formula termed "constructive engagement." However, as events in southern Africa have escalated into violence and destabilization, the Congress, under direct pressure from the nongovernmental wing of the Africa constituency, has sought to alter America's policy direction. This has been especially true since the beginning of 1983.

Another factor which limits the Africa constituency's effectiveness in influencing U.S. policy direction is the fact that it does not always see eye-to-eye with government authorities on American interests in southern Africa. While often sharing the U.S. official policy perception of what those interests should be (political stability, economic development and cooperation, decolonization of Namibia, curtailment of Soviet influence, the end of apartheid, prevention of nuclear proliferation, and so on), the constituency veers sharply from official policy in its views of how to prioritize, manage, and affect those interests. Nowhere are these differing perceptions more clearly manifest than on the issue of how to influence the process of change in South Africa.

For example, the Africa constituency argues that the United States, despite official disclaimers, does have leverage over South Africa. That leverage, it suggests, is partly psychological and partly material. For the last twenty-five years, South Africa has spent an inordinate amount of its resources trying to change its position as an international pariah, and to that end it has sought American approval and association. South Africa also wants to benefit from American and Western technological exchange and views having a closer association with the United States as a means to that end.

The Africa constituency therefore asserts that U.S. support for the South African regime has short- and long-term implications and potential costs, but very few benefits. According to their analysis, such support could result in a loss of African confidence in the political will of the U.S. government to use its power to make a significant difference in the region; in an expansion of Soviet influence, directly or through its proxies; and in further destabilization and deterioration of extant political states and economic infrastructure through extended military conflict. This prospect is what has prompted the Africa constituency to suggest other foreign policy options that would allow for maximal American influence on South Africa while it works out its own political destiny. In keeping with this view, the constituency has pressed for policy changes, many of which fall in the realm of congressional action, aimed at enhancing U.S. leverage on South Africa to encourage substantial changes internally and regionally.

The Reagan administration, however, by means of its constructive engagement policy, has assumed that through better communications and closer cooperation with South Africa, a transformation in that society would occur that is beneficial to American interests. Administration spokesmen have argued that through this policy approach, the United States could (1) support peaceful but fundamental change in South Africa; (2) move with increasing international acceptability to a more positive and reciprocal relationship with South Africa based upon shared strategic concern over Soviet and Cuban influence in the region; and (3) work to end South Africa's "polecat" status in the world and restore its place as a legitimate and important regional actor.

The Reagan administration has taken a number of steps to implement constructive engagement. A major step involved a change in export regulations under the Commerce Department to allow for the resumption of sales to the South African military of nonlethal items which had been curtailed during the Carter presidency. Items such as personal computers come under this category. Restrictions have also been relaxed to permit sales of computers to agencies of the South African regime that enforce apartheid, such as the ministries of Cooperation and Development, Interior, Manpower, and Justice, so long as the computers are used for internal administration rather than for direct enforcement of apartheid.

An illustrative example of what this relaxation of export controls can mean occurred in 1982. That summer the Department of Commerce issued a license to an American contractor to sell 2,500 shock batons (cattle prods) to a

South African buyer. The usual process of consultations among responsible U.S. government agencies was incomplete. When the sale received public exposure the Commerce Department acknowledged that the license should not have been approved, and attributed the error to "administrative inadvertence." The matter came to the attention of the Congress in September 1982, and the Africa Subcommittee held hearings on it in early December in connection with discussions on nuclear relations with South Africa. By then the Commerce Department had revoked the original license. However, the shipment of shock batons (described as flashlights with electrical circuits at the ends) had already been sent to South Africa. By legal precedent, once a license is revoked, it is up to the licensee to get the export items back, but this is usually impossible, as it was in this case. Fortunately, congressional action did mandate that shock batons be placed on the Commerce Department's crime control list so that this kind of travesty need not occur again.

The Reagan administration has also opened up a loophole in the Commerce Department regulations that permits the sale of medical equipment to the South African military, thus allowing potentially for the sale of Beechcraft and Piper aircraft designated as air ambulances to the South African air force. Such planes are frequently used for reconnaissance and intelligence-gathering purposes and could well be used in military conflict. Again, the administration has expanded nuclear cooperation with South Africa, overriding the fact that South Africa refuses to sign the Nuclear Nonproliferation Treaty or to accept safeguards on *all* of its facilities.

Most importantly, in March 1982, the Reagan administration granted an export license to Control Data Corporation to sell a high tech computer to South Africa's Center for Industrial and Scientific Research, a leading defense research group affiliated with the South African government. This advanced computer can be used to model nuclear explosions, a fact that prompted the previous administration not to approve the sale. Grave doubts about this sale were also expressed within the Reagan administration's Subnuclear Export Committee, known as SNEC.

American nuclear technicians have traveled to South Africa and South African nuclear technicians have visited the United States or trained at American facilities. The Reagan administration considered but did not implement the sale to South Africa of helium 3, a substance that can be used to make an ingredient of nuclear bombs. The administration also upgraded its military attache's office at the U.S. embassy in Pretoria and allowed the South African government to do the same in Washington, D.C. It has permitted South Africa to establish as many as five new honorary consulates in Seattle, Denver, Cleveland, Pittsburgh, and Phoenix, and it has trained the South African coast guard in the United States. The administration has only sporadically criticized South Africa's forced relocation of thousands of its black majority from urban centers to the so-called homelands, which comprise a mere 13 percent of the land. In 1981, half a dozen congressmen were in Capetown when South African authorities forced blacks from their squatter housing in the dead of winter and moved them to a so-called homeland 800 miles away in Transvaal. The congressmen urged the administration to speak out against this action but did not get an appropriate response.

In addition, the Reagan administration's record is poor regarding South Africa's aggression in the southern African region. South Africa has spent the last three years destabilizing its black-ruled neighbors, both economically and militarily. When South Africa invaded Angola in 1982, the United States vetoed the U.N. resolution condemning that invasion. On the very day that the House Foreign Affairs Subcommittee on Africa held a hearing on regional destabilization in southern Africa (December 8, 1982), South Africa attacked the capital of Lesotho, killing innocent civilians along with suspected African National Congress (ANC) insurgents. South Africa's attacks on Mozambique and Zimbabwe have also demonstrated its capacity to act violently against its weaker neighbors. Regarding Namibia, South Africa has used the American insistence on linking the removal of Cuban troops from Angola to moving ahead on implementation of U.N. Resolution 435 as a way to avoid granting independence to that illegally occupied territory. Direct South African rule has been reimposed upon Namibia once again and its northern provinces have been completely turned into a war zone. Namibia's freedom remains as elusive as in 1980. In the wake of these punitive military actions South Africa has exacted a series of nonaggression pacts in the region which delimit the sovereignty of the black-ruled states ringing its borders. At the same time it has sought to play down internal conflict within South Africa itself. The Reagan administration views these developments as positive and feels that constructive engagement has been a catalytic factor in the process of change in southern Africa.

The Africa constituency's response is that rhetoric is not enough to change the behavior of a powerful state like South Africa; therefore it favors a stronger approach toward white South Africa that would force the regime to make fundamental changes before it is too late. There appears to be a new determination on the part of the Africa constituency to join ranks with other public interest groups in order to enhance its role in shaping a renewed policy focus on this issue. And it is intent upon employing legislative action to disassociate American power and interests from the apartheid regime in the face of the Reagan administration's status-quo crisis management orientation.

Most significantly, the disparate wings of the Africa constituency have coalesced in the Congress to initiate, analyze, and pass a number of bills that begin to restrict American association with South Africa. In a modest way, the Congress has been pressed to consider seriously, perhaps for the first time, concrete options available to the United States to influence South Africa's political behavior. The passage of an act prohibiting loans to South Africa through the International Monetary Fund (IMF) (introduced by Julian Dixon, Democrat of California) and the pending bills (which were passed in the House of Representatives) to deny U.S. bank loans to the South African government (introduced by Stephen Solarz, Democrat of New York) and to deny any new corporate investment by U.S. corporations in South Africa (introduced by William Gray, Democrat of Pennsylvania) all point to a new concert of efforts to move the American nation-state away from financial ties with the apartheid regime.

These and other measures, if fully implemented, would begin a pattern of disassociation from the South African regime and posit a definitive U.S. stand that *only* the dismantling of the apartheid system is acceptable to the American people and their government. It is hoped that the Congress, by leading the way in introducing and passing such sanctions and penalties, can convince South Africa that the costs in both political and economic terms of maintaining its abhorrent system of racial domination are too high. In the absence of a will on the part of the Reagan administration to penalize Pretoria, the Africa constituency has come to view the American legislature as the most appropriate defender of U.S. national interests on the African continent. It has attempted, therefore, a wider and more sophisticated form of coalition-building to force a radical change in policy direction on South Africa. In that sense the Africa constituency has played a significant role in fostering these legislative gains and in keeping an Africa focus alive in the Congress. How the process will evolve remains an outstanding question in the conduct of U.S. policy on Africa.

5

Namibia and the Crisis of Constructive Engagement

ROBERT I. ROTBERG

In mid-decade Namibia still remained a part of South Africa. That it had not been launched toward independence testified as much to the complexity of the Namibian problem as it did to the growth in South African power and the failure of constructive engagement as an effective instrument of change. Namibia had become strategically central to the future of the southern African region; thus a solution to the Namibian issue depended more and more on a resolution of regional questions, and of South Africa's ultimate place in the region.

The carrots of constructive engagement had provided little definitive leverage on Namibia by late 1984 precisely because American policy had been focused on the narrow goal itself rather than on that same goal as an integral part of a comprehensive, regional objective. Clarity on the two key issues— South Africa's own future and South Africa's role as a regional power—had been subordinated to the achievement of tactical, if worthy, advances. Furthermore, an altered context of global as well as regional realities had given constructive engagement less salience and South Africa relatively more power compared to other local and international participants. In 1985 progress toward an internationally negotiated transformation of Namibia from a lapsed mandatory territory into a new, universally recognized nation appeared just as difficult as it had throughout the early 1980s.

Namibia, a land twice the size of California, is seven-eighths desert and semi-desert, with only its northern hinterland receiving crop-sustaining regular refreshments of rain. Nearly two-thirds of all Namibians, especially the dominant Ovambo and their Kavango and Caprivi neighbors, live in this northern sphere, growing sorghum and pulses traditionally and, more recently, maize amid the palm trees south of the Kunene and Kavango rivers. The Ovambo number about 600,000, the Kavango 100,000, and the Caprivi 40,000. In the arid west

are 11,000 Kaokovelders. Many Ovambo have become labor migrants, working either in the territory's mines, in its few cities and towns, or on farms
owned by others.

Central Namibia contains both Windhoek, the capital and the only main
city (population 120,000), a number of small towns, and—on the Atlantic
coast—both Swakopmund, a Hanseatic German-appearing and German-
speaking tourist community and, nearby, the South African enclave of Walvis
Bay, Namibia's only real port. This central belt of the country is the home of
about 83,000 Damara and 76,000 Herero, as well as 40,000 Coloureds (recent emigrants from South Africa), and nearly all of Namibia's 70,000 whites
(10,000 English-speakers and 25,000 German-speakers, with the remainder
using Afrikaans as a mother tongue). Of the whites, only 4,000 farm. Most are
employed in the civil service or by the South African–run railways, airways, and
other state bodies. About 9,000 Tswana and 35,000 San (Bushmen) live in the
eastern sections of this central region.

Southern Namibia—from Rehoboth to the Orange River border with
South Africa—is a dry grazing area inhabited by 45,000 brown-skinned
Nama (nineteenth-century conquerors from South Africa), 25,000 similarly
brown-skinned Baster farmers who live in and around Rehoboth (the Basters
also came from South Africa), and a few thousand whites.

In the far south, at the mouth of the Orange River, Namibia mines gem
diamonds. Taxes on these exports of the Consolidated Diamond Mines, a
wholly owned subsidiary of the De Beers Ltd. cartel of South Africa, in 1984
contributed about 20 percent of the total revenue of Namibia (an annual total
of about R1 billion). Although diamonds may in the future play a somewhat
less crucial role than they now do in the country's economy, it is hard to conceive of a modern Namibia which in this century does not live largely on their
glittering proceeds.[1]

There is coal, too, in Namibia's south, but it is not of high enough quality to
be exploitable in today's market. Instead, ranking second to diamonds is the
5,000 tons or so of yellowcake—uranium oxide—which is dug each year out of
a mountain east of Swakopmund by a company controlled by Rio Tinto Zinc of
Britain. (It has Canadian, French, German, and South African partners.) Although the world spot price of yellowcake was at mid-decade too low to justify
new mining of uranium in Namibia, the company had long-term contracts sufficient to make uranium a key contributor (about 10 percent) to Namibia's state
revenues and to its GNP throughout the remainder of the 1980s.

Copper, cadmium, lead, zinc, and arsenic, mined at Tsumeb and elsewhere in the country's central region, commanded such low world prices in
the first half of the 1980s that as national revenue producers or profit-making

1. For details on the economy and political economy of modern Namibia, see Robert I. Rotberg, ed. *Namibia: Political and Economic Prospects* (Lexington, Mass.: Lexington Books,
1983), pp. 29–99.

enterprises they had become unimportant. There are small tin mines, too. Only Tsumeb is a sizable enterprise, but it has returned little to its American owners (primarily Newmont Mining) or its South African partners since the middle 1970s.

Namibia once caught and canned fish, but the large schools of sardines and pilchards, are unlikely, Namibia will remain no unusually rich prize. Nor will it prosper except through the continued production and export of diamonds kul sheep also declined due to recession and changes in fashion. Namibia has never slaughtered much of its cattle, and its abattoirs are small. Nor has there been much internal production of food staples for interregional sale.

As an economic entity, Namibia is highly geared, with an outstanding infrastructure, and a first-rate service system for a country of small population and limited potential. The South African connection has clearly contributed to this modernity, giving Windhoek and the other towns a striking aspect in the midst of an arid and semi-arid grazing zone. But Namibia imports 70 percent of its food (predominantly from South Africa), and virtually all of its consumer durables. It adds little value to its major raw material exports, all of which are ultimately sold in the northern hemisphere.

If world markets for base metals improve dramatically over the next two decades, Namibian resources could be exploited more vigorously than at present. But the costs of proving new deposits under fifty meters of Kalahari sand are high. Likewise, known hills of uranium could be exported if world prices doubled. Since these eventualities, including the return of sardines and pilchards, are unlikely, Namibia will remain no unusually rich prize. Nor will it prosper except through the continued production and export of diamonds and uranium (the two industries that employ the largest numbers of local workers), an attempt to raise and slaughter more beef and sheep, and—if the terms of rural trade can be arranged satisfactorily—major new attention being devoted to the production of maize and rice for local consumption.

In addition to these several factors which put limits on Namibia's future growth, the country's most grievous impediment is its shortage of trained indigenous manpower. Because of German (until 1915) and South African failures to provide educational opportunities for the peoples of the territory, there were at mid-decade no more than 350 black Namibians who had graduated from a recognized university. There were one black lawyer, five black physicians, and a sprinkling of other trained professionals or technically qualified indigenous individuals. Indeed, in recent years, fewer than 100 indigenous Namibians have matriculated (graduated) annually from secondary school. In 1982 the number fell to 40.

Politically, there are two Namibias. Since the mid–1960s, the South West Africa People's Organization (SWAPO) has been the only indigenous party of national and international salience. Founded as an Ovambo group in the late 1950s and as SWAPO in 1960, it was anti–South African and Western-backed until about 1971, when it turned for funds and arms to the Soviet Union. Since then, and especially in the late 1970s, SWAPO has attempted to oust South Africa from Namibia by force, raiding first across the Zambezi River into the Caprivi region of Namibia from Zambia and then, after South Africa attacked Zambia and Angola became independent, from bases in Angola between the upper reaches of the Kunene and Kavango rivers. These guerrilla attacks have successfully disturbed northern Namibia as far south as Grootfontein and Tsumeb. Since the mid–1970s, South Africa has used 25,000 or more troops to defend its presence in Namibia and, in recent years, to push SWAPO well back into Angola as well.

In terms of battlefield strength, SWAPO probably can count about 3,000 to 5,000 trained guerrillas, down from 12,000 a year or two ago, and logistical support from the Angolan army, Cuban troops in Angola, and Soviet and East German advisers (*Star Weekly* 1983). Its arms are no match for those of South Africa. Nor can it interfere more than sporadically with South African control of the skies of southern Angola and northern Namibia. Yet as pronounced as is South African military might in the area, SWAPO is a guerrilla movement and continues to infiltrate small cadres into Namibia. There they mine roads, bomb administrative buildings, and assassinate collaborators. As an insurgent force, SWAPO certainly was weakened in 1983 and 1984. Yet it was not defeated and probably can never be. Nor, given conditions like those of today, can it ever bleed Namibia as thoroughly as the Patriotic Front did so dramatically in Rhodesia. SWAPO is unlikely to win the independence of Namibia by warfare.

As weak as SWAPO has become militarily, it remains the only Namibian political entity with unchallengeable legitimacy. Inside Namibia its organization is admittedly much more flaccid than it once was; some of its leaders are discredited, others have been detained or have fled. Yet just as the African National Congress (ANC) is still regarded by black South Africans as the only credible liberation movement in South Africa, so the standing of SWAPO has no equal inside Namibia. Bolstered by South Africa's vigorous opposition on the battlefield and by the number of times that South Africa's white leadership has called it the enemy, SWAPO has reservoirs of political strength among potential Ovambo, Kavango, Damara, and Nama electors. Even Herero, who traditionally have been anti-Ovambo, are well represented among the upper ranks of the Ovambo official hierarchy.

SWAPO's legitimacy was enhanced considerably in mid–1984, when South Africa finally released Andimba Toivo ja Toivo from prison after sixteen years. Although South Africa may have expected Toivo to assist its own attempts to obtain an internal solution to the Namibian problem, Toivo was soon elected secretary-general of SWAPO. He played a loyal second to Sam Nujoma, SWAPO's fiery president, at negotiating sessions with South Africa in Zambia and Cape Verde, and took an uncompromising position in opposition to the policies and pretensions of South Africa in Namibia. During the course of an interview he blamed the Reagan administration for consistently hampering progress toward Namibian independence."The so-called constructive engagement policy has served to camouflage Washington's open embrace of the oppressive apartheid regime. Washington's preoccupation is to keep southern Africa safe for continued plunder of natural resources, and unmitigated exploitation of labour. This selfish interest has led the Reagan Administration actively to support Pretoria in continuing its illegal and brutal occupation of Namibia" (quoted in Brittain, 1984).

Serious political alternatives to SWAPO are not now apparent. Although the once significant Democratic Turnhalle Alliance (DTA) remains in existence, its support among potential black electors is as weak as its appeal elsewhere continues questionable. As an amalgam of black and brown local groups led by an Afrikaner and supported from its inception in 1977 by South Africa, its real ability to counter SWAPO's inherent and historic appeal was always problematical. This became more and more apparent, especially to South Africa, leading early in 1983 to a final public rupture between South Africa and the DTA. Namibians and South Africans no longer regard the DTA as a prime vehicle for countering SWAPO in elections.

South Africa can now admit that no political grouping to which it gives birth and which it backs morally and financially will prove viable in Namibia in this decade. Theoretically, South Africa thus ought to declare that a new political era has commenced, and should begin readying the territory for its eventual emergence as a black, doubtless SWAPO-ruled, state. Such a move would enhance the likelihood that Namibia and South Africa could develop a mutually agreeable relationship as weak and strong neighboring nations after independence. But, as a result of domestic South African white political considerations, South African military successes, the diminished costs of a failure to please the West, and the political disarray within Namibia (and the lack of any viable indigenous alternative to SWAPO), South Africa cannot yet contemplate or accept the utility of such an alternative.

Instead, from 1983, South Africa has tried with little success to fashion a new political formula which could provide an internal alternative to the process of change prescribed by Security Council Resolution 435. It tried to collect representatives of the major political groups within the territory into a national council that would make recommendations about the future constitutional development of the territory, the result constituting an authentic Namibian voice. However, few of the local political parties, particularly the black-led ones, were prepared to accept nomination to such a council (Rotberg 1983b, 1–2).

A plethora of other non-SWAPO Namibian political parties still exist, most of which are and have been opposed to South African control of Namibia. They each disapproved of the DTA, and cooperated as little as possible with South Africa. Nearly all have come to accept the salience of SWAPO while eschewing the use of violence as a means to the mutually desired end of independence. Few reckon any more that alone or in combination they would emerge from a national election with a decisive bloc of votes.

From a historic point of view, the most important of these intermediate organizations is the South West African National Union (SWANU), which had Chinese and radical chic support throughout the 1960s. Now, however, it is a local organization with a predominantly Herero membership. Led first by Moses Katjiuongua and then by Nora Chase, in 1984 the Chase segment became realistic in its public view of SWAPO. Ottilie Abrahams, Chase's sister, and Dr. Kenneth Abrahams, her husband, run the very small Namibian Independence Party. SWAPO-Democrats (SWAPO-D), an equally tiny unit, is led by Andreas Shipanga, an Ovambo who rose to very high rank in SWAPO before breaking with the SWAPO hierarchy in 1976 (Rotberg 1980, 210–211). John Kirkpatrick and Brian O'Linn led the tiny white Federal Party. Most of these groups, along with the Damara Council, once were linked loosely as the Namibian National Front (NNF). But the Council now runs the second-tier (regional) Damara government and has retreated from the national scene, and the NNF is moribund. Additionally, each ethnic group or locality in Namibia is represented by one or more political vehicles of personal or group expression, but none is of national significance.

During 1983 and 1984, several of these organizations formed the Multi-Party Conference (MPC) and attempted to become a successful broker between South Africa and SWAPO. Despite dissent within SWANU, Katjiuongua's part of SWANU tried with little success to forge an alliance of internal parties which could accelerate the implementation of Security Council Resolution 435. The MPC took part in the Lusaka conference of 1984, which brought SWAPO, the Namibian administration, and the MPC together for the first time. But no agreement could be achieved.

Internally, Namibia in early 1985 constituted a political vacuum. SWAPO had revitalized its presence inside the territory by selecting Pastor Hendrik Witbooi, a distinguished Nama leader, as its organizational vice-president and titular chief. Otherwise, and despite a flurry of maneuvering connected with the attempt to appoint an interim government, such initiative as remained largely rested with South Africa's administrator-general. In accord with South African policy, he was continuing to avoid the political modernization of Namibia. He had refrained from altering the existing governmental direction of the territory and thus from weakening the power of the right-wing white parties. Instead of opting to prepare Namibia for independence in an expeditious manner by abolishing the framework of regional government which had enhanced ethnic identities and, particularly, given local whites' control over the educational, medical, and other services which would otherwise have been subject to multiracial influence, the administrator-general supported the status quo. By 1985 he had taken no steps to extend the scope or hasten the pace of desegregation. Nor had he initiated any bold moves to accelerate the education and training of Africans or to promote economic development, especially in northern Namibia.

As an agent of South Africa, the administrator-general's innovations in the early 1980s were tactical, not strategic. His mandate did not visibly include the readying of Namibia for a U.N.–sponsored form of independence. In that sense, and in the absence of any major new policy departures from South Africa, the fate of Namibia continues to be decided elsewhere—primarily in Pretoria and Luanda, and at a succession of international negotiating tables.

Despite much Sturm und Drang, the negotiations themselves were stalled throughout 1981–1984. Yet, in terms of the modalities of an overall settlement, or even the details of each modality, little separated South Africa from SWAPO and the Western Contact Group. Agreement on many items had been reached before the Carter administration left office. Its successor, ultimately hewing to the guidelines of Security Council Resolution 435, worked out a compromise over constitutional principles and the form of an eventual "free and fair," internationally validated, national election for a Namibian constituent assembly. The deployment, the numbers, and the approximate composition of the U.N. truce administering force were known. So were the numbers and dispositions of the South African troops who would remain during the transition period. The time periods between agreement and the stages of implementation were fixed. True, fine points still needed to be discussed; questions about the command and control of U.N. and South African forces required answers; the logistics of the exercise—never easy across such remote distances—needed to be planned; and the required funds were still to be found.

But as close as the several sides may have been over these and other issues, the negotiations in a real sense remained in a phase of prolonged pause—as they had often been—because South Africa was in no hurry to settle and, indeed, could not afford to agree to any simple conclusion to the Namibian question. To this long-term obstacle was added a further impediment: the presence of Cuban troops in nearby Angola.

Cuban troops came to Angola in 1975 to assist the Soviet-backed Popular Movement for the Liberation of Angola (MPLA) in its struggle for victory in Angola against two Western-supported armies: the National Front for the Liberation of Angola and the National Union for the Total Independence of Angola (UNITA). The Cubans also helped the MPLA counter a short-lived South African invasion of Angola in 1975. At mid-decade 30,600 Cuban soldiers still defend the MPLA government against UNITA, which has a secure base in southeastern Angola and is supplied and assisted by South Africa, and provide some logistical backing for SWAPO. They do little to help defend southern Angola from South African preemptive attacks, but their presence, together with that of the Angolan army, deters South African raids on central and northern Angola.

From 1982 the United States and South Africa linked the exodus of Cuban troops from Angola to decisive progress on a settlement of the Namibian problem. The removal of the Cubans would be seen as enhancing South Africa's sense of security in the southern African region. At least that is an assertion which can be argued plausibly, objective appraisals of known strategic balances to the contrary. The Cuban removal would also weaken the MPLA, and would therefore strengthen UNITA. An ideal arrangement, from the South African perspective, would be a takeover of the Angolan government by UNITA. Short of that transformation, the South Africans expect that once the Cuban shield is removed, a place will be found in the Angolan government for UNITA. They also assume, which perhaps they should not, that UNITA will remain pro–South African and antagonistic to the ideological goals toward which most African states incline. In terms of Namibia, a diminution of the Cuban presence would permit South Africa to regard any electoral victory of SWAPO with greater equanimity. If SWAPO won and the Cubans were still in Angola, the argument goes, the red flag would fly dangerously over Windhoek and Cubans in Namibia would pose an immediate threat to the security of South Africa itself.

The advantages which, it is claimed, would derive from a Cuban withdrawal are strategic. But the major advantage for the South Africans would be psychological. A Cuban exodus would support the government of South Africa's image as a negotiator obdurate enough to preserve white South Africa against external danger. Once the Cubans went, President Pieter W. Botha's South African government could end its control of Namibia without worrying overly much about adverse domestic political fallout, or about accusations that it had handed the territory, and the whites there, over to Marxism. Its inability to devise an effective internal political counterweight to SWAPO would be seen to be less fatal.

Another view suggests that these various pleadings are more or less irrelevant. A Cuban withdrawal is linked, by South Africa anyway, to the effective settlement of the Namibian question largely because the likelihood of such an outcome is remote. Although the Angolans have said time and again that they want the Cubans to go—and although there are good economic and political reasons why their government should, in fact, want the Cubans to leave—without a satisfactory prior elimination of, or accommodation to, the threat from UNITA, the present government of Angola would risk its very existence if the Cubans departed.

Bilateral direct talks between Angola and South Africa, which have been held intermittently since late 1982, need not be seen in the context of an eventual settlement. Construed as a separate initiative, leading to a possible cease-fire, the talks in 1984 produced benefits for both South Africa and Angola, isolated SWAPO, strengthened UNITA, and may have led away from, not toward, a resolution of the larger struggle for Namibia. Given the extent to which South Africa gained mastery in 1982–83 over southern Angola and has so thoroughly hamstrung the attacking ability of SWAPO, it was in Angola's interest to end hostilities. Otherwise Angola can exercise little effective hegemony over its southern reaches. With an end to the war, South African raids will presumably halt, and Angola can gradually assert itself to the farthest points of its own domain. Likewise, with SWAPO leashed, South Africa can pull back to the Namibian border and compel Angola to undertake the policing of SWAPO.

The cease-fire of 1984 thus acknowledged South Africa's current position of strategic superiority, diminished the stature of the Cubans, gave the image of the South African government a psychological boost, and deflected attention from the main settlement negotiations themselves. Moreover, behind the cessation of hostilities and the virtual end of guerrilla threat to Namibia, South Africa became more ideally placed to pursue the possibility of some kind of internal settlement. Whether or not those are South Africa's intentions, it should be clear that the cease-fire runs along the second of the two tracks that have long been followed by South Africa's negotiators. Furthermore, the cease-fire profoundly enhanced South Africa's international bargaining position.

South Africa, as a presumed rational actor in a rational world, should want to bring the long-running Namibian soap opera to an end. Large sums of expenditure could be foregone; the war on the border is estimated to cost at least $2 billion a year. Additional opportunity costs lost include the time underutilized by conscripts whose efforts could more productively be employed at home; industrial capacity diverted to armaments and other supplies of war; and the diversion of logistical resources away from the civilian economy of the republic and the region. The large budgeted sums saved could be devoted to underfinanced national needs like the expansion of black educational and training facilities, the raising of salaries in the black educational sector, and, say, the development of the impoverished rural homelands.

Although South African losses in the war have been few, eliminating the likelihood of casualties would still have widespread appeal in the white community of the republic. The border conflict cannot yet be considered unpopular, but only in a few quarters is it regarded as a fully "just war." From admittedly impressionistic evidence, it appears that white South Africans are less worried about the potential dangers of a black-run Namibia than are their political leaders. Already the possibility of an independent black Namibia has been discounted. Namibia is still remote, across a vast, largely uninhabited desert from the main South African population centers in the Transvaal, and north a long way across equally harsh terrain from Cape Town.

The West wants a Namibian settlement. Agreeing to it would, it has long been assumed, embellish South Africa's image in Western eyes and result in tangible as well as psychological benefits for South Africa, now the single

most difficult major hindrance to progress. There would also be domestic
political advantages to be gained by removing Namibia from the list of international disputes. The proposition is also advanced that South Africa can cut
its best deal—indeed, its only favorable deal—over Namibia only so long as
the Reagan administration is in office. A less constructively engaged American adversary would give South Africa poorer terms when and if South Africa
decides or is compelled to loosen its hold on Namibia. Within the republic,
too, politicians note that settling the Namibian issue becomes more and more
controversial the closer in time it is before a South African national election.

These are reasonable arguments which should help concentrate South Africa's official mind on a devolution of power in Namibia. However, there are
countervailing axioms; they seem to have held South Africa to its curmud-
geonly course despite the many explicit and the many more implicit carrots of
constructive engagement. Anxiety in the National Party about potential domestic political disgruntlement if Namibia becomes or seems to be becoming
a SWAPO-dominated state is a factor. The widespread acknowledgment that
SWAPO today has a likely marked electoral edge only accentuates that anxiety. No reassurances by Western observers about SWAPO's actual Marxist
commitment and no intelligence estimates of the extent to which a SWAPO
government would work effectively with South Africa in the post-indepen-
dence era have dampened the official enthusiasm to categorize SWAPO as
pernicious, its leaders as devils incarnate, and so on.

At least one influential group of South African decision makers is determined to permit an internationally validated election in Namibia only when a
surrogate political party has somehow developed sufficient popular appeal to
counter the undeniable attraction of SWAPO. Despite the demise of the DTA
and the weakness of the MPC alternative, the military and some of the politicians concerned with Namibia still wish to create such a client, even if to do
so from scratch will obviously take several years.

There is less sentiment at mid-decade than before to move South African
battle lines south from the Angolan border to South Africa's frontier along the
Orange River with Namibia. The military has demonstrated its ability to pursue an Israeli-like strategy of retaliation and preemption; politicians are comfortable for the most part with its unexpected success. For at least a year or two
they foresee few hindrances to pursuit of such a policy; the West has com-
plained only mildly, the Soviets and Soviet proxies are not spoiling for a fight,
and the Angolans (and SWAPO, too) have been sufficiently weakened to em-
bolden the most ambitious of the architects of South Africa's forward policy.
South Africa has even achieved the separate peace which has deescalated hostilities, saved costs, given South Africa enormous psychological advantages, and
provided a wall of time behind which to pursue the surrogate option.

Most of all, South Africa has several serious incentives for deferring a settlement as long as possible. The Reagan administration's posture has given

South Africa more freedom to pursue a policy of tactical realignment at home and destabilization abroad than was possible in the Carter years. By this logic, agreeing to a conclusion of the Namibian imbroglio makes no sense; as soon as Namibia ceases to be an issue of international concern, the West will—a fortiori—focus its attention on South Africa itself. This turn South Africa wants to avoid as long as possible. Given the success of South Africa's bargaining wiles since 1977, the argument that a subsequent American administration, or even this one, will become provoked enough to deal differently with South Africa is a risk which is thought to be worth running. The costs of doing nothing while sheltering behind the bogey of a Cuban presence in Angola are perceived to be less, probably far less, than the risks of giving up an advantage without clear gain. The fruits of Western gratitude cannot be sweet enough. For only the kinds of guarantees which no Western government could give to white South Africa would substitute for the broad power which South Africa continues to derive from its control of Namibia.

White-ruled South Africa wants to ensure its short- and long-term security. Western pressure for change internally, when combined with urban unrest and/or an upwardly escalating equilibrium of violence, poses the major threat to the perpetuation of white hegemony. (The Soviet threat is largely derivative, a function of the maintenance of apartheid and the failure to find viable channels for black political participation.) This being so, it is profoundly in white South Africa's self-interest to focus the attention of the West on Namibia. In this light, Namibia's main value to South Africa is as a psychological buffer, an object of bargaining contention. South Africa therefore gives up the position of bargainer in the great game of Namibia only at its own peril, or only when Namibia has outlived its usefulness to South Africa as a high card flush (Rotberg 1983a, 38–40). When Rhodesia was still an issue internationally, the question of Namibia seemed easier to resolve. And it was, because the West needed South Africa's help in that first arena. Today, only the existence of the Namibian problem keeps the West from South Africa's door. What, then, is the overriding South African incentive to settle?

Constructive engagement has reinforced South Africa's appreciation of its bargaining advantages. Instead of incentives, linking the Cubans to the process and withholding dramatic demarches about destabilization have given South Africa every reason to strengthen its borders and to negotiate a separate peace rather than the comprehensive settlement that the West wants.

South Africa and the United States have interests in Namibia which diverge fundamentally. The West wants to eliminate a potential source of East-West conflict by taking Namibia to independence. It also wants to strengthen ties to the nations of black Africa by fostering Namibia's transformation. Overall, it sees the achievement of Namibia's independence as the primary means of bringing stability to an otherwise volatile region. Stability is essential for economic development and political progress. Its spread also deprives the Soviet Union of new opportunities to fish in the turbulent waters of discontent. It could also make the Cuban contribution less conclusive. But the South Africans—erroneously from the American view, but nevertheless vitally—regard stability as inimical to their own existence as a white-ruled country. Black peace and prosperity on the South African periphery is seen to weaken the case for continued white tutelage within South Africa itself. There is an unsubstantiated notion that successes in the neighboring states will encourage South Africa's own black population and prove dangerous for the survival of white South Africa.

Constructive engagement was designed to do what it has not—to deliver Namibia, end globally connected and South African–inspired conflict in the region, and start South Africa down the evolutionary road toward fuller political participation for all. Constructive engagement stresses friendship and relaxed dealings with white South Africa. As a result, and despite the Reagan administration's reiterated abhorrence of apartheid, U.S. relations with South Africa since 1980 have been much more amicable than at any time since 1960. This closeness—this bonhomie and camaraderie—was intended to produce positive results.

Chester Crocker, assistant secretary of state for Africa and the architect of constructive engagement, summarized his personal approach in an interview with a South African magazine editor. He was asked how he perceived the relationship in 1984 between the United States and South Africa, "especially in view of past posturing?" Crocker replied:

> One develops personal familiarity with key decision-makers which pays dividends. We hope that we have achieved that with South Africa and with other key countries in the region. It's a two way street—a matter of developing a track record. Undoubtedly one can over time do business more effectively when one knows the people at the table, where they are coming from, and how they tend to think and operate. We take the South African Government as an important and serious partner. We share certain goals. We see clearly where we don't agree. The past few years have been a learning process. I believe each government takes the other seriously—which has not always been the case. (Murray 1984, 41)

Crocker persistently rejects claims that white control of South Africa has been strengthened during his time in office. "The dynamic we see," he recently told The Guardian, "is one of growing debate, open discussion and ferment in the white community, but also among Coloureds and Asians." He said that the South African government "has decided to test its own power base" by broadening the nature of its parliamentary representation. He believed that the Nkomati Accord dealt "a body blow" to the illusion that armed struggle would solve South Africa's problems. The Nkomati agreement was important because it endorsed sovereignty for South Africa's neighbors as well as itself, and showed the importance of statehood and survival. It also presaged economic cooperation. On Namibia, Crocker blamed the

Cubans for the failure to achieve independence. This was the rock on which constructive engagement had truly foundered. But Crocker explained: "There has to be something in it for everybody, including the party which controls Namibia today. There is no doubt in our minds that the South Africans would like to see a settlement in Namibia sooner than later" (*Guardian*, July 20, 1984).

To engage South Africa constructively was less venal than naive. The South Africans, confident of the power of their Namibian hand, simply dangled the specter of cooperation before game theorists who had foresworn sanctions (and therefore the employment of effective sticks). Crocker and his associates were left with carrots, each and all of which the South Africans were pleased to consume. The United States eased its commercial embargo, reaffirmed intelligence links, moderated public criticism at home and abroad, and affirmed closer relations in and with South Africa. But the biggest carrot of all was the Cuban issue. To have made the Cubans hostage for Namibia reversed the entire drift of negotiations, permitted South Africa to relax, and has delayed Namibian independence indefinitely. For no Angolan government could easily throw itself on the mercy of the West (and South Africa) while UNITA remained a clear and present danger.

Crocker and his associates still think that they can square the unholy triangle, but to believe so is optimistic. The United States has made dozens of concessions. South Africa has been rewarded. But there has been no attempt at operant conditioning or sanctions. The basic flaw in constructive engagement was and is its lack of an incentive structure. The concessions were made willy nilly, in no hierarchical sequence which might have commanded South African attention, if not positive performance.

What next? It *is* in the self-interest of a U.S. government which wants to minimize conflict in southern Africa, negate the influence of the Soviet Union in that region, and encourage conditions favorable to rising standards of living and broader political participation (not to mention justice, equity, and human rights) to devise a new policy that will achieve short- and long-term results without instantly forfeiting its ability to influence trends as they develop. The United States *does* want evolution rather than revolution to be South Africa's fate, providing that the evolution is progressive and that it commences soon and proceeds at a more than deliberate pace. It wants South Africa to remain prosperous, but in shared hands. It wants South Africa to continue producing minerals and crops, and to play a greater and more responsible role in the politics and economics of Africa.

The test of a new American policy will be its ability to spur South Africa's rulers to think anew about their country's real options in the world, in the region, and at home. By rewarding positive trends and withholding rewards or ensuring at least verbal unpleasantness for negative departures, South Africa could again begin to appreciate the real risks of acts and policies deplored by the West. Since 1980 the South African regime has borne almost no cost for its actions and suffered no shame or obloquy, while consolidating its position among whites at home. There are sanctions, mostly in the field of communications and transport, which can be threatened. If necessary, those threats could be made real, at minimal cost to the United States. Continued lending and investment could be contingent upon progress along defined paths, as Senator Paul Tsongas once proposed. Boycotts of various kinds are possible, but it is the aggregate of pressure that matters. It will prove influential only when the leaders of white South Africa count the cost of persisting in their present course too high and agree to sit down to talk with the true leaders of the black community. The point is not to hit out blindly at South Africa but to devise a carefully calibrated series of incentives which that country could reasonably be expected to seek and which would bring about the major policy shifts that black leaders in South Africa, many whites, and many foreigners so patently desire.

The United States can, in exchange for its continued friendship and the prospect of broadened trade relations and increased investments, expect the cessation of South African destabilization of its black neighbors, a swift finalizing of the independence arrangements for Namibia, and a beginning to the long and arduous process of dismantling apartheid and fostering the integration of Africans into the fabric of what is now a powerful, privileged white society. These overdue utopian steps will be wrenching, painful, and will take time. The United States has a role not as an arbitrator, but as a catalyst and, if absolutely necessary, as a facilitator. Since any reorientation of policy, American or South African, will take time and patience, there are a few interim postures which ought to be struck by official Americans in South Africa, and by the United States with regard to the South African question more generally. The United States should search for the pressure points of the white society, and make known its intention to push hard—but fairly—on those very spots. It should offer more vocal public and private criticism of South African misconceptions and missteps. If only for bargaining reasons, it should have expressed its outrage at South Africa's attempt to give KaNgwane and Ingwavumaland to Swaziland. The United States missed a similar opportunity at Dreifontein, after Saul Mkhize's death, to put white South Africa on the metaphorical rack. The American government can specify particular goals in the labor and industrial fields, quietly if necessary, but firmly. It can help find funds for black schooling. It can publicly resume contacts with black opponents of the white government, affirming friendships which have subtly been permitted to wither during the Reagan years. In other words, the United States needs to take black politics seriously, an element omitted in recent U.S. policy. It can talk to the ANC. It can fruitfully employ the multinational, Contact Group formula to give even more weight to any determined approach to South Africa.

Is this an efficacious formula? Its virtue is in stressing the obvious. Certainly a policy of carrots without sticks has been shown to be unworkable and foolish. A policy of sticks alone will, by definition, achieve nothing, but a middle course, employing both sticks and carrots, should have more effect. At any rate, such a shift is imperative if our own foreign policy needs are to be achieved.

REFERENCES

Brittain, Victoria. 1984. "A Hundred Years of Struggle." *Guardian* (London). September 14.

Guardian (London). 1984. July 20.

Murray, Hugh. 1984. "Crocker." *Leadership SA* 3, no. 2:41.

Rotberg, Robert I. 1980. *Suffer the Future: Policy Choices in Southern Africa.* Cambridge, Mass.: Harvard University Press.

_____. 1983a. "Political and Economic Realities in a Time of Settlement," pp. 29–40 in Robert I. Rotberg, ed. *Namibia: Political and Economic Prospects.* Lexington, Mass.: Lexington Books.

_____. 1983b. "Stalemate in Namibian Soap Opera." *Southern African Report* 1:1–2.

Star Weekly. 1983. January 8.

6

American Policy toward Angola: A History of Linkage

GERALD J. BENDER

Since the days of President Eisenhower, successive American administrations have linked U.S. attitudes and policies toward Angola to issues that lie outside the bounds of actual American interests in that country. Whether they perceived Angola merely as an extension of Portugal or focused on the issues of the Cuban presence today, every American administration (both Republican and Democrat) has shaped its policy toward Angola with reference to external factors.

At the heart of the matter lie American attitudes toward the cold war and, especially, toward the Soviet Union. As a consequence, American policy on Angola for the past three decades has been formulated almost exclusively around the question of what signal it would send to Moscow. Even the highly touted "domestic political constraint" against normalizing relations with Luanda owes its origins to cold war considerations. The Ford, Carter, and Reagan administrations all considered recognizing the People's Republic of Angola (RPA) but none did so. Each cited the fear of domestic political repercussions as their reason for maintaining the status quo. In other words, they were afraid that the Congress and the public would somehow judge them to be "soft" on the Soviet Union if the United States recognized the government in Luanda.

Eisenhower and Kennedy

John Foster Dulles, secretary of state and the principal architect of Eisenhower's foreign policy, perceived African nationalism as a tool of Moscow's creation rather than a natural outgrowth of the colonial experience. He maintained in the mid–1950s that Soviet leaders supported nationalism as a strategy to absorb colonial peoples in pursuit of their goal of world conquest. While Africa was peripheral to the Eisenhower administration's global concerns, there was a fear that if Europeans were forced to end colonialism in Africa, they would be replaced, ipso facto, by the Soviet Union (Emerson 1967; Nielsen 1965).

Until Eisenhower departed office in January 1961, the Portuguese colonies were considered part and parcel of Portugal. Dulles underscored this reality when, following India's takeover of Goa, he declared that "all the world regards Goa as a Portuguese province." He went even further when he argued that the United States and Portugal were united in a "common cause" to preserve Portugal's African colonies. In one of his last acts as president, Eisenhower abstained in the December 1960 U.N. vote on self-determination for the Portuguese colonies. The United States even abstained on the issue of requiring Portugal to submit reports on the conditions in its colonies (Mahoney 1979; 1983).

One of the few congressional challenges to the Dulles/Eisenhower perception of African nationalism came from Senator John Fitzgerald Kennedy. In a July 1957 speech from the Senate floor, Kennedy startled the administration as well as Western European governments when he strongly criticized U.S. support for the French in Algeria. He saw nationalism as the wave of the future in Africa and did not believe that it could be stopped or that Moscow should be seen as the only major supporter of this phenomenon.

With the outbreak of the anticolonial war in Angola less than one month after Kennedy was inaugurated, he had an immediate opportunity to dramatically shift the entire thrust of American policy toward colonialism in the Third World. He instructed his ambassador to the United Nations, Adlai Stevenson, to vote in favor of all U.N. resolutions which condemned Portugal, including those which called for an end to Portuguese colonialism in Angola; he also ordered the CIA to send arms and money to the most powerful Angolan nationalist movement at the time, the FNLA (the National Front for the Liberation of Angola, then called UPA), led by Holden Roberto.[1]

The underlying rationale of Kennedy's Angola policy was that the longer the war for liberation endured the greater the opportunity for the Soviets to gain influence over the nationalist parties. (Ironically, this was the same logic which the Carter administration initially adopted toward Angola a decade and a half later.) One should note that the motivation behind the policy was well grounded in cold war thinking—it was merely a different approach to fighting the same cold war.

Kennedy's volte-face on Angola was short lived, however. Almost immediately the policy came under attack by many in his administration (for example, Dean Acheson, Dean Rusk, and General Maxwell D. Taylor) who argued

1. It should be recalled that Roberto's movement was viewed by much of the world at this time as the most radical of the Angolan parties. When the CIA began to assist the FNLA, Roberto enjoyed the support of many radical leaders at the time, including Patrice Lumumba, Kwame Nkrumah, Sékou Touré, and even Franz Fanon.

that the policy weakened the NATO alliance and jeopardized U.S. strategic military interests in the Azores. By Kennedy's second year the policy was already slipping as he asked his aides to try to find a way to "balance" support for Angolan nationalists and Antonio Salazar's government in Lisbon. The dilemma, as Arthur Schlesinger, Jr., stated it in a memorandum to Attorney General Robert F. Kennedy, was that the United States faced a choice between "the military risk of losing the Azores and the [NASA] South African tracking station and the political risk of losing Africa" (Schlesinger 1963).

The result was that a two-track policy was developed which tried to appeal to both the Portuguese and Angolan nationalists but ultimately satisfied neither. Kennedy did use some imagination in attempting to end Portuguese rule in Angola (for example, in his plan to reward Portugal with half a billion dollars in aid for the promise to get out of Angola within five years and in his support of an abortive coup by younger, more enlightened, military officers— led by Botelho Moniz, then minister of defense), but by the end of his life in November 1963 the "pro-NATO" (and anti-Angolan nationalism) elements in his administration had gained the upper hand.

The Johnson administration attempted to pursue the same two-track policy but tilted even further in the direction of Lisbon. Those who emphasized strategic military interests in Europe over those in Africa predominated. In 1965 the Johnson administration went so far as to start delivering twenty B–26 planes equipped for jungle warfare to Portugal. No less than thirteen government agencies were aware of this covert CIA plan (Operation Sparrow), which came to an abrupt end when one of the CIA pilots, apparently drunk, buzzed the White House with one of the B–26s and revealed the operation after being arrested (Welsh 1966). By the end of Johnson's term little material or rhetorical support for Angolan nationalists could be found. Only the pretense remained.

Nixon and Kissinger

At a White House reception shortly after Richard Nixon's election, the new American president assured Portuguese Foreign Minister Franco Nogueira that Lisbon now had a friend in Washington and that they would no longer be kicked around as in the days of Kennedy.[2]

Roger Morris (1977, 110), who served on Kissinger's National Security Council, writes that Kissinger and Nixon were convinced that the United States could best protect its material and strategic interests in Africa by supporting the white-ruled regimes. They also believed that the main historical lesson from colonialism in southern Africa was that outside coercion only united and hardened the repressiveness of the white dominated states.

2. For a fascinating study of Kennedy's Africa policy, see the recent book by Richard Mahoney (1983). Mahoney's study is filled with new revelations on this period, including the story of the Nixon-Nogueira discussion noted above.

The result of this belief was the now infamous National Security Study Memorandum 39 (NSSM 39), which has been widely discussed in recent years (Bender 1981; El-Khawas and Cohen 1976). In essence, Nixon and Kissinger bet on the tenacity and staying power of the white regimes to protect American security interests, but it was a losing bet from the start. Four years after they concluded that Africans could never gain power in Angola through the use of violence, the Caetano regime in Lisbon was overthrown by a military which had grown weary of the fighting in Africa.

The Lisbon coup on April 25, 1974, presented Kissinger with an opportunity to reevaluate his policies, but he did not take advantage of it. In fact, he never really changed his basic goal of trying to prevent any Soviet gains at all costs. When it became clear that he could not stop the Armed Forces Movement in Portugal from carrying out its pledge to decolonize, Kissinger looked for an "anticommunist" faction to back in Angola. He thought that he had found it in the old U.S. ally, the FNLA.

It appears that Kissinger was initially unaware of the complexity of external support for the Angolan parties at the time he entered the imbroglio. While these complexities precluded simplistic cold war breakdowns, Kissinger did not factor them into his Angolan policy. For example, he never took into account the fact that the Soviet Union had dropped all support for the Popular Movement for the Liberation of Angola (MPLA) only one month before the Portuguese coup or that the Soviets continued to withhold support for a period of approximately seven months. Nor did it apparently bother him that the "anticommunist" party he chose to back was receiving most of its support from the People's Republic of China, Rumania, and North Korea. Kissinger called this the "pro-Western faction," an appellation which few Americans questioned (Bender 1978a; 1981). When the British mercenaries were executed following the civil war, Kissinger, visibly angry, vowed that the United States would never recognize the RPA.

The Carter Administration

Those who supported a new American attitude and policy toward Angola were greatly encouraged by the position taken by Jimmy Carter during the 1976 presidential campaign. In an interview with the magazine *Africa Report* (May-June 1976, 19) Carter argued:

> I think that the United States' position in Angola should be one which admits that we missed the opportunity to be a positive and creative force for good in Angola. . . . We should also realize that the Russian and Cuban presence in Angola, while regrettable and counterproductive of peace, need not constitute a threat to United States interests, nor does that presence mean the existence of a satellite on the continent.

Carter appointed a number of high officials who not only agreed with this position (such as Andrew Young, Donald McHenry, Richard Moose, and

Anthony Lake) but who had testified before Congress in 1976 that the United States should recognize the RPA immediately. They were joined by Secretary of State Cyrus Vance (Bender 1978b), who during the first year of the Carter presidency maintained:

> The most effective policies toward Africa are affirmative policies.... A negative, reactive American policy that seeks only to oppose Soviet or Cuban involvement in Africa would be futile. Our best course is to help resolve the problems which create opportunities for external intervention.

Yet, despite these enlightened words, Vance (in an interview with the *New York Times* in 1979) stated after his resignation that his greatest regret was that the United States did not recognize the RPA. His words echoed those of Andrew Young, who said retrospectively that not recognizing the RPA was the biggest mistake of the Carter administration. The question is why, given these attitudes, was recognition withheld?

Carter and some key aides—especially National Security Adviser Brzezinski—were afraid that the administration would be strongly attacked for being "soft on Communism" if it recognized the RPA. It never abandoned its intention to normalize relations but merely hoped to do it at the "right moment." Conventional wisdom held that this moment should not be at a time when other important issues were being debated, which might leave the administration open to the charge that it was weak on communism. So once again Angola became linked to a number of issues that were totally extraneous to U.S.–Angolan relations. It was argued, for example, that recognition could not take place before relations were normalized between the United States and the People's Republic of China. The same argument was advanced with respect to the Panama Canal Treaty, SALT negotiations, the 1978 congressional elections, the Zimbabwe negotiations, and so on. Finally, a plan to recognize the RPA after Carter's electoral defeat (November 1980) and before he left office (January 1981) was abandoned after the Soviet invasion of Afghanistan. So, once again, American-Angolan relations were held hostage to linkage. This time, however, they were not only linked to the Cuban presence but also to a series of international issues which had no direct bearing on American interests in Angola.

The Reagan Approach

Conventional wisdom held that the election of Ronald Reagan would lead to a return to the policy of U.S. military intervention in Angola. Practically all of the signs pointed to it. In perhaps his only reference to Africa during the campaign, Reagan told the *Wall Street Journal* (May 6, 1980) that he favored military support for the National Union for the Total Independence of Angola (UNITA) and its leader Jonas Savimbi, who, he argued erroneously, controlled over half of Angola. Secretary of State Alexander Haig, Assistant Secretary for Africa Chester Crocker, National Security Adviser Richard Allen, National Security Council Deputy for Africa Frederick Wettering, CIA Director William Casey, and many other key officials had written or made statements prior to the election which could be interpreted as supporting Reagan's stated goal of providing military aid to UNITA. Savimbi was so convinced of this support that some at the State Department joked that his suitcase was packed in anticipation of a trip to Washington for the day after Reagan's inauguration.

Crocker, however, the first U.S. assistant secretary of state for Africa with acknowledged expertise on southern Africa, moved cautiously in the early months of the Reagan administration. In his numerous previous publications Crocker's position on the question of providing aid to Savimbi was ambiguous. In an article entitled "A U.S. Policy for the '80s" (Crocker et al. 1981), published by Freedom House just prior to the 1980 election, he argued that the United States should admit publicly "the legitimacy of the UNITA struggle," but he also cautioned that if the United States were to back UNITA outright "it is not obvious how this path would lead to reconciliation. . . . It could produce an escalation of conflict, and it would probably rule out responding to frequent hints from the MPLA of a desire to reduce sharply its Soviet-Cuban ties."

For Crocker, then, the "ultimate goal" should be to "reduce or eliminate the Communist combat presence," and he did not see provision of military support to UNITA as necessarily equivalent to that goal. Crocker's insistence on focusing on his ultimate goal has had a healthy effect on the formulation of the administration's Angola policy. Too many, both within and outside the administration, have failed to recognize the critical question about U.S. military support for UNITA: Does this support serve the desired goal? If the goal were to bloody the Cubans as much as possible, tie them down in an African quagmire, or show the world that Washington will back its "friends"—professed anti-Soviet rebels from Afghanistan to Angola—then military support for UNITA makes perfect sense. Savimbi commands a force inside Angola of over 15,000 veteran guerrillas, who have demonstrated over the years a military capacity to inflict relatively serious military and, more importantly, economic damage in Angola. American support would not enable UNITA to win a military victory but it certainly could enhance Savimbi's capacity to raise the level of violence and disruption for both the MPLA and the Cubans.

If, on the other hand, the goal is to reduce or eliminate the Cuban presence, then aiding UNITA is probably the worst thing the United States could do. Enhancing UNITA's military capacity would almost certainly produce an increase not only in the number of Cuban combat troops in Angola but in Cuba's influence over the MPLA. All who have closely followed post-independent Angola have noted a close correlation between the number of Cuban combat troops and the level of external threats either actually faced or perceived by the MPLA. Because of the importance the Reagan administration has attached to the issue of Cuban troops in Angola, a closer look is in order.

Cuban Troops in Angola

During the past quarter century few, if any, foreign troops stationed in Africa have attracted U.S. attention and condemnation as have the Cubans in Angola. The past three American administrations have made the demand for withdrawal of the Cuban troops from Angola a top priority. It has been assumed that their presence complicates American relations with Angola and Africa in general and argued that they are one of the most divisive factors in East-West relations. In fact, many Americans mark the end of detente with the arrival of the Cubans in Angola (Bender 1978b; 1980).

Given the importance which has been attached to the Cuban troops in Angola, it is amazing that more than a decade after their arrival the level of discussion and debate remains more rhetorical than factual. Evidence is rarely introduced and key questions are usually ignored. What international principles, for example, do the Cuban troops violate? Why does the United States accord the right to any African nation to request French, Moroccan, British, and even American troops when its sovereignty is threatened by external aggression (for example, Chad and Zaire), but not grant Angola the same right when it is threatened by South Africa? Is it because French, Moroccan, British, and American troops are ipso facto "good" and Cubans are ipso facto "bad"? Does a sovereign nation such as Angola, recognized by all countries in the world except the United States, have the right to invite outside assistance to protect itself from external (that is, South African) aggression?

Finally, if it is truly in the American interest that the Cuban military presence in Angola be greatly reduced or eliminated, what is the best way for the United States to achieve this? The two most frequently debated strategies revolve around military versus diplomatic options. It should be noted here that whether one endorses the military or diplomatic options depends to a large extent on what one believes about the motives for the Cubans' presence. Thus, those who believe that they are there to repel outside aggression endorse diplomatic options designed to greatly reduce or eliminate that external threat. On the other hand, those who believe the Cubans intend to stay permanently to further Soviet expansion back military measures to eliminate them. After eleven visits to Angola in the last eleven years, during which I discussed all of these questions with most of the Angolan leadership, I am convinced that the Cuban troops will be sent home as soon as South Africa ceases its aggression against Angola. Moreover, after many talks with officials in the Reagan administration, I am certain that no efficacious plan exists for the United States to eliminate the Cubans militarily. In fact, it is clear that any attempt to do so would merely raise their number in Angola. Ultimately, then, diplomacy is the only realistic option for the United States to pursue.

Crocker apparently reached this very conclusion by the end of the first phase of formulating the Reagan administration's policy. Despite all the signals associated with the so-called tilt toward South Africa—especially the push to repeal the Clark Amendment, which prohibits U.S. military support to factions in Angola—the Reagan administration decided in March 1981 that the "ultimate goal" was the reduction or elimination of Cuban troops from Angola and not military support for UNITA. It appeared to recognize that the ultimate goal could not be achieved if a secondary goal of military support for UNITA were also pursued.

Once there was agreement on this ultimate goal, the question turned to how it could best be accomplished. The immediate answer was to link the withdrawal of the Cuban combat troops in Angola with the removal of South African troops from Namibia as part of an overall settlement of the Namibian question. But this proved to be a sticky and divisive issue for the other four members of the Western Contact Group (Great Britain, France, Germany, and Canada), to say nothing about the universally negative response toward this linkage from the African Front Line states (Angola, Mozambique, Botswana, Zambia, Zimbabwe, and Tanzania). Only South Africa stands with the United States in its desire to bring the issue of the Cuban withdrawal into the Namibian negotiations.

During Carter's four years in office, Namibia and the Cuban troops were the two issues dominating all U.S.–Angola contacts, but they were never linked. The Carter administration, like the other members of the Contact Group, was convinced that the Cuban troops would not leave Angola until South Africa ceased its attacks in southern Angola against the South West Africa People's Organization (SWAPO) and Angolan citizens, and that this would not occur until after Namibian independence. All agreed that it would be a grave mistake to link the two issues as it would almost certainly delay and jeopardize a Namibian settlement. Even Pretoria had never suggested such a linkage.

It was only after the initial talks between the Reagan administration and the Botha regime that both the United States and South Africa insisted on this linkage—over the strong objections of all other parties concerned with the Namibian issue. Moreover, there has been widespread optimism that it is working. Former Secretary of State Alexander M. Haig, Jr., even predicted (in mid–1981) that South Africa would end its illegal occupation of Namibia and accept Namibia's independence by the end of 1981. In fact, the administration's initial defensiveness over its alleged tilt toward Pretoria gave way to confident, almost self-righteous assertions that the strategy will be successful. In 1982 and 1983, President Reagan evoked the Namibian negotiations as an example of his diplomatic success during his first term. As the first four years of the Reagan administration came to a close, Secretary of State George Shultz touted the success of constructive engagement.

The Reagan administration's focus on Namibia is part of its overall goal of reducing, if not eliminating, the Soviet and Cuban presence throughout southern Africa. By including Namibia in a larger regional package the Reagan administration would like, simultaneously: (1) to see an internationally acceptable independence obtained in Namibia; (2) to eliminate Cuban combat troops in Angola and promote unity between the ruling MPLA and Jonas Savimbi's UNITA; and (3) to establish strategic ties with South Africa, a task which is viewed as impossible without South African cooperation on Namibia and racial reform at home.[3]

In order to accomplish these complex goals, former Secretary of State Haig fashioned a two-track policy. Along one track the United States entered into a dialogue with South Africa and was ready to take those steps necessary to ensure South African cooperation in Namibia. On the second track Washington was supposed to have entered into a dialogue with the Angolan government with the aims of ensuring its cooperation on Namibia, drastically reducing the number of Cuban combat troops in Angola, and promoting unity between the MPLA and UNITA.

Haig believed the second track imperative in order to garner Pretoria's cooperation, despite the objections of the other Contact Group members. Their concern has been that tying or connecting the two withdrawals (the administration is reluctant to say they are "linked") will eventually abort the Namibian negotiations. In essence they do not believe that the Angolan government can or should agree to send the Cubans home before Namibian independence rather than after, as Luanda has already promised. As a result they have disassociated themselves from the Reagan administration's second track, believing that if negotiations break down over this issue, it will then be Washington's fault, not theirs.

Interestingly, while the administration propounded its two-track policy, during 1981 it was actually active along only one track. A series of almost monthly meetings were held between high-level American and South African officials to spell out the terms of the quid pro quo which Washington was offering Pretoria. That is, what kind of cooperation would South Africa provide in Namibia in exchange for what kind of relationship with the United States?

The train on the second track, however, did not even leave the station during the entire first year of Reagan's administration. By late September, when the Contact Group foreign ministers met at the United Nations to discuss Namibia, only one extremely brief and superficial conversation had occurred between senior American and Angolan officials. Haig actually gave orders that no one in the administration was to have any contact with Angolan officials. He vetoed Crocker's proposal to meet with Alexandre Rodrigues

---

3. Parts of this section appeared in my article in the *New York Times* (Bender 1982).

(Kito), who headed the Angolan delegation to the opening of the United Nations in September 1981. The same veto was extended to Foreign Minister Paulo Jorge, who replaced Kito as head of the delegation.

Haig's prevention of contacts with Angolan leaders raised concern and even anger among the other members of the Contact Group (who were all present for the opening of the 1981 U.N. session). Haig was strongly admonished by his counterparts and warned that his attitude threatened to sabotage the entire Namibian settlement. As a result Haig hastily arranged a meeting with Paulo Jorge as he was packing his bags to return to Angola. Although both sides reported that the meeting went well, the second track was not even broached. At best it might have been brought up by Chester Crocker when he returned to Luanda in November to meet Jorge and President José Eduardo dos Santos, along with delegations from the other Contact Group countries. (See Table 6–1 on p. 120 for a list of all meetings between the United States and Angola during the Reagan administration.)

The contrast in the way Haig pursued the two tracks of the Namibian policy during 1981 was startling. The frequent and substantive talks between Washington and Pretoria were justified on the grounds that "we believe that the chance for influencing governments is better if we have reasonably good relations with them." Why this logic was limited to South Africa and not extended to Angola was never made clear. To many it appeared that the Reagan administration had different principles for white- and black-ruled states in Africa.

One of the most highly touted and controversial elements in the Reagan administration's approach toward southern Africa has been its insistence on taking into account "South Africa's legitimate security concerns and needs." Pretoria's concerns are indeed numerous, ranging from the presence of Cuban troops in Angola and Soviet influence on SWAPO to minimizing the African component of any U.N. peace-keeping force during the transition period in Namibia. The Reagan administration argues that South Africa cannot be expected to make concessions which it believes would greatly jeopardize its security. No matter how unrealistic or paranoid one may consider these security concerns, one must address them and not merely dismiss them out of hand. On this point there is broad agreement because to ignore these concerns is to invite failure.

Once again, however, the same logic or strategy has not been applied to the Angolan side of the equation. Not only has the Reagan administration essentially ignored Angola's "legitimate security concerns and needs" but, on the contrary, at times it went out of its way to unnecessarily exacerbate Luanda's fears. It justified these actions on the basis of "principle," ignoring the negative impact on Angola and Angolan perceptions of them as threatening gestures.

Following the Haig-Jorge meeting at the United Nations in late September

TABLE 6–1 Bilateral Meetings between the United States and the
People's Republic of Angola during the Reagan Administration

Date	Place	Principals
July 21–24, 1982	Luanda	President dos Santos and Vernon Walters
August 17, 1982	Luanda	President dos Santos and Frank Wisner–USA
September 27, 1982	Luanda	Paulo Jorge–RPA and Frank Wisner–USA
October 5, 1982	New York	Paulo Jorge–RPA and George Shultz–USA
January 26, 1983	Luanda	Paulo Jorge–RPA and Nicholas Platt–USA
March 16, 1983	Paris	A. Rodrigues–RPA and Frank Wisner–USA
April 13–14, 1983	Wash. D.C.	A. Rodrigues–RPA and G. Bush/ G. Shultz–USA
October 6, 1983	New York	Paulo Jorge–RPA and Chester Crocker–USA
January 20–22, 1984	Cape Verde	V. da Moura–RPA and Frank Wisner–USA
February 16–17, 1984	Lusaka	A. Rodrigues–RPA and Chester Crocker–USA
May 28, 1984	Lusaka	A. Rodrigues–RPA and Chester Crocker–USA
July 24–25, 1984	Cape Verde	A. Rodrigues–RPA and Frank Wisner–USA
September 6–7, 1984	Luanda	A. Rodrigues–RPA and Chester Crocker–USA
September 28–29, 1984	Luanda	A. Rodrigues–RPA and Frank Wisner–USA
October 15–16, 1984	Luanda	A. Rodrigues–RPA and Frank Wisner–USA
December 3–5, 1984	Luanda	A. Rodrigues–RPA and Frank Wisner–USA
January 29–30, 1984	Luanda	A. Rodrigues–RPA and Frank Wisner–USA
March 18, 1985	Cape Verde	A. Rodrigues–RPA and Chester Crocker–USA

1981, the American secretary of state became anxious to get the train started on the second track but did not know quite how. An opportunity arose on December 10 when Angolan President José Eduardo dos Santos chose to mark the important twenty-fifth anniversary of the MPLA in the oil-rich Angolan enclave of Cabinda (with Gulf Oil officials present). While attacking the ongoing visit of Mr. Savimbi to the United States, dos Santos nevertheless reaffirmed his "readiness to hold talks with the United States at any time on problems of common interest that would lead to the normalization of relations between our two countries." The State Department responded immediately and the first substantive talks were held a month later in Paris on January 15–16, 1982.[4] There have been numerous bilateral discussions since then (see Table 6–1).

American-Angolan Dialogue

The results of the first four years of the Angolan-American dialogue, consisting of almost two dozen meetings, can be summarized by the Portuguese saying: *Tudo esta cada vez mais na mesma* (Everything is more and more the same). While the United States has shifted its position during these four years somewhat closer to reality, the bottom line remains the same—the Cubans must go. Initially they had to start their withdrawal before South Africa began its own from Namibia; now the Reagan administration insists that the Angolans "only" have to sign a calendar for that withdrawal before U.N. Resolution 435 begins to be implemented. This is as far as Washington appears prepared to go in addressing Angola's security needs.

Naturally, the American plan for movement along the second track is dependent upon the cooperation of South Africa. And it is here that the entire process has broken down, for South Africa has made sure, through its massive military escalation in Angola, that no Angolan government official would seek withdrawal of Cuban troops. To do so would be to commit political (or perhaps physical) suicide.

Military Developments

South Africa's deep penetration into Angola to provide logistical assistance for UNITA's August 1983 attack against Cangamba, an MPLA-held town in eastern Angola, greatly alarmed the MPLA leadership and confounded their previous assessments of how far South Africa would go in Angola.[5] By September 1983, the MPLA perceived that it was caught on the

4. A reputedly accurate version of the first round of talks was leaked in *Afrique-Asie;* see Malley (1982, 7–10).

5. The remainder of this paper is largely drawn from Bender (1984, 235–247).

horns of a terrible dilemma, forced to choose between equally unpromising military and diplomatic options. The increased South African/UNITA threat required a decision either to (1) go the military route of accepting greatly increased supplies of Soviet military equipment and Eastern European military technicians, as well as a modest increase in the number of Cuban combat troops; or (2) go the diplomatic route of accepting the Reagan linkage.

Neither option appeared to hold serious prospects for "victory," but the military option seemed infinitely less risky. It could buy years (in terms of preserving the stalemate), while the diplomatic option could mean defeat within a matter of months. In other words, if the mutual pullouts actually proceeded as envisioned under linkage, Angola would be left without its Cuban protective shield. To go this route would require a tremendous leap of faith—that both South Africa and the United States would live up to their words and not take advantage of the increased vulnerability of the MPLA under those circumstances.

Angolan anxieties about the true intentions of Pretoria and Washington were exacerbated in December 1983, when South Africa once again launched an invasion of Angola—the twelfth since 1976. The United States was the sole member of the Contact Group not to vote for condemnation of South Africa's action.

In early January 1984, the Soviet Union announced new military accords with Angola to strengthen Angola's "defenses, independence and territorial integrity." To some, it appeared that the MPLA had made its choice and the big question was now the price. Short on oil revenues, the MPLA could no longer pay for the Soviet arms within a short period, as had been its custom. Another major question was: Given the new military accords, would the MPLA be more or less disposed to negotiate seriously about linkage?

The Cease-Fire

The United States, seeing its opportunity to influence the Angolans slipping away, tried to capitalize on the negotiating option. Prior to embarking on his two-week trip to southern Africa and Western Europe in January 1984, Assistant Secretary of State for Africa Chester Crocker stated that the South African call for a cease-fire opened a "window of opportunity." It might have been more appropriate to say "the last opportunity."

Given the dramatic escalation in the number, size, and scope of South African military operations against Angola (most of which appeared to the MPLA and many others to have Washington's tacit support), it taxed the faith of even those in the MPLA who are sometimes considered "pro-Western" to trust American and South African intentions in southern Africa.[6] With their very

6. What many in the West often forget in their indefatigable search for "moderate" or "pro-Western" factions in Marxist parties such as the MPLA (or Nicaragua's Sandinistas) is that the moderates have as much to lose as the so-called hardliners if the party is overthrown by common enemies such as South Africa (or the Contras).

survival at stake, the MPLA required at least some small signal that might justify placing trust in Washington and Pretoria.

Unfortunately, the Reagan administration has tended to send just the opposite signals, reinforcing the so-called hardliners' admonitions not to trust plots hatched in Pretoria and Washington. In addition to Reagan's unsuccessful attempt to repeal congressional restrictions prohibiting covert military aid to UNITA, his administration has hosted UNITA leaders at the highest levels in Washington, provided the South African military and police with aid banned by previous administrations, and has continued to withhold recognition of the Angolan government—a decade after its independence—making the United States the only country in the world to do so.

The United States has vetoed Security Council resolutions condemning South African invasions of Angola, and in 1983 it abstained on a key vote in the African Development Bank which cost Angola an important loan for agricultural development. The abstention was defended on bogus human rights grounds by Eliot Abrams, assistant secretary of state for human rights, and Frank Wisner, deputy assistant secretary of state for Africa and a key administration negotiator with the Angolans. Wisner infuriated some Angolan officials when he argued that no significant improvement in human rights had occurred in Angola since 1977 (when there were numerous and serious human rights violations by the MPLA).[7] One Angolan official who has had extensive dealings with Americans remarked that with the vote in the African Development Bank, "the United States abandoned Angola."

The State Department was aware of the MPLA's dilemma over military versus diplomatic options and understood that unless Washington did something dramatic to win the MPLA's trust, there was little likelihood of its accepting linkage. The administration, however, considered and then rejected all "dramatic" moves, ultimately deciding that demonstrating its "leverage" over South Africa would entice the Angolans back to the negotiations. The result was the Crocker-Botha meeting in December 1983 in Rome, where it was agreed that South Africa would offer a cease-fire and withdrawal of its troops from southern Angola.

These steps were intended to convey to the Angolans that the United States was willing and able to restrain South Africa; at the same time Pretoria's behavior in southern Africa also became the direct responsibility of the Reagan administration. Both South Africa and Angola thus look to the Reagan administration as a kind of "guarantor" of the other's behavior. After Wisner obtained Angola's agreement in Cape Verde in late January 1984 not to exploit the cease-fire, Crocker delivered it to the South Africans. Armed with this assurance, Pretoria agreed to proceed with its military pullout from Angola and implementation of the cease-fire.

---

7. The State Department's annual reviews of human rights in Angola and annual reports by Amnesty International underscore clear improvement in human rights in Angola since 1977.

South Africa and Angola have equally strong interests in seeing a cease-fire endure. The cessation of South African attacks inside Angola not only preserves life and property but could produce a savings of hundreds of millions of dollars a year. The withdrawal of South African troops also permits the MPLA to reoccupy parts of southern Angola not seen by government officials for over two years. It has also lifted the sagging morale of the MPLA army.

South Africa, for its part, accomplished its main goal in occupying parts of southern Angola—to neutralize SWAPO raids into Namibia from Angola. It had been unable to achieve this with the dozen military invasions and recent occupation. A cease-fire also allows Pretoria to greatly reduce military expenses and casualties. The twenty-one soldiers killed during the December 1983–January 1984 invasion was a record number of fatalities in the Angolan operations and gave rise to considerable domestic criticism of South Africa's "Angola policy" in both the English-language and Afrikaans press.

While a cease-fire clearly serves Angolan and South African interests, its effect on the fortunes of SWAPO and UNITA are less certain. Savimbi's guerrillas have demonstrated many times that they can be militarily effective without South African logistical support, but many of their operations will be hampered in size and effectiveness. Nothing in the cease-fire agreement rules out continued combat between UNITA and the MPLA, and it will undoubtedly persist in areas away from the Namibian border.

SWAPO, expected to remain idle militarily during the cease-fire period, runs the danger of being eclipsed if Pretoria drags its feet on negotiations on Namibian independence. A joint Angolan–South African monitoring commission was established in southern Angola to guarantee that SWAPO respected the cease-fire and stayed on the Angolan side of the border. On at least three occasions during the spring of 1984, Angolan troops in the joint monitoring commission militarily engaged SWAPO, resulting in deaths on both sides. One senior State Department official intimately involved in the negotiations noted that South Africa had entered the joint monitoring commission highly skeptical of being able to depend on the MPLA to monitor SWAPO, but that the comportment of the Angolan troops in the commission was so exemplary that it turned out to be a major "confidence builder for South Africa—with a capital C"!

It was initially thought that Pretoria would withdraw from Angola within roughly a month, that is, by the end of March 1984, and that as soon as this was accomplished, the Angolans would return to the negotiating table with a new attitude. But once again Pretoria has undermined American efforts, by greatly prolonging the final withdrawal.

The Question of South Africa's Strategy

The same South African Defense Forces which, in October 1975, had advanced almost 500 miles into Angola in only two weeks, took more than a year to withdraw a mere 100 miles. Not only was the slow pace of the withdrawal troublesome for Luanda, but the arrest by the South African forces of some thirty key leaders from SWAPO's internal wing at the very time Chester Crocker was meeting with P. W. Botha in Europe further undermined the notion that Washington could keep South Africa under control. To make matters worse, Pretoria's attempt to float three settlement proposals which would have skirted the U.N. plan caught the United States off guard, lending further credibility to the old adage about good friends being "the last to know." By mid–1984, following the aborted talks in Lusaka among the South Africans, SWAPO, and internal Namibian parties in May, and Prime Minister P. W. Botha's visit to Western Europe in June, no one appeared to have a handle on South Africa's intentions toward Namibia.

Confusion over this question has been the normal state of affairs even since Pretoria accepted U.N. Security Council Resolution 435 for Namibia in April 1978. South Africa could have withdrawn from Namibia at any time, but thus far, it has not chosen to do so.

Some in the Carter administration thought that they could parlay the Rhodesian success into a Namibian settlement, but their final effort collapsed in Geneva in January 1981. South Africa's ready excuse for the Geneva debacle was its doubts about U.N. impartiality in administering the transition to independence. Ambassador Donald McHenry, who headed the American delegation in Geneva, was told by a South African delegate to the conference, however, that Pretoria needed about two more years to build up the Democratic Turnhalle Alliance, or DTA (the coalition of internal Namibian parties backed by South Africa), so that it could make a credible showing in an election against SWAPO.

Before the two years had elapsed and despite South Africa's efforts, the DTA collapsed from its own ineptness and inability to gain political credibility. Pretoria then tried to piece together another coalition of internal Namibian parties, the Multi-Party Conference (MPC). Suffering from the same weaknesses and vulnerabilities as its predecessor, the MPC has thus far not exhibited any signs of being able to compete effectively against SWAPO in an open and democratic election. Whether P. W. Botha is willing to follow through with a plan which would result, at least for the next few years, in a SWAPO victory is a key question. He would suffer some political loss to his right wing at home, but just how much is a matter of speculation. Ironically, according to some close observers, the Lusaka talks in May 1984 collapsed for almost the same reasons as did the Geneva talks of January 1981.[8]

The Reagan administration launched its constructive engagement policy buoyed with the confidence that it would be able to succeed where the Carter

---

8. This position is argued persuasively in "The Story Behind the Collapse of the Namibia Talks" (Legum 1984).

administration had failed. It was convinced that South Africa did want to get out of Namibia, and it offered Pretoria more cordial relations and respectability than any other American administration since Eisenhower. Riding the tide of this respectability, the Botha regime may believe that it can enjoy improved relations with the United States without actually having to withdraw from Namibia. Certainly it has been in no hurry to withdraw.

The Need for Positive American Action

So the debate and speculation continue, often assuming the character of competing faiths. For many involved in the debate, the stakes are relatively minor; if one is wrong, the worst that can result is a tarnished political or academic reputation. For those who live in Angola or Namibia, however, the stakes involve life and death. Misplaced faith in South Africa's sincerity or intentions could cost them their lives.

This is why the Angolan government has had such a difficult time accepting linkage. For Luanda to accept linkage requires that it must have faith— *and risk its fate on*—the sincerity of both Pretoria and Washington. Thus far it has felt more secure not giving up the Cuban card. As President dos Santos made clear during a June 1984 meeting with Zambian President Kenneth Kaunda, "The presence of Cuban forces in Angola is a counter-balance and deterrent in view of the military superiority of some branches of the South African armed forces."[9] In fact, for the past four years, the Angolans have clung tenaciously to the same four conditions for the Cuban withdrawal: (1) the total withdrawal of South African forces from Angola, (2) the cessation of all aggression or threats of aggression by South Africa, (3) the independence of Namibia on the basis of U.N. Resolution 435, and (4) the cessation of all types of South African support for UNITA.

The cease-fire and South Africa's troop withdrawal from southern Angola went half way toward fulfilling these conditions. Yet in effect, these measures only returned the situation to approximately what it was prior to the Reagan administration, when South Africa did not occupy Angola or direct most of its attacks against MPLA troops and equipment. If Luanda did not feel secure enough then to relinquish its Cuban protection, there is little reason why it should be more prepared to do so today. President dos Santos's final two conditions undoubtedly contain some flexibility (for example, Namibia would not have to be totally independent before the first phase of a Cuban withdrawal could begin). South Africa and the United States, however, will have to offer more than a return to the status quo ante to persuade the MPLA to sign a calendar for Cuban withdrawal. It would appear that negotiations have come full circle, once again paralyzed by the linkage question.

The negotiations over linkage were carried on briefly in public in late 1984, when Angolan President dos Santos spelled out Luanda's position in an

9. Angolan Press Agency (ANGOP), Luanda, June 6, 1984.

open letter to the U.N. secretary general. South Africa countered by publishing its own position in the press. The gap between the two remained almost as wide as when the negotiations began in 1981. Angola still insisted on removal of most South African troops from Namibia before it would begin its slow withdrawal of the bulk of the Cuban troops. South Africa, on the other hand, called for prior Cuban withdrawal in a matter of months, not years, before it would consider removing its forces from Namibia. Deputy Assistant Secretary of State Frank Wisner's trip to Pretoria and Luanda in early 1985 did not succeed in significantly closing the gap between the two sides. Increasingly, it appears that a new approach by Washington will be necessary to bridge this intractable chasm.

The time has come for the United States to transcend its phobias, myths, and paranoia about the Soviets and Cubans in Angola and to deal with Angola directly, as a recognized independent country, on the basis of mutual interests rather than unilaterally imposed linkages.

REFERENCES

Africa Report. 1976. "Jimmy Carter on Africa." May-June: 18–20.

Bender, Gerald J. 1978a. "Angola: A Story of Stupidity." *New York Review of Books* (December 21):26–30.

———. 1978b. "Angola, the Cubans and American Anxieties." *Foreign Policy,* no. 31 (Summer):3–30.

———. 1980. "Past, Present, and Future Perspectives of Cuba in Africa." *Cuban Studies* 10 (July):44–54.

———. 1981. "Kissinger in Angola: Anatomy of Failure," pp. 63–144 in René Lemarchand, ed. *American Policy in Southern Africa: The Stakes and the Stance.* 2d ed. Washington, D.C.: University Press of America.

———. 1982. "Why Optimism About a Namibian Settlement." *New York Times,* January 8.

———. 1984. "The Reagan Administration and South Africa." *Atlantic Quarterly* 2, no. 3 (Autumn):235–247.

Crocker, Chester A., et al. 1981. "A U.S. Policy for the '80s." *Africa Report* (January–February) :7–14.

El-Khawas, Mohamed A., and Barry Cohen, eds. 1976. *The Kissinger Study of Southern Africa.* Westport, Conn.: Lawrence Hill.

Emerson, Rupert. 1967. *Africa and United States Policy.* Englewood Cliffs, N.J.: Prentice Hall.

Legum, Colin. 1984. *Colin Legum's Third World Reports.* May 18.

Mahoney, Richard D. 1979. "The Kennedy-Salazar Skirmish over Portuguese Africa." Paper presented to the International Conference Group on Modern Portugal, University of New Hampshire, June 21–24.

———. 1983. *JFK: Ordeal in Africa.* New York: Oxford University Press.

Malley, Simon. 1982. "Angola–Etats-Unis: Les Secrets de la Rencontre de Paris." *Afrique-Asie,* no. 258 (February 1):7–10.

Morris, Roger. 1977. *Uncertain Greatness.* New York: Harper and Row.

Nielsen, Waldemar A. 1965. *African Battleline: American Policy Choices in Southern Africa.* New York: Harper and Row.

Schlesinger, Arthur, Jr. 1963. "Memorandum for The Honourable Robert Kennedy." Subject: Our Policy in Africa, July 1, The Declassified Documents Reference System (Carrollton, Texas: The Carrollton Press, 1979), p. 327A.

Wall Street Journal. 1980. May 6.

Welsh, David. 1966. "Flyboys of the CIA." *Ramparts* (December):11–18.

7

Mozambique: Tugging at the Chains of Dependency

ALLEN F. ISAACMAN

The South African regime, a few days ago, alleged that Mozambique threatened it by concentrating sophisticated arms on its frontiers. What are the arms to which they refer? Neither economically nor militarily do we represent a threat to anyone. No reasonable person can think that an underdeveloped country as poor as we, still bloodied from the wounds of war, can pose a threat to the sovereignty, and territorial integrity, the stability of another state, particularly one as powerful as South Africa. In fact, the only thing that the regime can fear is our example of creating a non-racial society. (President Samora Machel quoted in *Notícias,* August 24, 1982)

If anything, Machel's sobering assessment, in response to a South African invasion threat, understates the asymmetrical relationship of power. By almost any conceivable measure, Pretoria's hegemony extends not only over Mozambique but over all of southern Africa. Consider the fact that South Africa outproduces all of its ten neighbors combined and that the 1978 per capita GNP of South Africa was more than tenfold that of Mozambique (Grundy 1982, 148). When translated into military terms, this gap becomes even wider. South Africa has been able to amass some of the most advanced weapon systems in the world, underwritten by a $2.75 billion military budget, while Mozambique's military has had to rely essentially on a handful of Korean War vintage jets, tanks, and artillery, and a defense budget of only $150 million (Isaacman and Isaacman 1983, 174).

Given this asymmetrical power relationship, the South African leadership would seem to enjoy enormous leverage with which to perpetuate its regional domination. Conversely, the Mozambican government's attempts to break the chains of dependency forged over the past century would seem to be futile. Nevertheless, an intense struggle, waged simultaneously at an economic, mil-

129

itary, political, and ideological level, is taking place in southern Africa. More-over, the Reagan administration has entered this arena by attempting to bro-ker a new, "more stable," relationship between Pretoria and Maputo. This paper examines the historical roots of Mozambique's dependency and the changing character of this struggle, which carries profound implications ex-tending well beyond the continent to Washington, Moscow, and other parts of the globe.

The Chains of Dependency Forged: ca. 1900–1975

Although Lisbon had maintained a nominal presence in Mozambique since the sixteenth century and Portuguese merchant capital had profited handsomely from the ivory and slave trade, Lisbon did not begin actively to occupy the country until after the Conference of Berlin in 1885. During the next thirty years the people of Mozambique—peasants and chiefs, women and men, old and young—valiantly resisted foreign domination. By 1919 Mozambique had been pacified.[1]

From the outset, the most salient feature of Portuguese colonialism was the absence of development capital. This lack provided South African and British investors with a strategic entry point from which to dominate the Mozambi-can economy. Although a few Portuguese financiers maintained a powerful position through the Banco Nacional Ultramarino, foreign mining, and in-dustrial and merchant capital quickly came to prevail. Even in the capital city of Lourenço Marques, only 27 percent of investments in 1900 consisted of Portuguese capital (Penvenne 1979, 3–4). Without substantial investments, Portuguese interests, both in the metropole and in Mozambique, could only hope to extract a portion of the colony's resources by transforming the rural area into a labor reserve. This transformation would, through state interven-tion, generate a large bound and ultra-cheap labor force. An 1899 govern-ment commission, whose task it was to analyze the prospects for development in Mozambique, concluded:

> We need native labor, we need it in order to better the conditions of these labor-ers, we need it for the economy of Europe, and for the progress of Africa. Our tropical Africa will not grow without the Africans. The capital needed to ex-ploit it, and it so needs to be exploited, lies in the procurement of labor for

---

1. Superior firepower, the use of black mercenaries who often comprised more than 90 per-cent of the invading army, intense ethnic rivalries exploited by the colonial regime, and growing class cleavages within the indigenous societies all combined to undermine the ability of the Mo-zambican people to resist. Once in power, Lisbon imposed a highly structured administrative system in which the instruments of oppression were used to suppress all forms of opposition and to appropriate the colony's human and natural resources.

exploitation. Abundant, cheap, solid labor . . . and this labor, given the circumstances, will never be supplied by European immigrants. (quoted in Silva Cunha 1949, 144)[2]

Colonial officials anticipated that by forcing male members of the rural population to pay a tax in European currency and by imposing artificially low prices that strangled peasant initiatives, they would be compelled to seek employment on Portuguese plantations, in the embryonic light industrial sector, and in the port towns of Lourenço Marques and Beira. While the tax laws did provide the state with a new source of revenue, they initially failed to generate a cheap labor force on a sufficient scale, requiring the colonial state to resort to undisguised coercion known as *chibalo*.[3]

But just as the lack of Portuguese capital provided an opening for South African investors, so the forced labor policy, designed to remedy this situation, drove thousands of Mozambican migrant laborers to the relatively better paying South African gold mines. The result was to reinforce Mozambique's dependence on its southern neighbor.[4]

Anxious to secure "rent" for the loss of its "natives," Portugal signed a formal agreement in 1901 with the Witwatersrand Native Labor Association (WNLA), official representative of the South African mining industry. Under this accord, the colonial state received 13 shillings per mineworker plus 6 pence more for each month's service beyond the initial one-year contract period. As a result of subsequent agreements in which a portion of the workers' salaries was paid directly to the state in gold at a fixed rate of exchange, which was well below the market rate, labor "rent" for 80,000 to 100,000 miners became the colony's major source of income (see Table 7–1). Thus the colony became inextricably linked to South Africa.

2. More than a decade before this commission had been established, the colonial state had introduced a number of tax laws designed to drive many African peasants off their land and, in doing so, created a pool of cheap labor (AHM 1886).

3. Article 1 of the 1899 native labor code spelled out the legal rationale for *chibalo* which continued under varying guises until 1961: "All native inhabitants of the Portuguese overseas are subject to the moral and legal obligations to seek to acquire through work those things which they lack to subsist and to improve their own social conditions. They have full liberty to choose the means through which to comply with this obligation, but if they do not comply in some way, the public authorities may force them to comply." (quoted in Silva Cunha 1949, 151)

4. Although the unique cost structure of the South African mines required cheap labor, wages on the Rand were still 200–300 percent higher than those paid in Mozambique (Johnstone 1976). As early as 1893 it was reported that "tens of thousands of natives immigrated spontaneously from the southern Mozambican districts of Inhambane and Lourenço Marques" (Katzenellenbogen 1982, 38). The presence of impoverished and desperate immigrants helped to suppress wages of South African workers to the delight of the mine owners who began to recruit large numbers of migrant laborers from the Portuguese colony. By 1899, it was estimated that 60,000 miners, 60 percent of the total work force, came from Mozambique.

TABLE 7–1 Mozambican Mineworkers Employed in South African
Gold Mines (Legal Exports, Select Years)

Year	From Mozambique	Total Number of Mineworkers
1902	38,635 *	—
1903	43,595	—
1904	50,997	77,000
1905	59,284	81,000
1908	81,920	149,000
1909	85,282	157,000
1912	91,546	191,000
1913	80,832	155,000
1915	83,338	198,000
1918	81,306	158,000
1920	96,188	173,000
1922	80,959	183,000
1927	107,672	215,000
1929	96,667	205,000
1931	73,924	226,000
1932	58,483	233,000
1933	88,499	318,000
1939	84,335	323,000
1942	74,507	310,406
1945	78,806	320,147
1946	96,300	305,400
1951	106,500	306,100
1956	102,900	334,500
1960	95,500	396,700
1961	100,200	413,900
1973	99,424	422,181
1978	45,168	453,721

*From February to December.

SOURCES: Centro Estudos Africanos, *The Mozambican Miner* (Maputo, 1977), 24; A. Rita Ferreira, *O Movimento Migratório de Trabalhadores Entre Moçambique e a África do Sul* (Lisbon, 1963), 68; Colin Murray, *Families Divided* (Cambridge, 1981), 30.

The 1901 labor treaty also laid the foundation for another form of dependence on South Africa. In return for cheap labor, South Africa agreed to divert from Capetown to the port of Lourenço Marques a specified percentage of imports to and exports from the Transvaal. Lisbon's capitulation in 1928 to

South African demands that the congested port of Lourenço Marques be managed more efficiently and that Mozambique continue to export a prescribed number of mineworkers suggests the extent to which it had become an economic satellite of its southern neighbor.[5]

The same year that this agreement was signed, an obscure professor of economics, Antonio Salazar, became Portugal's finance minister and shortly thereafter prime minister, heralding a forty-year legacy of fascism (Smith 1974). Salazar's colonial policy rested on two interdependent propositions which theoretically placed him in direct opposition to South Africa. Fiercely nationalist, he insisted that the colonies had to remain under the firm grip of Lisbon. Second, the human and natural resources of Mozambique had to be more effectively and directly exploited for the benefit of the metropole and the nascent Portuguese capitalist class rather than for the benefit of foreign investors including the South Africans. To achieve this goal, he promoted a neomercantilist policy in which state intervention figured prominently at all levels of the economy.

Beginning with the Colonial Act of 1930, the Salazar regime imposed a restrictive foreign investment code, high tariffs on foreign goods, and limits on specific foreign commodities that could be imported into the colony (Mittleman 1981, 29–30; Smith 1974). The state also strengthened the position both of Portuguese industrial capital and of local Portuguese investors by withholding permits for foreign goods that competed with those manufactured in the metropole or in Mozambique itself. A new labor code was introduced that disguised the *chibalo* system and more than 750,000 peasants were forced to cultivate cotton in order to fuel the Portuguese textile industry (Isaacman, Stephen, et al. 1980).

Through such state policies Portugal increased its share in Mozambique's trade fourfold and by the mid–1940s had replaced Britain and the British empire as the colony's major trading partner. Moreover, Mozambique imported appreciably more than it exported to the metropole, thereby serving as a net contributor of foreign currency to the embattled Portuguese economy, while suffering itself from a progressively deteriorating balance of payment problems (see Table 7–2).

Yet, for all Salazar's rhetoric of economic nationalism and his neomercantile policies, which had the effect of further distorting the Mozambican economy by blocking virtually all industrial development in the colony, his regime failed to undermine South Africa's economic hegemony. To the contrary, as the colony's balance of payment problems expanded, Mozambique's dependency on South African "invisible income"—generated by wage remittances

---

5. In 1928, a new labor and port agreement was signed requiring Mozambique to export up to 100,000 workers annually and the following year the Portuguese government agreed to nationalize the port and railroad system in order to improve its efficiency.

TABLE 7–2   Balance of Payments, 1960–1973 (in thousand contos)

Year	Imports	Exports	Balance	Relation Between Imports and Exports
1950	1,753	1,221	- 522	0.70
1960	3,646	2,099	-1,547	0.58
1961	3,720	2,548	-1,172	0.69
1962	3,908	2,616	-1,292	0.67
1963	4,075	2,896	-1,079	0.71
1964	4,488	3,042	-1,446	0.68
1965	4,984	3,106	-1,878	0.62
1966	5,967	3,223	-2,753	0.54
1967	5,725	3,500	-2,225	0.61
1968	6,735	4,450	-2,276	0.66
1969	7,491	4,081	-3,410	0.54
1970	9,363	4,497	-4,866	0.48
1971	9,639	4,613	-5,026	0.48
1972	8,912	4,768	-4,144	0.54
1973	11,415	5,541	-5,874	0.49

SOURCE: *Estatística do Comércio Externo: Moçambique, Economic Survey* (Lourenço Marques, 1975).

from the miners and port and transit fees—became increasingly significant.[6] And despite continued complaints from representatives of settler agriculture about the lack of cheap African labor, the Salazar regime permitted an increasing number of Mozambicans to work in the mines.

The formation of the Mozambique Liberation Front (FRELIMO) in 1962 and its initiation of armed struggle two years later increased the South African presence in Mozambique. In order for the Salazar regime to finance its military operations against FRELIMO as well as against liberation movements in Angola and Guinea-Bissau, it was forced to reverse its protectionist policies and seek foreign investments in its colonies. Beginning in 1965 gener-

6. Until 1957, this invisible income offset the colony's negative balance of payments and subsequently reduced it to a few million dollars. Lisbon's recognition of the critical position which South Africa played was reflected in the 1953 Six–Year Development Plan in which the bulk of the state's investment capital went into harbors and railways linking Mozambique to her English-speaking neighbors rather than building an integrated national economy (Mittleman 1981, 30).

ous tax holidays and liberal terms for the repatriation of profits were offered. A United Nations' study completed in the early 1970s found that these incentives enabled foreign investors to enjoy some of the highest profits in the world (U.N. General Assembly 1973, 3). Given such favorable conditions, South African as well as other Western investors were increasingly attracted to Mozambique.

The major South African investment was in the construction of Cabora Bassa Dam—the largest new project begun after Salazar liberalized the investment codes (Middlemas 1975). ZAMCO, an international consortium of South African and Western capital under the direction of the Anglo-American Corporation, planned to invest $515 million to build the dam, which would be the largest in Africa. Cabora Bassa served the strategic needs of both South Africa and Portugal. Colonial authorities predicted that the dam would facilitate the settlement of one million Portuguese in the strategic Zambesi Valley. These settlers would be the first line of defense against the advancing FRELIMO guerrillas. For its part, South Africa was the major investor, providing more than two-thirds of the capital during the first phase, and the principal beneficiary, with 87 percent of the dam's output slated to ease its energy shortage (*Times,* May 29, 1973).

Expanding economic ties and a shared racist ideology motivated Pretoria to provide military assistance as the threat from FRELIMO increased. Although South African assistance was never as great as that provided by Rhodesia, there is evidence of covert security ties between South Africa and Portugal.[7] Whatever the degree of direct South African military involvement, it was certainly increasing in April 1974, when the Armed Forces Movement launched its successful coup in Portugal, which ended forty years of fascism and raised the possibility of Mozambican independence.

In the aftermath of the coup, policymakers in Pretoria, who had been forewarned by their own intelligence services of the deteriorating war situation in Mozambique and the growing antiwar sentiment in Portugal, were faced with the difficult decision of whether or not to intervene militarily. The Lusaka

7. In 1967, the commander of the South African Joint Armed Forces conferred with Portuguese military commanders on counterinsurgency strategies and, shortly thereafter, Pretoria began to send jeeps, radio equipment, tracking dogs, and other material which complemented the heavy equipment Portugal received from NATO (Henriksen 1983, 178–179; Munslow 1983, 115). South African police and troops were also sent to guard Cabora Bassa dam. FRELIMO claimed that as early as 1968 there was a full battalion protecting the site and five years later the number had increased threefold. Although Pretoria and Lisbon both denied the accusations, United Nations reports confirmed the presence of South African troops in Tete Province (U.N. General Assembly A/AC. 109/L. 919, February 8, 1974, 23). There is also documented evidence of South African civilian pilots spraying FRELIMO-held areas with defoliants as well as suggestions that South African troops were integrated within the ranks of the Rhodesian forces which regularly crossed into Mozambique on "search and destroy missions" (Henriksen 1983, 179; Martin and Johnson 1982).

Agreement in September 1974, in which the new Portuguese government reluctantly acceded to FRELIMO's demand for independence after a nine-month transitional phase, precluded a neocolonial solution which would have allowed Pretoria to exercise maximum leverage without intervening. With this option denied to it, Pretoria had to make a difficult decision. Powerful forces both within the military and the right wing of the Nationalist Party called for intervention (Leonard 1983, 13–14; *Observer,* August 4, 1974). The chief of the defense forces, Admiral Hugo Bierman, voiced concern about the threat which FRELIMO posed: "There certainly has never been a precedent to the current vast number of events with its potential impact, individually and collectively on our national security" (*Times,* July 12, 1974). Moreover, the South African government provided sanctuary and support for Portuguese former secret police officials and former settlers who had fled Mozambique and organized FICO ("I Stay"), a right-wing movement to prevent FRELIMO from coming to power (*Observer,* August 4, 1974). On September 7, 1974, FICO supporters seized the radio station in Lourenço Marques and urged all Portuguese to rise up while appealing for direct South African intervention. Although Pretoria is reported to have mobilized some troops on the Mozambican border (*Star Weekly,* September 19, 1974), to the dismay and disbelief of the insurgents (*Observer,* September 15, 1974) no military assistance was forthcoming and a joint FRELIMO-Portuguese force crushed the coup.

The government of John Vorster had resisted the immediate temptation of direct intervention when it became clear that there was no real "moderate alternative" who could guarantee political stability on its northern border. Vorster acknowledged this sober reality: "All that we are really interested in is good rule. It is not in our interest that there should be chaos in any neighboring country. We want stability. It is not for us to prescribe what sort of rule" (*Financial Times,* May 30, 1974).

But short of direct intervention, Pretoria could still exercise enormous economic and military leverage in order to narrow FRELIMO's more radical options and to perpetuate its own regional domination. Vorster warned FRELIMO leaders that despite Mozambique's economic potential, "it cannot stand on its own legs without the cooperation of South Africa" (*Guardian,* April 30, 1974). And he was right. By the end of the first half of 1974, Mozambique's faltering economy derived half of all its hard currency from economic relations with South Africa. Moreover, Vorster did not preclude future military intervention: "We have no plans to invade Mozambique as is being alleged in some quarters. All South Africa will ever do is to defend itself with its full-striking power if it is ever attacked. This is South Africa's right and no country and no organization can deprive us of it" (*Star Weekly,* October 5, 1974).

For its part, despite an increasing revolutionary ethos, during the transitional period from September 1974 to June 1975, FRELIMO's leaders were not in a position to confront South Africa or even to begin to extract Mozambique from the historic web of dependency. While President Machel tried to negotiate substantial aid agreements with the USSR, China, and the United Nations to achieve greater economic authority, nothing significant ever materialized from these initiatives (*Observer,* August 18, 1974). Because FRELIMO had to devote almost all of its energy before independence to the immediate problems of consolidating its power over the southern half of the country—where its presence had been minimal—and establishing the structures of government, relations with Pretoria assumed a secondary importance.

Shifting the Terrain of Struggle: 1975–80

With independence and state power, FRELIMO was theoretically positioned to set in motion policies which, over time, could reshape Mozambique's relations with South Africa. But even before such policies could be considered, forces beyond the government's control foreclosed such an option. A combination of natural calamities which destroyed much of the nation's agricultural output, extensive sabotage of factories, trucks, and farm equipment by Portuguese settlers, and the massive exodus of technicians and professionals left Mozambique's fragile economy in disarray. FRELIMO's decision to support U.N. sanctions against Rhodesia cost it more than $150 million annually (U.N. Economic and Social Council 1976, 24) and precipitated a major Rhodesian military campaign against Mozambique that destroyed key rural projects and infrastructure valued at $350 million.

The effect of these economic setbacks that Mozambique experienced during its first two years heightened the young nation's dependence on its powerful neighbor. By 1977 South Africa had replaced Portugal as Mozambique's principal source of imports, including such critical commodities as machinery, iron, steel, fertilizers, and wheat. Moreover the proportion of hard currency earnings coming from South Africa had skyrocketed to 80 percent.

Mozambique's difficulties strengthened Pretoria's hegemonic position and increased the prospects of aborting Mozambique's socialist experiment, which was only formally initiated at the end of 1977.[8] The simplest way to squeeze the FRELIMO government was to reduce the number of Mozambicans working in the mines. Between 1975 and 1982 Mozambique lost $3.2 billion because South Africa slashed the number of Mozambicans working in its gold mines from 120,000 to 45,000[9] and ceased its long-standing practice of remitting their wages to the Mozambican government in gold at a prefer-

8. It was only at the Third Party Congress held in 1977 that FRELIMO explicitly made a commitment to lead Mozambique along a socialist path of development and to organize the worker-peasant alliance to "crush the class enemy" (Mozambique, Angola and Guinea Information Center 1978).

9. To compensate for the reduction of Mozambican labor, larger numbers of migrants from Swaziland, Botswana, and especially Lesotho were recruited. The percentage of South Africans employed in the mines also increased (Murray 1981, 30).

ential rate (Murray 1981, 30; AIM 1982). The young nation also lost $250 million in fees from South Africa's reduction in the level of commerce moving through the port of Maputo[10] which fell during the same period from approximately 600 million to 100 million tons (Isaacman 1985, 11). And to emphasize how vulnerable Mozambique actually was, Pretoria again raised the specter of terminating all trade links and building a new Indian Ocean port.

At the same time that it tightened its economic grip, South Africa made menacing military gestures and warned about the growing communist menace on its borders. South Africa's planes regularly violated Mozambican airspace, its ships entered Mozambican waters with impunity, and there were reports of an undetermined number of border crossings. Most ominous was Pretoria's support of the Mozambican National Resistance (MNR), which after 1980 was to become South Africa's principal weapon against Mozambique.

Indeed, Pretoria did more than just support the MNR. According to Gordon Winter's *Inside Boss* (1981, 545), which documents his career as a South African spy, the idea for forming the MNR came from South African intelligence.

> The best example of South African involvement in the affairs of another country came in 1976, when South Africa's Army Chief Magnus Malan and his military intelligence apparatus set up a fake Black Liberation Movement in league with Rhodesian intelligence. I know all about this movement because I was its number one propagandist from the start. ... Its name was the Mozambique National Resistance and when I first started glorifying its exploits in July 1977 it existed in name only.

Ken Flowers, the head of Rhodesian intelligence, on the other hand, claimed that the idea for the MNR came from his organization, a proposition tacitly acknowledged by MNR officials (Fernandes 1983).

Whatever the case, from 1976 onward South African security, working with its Rhodesian counterparts, recruited Portuguese settlers and mercenaries, black and white secret police agents, and former African members of the elite special forces of the colonial army (GE) who had fled to South Africa and Rhodesia after Mozambican independence. Three former agents of the Portuguese Secret Police (PIDE) figured prominently in the formation of the MNR. The principal figure was Orlando Cristina. A prominent PIDE official, he became the secretary general of the MNR. Evo Fernandes, who infiltrated the antifascist student movement in Lisbon during the 1950s and subsequently rose to an influential position within the PIDE hierarchy in Mozambique, became MNR spokesperson in Europe. Casimiro Monteiro, a professional assassin implicated in the 1965 murder of Portuguese opposition

---

10. Part of the drop in exports was due both to Mozambique's decision to close its ports to Rhodesia and to the decline of iron-ore mining in Swaziland. As part of the South African squeeze, the proportion of low-value high-bulk commodities which generated lower rail and port fees was substantially increased.

leader Huberto Delgado and probably involved in the murder of FRELIMO's first president, Eduardo Mondlane, took over as liaison with South African security. To this initial group were added ex-FRELIMO guerrillas who had been expelled for corruption or had left because of unfulfilled personal ambitions. André Matzangaiza and Alfonso Dhlakama, two former FRELIMO soldiers, received prominent positions to give the MNR visible black leadership (*Africa Confidential* 1981, 1–5; *Sunday Times,* January 26, 1975; *Domingo,* January 10, 1982).

From 1976 the Rhodesian government provided the MNR with arms and bases along the Mozambican border and logistical support.[11] In retaliation for Mozambique's imposition of U.N.–backed sanctions against Rhodesia, the latter sent MNR bands repeatedly into Mozambique to burn villages, plunder agricultural cooperatives, attack railroad lines and road traffic, disrupt commerce, and raid reeducation camps, from which they recruited additional members (Dhlakama 1980b). They also collected valuable intelligence data on Zimbabwe African National Union (ZANU) forces in Mozambique and intimidated Zimbabwean refugees. For its part South African security planted in *To The Point* and *The Citizen* a number of accounts of the "heroic efforts" of the MNR against the Marxist regime of Samora Machel (Winter 1981, 545–547). These were often reproduced uncritically in the Western press.

Between 1976 and 1979 Mozambique suffered from more than 350 MNR and Rhodesian attacks. In the face of this escalating threat, the country was put on a war footing and discussion on how to reduce South Africa's long-term hegemony had to be deferred again. Instead, the government utilized its energy and limited resources to transform its poorly armed guerrilla force into a national army that it hoped would be capable of protecting its territorial integrity. Tanks, planes, and artillery were purchased from the socialist countries as part of a national campaign of military and political mobilization.

By 1979, the tide had turned against the MNR and its Rhodesian sponsors. Zimbabwean freedom fighters, working in close collaboration with the Mozambican military, had scored a number of important victories against the Rhodesians. In October FRELIMO forces overran the main MNR base in Mozambique killing the MNR leader André Matzangaiza and precipitating a violent power struggle among his lieutenants. The Lancaster House Agreement signed in late 1979, guaranteeing the end of minority rule in Rhodesia, forced the MNR to abandon its Rhodesian sanctuaries and bases. "It was,"

---

11. In return for its assistance, Rhodesian security demanded MNR subservience—as is clear from MNR documents found stuffed down a latrine when the Mozambican army captured the MNR's Garagua base in Manica province. In the words of Dhlakama, "We were opposed by the Rhodesians, and the leaders of our movement were not allowed to make any of the decisions. . . . We worked for the English, neither I nor the deceased André could plan any military operations. It was the English who determined the areas to attack and where to recruit" (Dhlakama 1980b).

according to a captured MNR document, "a disastrous period in which many soldiers and leaders were killed" (Dhlakama 1980b).

With the independence of Zimbabwe and the prospect that the weakened and divided MNR would crumble, the Mozambican government turned its energy to national reconstruction after five years of war. By diversifying its economic ties and attracting new investment capital to build an industrial base, Mozambique's leaders felts confident that they could begin to free their country from South Africa's grip. It was precisely during this period that Mozambique signed important economic agreements with England, France, Italy, Bulgaria, West Germany, and the Soviet Union worth more than $700 million (Isaacman and Isaacman 1983, 182, 186–187). It was also during this period that Mozambique played a critical role in transforming the loose political alliance of frontline states into an integrated regional alliance, the Southern African Development Coordination Conference (SADCC), which included newly independent Zimbabwe, Swaziland, Lesotho, and Malawi, in addition to Mozambique's historic allies, Tanzania, Zambia, and Angola. SADCC adopted as its overarching objective the reduction of the member states' structural dependence on South Africa. Strengthening the transportation and communication networks, without which all forms of regional cooperation would be impractical, received the highest priority. Of the $800 million pledged to SADCC in 1980 (AIM 1980, 1–11), $650 million was allocated to transportation projects primarily in Mozambique. Deepening the ports of Beira, Maputo, and Nacala and increasing their capacities could reduce the dependence of landlocked Swaziland, Botswana, Zimbabwe, Malawi, and Zambia on South African ports. For Mozambique, the prospect of a sharp increase in rail and port fees held out the hope of alleviating the nation's shortage of foreign exchange and development capital. Anticipating a substantial increase in traffic, the government spent one-third of its total investment budget on upgrading railway lines and ports in 1979 and 1980 (Santos 1982).

Preliminary indications suggest that through the SADCC transportation network international commerce was gradually redirected away from South African ports. Zimbabwe, for example, totally dependent on South African ports before independence, exported 30 million tons through Maputo in 1980 and 203 million tons in 1981, as well as an additional 166 million tons through the adjacent port of Matola (Santos 1982). Exports to Beira, although a fraction of what they were before the 1976 international boycott, nevertheless jumped from 15 million to 60 million tons in the same period (Ministério de Portos e Transportes 1981, 3). For Mozambique the port duties and transportation fees from Zimbabwean commerce replaced those from South Africa as the country's principal source of invisible income (Santos 1982). With the ties to Swaziland, Botswana, and Malawi expected to increase, the beginnings of a regional transportation system had been created. By the end of 1981 it had become increasingly clear that, for all the structural problems[12] which SADCC still had to resolve, it posed a long-term threat to South Africa's regional hegemony.

The Escalating Conflict, 1980–84

With its attention riveted on national reconstruction Machel's government failed to anticipate either that the remnants of the MNR would be given sanctuary in South Africa or that Pretoria would use the defeated guerrilla force as its covert military arm to disrupt SADCC and sabotage strategic economic projects. But this is exactly what happened. With the fall of the Ian Smith regime in Rhodesia, the South African military transferred MNR headquarters and bases to the Transvaal, a northern province adjacent to Mozambique. These operations were witnessed at the time by a British military team under Lieutenant General John Acland who was supervising the transition to independence in Zimbabwe (Legum 1983, 2). Shortly thereafter, MNR Commander Alfonso Dhlakama boasted to Portuguese journalists that South African Defense Minister Magnus Malan had made him a colonel and assured him that "your army is now part of the South African Defense Force" (quoted in Legum 1983, 13).

Whereas the Rhodesian government had used the MNR to collect information on Zimbabwean nationalist operations and to intimidate refugees who had fled to Mozambique, South Africa saw the roving bands as instruments of havoc. At a meeting between Dhlakama and Colonel Van Nierok of South African security on October 25, 1980, at Zoabostad, a military base in the Transvaal, the MNR Supreme Commander unveiled plans to reestablish bases in Sofala and Manica, and to attack both the railroad lines between Beira and Umtali and road traffic on the north-south highway. Van Nierok insisted that this was not sufficient. By the end of 1981 he ordered them to "interdict rail traffic from Malverne-Gwelo [southern Mozambique], establish bases inside Mozambique adjacent to the South African border, open a new military front in Maputo province, and provoke incidents in Maputo and Beira" (Dhlakama 1980a). The South African strategy was clear—the MNR must extend its activity to the strategic southern provinces, thereby discouraging Zimbabwe and Botswana from exporting their commodities through Maputo. Ten days later Orlando Cristina urged Dhlakama to "destroy power lines which transport energy from Cabora Bassa Dam to South Africa in order to deflect charges that South Africa was aiding the MNR" (Domingos 1980). To accomplish these broader objectives, South African officials agreed to provide larger supplies of war material, including rockets, mortars, and small arms, as well as instructors "who will not only teach but also participate in attacks" (Dhlakama 1980a).

---

12. Interregional coordination of investment projects or trade is much more problematic, as Mozambique and Angola reject "market forces" in favor of socialist state planning and most of the other SADCC countries are committed to a capitalist economy. The positions of Zimbabwe and Tanzania, although distinctly different from each other, are somewhat ambiguous.

Initially South Africa trained MNR forces at military bases in the Transvaal and provided supplies and logistical assistance to the guerrillas inside Mozambique. According to Mozambican field commanders in Tete and Manica provinces, MNR forces were regularly resupplied at night, and FRELIMO troops lacked the communications and air support to prevent these airdrops. Mozambique's long coastline is also ideally suited for naval landings, which became more frequent. Captured MNR documents suggest that this is the preferred route (Dhlakama 1980a). It is much cheaper for South Africa, and Mozambique's fledgling navy cannot patrol effectively. In addition to the small arms, mortars, mines, and anti-aircraft weaponry, Mozambican officials acknowledged that the MNR receives communications equipment which is far more sophisticated than that available to its own forces (Guebuza 1982). This enabled MNR bands to maintain contact with South Africa, whose reconnaissance planes flew inside Mozambique to provide valuable information on Mozambican troop movements.

In 1983 Western diplomats in Maputo estimated the MNR numbers to be between 5,000 and 10,000—appreciably lower than Dhlakama's claim of 17,000 armed soldiers (*Washington Post,* April 6, 1983). Many MNR recruits seem to have been coerced into joining. According to Sara Muchalima, "The bandits came to my house and told my parents I had to go with them. My father refused, but they beat him up, tied my hands, and with a gun to my head took me to their base at Garagua" (quoted in Isaacman and Isaacman 1982, 6). John Burleson (1982), a British ecologist held prisoner by the MNR for several months, reported seeing hundreds of forced recruits who were kept under armed guard.

Nevertheless, Mozambique's serious economic problems made MNR recruitment that much easier. Extensive droughts, which the MNR attributed to the alienated ancestors, the Mozambican government's failure to provide sufficient support for the family farming sector, and the lack of consumer goods in parts of Manica, Sofala, and Inhambane, provided fertile ground for MNR overtures. So did the MNR's manipulation of tribal divisions and appeals to Shona chiefs, spirit mediums, and "traditional"[13] Shona values.

Whatever the initial attraction of these appeals, widescale plundering and increasing terrorism quickly evaporated support for the MNR and alienated the rural population which, above all else, wanted to be left alone. Western missionaries living along the Mozambican-Zimbabwean border reported that in December 1980, the MNR launched a terrorist campaign around Espangabera in Manica "beheading Machel loyalists, abducting girls, and press-ganging young men into service" (*Guardian,* December 16, 1980).

13. FRELIMO's campaign against polygamy, bride-price, female rites of initiation, and other customs which either exploited women or reproduced obscurantism, was bitterly opposed by a number of chiefs and male elders. The MNR was able to appeal to this dissatisfaction with a degree of success.

Some, such as Daniel Manhique, an agricultural worker living in the southern part of the country, have suffered from repeated MNR raids. "They beat me and beat me until I lost consciousness," and two months later they returned and asked "us if we didn't know that they had given us a warning not to work, whereupon they beat me again for defying them" (quoted in *Notícias,* May 10, 1983). Peasants from Gaza who fled to Zimbabwe also spoke of repeated MNR atrocities: "At Madura, they came and demanded money and food. They accused some people of being informers for government forces and cut off the nose, lips and ears of a number of people. Then they told them to go and report to FRELIMO" (quoted in *Africa News,* August 9, 1982).

Reports filtering in from the bush made it clear that these were not isolated acts by a few disaffected MNR members, but rather reflected the underlying strategy of an organization committed to banditry and marauding. The August 1982 attack on a packed passenger train, in which sixty-four civilians were shot after the train had come to a halt, epitomized this campaign of terrorism (*Guardian,* August 14, 1982).

These tactics, together with the MNR's reliance on narrow tribal appeals directed primarily at Shona-speaking peoples, only one of a dozen ethnic and cultural groups in the country, belie its claim that it is a nationalist movement of freedom fighters disillusioned with the FRELIMO party's Marxist strategy (MNR 1982). Apart from its anticommunist rhetoric, it lacks any political program and has made no effort to organize the peasants in those areas in which it operates. "Its raison d'être," noted Jay Ross of the *Washington Post* (August 6, 1983), "seems mainly to oppose Machel's Marxist government with a vague appeal to capitalism and to return to more traditional ways such as polygamy and tribal chieftainship." Western diplomats in Maputo agreed unanimously that the MNR was little more than an arm of South African security (*Guardian,* April 18, 1983). A senior member of the diplomatic corps, who insisted upon anonymity, characterized the MNR as "a disparate group of gunslingers, thugs, white Portuguese opportunists and other assorted anti-FRELIMO types who lack any vision or program for the future."

Nevertheless, the MNR has played a significant role in Pretoria's undeclared economic, political, and psychological war against Mozambique and its SADCC allies. Roving bands have repeatedly attacked strategic economic targets, cutting railroad lines, mining roads and bridges, interdicting traffic, plundering communal villages, state farms and shops, and sabotaging key development projects. Mineral prospecting and geological surveys in Sofala, Manica, and Zambezia have also been disrupted, and a number of technicians, from both Eastern and Western European countries, have been captured or killed.

But South Africa's principal economic target was the SADCC transportation network, especially the railway lines from Mozambique to Zimbabwe, which came under repeated attack. As a result, many Zimbabwean companies have decided to continue relying on the South African port of Durban, despite the appreciably lower cost of shipping through Maputo and the ten-day shorter turnaround time there, when all runs well. Beira, historically Zimbabwe's major international outlet, has suffered the most. In 1982 Zimbabwe exported only 55,000 tons through Beira, a mere fraction of pre-sanction trade (Santos 1982). The MNR also stepped up its attacks on rail traffic between Beira and Malawi, resulting in serious fuel and fertilizer shortages just before the 1982 agricultural season (*Rand Daily Mail,* October 29, 1982). There were also indications that Pretoria's surrogate was increasing pressure on the Nacala railroad line, Malawi's only other link to the outside world besides the South African ports.

As the economic stakes increased, South African commandos no longer even bothered to maintain the facade as "instructors." In November 1981 marker buoys at the entrance of the Beira harbor were blown up. This was a sophisticated operation, which Western diplomats in Mozambique agreed was obviously beyond the technical capacity of the MNR. Similarly, South African commandos destroyed the strategic bridge across the Pungue River, blocking road communications to Beira, and periodically mined the railroad lines linking that port city to Zimbabwe (*Observer,* February 20, 1983). On December 9, 1982, South African raiders destroyed thirty-four oil storage tanks in Beira valued at more than $40 million, causing severe shortages in Zimbabwe (*Washington Post,* January 7, 1983; *Financial Times,* January 6, 1983).

At the same time that South Africa intensified its military pressure, it expanded its long-term objectives. Fearing both the increasing popularity of the African National Congress (ANC) and the liberation movement's ability to attack strategic points within South Africa, Pretoria embarked upon the campaign to compel Mozambique not to provide any sanctuary or support for the freedom fighters. The first indication of this policy was the 1981 attack on the homes of South African refugees, some of whom were ANC members, living on the outskirts of Maputo. The August 1982 assassination of Ruth First, a leading member of the ANC and an outspoken critic of the apartheid regime, and increased South African border violations were other indications of Pretoria's intent. In a rare interview, South African Prime Minister Botha was even more explicit on the question of linkage.

> We say two can play this game. We say two can make war. But also two can make peace. If Mozambican leaders will say "We are socialist but we won't fight against South Africa militarily and we will cooperate economically"—and they mean it—that they won't undermine South Africa by letting their country be used by people who fight against South Africa then surely we can cooperate. (quoted in *New York Times,* February 17, 1983)

Most ominous was the explicit warning of South African Defense Minister General Magnus Malan in August 1982 that his country might find it necessary to initiate a "Lebanese-type invasion" of Mozambique to rid it of "ANC terrorists" (*Reuters,* August 22, 1982). In subsequent meetings with Mozambican officials at the Nkomati (Komatiport) border town, South African Foreign Minister Pik Botha reportedly warned of escalating attacks unless ANC personnel were removed from Maputo (*Washington Post,* April 4, 1983; *Economist,* July 18, 1983; *Guardian,* January 11, 1983).

The brazen December 1982 raid against ANC homes in Maseru, Lesotho, coming precisely at the same moment when the Beira oil facilities were attacked, was meant as a clear warning to Mozambique that Maputo would be next. Indeed, in January 1983 the MNR initiated an unsuccessful offensive to capture or at least isolate southern Mozambique, including the capital. Five months later the South African air force bombed the industrial outskirts of Maputo ostensibly in reprisal for an ANC attack in Pretoria several days earlier (*Star,* May 30, 1983; *Financial Times,* May 25, 1983). The message was unmistakable. Mozambique's fragile economy would be held hostage. The October 1983 South African commando attack on an ANC house located only a few blocks from the presidential palace was deliberately meant to further demonstrate the vulnerability of the FRELIMO government (*Times,* October 18, 1983).

Early in 1982 the Mozambican leadership turned its attention to combating the escalating South African MNR threat. It finally acknowledged the need for a new military and political strategy, one that would incorporate aspects of guerrilla warfare and peasant mobilization that FRELIMO had previously used successfully.

Shortly after independence, in the face of impending attacks from the Smith regime, the government had disbanded most guerrilla units and begun to organize a conventional army composed of draftees, believing that tanks, artillery, and jets—however antiquated—would be an effective deterrent. Then, in late 1979, euphoric about Zimbabwean independence, Mozambique disbanded many rural militia units thinking that MNR activity would cease. As a result, it was unprepared for the MNR's resurgence in late 1980. FRELIMO, which during the armed struggle had been so effective as a guerrilla movement, found itself trying to contain guerrillas—who had sophisticated logistical support from Pretoria—with a relatively inexperienced, poorly equipped conventional army relying on dated Soviet equipment. To remedy this situation the government, in May 1982, activated more than 1,500 former freedom fighters, many of whom were organized into counterinsurgency forces whose job was to harass the terrorists deep in the bush (Mabote 1983). Others, working under newly appointed provincial military commanders, all with substantial experience in the armed struggle and deep familial and ethnic ties to the provinces in which they were assigned, assumed responsibility for revitalizing the civilian militias in the war zones. By August 1982, about 40 percent of the adult rural population in Sofala was armed, and in the capital the newly formed militia boasted upward of 30,000 men and women. Although the quality and performance of the militia are varied, they have blunted several MNR attacks in Inhambane, Sofala, and Manica (Thai 1982).

Restructuring the military and reinvigorating the militia, according to Mozambican sources, proved decisive in thwarting the major MNR offensive at the beginning of 1983. During a six-month campaign more than 420 South African–backed troops were killed or captured and government troops over-ran the principal MNR supply and logistical base in Inhambane (*Tempo*, October 16, 1983, 17–23). Yet despite its success in the south, FRELIMO forces were unable to prevent the MNR from intensifying its military operations in Nampula and Zambezia—the nation's most populous and economically important provinces. The capture of twenty-four Soviet geologists in August 1983, the removal of the entire Zambezian military command, and the appointment of a leading member of the Central Committee as provincial governor of Zambezia suggested the gravity of the situation (*Observer*, August 28, 1983; *Star*, September 19, 1983).

It also suggested that the problem of the MNR defied a simple military solution, a fact which Mozambique's leaders had increasingly come to realize. At a minimum what was required was to regain the confidence and support of the peasantry, who constitute 90 percent of the population, and to mobilize international support in opposition to South Africa's escalating military campaign. Neither of these was a particularly easy task.

For more than five years, peasants in the affected areas had been subjected to periodic attacks, first from Rhodesian forces and then from the MNR, from which the Mozambican army could not protect them. As one close adviser to President Machel acknowledged, "FRELIMO used up a lot of its political capital during the Zimbabwean war" (Cabaço 1983) by assuring peasants that peace in Zimbabwe would bring prosperity to Mozambique. That the peasants had legitimate grievances that the government must address was also stressed by Armando Guebuza (1982), ranking member of FRELIMO's Central Committee, and then resident minister of war-torn Sofala: "We cannot stand idly by but must attack the economic and social problems, especially the lack of material goods." His words were echoed by another senior party official summarizing the public sentiment expressed at meetings held in villages and work places throughout the entire country in preparation for the April 1983 Fourth Party Congress. "We were deluged with complaints of bureaucratic indifference, of corruption, of the absence of state support for the family sector and communal villages and, above all else, of the lack of basic consumer goods" (Cabaço 1983). The official summary of these meetings, which was presented at the Congress, confirmed the magnitude of the problem. In honest self-criticism, which has always characterized FRELIMO, it concluded that the quality of life of many Mozambicans had been adversely affected "by our own shortcomings and mistakes" (FRELIMO, "Report on the Preparation for the Congress," 14).

Empowering the peasantry was the central theme of President Machel's thirteen-hour report to the Fourth Party Congress. He was especially critical of the lack of state support for the rural population and the excessive centralization of authority which stifled peasant initiatives. Whereas the previous Congress held in 1977 had concluded that organizing massive Eastern European–style state farms was the most effective way to end Mozambique's food shortages and to generate cash crop exports, Machel articulated a very different set of priorities this time.

> Small-scale projects are a method of making full use of locally available resources, and of taking full advantage of existing productive capacities. Their achievement develops the people's confidence in their own abilities, combats passivity, and a spirit of dependence, frees the imagination and creative initiative. (FRELIMO, "Report of the Central Committee," 27)

He went on to note that in the struggle against hunger, "the family sector in the countryside warrants immediate priority." Privately, leading members of the Central Committee admitted that the expensive state farms had not produced the anticipated output and had created serious organizational problems. Moreover, by locating all the country's resources in this sector and promising peasants technical inputs which were not forthcoming, the state "repressed local initiatives because the peasants were reluctant to clear their fields with hoes, waiting for the day when the tractors would come" (FRELIMO, "Report of the Central Committee," 27). Together with assurances of greater state support at the grassroots level, higher prices for agricultural products, and more consumer goods, the Central Committee report emphasized the need to revitalize local political institutions.

The composition of the new Central Committee suggested the high priority which FRELIMO placed on peasant mobilization. Several of the most outspoken peasant critics of the state's agricultural policies were elected to the Central Committee, while a number of junior ministers and national directors responsible for major economic projects were not. While this decision represents, in part, the desire to separate the party and state apparatus, it also reflects FRELIMO's intention to have greater grassroots representation. The doubling of the Central Committee from 65 to 130 members, with most new members coming from the countryside, demonstrates this (*Christian Science Monitor,* June 15, 1983). So does the decision to elect a significant number of disillusioned former freedom-fighters who had been overlooked at the previous Congress, people who had been frozen out of positions of responsibility since independence because of their lack of formal education.

But even if FRELIMO's aggressive military strategy and policy of returning to the grassroots could isolate the MNR, the formidable problem of South African hegemony remained. Indeed, despite a substantial increase in trade with the socialist countries, eight years after independence Mozambique had not been able to restructure its economy and break the chains of dependency.

As of 1983 there were still some 45,000 Mozambican workers in the South African mines, South African transit traffic through the port of Maputo remained a major source of hard currency, and almost 90 percent of the hydroelectrical power from Cabora Bassa went south (*Guardian,* May 27, 1983). South Africa's awesome military might posed a reality with which Mozambican leaders had to contend on a daily basis. Relatively modest military assistance from the socialist countries, which nevertheless have been the only reliable source of weapons and advisers, and the presence of more than 1,000 Zimbabwean and Tanzanian troops (*Guardian,* January 4, 1983) guarding the railway and pipelines to Zimbabwe clearly did not represent a sufficient deterrence.

Mozambique's Opening to the West

In an attempt to weaken South Africa's stranglehold, since 1982[14] Mozambique has turned increasingly and more publicly to the West for economic, diplomatic, and even military assistance. This strategy does not represent a reversal of its commitment to a socialist path of development nor to an autonomous foreign policy that best serves its national interest. It does, however, reflect a careful calculation that the socialist countries were either unwilling or unable to provide the aid and development capital which Mozambique desperately needed and that only the West can pressure South Africa to cease its military aggression. For their part, the Western European countries have increasingly shied away from their cold war stereotypes and have begun to accept Mozambique's domestic and international stance on its own terms. President Machel's highly publicized trip to the European Common Market headquarters in Brussels and his extensive discussion with Portuguese, British, and French leaders in the fall of 1983 were just the most visible features of Mozambique's "opening to the West." This policy poses new sets of contradictions but is nevertheless perceived in Maputo as a necessary risk if Mozambique is to break out of Pretoria's grip.

Mozambique has had to make a number of strategic concessions in an effort to attract foreign capital. After years of adamantly refusing to agree to the "Berlin Clause," in 1982 Mozambique signed a commercial agreement with West Germany that included a modified version of the clause. While the agreement did not please the East Germans, it opened the way for increased economic ties to both the Bonn government and West German capital and removed an important barrier to closer relations with the EEC countries (Isaacman and Isaacman, 1983, 188). An additional step was taken in that direction when, on his visit to Brussels, Machel's delegation announced that it would probably sign the Lomé agreements, which it did in September 1984,

---

14. As early as 1978, the Mozambican government quietly initiated efforts to improve relations with the West and attract foreign capital, but these efforts met with very little success.

formally linking Mozambique to the EEC. Mozambican officials have agreed to introduce a standardized foreign investment code to replace its somewhat ambiguous private-capital laws,[15] which have tended to discourage potential investors concerned about Mozambique's socialist path of development. Indications that the principles embodied in the new code would be similar to those in the $60 million oil exploratory agreement signed with Esso and Shell in the summer of 1983 were also well received in Western business circles. After a year's discussion with World Bank officials, Mozambique joined the IMF in the fall of 1984.

No less important has been Mozambique's effort to mobilize Western opposition to the South African–MNR attacks. Great Britain adopted a more sympathetic posture in the aftermath of the Lancaster House agreement and has even considered providing Mozambique with an advanced ground-to-air communication system critical to coordinate counterinsurgency activities (*Observer,* November 19, 1983).

Maputo has focused its attention on Portugal and the United States, two unlikely supporters. Since the MNR's inception in 1977, right-wing elements living in Portugal have operated a highly visible and elaborate recruiting and propaganda network which Lisbon had allowed to function unimpeded. For their part both American economic and military interest groups have historically had close ties to Pretoria, and there are reports, which Washington has never denied, that the CIA provided the South Africans with strategic information that facilitated their attack on Maputo in 1981 (Muthemba 1981).

Paradoxically, it was the awareness of these close connections which shaped Mozambique's diplomatic campaign—a campaign which by the middle of 1983 had produced some significant results. As part of a broader agreement signed in April 1982, Lisbon attacked the South African raids and agreed both to monitor right-wing activity in Portugal and to provide some military assistance to thwart the MNR–South African attacks (AIM 1982, 5–6; *International Herald Tribune,* October 3, 1983). The agreement probably marked the first time that Mozambique has turned to the West for any military assistance and certainly represented the first positive response to such an initiative. It reportedly includes war materiel, logistical support, and training for Mozambican officers in Portugal. In late October 1982, the minister of defense, Alberto Chipande, went to Lisbon to continue negotiations with his Portuguese counterparts. Asked by a Mozambican journalist if this

15. Private property is guaranteed in Article 12 of the Constitution and Law no. 18/77 promulgated on April 28, 1977, explicitly welcomes private companies in Mozambique as long as they "operate within the framework of the State's economic plan." What concerned foreign investors was the lack of specific laws that regulated such issues as nationalization, repatriation of profits, etc. The new legislation is intended to address these issues. In September 1984, Mozambique joined the World Bank and the International Monetary Fund in an effort to attract development capital and to resolve its increasing indebtedness.

agreement with a NATO country would not compromise Mozambique's socialist integrity, Chipande responded:

> We are not going to be prevented from cooperating with the Portuguese merely because we are a socialist country. They left infrastructures and equipment here that could be used for military objectives. We cannot spend millions and millions of dollars merely because we do not want to buy a part from a country that is a member of NATO. (*Tempo,* June 20, 1982, 22–23)

In addition, the Portuguese military possessed maps and other strategic information collected during the armed struggle that would be of invaluable assistance to Mozambique. For its part, Lisbon was anxious that its citizens working in Mozambique, who had been the target of MNR attacks, be protected. Portuguese officials also saw Machel's 1983 visit as an opportunity to rebuild economic and cultural relations with their former colony.

Since 1982 there has been a perceptible thaw in relations with Washington and a discernible increase in diplomatic activity. Speaking to the Portuguese newspaper *Diário de Notícias* (October 6, 1983), Machel emphasized that "The American administration now has, without doubt, a more lucid attitude toward cooperation with Mozambique. They discuss things with us frankly and we appreciate this." This activity seems to have produced some tangible results. The United States condemned South African aggression against Lesotho, and in a departure from past policy the Reagan administration, through a State Department spokesperson, acknowledged and tacitly criticized Pretoria's support of the MNR (*Africa Report* January-February 1983, 48). In January 1983 the U.S. chargé d'affaires in Maputo joined with representatives of England, France, the Soviet Union, and China to condemn South African aggression (*Washington Post,* April 6, 1983), and the American government increased its food aid to Maputo.

Nkomati and After

By 1982 FRELIMO had realized that, unless it reached some sort of accommodation with South Africa, peace would not be possible. Faced with a deteriorating military situation resulting from the South African–backed MNR offensive begun two years earlier, the leaders were forced to acknowledge that the socialist countries were either unwilling or unable to provide the military assistance Mozambique had been led to expect. Soviet weapons— with the exception of a handful of MIG–21s, MI–24 helicopter gunships, and SAM–7s—were out of date and costly, a fact not lost on the Mozambicans. Moreover, there was growing dissatisfaction with the quality of the conventional military training provided by Eastern-bloc advisers which proved ineffectual against the MNR guerrillas (*Africa Report,* January-February 1983). South Africa's undeclared campaign of economic strangulation, together with the escalating MNR attacks, had made a shambles of Mozambique's economy.

Mozambican analysts concluded that South Africa's deepening economic crisis, brought about by the steep decline in the price of gold and the skyrocketing costs of petroleum, would make Pretoria more receptive to peace overtures (Cabaço 1984). By 1982, South Africa's balance of payments deficit had grown to over $500 million and its foreign debt to $13 billion (Isaacman 1985, 11). At the end of that year, Mozambican officials, dangling new markets and investment possibilities as an incentive to negotiate, raised the prospect of a nonaggression pact.

Initially, South Africa rejected the proposal, offering instead aid to revitalize the Mozambican economy in return for FRELIMO's expulsion of the ANC, a condition which was unacceptable to the Mozambicans (Cabaço 1984). Only after a year-long campaign by Mozambique, aimed at convincing NATO governments that it was not a pawn of the Soviet Union and that the interests of the West were not served by allowing Pretoria to transform southern Africa into a new zone of cold war conflict, did the West pressure Pretoria to reconsider.

A secret meeting of senior South African and Mozambican officials took place in Swaziland in December 1983. After some difficult negotiations, which included a South African walkout after the Mozambican delegation denounced the long history of racist aggression, Pretoria finally accepted the idea of a nonaggression pact. On March 16, 1984, at the border town of Nkomati, each side formally promised "not to allow its territory to be used for acts of war, aggression or violence against the other state" (*Africa News*, March 26, 1984.)[16]

It is clear in retrospect, however, that hard-line members of the South African military and security forces had no intention of living up to the agreement. Reluctant to see the MNR decline significantly as a threat to Marxist Mozambique, South African intelligence, just before March, stockpiled the MNR with enough military equipment to last for two years. At the same time,

16. The three major articles of the accord of Nkomati are:

ARTICLE ONE. The High Contracting Parties undertake to respect each other's sovereignty and independence and, in fulfillment of this fundamental obligation, to refrain from interfering in the internal affairs of the other.

ARTICLE TWO. (1) The High Contracting Parties shall resolve differences and disputes that may arise between them and that may or are likely to endanger mutual peace and security or peace and security in the region, by means of negotiation, enquiry, mediation, conciliation, arbitration or other peaceful means, and undertake not to resort, individually or collectively, to the threat or use of force against each other's sovereignty, territorial integrity or political independence. . . .

ARTICLE THREE. (1) The High Contracting Parties shall not allow their respective territories, territorial waters or air space to be used as a base, thoroughfare, or in any other way by another state, government, foreign military forces, organizations or individuals which plan or prepare to commit acts of violence, terrorism or aggression against the territorial integrity or political independence of the other or may threaten the security of its inhabitants. . . .

according to Western diplomats, between 1,200 and 1,500 MNR soldiers and paratroopers were infiltrated into the area surrounding Maputo, the capital, to create havoc and to increase South Africa's bargaining power in the post-Nkomati period (*Guardian*, May 29, 1984).

Six months after the agreement was signed, Mozambique's vice minister of security, Teodato Hunguana, charged that the South African military was still sending hundreds of MNR troops into Mozambique and continuing to resupply the insurgents already fighting there (Hunguana 1984). Another high-level Mozambican told me that South African intelligence used Portuguese import-export firms as a conduit to supply arms to the MNR. The Mozambicans also contend that South African agents operate freely from Malawi, providing MNR forces in central and northern Mozambique with war materiel. These claims seem to be borne out by the fact that, since the Nkomati Accord, the fighting has been heaviest in those areas adjacent to the Malawian border. To try to stem this flow of men and war materiel, President Machel flew to Blantyre in October 1984, to meet with President Banda and high-level Malawian military officials (*Africa News*, October 5, 1984; *Guardian*, October 24, 1984).

Although the military situation had improved in the central part of the country, the MNR offensive continued in the strategic Maputo province, and for the first time the insurgents began operating in Cabo Delgado in the extreme north of Mozambique (*Guardian*, August 15, 1984). This move into Cabo Delgado enabled the MNR to score a propaganda victory by claiming that it was now fighting in all ten Mozambican provinces. The escalation of hostilities, combined with the continued drought, greatly heightened Mozambique's economic crisis. There were serious food shortages throughout the southern half of the country, where it is estimated that more than 100,000 Mozambicans died from the famine in 1983 and an even greater number in 1984.

Pretoria, too, faced serious problems in the post-Nkomati period. Its failure to enforce the nonaggression pact created difficulties at home and undercut South Africa's credibility in the larger international community. A number of prominent organizations, including the Conference of Catholic Bishops, condemned the MNR for committing atrocities and demanded that the Botha government cease supporting it (*Domingo*, September 30, 1984).

More important, powerful industrial and financial interests, which had applauded the Nkomati agreement and saw increased trade and investment possibilities with Mozambique as a way for South Africa to reverse its deteriorating economic situation (by 1983 the international debt had shot up to $15 billion), criticized the continued policy of destabilization as counterproductive (Isaacman 1985). Several large multinational corporations based in South Africa, most notably the Anglo–American Corporation, which had begun negotiations with the Mozambican government to revitalize both the once lucrative tourist industry and the port of Maputo, were informed in the spring that Mozambique would not sign any formal agreements until the problems of security had been resolved. Explaining his government's refusal to finalize negotiations, the Minister of Information, José Luís Cabaço (1984), was quite blunt: "Frankly, it is the only weapon we have." Major South African trading firms, which were anxious to once again realize the 14 rand per ton savings by trading through Maputo rather than Durban, also demanded that their government stop supporting the MNR.

Moreover, energy-starved South Africa had additional reasons for wanting peace. Recently discovered additional deposits of natural gas in southern Mozambique could easily be consumed by South African industry. Indeed, immediately after the Nkomati Accord, South Africa and Mozambique had begun discussing the possibility of constructing a pipeline from the gas deposits at Pande to South Africa. A stable government in Mozambique could help South Africa substantially reduce its energy problems, not only by providing natural gas but also by ensuring the uninterrupted flow of electricity from the large dam at Cabora Bassa, the power lines of which the MNR has regularly disrupted. In addition, Mozambique's likely oil reserves, both in the far north and off the southern coast, although potentially beneficial to South Africa, will not become accessible to Pretoria until there is peace.

South Africa's Western allies also pressured Pretoria to curtail the MNR's activities. Great Britain and the United States were especially dismayed at South Africa's reluctance to adhere to the terms of the nonaggression pact. For the Reagan administration the unraveling of the Nkomati agreement would destroy the only modest triumph it could claim from its much heralded policy of constructive engagement, inasmuch as Washington had failed to resolve the issue of Namibian independence or to remove the Cubans from Angola. Moreover, the Reagan administration, which had given Mozambique over $100 million worth of food aid in 1984 to encourage it to continue pursuing an independent political line, feared that the failure of Machel's diplomatic initiative might ultimately force him to succumb to the Soviet Union's often repeated request for military bases.

After a number of unproductive discussions concerning the implementation of the nonaggression pact, Jacinto Veloso, the head of the Mozambican delegation, warned on September 27, 1984, that continuous MNR activity "could seriously endanger the Nkomati accord" (*Notícias*, September 28, 1984). Apparently, the South Africans took him at his word, because a new round of negotiations began in Pretoria the following week. Although the meetings were tense, both sides made the necessary concessions. South Africa, which at first had refused to take public responsibility for the MNR, finally did so. It also seems to have dropped the MNR's insistence on a government of national unity in which the insurgents would receive several ministerial posts,[17] a demand Mozambique refused even to consider. For its part, Machel's government had to accept the equal billing given to the MNR at the signing ceremony and the fact that at least one MNR member would serve on the commission to be formed to monitor the cease-fire and to guarantee amnesty to the insurgents. South Africa also benefited by being able to claim to the international community that it was serving as peacemaker.

To be sure, many problems remain. South Africa's commitment to the principles of Nkomati is suspect itself. The actual role of the Cease-Fire Commission is ill defined. Moreover, unless Pretoria forcibly pressures the MNR, there is little reason to believe that the MNR leadership will accept the agreement. Mozambican officials fear that the MNR will intensify its military operations in order to improve its influence on the commission and that Pretoria's representatives to that body will stall its work in order to give the MNR this opportunity. This fear seems well founded since, one day after the agreement, Evo Fernandes, the Portuguese Secretary General of the MNR, proclaimed that "the war continues" (*Financial Times,* October 5, 1984). Even if South Africa and the MNR leadership ultimately act in good faith, however, they are believed by Western analysts in Maputo to control only 30 to 50 percent of the several thousand guerrillas operating in Mozambique, and, at the moment, there is little incentive for the remainder, who move in small autonomous bands, to put down their arms.

In the last analysis, an effective cessation of hostilities might even require the involvement of South African troops at least to monitor the cease-fire. The presence of South African soldiers in Mozambique would raise a number of questions. Is the South African military prepared to abandon the MNR and to help disarm the insurgents if they refuse to comply with the agreement? How can the Mozambican government limit the role of the South Africans and guarantee that they do not actively promote destabilization? If South Africa abandons the MNR, what message will it be sending to UNITA, its ally in Angola, and to the antigovernment forces it reportedly supports in Zimbabwe and Lesotho? Whatever the ambiguities for South Africa, however, President Machel maintains that "South Africa must destroy the monster it created" (Machel 1984).

Unless the United States pressures Pretoria to do so, Mozambican leaders might well be forced to scrap the Nkomati agreement and to become dependent on Soviet military assistance, whatever the cost. This would constitute a

17. Before the talks began in Pretoria, the MNR insisted on a government of national conciliation in which it would hold several ministries, including the position of foreign minister and senior economic cabinet positions. Although the MNR did not participate directly in the Pretoria discussions, its leadership met daily with the South African negotiating team which initially advanced the MNR plan for a government of national recognition. After the Pretoria agreement, which left the MNR without any political power, a spokesman for the MNR criticized P. K. Botha "as an unconditional ally of the Marxist-Leninist regime" (*International Herald Tribune,* October 3, 1984).

major setback for the Reagan administration's highly publicized policy of constructive engagement, since Nkomati is the one success Washington has claimed. It would also virtually preclude the possibility of an agreement with Angola, thereby leaving little hope for a settlement of the Namibian crisis.

REFERENCES

Africa Confidential. 1981. July 21.

Africa News (Durham, N.C.). August 9, 1982; March 26, 1984; October 5, 1984.

Africa Report (New York). 1983. January-February; May-June.

AHM (Arquivo Histórico de Moçambique). 1886. Fundo do Século XIX, Governo Geral, CX.1, Governador de Quelimane to Secretario Geral do Governador, February 4.

AID (Agency for International Development). n.d. "PL 480, Title 2, Africa: Historical Trends." Washington, D.C.: U.S. Government Printing Office.

————. 1984. "Approved FY 84 PL 480 Title 2 Emergency Program in Africa." (February 23). Washington, D.C.: U.S. Government Printing Office.

AIM (Agência de Informação de Moçambique) (Maputo). 1980. *Information Bulletin 53.*

————. 1982. *Information Bulletin 75–76.*

Burleson, John. 1982. Transcripts of interview, May 27.

Cabaço, José Luís. 1982. Mozambican Minister of Information, personal interview, August 9.

————. 1983. Mozambican Minister of Information, personal interview, May 4.

————. 1984. Mozambican Minister of Information, personal interview, October 7.

Chissano, Joaquim. 1983. Mozambican Minister of Foreign Affairs, personal interview, October 7.

Christian Science Monitor (Boston). 1983. June 15; October 7.

Dhlakama, Alfonso Macacho Maresta. 1980a. "Relatório Referente a Sessão do Trabalho de R.N.M. e do Representativo do Governo Sul Africano." MNR (Resistência Nacional de Moçambique) document, October 25.

————. 1980b. "Commando Geral." MNR document, November 28.

Diário de Notícias. 1983. October 6.

Domingo (Maputo). January 10, 1982; September 30, 1984.

Domingos, Raul Manuel. 1980. Untitled Summary of Conversations with Orlando Christina. MNR document, Zoabostad, November 4.

Duffy, James. 1961. *Portuguese Africa.* Cambridge, Mass.: Harvard University Press.

Economist (London). 1983. July 18.

Fernandes, Evo. 1983. MNR Spokesman in Lisbon, transcripts of interview, April 4.

Financial Times (London). May 30, 1974; January 6, 1983; May 25, 1983; October 5, 1984.

FRELIMO. n.d. "Report on the Preparation for the Congress." FRELIMO Archives, Maputo.

————. n.d. "Report of the Central Committee." FRELIMO Archives, Maputo.

Grundy, Kenneth. 1982. "South Africa in the Political Economy of Southern Africa," pp. 148–178 in Gwendolen M. Carter and Patrick O'Meara, eds. *International Politics in Southern Africa.* Bloomington: University of Indiana Press.

Guardian (London). April 30, 1974; December 16, 1980; August 14, 1982; January 4, 1983; January 11, 1983; April 18, 1983; May 27, 1983; October 10, 1983; May 29, 1984; August 15, 1984; October 24, 1984.

Guebuza, Armando. 1982. Resident Minister of Sofala Province, personal interview, September 2.

Henriksen, Thomas. 1983. *Revolution and Counterrevolution: Mozambique's War of Independence, 1964–1974.* Westport, Conn.: Greenwood Press.

Hunguana, Teodato. 1984. Mozambican Vice Minister of Security, personal interview, October 5.

International Herald Tribune (Paris). 1983. October 3.

Isaacman, Allen, and Barbara Isaacman. 1982. "South Africa's Hidden War." *Africa Report* (November-December):4–8.

———. 1983. *Mozambique: From Colonialism to Revolution, 1900–1982.* Boulder, Col.: Westview Press.

———: 1985. "After the Nkomati Accord." *Africa Report.* January-February: 10–13.

Isaacman, Allen; Michael Stephen; Yussuf Adam; Maria Joxo Homen; Eugénio Macamo; and Augustinho Pililão. 1980. "Cotton is the Mother of Poverty." *International Journal of Africa Historical Studies* 13, no. 4:581–615.

Johnstone, Frederick A. 1976. *Class, Race and Gold.* London: Routledge and Kegan Paul.

Katzenellenbogen, Simon E. 1982. *South Africa and Southern Mozambique.* Manchester, England: University of Manchester Press.

Legum, Colin. 1983. "The Counter Revolutionaries in Southern Africa: The Challenge of the Mozambique National Resistance." *Third World Reports* (March): 1–22.

Leonard, Richard. 1983. *South Africa at War.* Westport, Conn.: Lawrence Hill.

Mabote, Sebastião. 1983. Chief of the General Staff and Deputy Minister of Defense, personal interview, May 5.

Machel, Samora Moises. 1984. President of Mozambique, personal interview, October 5.

Martin, David, and Phyllis Johnson. 1982. *The Struggle for Zimbabwe.* New York: Monthly Review Press.

Middlemas, Robert Keith. 1975. *Cabora Bassa: Engineering and Politics in Southern Africa.* London: Weidenfield and Nicolson.

Ministério de Portos e Transportes, Departamento Estatístico. 1981. *Informação Estatística* (Maputo) 4.

Mittleman, James. 1981. *Underdevelopment and the Transition to Socialism: Mozambique and Tanzania.* New York: Academic Press.

MNR (Resistência Nacional de Moçambique). 1982. *A Luta Contínua* 3.

Mozambique, Angola and Guinea Information Center. 1978. *Central Committee Report to the Third Party Congress of FRELIMO.* London.

Munslow, Barry. 1983. *Mozambique: The Revolution and Its Origins.* London, New York: Longman.

Murray, Colin. 1981. *Families Divided.* Cambridge: Cambridge University Press.

Muthemba, Abel. 1981. *Como Uma Reda da CIA Foi Desmentalada im Moçambique.* Maputo.

New York Times. 1983. February 17.

Notícias (Maputo). August 24, 1982; May 10, 1983; September 28, 1984.

Observer (London). August 4, 1974; August 18, 1974; September 15, 1974; February 20, 1983; August 28, 1983; October 19, 1983; November 19, 1983.

Penvenne, Jeanne. 1979. "Forced Labor and the Origins of an African Working Class, Lourenço Marques, 1870–1962." Boston University African Studies Center Working Paper no. 13.

Rand Daily Mail. 1982. October 29.

Reuters. 1982. August 22.

Ross, Edward. 1925. *Report on Employment of Native Labor in Portuguese Africa.* New York.

Santos, Luís Maria Alcatara. 1982. Minister of Ports and Surface Transportation, personal interview, September 6.

Silva Cunha, J. M. da. 1949. *O Trabalho Indígena: Estudo do Direito Colonial.* Lisbon: Agência Geral das Colonias.

Smith, Alan. 1974. "António Salazar and the Reversal of Portuguese Colonial Policy." *Journal of African History* 15:653–668.

Star (Johannesburg). 1983. May 30; September 19.

Star Weekly (Johannesburg). September 19, 1974; October 5, 1974; March 30, 1983.

Sunday Times. 1975. January 26.

Tempo (Maputo). June 20, 1982; October 16, 1983.

Thai, António. 1982. Personal interview, September 13.

Times (London). May 29, 1973; July 12, 1974; October 18, 1983.

U.N. Economic and Social Council. 1976. E/5812, April 30.

U.N. General Assembly. 1973. A/AC. 109/L.893, July.

————. 1974. A/AC. 109/L.919, February 8.

Vail, Leroy, and Landeg White. 1979. "The Struggle for Mozambique: Capitalist Rivalries, 1900–1940." *Review* 3:243–275.

Washington Post (Washington, D.C.). January 7, 1983; April 4, 1983; April 6, 1983; August 6, 1983.

Winter, Gordon. 1981. *Inside Boss.* Harmondsworth, England: Penguin.

PART II

The Horn of Africa

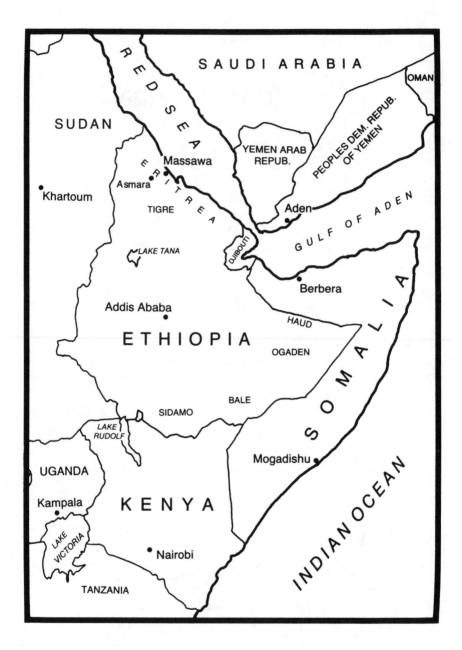

Map 3.   The Horn of Africa

In Africa's proverbial Horn, comprising Ethiopia, Somalia, and Djibouti, the dread horsemen of the apocalypse—famine, war, pestilence, and death—have ridden without respite for the better part of two decades. Whatever prospects there might have been for economic development in these impoverished lands were virtually extinguished for the present generation by destructive conflicts between rival nationalisms. Indeed, physical survival itself has become problematic for millions of starving and homeless people.

Northern Ethiopia is ravaged by warfare between the forces of the central government and two dissident nationality movements, namely, the secessionist Eritrean People's Liberation Front and the autonomist Tigré People's Liberation Front. Insurgency in Eritrea dates from 1962, when Emperor Haile Selassie abrogated the federal status of that former Italian colony on the Red Sea to impose direct imperial rule. Despite its own orientation toward socialist revolution, the Eritrean movement gained nothing from the Ethiopian revolution of 1974. Haile Selassie's revolutionary successors, who adhere to the tenets of Marxism-Leninism, have not abandoned the fallen emperor's resolve to incorporate Eritrea within a unitary state. Yet the military regime in Addis Ababa has been unable to subdue its secessionist opponent and the war continues with no end in sight.

Meanwhile, military campaigns mounted against the Eritreans have been obstructed by the growth of rebellion in the adjacent Tigrean region, which has been desolated by drought and massive starvation. The combined effects of war and famine have driven half a million people out of northern Ethiopia into the refugee camps of Sudan. Elsewhere in strife-ridden Ethiopia, the beleaguered central government confronts rebellions by dissident Oromo people, who constitute 40 percent of the population, because it, like its predecessor, is identified with Amhara domination. Moreover, the Western desert, known as the Ogaden, is claimed by Somalia on the irredentist ground that it properly belongs to the historic Somali nation.

Under Siad Barre, who seized power in 1969, Somalia had been aligned with the Soviet Union until 1977, when Moscow opposed its attempt to annex the Ogaden. The genuine social revolution in populous Ethiopia (with its more than 30 million people by comparison with 4 million to 5 million Somalis) was too great a prize for the Kremlin to forego in deference to the alliance with Somalia. However, Fidel Castro did try to mediate both the Ogaden and the Eritrean disputes in conformity with Soviet interests when he visited the Horn and its environs in March 1977. His efforts to promote an "anti-imperialist" federation, reported in some accounts to include both Eritrea and Djibouti as well as Ethiopia and Somalia, and, in other accounts, the People's Democratic Republic of Yemen as well, were unproductive. Eventually, 15,000 to 18,000 Cuban troops played a major part in driving the Somali forces from the Ogaden in 1978. Thereafter, Somalia, with ample support in the form of petroleum supplies and encouragement from Saudi Arabia, became an ally of the United States while Ethiopia has moved toward the creation of a Leninist party-state and, like Cuba and Vietnam, full membership in the Soviet-led economic bloc, COMECON. However, Cuba has refused to commit its own forces to operations against the Eritrean secessionist movement, for which Havana, unlike Moscow, continues to profess revolutionary respect.

The chapters in Part II analyze challenges to U.S. foreign policy in connection with the Ethiopian revolution, the Eritrean war, and the irredentist dilemmas of Somalia. Human tragedies—famine, warfare, and displacement of populations, including refugees—persist in this region without abatement. While grand patrons, namely the Soviet Union and the United States, pursue their respective strategic interests, the grim horsemen of the apocalypse ride on.

8

The American Dilemma on the Horn

BEREKET H. SELASSIE

The conflict in the Horn of Africa and its internationalization since 1977 has stimulated much debate in American policymaking circles on whether the costs of expanded U.S. involvement in the region are coming to outweigh the strategic and other benefits. This question has defined the terms of the debate since congressional hearings began in early 1976 (U.S. Senate Foreign Relations Committee 1976). The most intense phase of this debate has followed the post-1978 realignment of forces in the region which transformed Somalia into a U.S. ally and Ethiopia—long close to the United States—into a Soviet ally.

The larger debate has sometimes been summed up in terms of two seemingly opposed perspectives: a globalist view stressed by those who favor an expanded U.S. military presence, and a regionalist view advanced by those who advocate that U.S. policy in the region should be oriented primarily toward developmental and humanitarian goals (Wolpe 1982). A central but often neglected aspect of this debate is the tendency for both globalists and regionalists to underestimate, if not ignore, the autonomy of local, national (or indigenous) social and political forces in the region. Both tend to overstress the power of intervening external actors and factors in the political and economic arenas.

Indigenous Forces and Foreign Intervention

The conflict in the Horn of Africa arises from indigenous forces contending over issues which have complex, historical origins. External forces have intervened on behalf of one or more of these regional, indigenous forces, particularly in the recent past. A greater understanding of these indigenous social and political forces, and of their historical roots, is needed. To minimize their importance and lay undue stress on external factors—to force the region's reality into the mechanistic/Manichean context of East-West strategic polarity—is to ignore the objective potency of indigenous local and national socioeconomic forces. It is to risk perpetuating the erroneous assumptions on which the disastrous American foreign policy toward Vietnam was based.

The crisis in the Horn of Africa—a crisis encompassing several armed conflicts within the region—reflects two interrelated historical processes: (1) a continuing "crisis of empire" within the borders of the Ethiopian state, a state created through military expansion and subjugation of national groups in the area from the late nineteenth century onwards; and (2) the persistence of unresolved national and social questions and contradictions shaped by, and inherited from, the European colonial era in Ethiopia, Somalia, and Kenya.

U.S. foreign policy experts can learn certain lessons from the Soviet/Cuban intervention on Ethiopia's behalf in 1977–78. Not the least of these is the primacy of indigenous struggles over East-West divisions in shaping the dominant course of events in that region. The Soviet/Cuban intervention in Ethiopia, the Iranian revolution of 1979, and the Soviet invasion of Afghanistan in 1980 have all underlined the limits of foreign intervention in reshaping local forces.

These events were the culmination of a series of local struggles throughout the Third World in the mid- and late 1970s which signaled a changing reality within which U.S.–Soviet global contention was taking place. While the boldness, speed, and efficiency of Soviet intervention in Ethiopia seemed at first—in contrast to President Carter's feeble response to the Iranian crisis—to prove the dominant importance of external over internal forces, in fact this intervention has been unable to suppress or eliminate the historical contradictions between indigenous forces within the region or boundaries of the "empire."

Military force, and the manner and scale of its use, is often a product of the technological capability of the big power involved, as well as of its attitude toward prevailing norms of international conduct. Such norms constrain big powers only to the extent that they have been adhered to by the international community as a whole. The international community has become more aware of the limits of military power and the value of restraint and carefully weighed conduct. The risk of nuclear confrontation and the failure of the United States to win the Vietnam War have further sharpened awareness of the limits of external military action.[1]

The emergence in the Third World of a group of nonaligned countries actively opposed to being ensnared in the web of East-West tensions and desperately seeking to maintain their autonomous definition of the problems they face has added a new dimension to international relations. It is also true that the manner and degree of Soviet and U.S. intervention overseas reflects, in turn, their respective domestic circumstances. Carter's diffident response to

1. For a comparative study of the nuclear weapons development of the United States and the USSR see Daggat (1981) and Volman (1980).

the situations in Iran, Afghanistan, and Ethiopia was in great part a result of the post-Vietnam and post-Watergate climate in the United States. The upcoming election also conditioned his responses as Iran, in particular, became an election issue. Thus, an overseas conflict—a local conflict caught up in big-power rivalries—became a domestic issue in the United States which helped shape the outcome of U.S. domestic policies.[2]

President-elect Reagan sought to counter these reverses and repair the damage to America's image. Through an aggressive posture and strident language, he has sought to prove to friends and foes that America would respond effectively to any challenges to its perceived interests. This is seen most clearly today in Grenada and the Lebanese situation.

Where external intervention has been successful, it has been so because the external power's interests coincided with those of the local people. The Soviet intervention in Angola in 1975, for example, undoubtedly owed its success in part to the presence of Soviet naval forces in the area, the timely delivery of critically needed weapons, and the capability to airlift Cuban forces. But all this military capability would have come to naught if their interests had conflicted with those of indigenous Angolan social and political forces resisting the threat of South African occupation.

Nature and Sources of the Horn's Conflict

The conflict in the Horn of Africa is rooted in its history and geography. At the heart of the region and the center of the several regional conflicts lies the continuing historical reality of the Ethiopian empire. This reality has unified social and national groups within its boundaries to struggle against it, for its creation and maintenance has meant their continued suppression and exploitation.

The four central indigenous facets of the conflict in the Horn of Africa are: (1) the Ethiopian state; (2) the Eritrean liberation struggle; (3) the struggles for national self-determination of the people of Tigré (in northern Ethiopia) and of the Oromo (in south and southwest Ethiopia); and (4) the Somali-Ethiopian fighting over the Ogaden. Foreign intervention constitutes an additional factor. The first three factors are discussed in turn below. The fourth is taken up later in conjunction with the discussion of U.S. policy toward the Horn, with which it is intertwined.

The Ethiopian State. It is not commonly known that there are two Ethiopias, historically speaking. The Ethiopia of ancient history and mythology goes back three thousand years. The reference to three thousand years, though mythically based, has important political connotations in official Ethiopian

---

2. "America Held Hostage" was the title of an ABC nightly report and commentary lasting for several months, following the seizure of the American hostages.

accounts. Its starting point in the misty distant past is the visit of the Queen of Sheba from Northern Ethiopia to King Solomon. Later Ethiopian Christian scribes, the ideologues of the monarchy, developed the legend connecting the Ethiopian kings by blood kinship to Solomon, the progenitor of Jesus Christ, in an effort to further legitimize these kings. This legend as expressed in the quasi-sacred book the "Kabra Nagast" (Glory of Kings) has been a powerful tool in efforts to preserve the Ethiopian monarchy.

The second Ethiopia is historical Ethiopia, shorn of legends. Menelik II of Shoa, who assumed the imperial throne in 1889, is the father of modern Ethiopia. After the fall of Axum in the seventh century Ethiopia was a small highland kingdom comprised of the central Shoan, Gondarin, and Tigrean highlands. The outlying lowland areas, including the bulk of the lands inhabited by Oromos and Somalis today, were not integrated into or ruled by the Christian highland kingdom.

Menelik II acquired enormous quantities of arms through contacts and astute diplomacy with European colonial powers. With these arms, he was able to conquer the outlying areas to the south, west, and southeast of Shoa (Perham 1948). The people incorporated in this process of conquest include the Oromo, the majority nation in Ethiopia today, as well as the Somali in the Ogaden.

Menelik's eventual successor, Emperor Haile Selassie, further consolidated this new empire after coming to power as crown prince in 1916 and as emperor in 1930. His supposed "modernization" of Ethiopia, which began in 1931 with the introduction of a European-style constitution, was seen by various national minorities as only modernizing their own oppression. The constitution allowed him to further centralize imperial power. An ultimate irony was that many of the forces that emerged in 1974 to challenge and eventually overthrow the emperor were products of his modernization efforts— students, teachers, labor unions, and the military.

The military who now control Ethiopia's centralized and still imperial state are not different from their predecessor, for they have been indoctrinated and trained to maintain the empire's territorial integrity as part of a sacred trust.

Thus the central reality of Ethiopian state/empire politics has been and remains today the refusal of an imperial elite to share power with other nationalities, even when those were willing to accept the legacy of imperial conquest in return for peaceful and cooperative reconstruction and some degree of autonomy and democracy.

Mengistu Haile Mariam, the leader of the Derg, is an interesting compromise. By culture and upbringing he is Amhara, although his parents are of diverse minority background. But the entire structure of the Ethiopian ruling elite—the bureaucracy, the officer corps, and the cabinet—is predominantly Amhara. Mengistu, who admires Menelik, continues to serve the imperial purpose. His slogan, "revolutionary motherland or death," served that purpose in 1977–78, being instrumental in mobilizing public support for the Derg at a time when the country was facing a crossroads—either continuation of an unreconstructed empire state or real transformation through full, democratic participation of all the people. Mengistu's socialist rhetoric masked his opting for the first.

The Soviets tragically supported his choice of this first route (Simes 1978). As a result they have become allied with an imperial state against the national aspirations of peoples demanding self-determination in all parts of Ethiopia. The latter have cogently argued that this stance has undermined the credibility of the USSR's professed motives for intervening. Because a defeat for the Ethiopian elite would represent a disaster for Soviet diplomacy, the Soviets have continued to support a politically and morally bankrupt and increasingly unpopular military junta. The real tragedy is that they have foreclosed any possible role they might have played as conciliators. Armed struggle seems to be the only means of effectively resolving these contradictions for the peoples of Tigré, Oromoland, the Ogaden, and Eritrea.

The Eritrean Liberation Struggle.   The Eritreans have waged a war of national liberation since September 1961. Of all the peoples victimized by strategic power manipulation in the post–Second World War era, the Eritrean people are a prime example.[3]

The essence of the "Eritrean question" is that Eritrea—a former Italian colony—was denied independence contrary to the principles of self-determination recognized by the United Nations since 1945 and the OAU since 1963.

Eritrea, like most of today's African states, was a creation of colonial history. Italy colonized the country, consolidating its military control between 1882 and 1890, and baptized the colony "Eritrea." A treaty with Emperor Menelik delineated Eritrea's border with Ethiopia. Italian rule continued until 1941, when British and allied forces defeated Italian forces and declared Eritrea a British protectorate (Trimingham 1952; Trevaskis 1975).

For over a decade after that the Eritrean people were ruled by the British, while the future of Eritrea and the other former Italian colonies—Libya and Somalia—was the subject of international debate and national agitation after the Second World War. The U.N. General Assembly resolved to grant Libya independence by 1953, and Somalia by 1960, after a ten-year period of U.N. trusteeship with Italy as the administering authority. The case of Eritrea proved to be more contentious. Ethiopia demanded that Eritrea should be joined to it. Ethiopia's ambitions and U.S. interests in the area prevailed. Emperor Haile Selassie was regarded as an ally of the United States. At that time the United States dominated the United Nations to a great extent.

3. For a differing view of Ethiopian history or the disputed territory of Eritrea and Ethiopia's claim to Eritrea, see Spencer (1984).

In 1950, the United Nations passed a resolution[4] making Eritrea an autonomous unit "under the sovereignty of the Ethiopian Crown." The Eritrean people's demand for self-determination was ignored.

A year after the federation between Eritrea and Ethiopia came into force, Ethiopia and the United States entered into a twenty-five-year agreement which lasted until the overthrow of Emperor Haile Selassie. In 1962, on the eve of the founding of the OAU, the emperor abolished the federation, incorporating Eritrea into Ethiopia as a province (Selassie 1981). The federation was abolished in order to forestall citing of expected OAU principles in support of self-determination for the people of Eritrea.

The Eritrean Liberation Front (ELF) grew from a handful of armed bands in 1961 to a sizable, well-armed, guerrilla group by 1965 (Sherman 1980). Ethiopian efforts to stop this growing resistance led to massacres which created the first flows of Eritrean refugees into neighboring countries. (By 1982, this flow had grown tenfold to 500,000, most of whom had fled to the Sudan.) As a patriotic fighting force, the ELF commanded broad support. But the inability of its leadership to open up to more democratic forces led many of the more educated and politically conscious elements in its ranks to form the Eritrean People's Liberation Front (EPLF) in 1970. By 1976, the size of the EPLF had more than quadrupled and its military predominance was shown by its ability to survive a series of offensives by a much stronger Ethiopian army, first in 1973–74 and again in 1975–76.

The EPLF has repulsed six major Ethiopian offensives since its founding barely thirteen years ago. It owes its successes primarily to its widespread popular support, based on its understanding of the social, political, and economic realities of the majority of the people of Eritrea, and to its leaders' ingenuity, administrative efficiency, and military capability. Outside observers[5] have remarked on its impressive infrastructure and social services—hospitals, workshops, cooperatives, schools, and a network of popular organizations for women and youth.

The Tigrean and Oromo Liberation Struggles.   The Tigrean People's Liberation Front (TPLF) represents the latest armed phase of the Tigrean people's resistance to a central Ethiopian state. Tigré forms part of the highland of Ethiopia and historically has been part of the Ethiopian empire. However, resistance to this domination broke out at various times, including in 1943, when a Tigrean revolt was suppressed by the emperor with British help. Tigreans continued to resist, in part through underground activities. The TPLF was formed in 1975, growing in strength and popularity as it successfully

4. Resolution 390 (A) V.

5. Among these were Dan Connell (*Washington Post, The Guardian, Le Monde,* and Reuters); Guido Bimbi (Italian newspapers, e.g., *Unita*), Mary Dines (*War on Want*); J. L. Peninou (*Liberation*); G. Chaliand; and others.

engaged the Ethiopian army. It has organized a militia and peasant self-governing bodies and its land reform and social services in the countryside have improved peasant conditions, drawing more support to its side despite Ethiopian efforts to end this "insurgency."

The Oromo Liberation Front (OLF) is the latest expression of the Oromo people's resistance to Ethiopia's imperial conquest and rule, which began for them in the nineteenth century. The Oromo are the most populous minority national group in Ethiopia, inhabiting most of the central highlands. Their social structure is based on the *gada* system—a democratic form of social and political organization that ensures participation in public life according to age groups (Baxter 1978).

Oromo resistance to Ethiopian rule has been sustained since the 1890s in various forms. They particularly opposed confiscation and redistribution of their land among occupying Ethiopians. The Oromo movement was galvanized by the overthrow of the emperor. Formed in 1974–75, the OLF began launching armed attacks against military outposts, expanding until in 1981 it opened a new front in the western area of Oromoland.

U.S. Policy toward the Horn of Africa

U.S. policy toward the current crisis in the Horn is conditioned first by American strategic and geopolitical interests in the region, and second by American perceptions of an aggressive Soviet policy in Africa since 1975 and in the region since 1977. Evidence of American interest in the region began with the debate among the allies on the "disposal" of the former Italian colonies following the defeat of the Axis powers in 1945. In 1952 John Foster Dulles, U.S. secretary of state, bluntly expressed U.S. concerns when he said:

> From the point of view of justice, the opinions of the Eritrean people must receive consideration. Nevertheless, the strategic interests of the United States in the Red Sea Basin and considerations of security and world peace makes it necessary that the country has to be linked with our ally Ethiopia.

This interest climaxed in 1980 with the signing of a Somali–U.S. military agreement.

The history of American interest in the region may thus be divided into three phases:

1. American attempts successfully to step into the shoes of the British.

2. The departure of the British from Eritrea, the decline of their influence in Ethiopia, and the signing of the Ethiopian–American Treaty of May 23, 1953. That treaty ended in February 1977 when the military government in Ethiopia aligned with the Soviet Union (formally, in November 1978).

3. A new alignment of forces formalized with the Somali–U.S. agreement of August 1980.

U.S. Policy 1945–77. Beginning in the aftermath of the Second World War and continuing through the end of the 1940s, the United States, in pursuit of its strategic and geopolitical interests in the Horn, forged an alliance with Ethiopia, which it regarded as the most important state in the region.

The convergence of U.S. strategic interests with the social and political interests of the ruling Ethiopian elite was articulated most clearly in the twenty-five-year treaty concluded in May 1953 between Ethiopia and the United States. The treaty granted the United States naval and air facilities and control of a communications base in Asmara, the capital of Eritrea. It formalized what would be the dominant role of the United States in the entire region for the next quarter century; Ethiopia was the linchpin for anchoring U.S. policy in the region among competing European powers. U.S. dominance—which only ended with the demise of Emperor Haile Selassie's regime—was enforced through the use of economic and military aid, backed up by an expanding cultural presence and influence.

Between 1953 and 1977 Ethiopia received some $279 million in U.S. military aid, and more than 3,500 Ethiopian military personnel were trained in the United States. The Kagnew Communications Center in Asmara was central to America's worldwide communications system—stretching from U.S. bases in Morocco to the Philippines—used to monitor Soviet activities during the cold war. Kagnew was a critical listening post for U.S. intelligence-gathering in the Middle East and the Indian Ocean as well as Africa. It played a vital role during both the Korean and Vietnam wars. The development of satellite communications technology, however, and the U.S. decision to expand its presence in the Indian Ocean, reduced the significance of the Kagnew base and led to a progressive decline of U.S. military aid. By 1976 U.S. personnel at Kagnew had been reduced to 35 from a 1971 peak of 3,000 (Halliday and Molyneux 1981).

After the mid–1950s, an increasing amount of U.S. economic aid was given to Ethiopia. Point Four and later AID-funded education, health, and agricultural projects were among the programs funded. U.S. economic aid was based on the idea of "modernization"—a multidimensional concept including administrative reform, land and law reform, and the progressive opening up of the feudal country to market forces which would reshape the country and its social forces in the direction of the American pattern. The overthrow of the emperor and the escalation of struggles for national liberation were to show how naive and how oblivious of indigenous realities these presumptions were.

Why did U.S. military and economic aid, though significant by African standards, fail to bring about the expected changes in the country? There are at least two significant reasons:

1. Despite the lip service accorded modernization, priority was in fact given to U.S. military and strategic considerations. Insufficient atten-

tion was devoted to developing economically productive resources and concomitant social changes, leaving intact the historical inequities that fueled rebellion and resistance to feudal rule.

2. The aid given failed to alter the semifeudal system of centralizing all critical decision making in the hands of the emperor and his hand-picked ministers and governors, leaving intact, if not reinforcing, traditional antagonisms to the exercise of imperial power. The U.S. ambassador to Ethiopia during the 1960s, Edward Korry, expressed this American dilemma in his testimony before the African Affairs Subcommittee of the U.S. Senate in 1976:

> The U.S. interest in Ethiopia was simple then for Washington. The government defined it as "the unhampered use of Kagnew Station." The facility was deemed then to be strategically vital to the United States . . . the reports on the use of our military aid to Ethiopia were depressing . . . and if the emperor wanted it [i.e., Kagnew rent money] in solid gold cadillac that was his term and he could have it that way. (U.S. Senate Foreign Relations Committee 1976)

The United States made several attempts to encourage the emperor to introduce reforms. The 1960 coup attempt and President Kennedy's appointment of Korry as ambassador added some urgency and momentum to these efforts. Despite Korry's energetic commitment to modernization (and the assumption that societies could easily be reshaped from outside with predictable results), he did little to speed up needed reforms.

Korry was assiduous in cultivating contact with young bureaucrats at the cabinet and subcabinet levels, organizing seminars on a range of issues, and unofficially hosting meetings of future decision makers, maintaining all the while an active official dialogue with the emperor and his prime minister. Yet the clamor for change was taking on more radical overtones throughout the country outside this quiet "development diplomacy."

The United States tried to straddle the fence—both supporting the emperor's government and trying to distance itself from his policies. While trying to identify and control the forces of change, it continued to defend the imperial regime from alleged "communist" subversion. The contradictions of U.S. policy—which subordinated Ethiopian realities to American geopolitical interests—were sharpened by the growing numbers of U.S. Peace Corps volunteers in Ethiopia. Because their projects often brought them closer to Ethiopian realities, they frequently aligned themselves with the aspirations of the emergent social forces. Some Peace Corps members were found helping student protestors and were expelled within forty-eight hours, further straining U.S.–Ethiopian relations.

Although the U.S. attitude began to cool toward the emperor's regime—he failed in his 1973 visit to Washington to gain new jets and tanks—its commitment to Ethiopia's territorial integrity remained unchanged despite the growing Eritrean struggle for self-determination. Increasing Soviet assistance to and training of Somalia's army reinforced U.S. commitment to the anticommunist regime in power in Ethiopia, however unpopular it might be internally.

U.S. Policy in Crisis.   From the 1972–73 famine onwards, U.S. policy vacillated, somewhat leaning toward attempts to disassociate itself from a regime clearly doomed to fall. The emperor's failure to alleviate the effects of the famine, despite his power to do so, unleashed both international outrage and domestic popular unrest. The Yom Kippur War, which caused Ethiopia to join the rest of the OAU in breaking ties with its former ally, Israel, further complicated the picture for U.S. policymakers.

The spring 1974 revolution which shook the empire threw U.S. policy into turmoil. The shadowy coordinating committee that seized power began to articulate a social and political agenda that jolted American expectations. This military group, known as the Derg, was still very much dependent on American aid in the military area, however, since it faced accelerating liberation movements in Eritrea and the Ogaden. By early 1975, the Eritrean liberation was mounting attacks in and around Asmara.

In February 1975 the United States decided to continue aid to Ethiopia's new regime, as long as it retained some pro-Western orientation, for three strategic reasons:

1. The United States feared that if it terminated its aid Ethiopia would become more independent and align itself with radical Arab forces, thereby cutting off Israeli access via the Red Sea to the Indian Ocean.

2. Without continued aid, Ethiopia might join the growing bloc of African countries critical of U.S. policies, thus undermining U.S. credibility in the continent.

3. Only Ethiopia could serve as an effective counterweight to a Somalia aligned with the Soviet Union.

As early as February 1975, Secretary of State Kissinger authorized continued aid to Ethiopia. In the midst of the brewing Angola crisis, he argued that the United States should support the Derg as long as it retained some pro-Western orientation (U.S. Senate Foreign Relations Committee 1976, 114). Thus U.S. policy was guided not by an understanding of the brewing social contradictions within Ethiopia but by broader external factors such as the American conflict with the USSR. As the Derg's ties with the USSR grew, so did pressure for the United States to stop aid to Ethiopia. Although the Carter administration evoked human rights as the reason for ending U.S. aid to the Derg, its willingness in 1977 to arm a not much more progressive Somalia and Sudan—once they had expelled Soviet advisers—reflected the continuation of a historic realpolitik tendency to evaluate events and conduct policies along predetermined lines.

A Changing U.S. Policy: 1977 to the Present. In February 1977, Mengistu Haile Mariam emerged as the leader of the Derg, after eliminating many rivals and massacring those who protested his use of violence to advance his own position. The Carter administration quickly announced it would suspend all U.S. aid, citing as its reasons human rights violations. The Derg responded by closing all U.S. installations in April 1977 except for the embassy and the AID office. The United States soon halted previously ordered arms deliveries and announced its intention to sell arms to two of Ethiopia's neighbors.

The U.S. switch from supporting Ethiopia to supporting Sudan and Somalia was primarily a response to changing political and military developments in the region altering U.S. strategic interests vis-à-vis the USSR. Of primary concern to the United States was the Saudi interest in weaning Somalia away from Soviet influence and back to the Islamic fold. The alienation of Somalia from the USSR because of growing Soviet ties with Ethiopia, combined with the Derg's expulsion of U.S. military personnel, reinforced the convergence of Saudi and U.S. interests.

U.S.–Somali Relations. In looking at the U.S.–Somali alliance that emerged after 1977, it is crucial to understand the nature and source of Somali claims and interests in the region. Until 1977, U.S. interests had already led it to back Ethiopia on the issue of autonomy for the Ogaden. The United States turned down Somali requests for military aid in the early 1960s as a possible threat to Ethiopian security interests. The creation of the OAU in 1963 and the adoption of the Cairo Resolution in 1964 accepting the inviolability of colonial boundaries reinforced this U.S. position.

Three issues are intertwined in the Ogaden question: (1) the border dispute between two sovereign states, Ethiopia and Somalia, over boundaries left undemarcated by Ethiopia and Italy; (2) the Somali claim to western Somalia, including the Ogaden and sections of the Haud and Bale; and (3) the right to self-determination of the Somali people in these territories as expressed in the struggle of the Western Somali Liberation Front (WSLF).

Somalia was originally formed by the unification of the former British and Italian Somalilands in 1960. It is one of Africa's few authentic nation-states, its people sharing a common language, culture, history, and religion (Islam). At the time Somalia was formed, however, large numbers of ethnic Somalis inhabited the Haud, Ogaden, and Bale provinces of imperial Ethiopia as well as the northern frontier district of Kenya and parts of Djibouti.

Several wars have been fought between Somalia and Ethiopia, first in 1960 and again in 1964. Starting in 1965, Somalia strengthened its ties with the

Soviet Union and sent its air force pilots there for training. It also increased the size of its army. The regime of Siad Barre, which seized power from civilians in 1969, more than doubled the size of Somalia's armed forces by 1976. Somalia signed a Treaty of Friendship with the USSR in 1974 and Soviet military advisers were present in Somalia until the Somali invasion of the Ogaden in 1977.

The 1977–78 Somali–Ethiopian War marked a significant realignment of forces in the region. It was affected by several other regional developments, including the suspension of U.S. military aid to Ethiopia; the mutual defense pact concluded between Egypt and Sudan in 1976 following the abortive coup attempt against Numeiri with alleged Libyan and Ethiopian assistance; the U.S. agreement to supply Kenya with twelve F–5 jets; Sudan's expulsion of Soviet advisers in 1977; and Ethiopia's growing ties to the USSR. In late 1977, Somalia broke its treaty with the USSR and expelled all Soviet advisers. By then Somali armed forces supporting the WSLF were suffering serious defeat at the hands of Ethiopian troops newly armed and trained by the USSR and aided by Cuban troops. By March 1978, Somalia withdrew its troops from the Ogaden, though it continued to support the WSLF guerrilla struggle.

The United States during this period was preoccupied with trying to prevent an Ethiopian invasion of Somalia and avert the overthrow of the Siad Barre government in favor of one more closely aligned with the Soviet Union. Barre, despite contrary predictions, survived this period. However, the remarkable gains in development achieved during 1969–75 were thrown into jeopardy by the diversion of most national resources to meet the survival needs of huge influxes of refugees from the Ogaden, by fiscal mismanagement, and by the expenditure of vast sums to sustain internal and external security. Human rights violations reportedly rose as Barre sought to stifle Somali protest over the outcome of the Ogaden adventure (Wolpe 1982).

In part because he was able to survive, Barre eventually came to reap the fruits of U.S. realignment toward Somalia. In 1978 the United States as a precaution had sent a naval task force to the Indian Ocean and the Red Sea. In March Assistant Secretary of State for African Affairs Richard Moose came to Somalia to discuss the possible supply of defense weapons. By then the United States had begun to accept the fait accompli of a consolidated Soviet presence in Ethiopia, its former ally. Ethiopia and the USSR signed a treaty of friendship in late 1978 which included provisions for military aid.

By 1979 the United States and Somalia were moving toward signing an agreement that would allow the United States access to Somali ports and airfields in return for financial and military assistance. This movement occurred as Ethiopia was carrying out a new offensive in the Ogaden, setting off new waves of refugees fleeing into Somalia, and a new offensive in Eritrea; at the same time the newly independent Djibouti was appealing for help in defending itself against an alleged Ethiopian plot to overthrow its government. The

United States responded by sending an aircraft carrier into the Indian Ocean to underline U.S. concerns in the region. Such projections of power continued well into early 1980.

In that year the new U.S.–Somali alliance was cemented by a formal agreement. Initial congressional concern was overcome though written assurances that the U.S.–supplied weapons would not be used in the Ogaden.

The U.S. Defense Department proposed the sale of $42 million worth of defensive military equipment to Somalia. The U.S. Navy proposed to spend $24 million in Somalia in fiscal 1982 for port and airfield expansion and $400,000 for refurbishing the Berbera airfield. Some 250 U.S. military personnel were sent to Somalia as part of the November-December 1980 "Operation Bright Star" military maneuver in the Middle East (Wolpe 1982).

In fiscal 1982, the United States was expected to provide $20 million in development assistance and $25 million in food aid, but Congress approved an additional $5 million for Somalia for that year under the supplemental appropriations bill (P.L. 97–257, Legislation Section). The Reagan administration's 1983 foreign aid proposal called for a $1 million drop in economic assistance and a hefty $10 million increase in security assistance (Wolpe 1982).

Reagan and the U.S.–Soviet Strategic Struggle

The Reagan administration brought to U.S. policy an intensified fear of growing Soviet influence in the region. The continued role of Cuban forces in Angola and Ethiopia caused increasing U.S. concern that Ethiopia would be "converted into an armory, conference center, training ground and military sanctuary for dissidents" (Farer 1978, 4).

The USSR, meanwhile, has certainly demonstrated its determination to keep the Mengistu-dominated Derg in power. Hence, U.S. fears for the stability of pro-Western regimes bordering on Ethiopia, such as that of Numeiri, have grown with the role of Soviet advisers and military aid. Yet the United States may still hope to be able to "retrieve" Ethiopia from Soviet dominance, for several reasons: (1) Ethiopia's position on the question of nationalities is generally supported in Africa, though some support the Eritreans; Ethiopia has more valuable resources than Somalia and is of equal if not greater strategic importance; (2) there are still many social forces within Ethiopia strongly favoring reassociation with the West for political, economic, and cultural reasons; (3) the Derg's nationalism far outweighs its "proletarian internationalism" when it comes to concrete policies and programs; (4) the USSR has proven no better than the United States in resolving the economic, social, and political contradictions of Ethiopia represented by the continued wars of liberation in Eritrea, the Ogaden, Tigré, and Oromoland; (5) Soviet economic models for a "non-capitalist road to development" have produced very little; and (6) the USSR has been unable to help the Derg win the war in Eritrea and elsewhere, creating disaffection and recriminations and leading to growing desertions. The continuing ambivalence in U.S. policy toward Ethiopia is shown by the fact that it has maintained diplomatic relations and has not actively opposed loans to Ethiopia from multilateral institutions such as the IMF and World Bank, in contrast to its intransigent opposition to loans to Vietnam or Nicaragua. At the same time it has continued to strengthen Somalia's defense capability, providing increased aid in 1981 and 1982 to counter growing Ethiopian attacks on Somali territory and Ethiopia's agreement with Libya and South Yemen on financial aid. The dilemma facing U.S. policymakers who desire to "regain" Ethiopia is that military maneuvers designed to strengthen their allies in the region—such as Egypt, Sudan, and Somalia—may have the effect of increasing Ethiopian and Libyan reliance on Soviet support.

Conclusion

What can we conclude from this review of U.S. policy options and decisions?

First, the Horn of Africa remains of great strategic importance to the United States and its allies.

Second, recent U.S. policy has been primarily reactive to external, not indigenous factors. It has been guided by responses to real or perceived Soviet expansion. In neglecting the indigenous roots of most of the changes taking place, the United States is increasingly viewed by Africans as opposing such changes and even trying to reverse many of them. The Soviets have been equally insensitive to self-determination in the region, but more decisive in supporting their ally of the moment militarily.

Third, the conflict in the Horn has been conditioned by the continued reality of the Ethiopian empire—the unresolved national struggles in the region, the unresolved colonial question posed by Eritrea, and the unresolved Ethiopia-Somali conflict over the Ogaden.

Fourth, colonial history, as in the case of Eritrea, forges a national consciousness and socioeconomic formations that cannot be ignored or suppressed.

Fifth, military solutions are no substitute for political solutions. The continued inability of Ethiopia to impose a military solution on the Eritrean conflict, despite U.S. aid from 1953 to 1977 and Soviet aid from 1977 on, is a cogent example.

Finally, the future of the region may be predicted more accurately from careful analysis of the popular mass movements in the region and the new institutions, politics, and culture they are creating and consolidating than from general strategic analysis of the area.

REFERENCES

Baxter, P. T. W. 1978. "Ethiopia's Unacknowledged Problems: The Oromo." *African Affairs* 77, no. 309 (July):283–296.

Daggat, Stephen. 1981. *The New Generation of Nuclear Weapons.* Washington, D.C.: Institute for Policy Studies.

Farer, Tom. 1978. "Soviet Strategy and Western Fears." *Africa Report* (November–December): 4–8.

Halliday, Fred, and Maxine Molyneux. 1981. *The Ethiopian Revolution.* London: NLB.

Perham, Margery Freda. 1948. *The Government of Ethiopia.* New York: Oxford University Press.

Selassie, Bereket H. 1981. "Eritrea and the United Nations," in *The Eritrean Case.* Proceedings of the Permanent Tribunal, Session on Eritrea, Milan, Italy, May 24–26, 1980. Brussels: 1981; Rome: Research and Information Centre on Eritrea, 1982.

Sherman, Richard. 1980. *Eritrea: The Unfinished Revolution.* New York: Praeger.

Simes, D. K. 1978. "Soviet Intervention in the Horn." *The Washington Quarterly.* April.

Spencer, John. 1984. *Ethopia at Bay: A Personal Account of the Haile Selassie Years.* Algonac, Mi: Reference Publications.

Trevaskis, Gerald K. 1975. *Eritrea: A Colony In Transition, 1941–52.* Westport, Conn.: Greenwood Press.

Trimingham, J. Spencer. 1952. *Islam in Ethiopia.* London, New York: Oxford University Press.

U.S. Senate Foreign Relations Committee. 1976. "Ethiopia and the Horn of Africa." Hearings before the Sub-Committee on African Affairs of the U.S. Senate Foreign Relations Committee.

Volman, Daniel. 1980. *A Continent Besieged: Foreign Military Activities in Africa.* Washington, D.C.: Institute for Policy Studies.

Wolpe, Howard. 1982. *The Horn of Africa and the United States.* Washington, D.C.: Library of Congress, Congressional Research Service, October 22.

9

United States Foreign Policy on the Horn of Africa: Policymaking with Blinders On

EDMOND J. KELLER

Increasingly, students of American foreign policy in the Third World stress the need for a more regionalist perspective as opposed to the predominantly globalist orientation that has historically characterized official policy. The point is not that regionalist considerations should override globalist ones. In fact, the keys to any successful foreign policy are, first, a clear perception of vital global concerns, and second, a prudent and flexible balance between regionalist and globalist interest (Bienen 1980; Price 1978). Simultaneously, there must be a realistic perception of the interplay of the regional social forces at work at a given moment in history. Such considerations would allow policymakers to rank-order globalist as well as regionalist objectives, to evaluate their relative compatibility, and then to engage in the necessary trade-offs to fit the circumstances. Failure to initiate foreign policy in any region in this way could have disastrous consequences. A particular danger of errant policymaking exists where the priority ranking of globalist and/or regional interests is for whatever reason difficult to discern.

Throughout the Carter administration political tensions in the Horn of Africa brought its globalist objectives into conflict with its more regionally based Africa policy. On the one hand, Carter wanted to demonstrate to Africa in no uncertain terms that, in contrast to previous American presidents, he recognized Africa's importance in the world and was committed to a more affirmative and activist U.S. involvement in helping Africans address their problems as they themselves defined those problems. On the other hand, at an early date the Carter administration identified human rights as its preeminent foreign policy objective. Theoretically, human rights interests were to serve as the foundation of Carter's total approach to foreign policy, and to overlay his administration's more regionally based objectives. Under normal circumstances—instances where violations of human rights were not gross—regionalist goals were only slightly or not at all affected by this global interest. However, Carter made it clear that where gross violations of human rights existed, a cessation of such violations would have to precede the normal application of regionally based policies.

In practice the administration's human rights policy was only selectively applied (Vogelgesan 1978, 833). Some countries, known to be guilty of gross human rights violations, were almost entirely untouched because of the perceived overriding economic or strategic interests involved. Other countries, deemed to be less "important," were singled out for sanctions in order to demonstrate that the administration was serious about human rights. Ethiopia was one of the latter countries. The assumption seems to have been that the United States—Ethiopia's most important trading partner and arms supplier—had enough leverage to force a change in that country's human rights policy. This assumption turned out to be mistaken. Not only did human rights violations not cease, they increased. What is more, the deterioration in U.S.–Ethiopian relations opened up a Pandora's box which internationalized the crisis in the Horn. This was clearly an alternative Carter would have preferred to avoid. Yet, because he failed to calculate the power of the regional forces at work at the time and was guided by the more global concern of human rights, policy contradictions emerged which might have been avoided if a more balanced globalist-regionalist perspective had been applied.

The purpose of this essay is to analyze American foreign policy toward Ethiopia from a perspective that takes both the historic and contemporary realities of Ethiopian society and the entire Horn region into account. An effort is made to show how America's fundamentally Americocentric, globalist approach to foreign policy in Africa blinded it from the very beginning to the potential political liabilities of such a narrow view. Further, I analyze the ongoing dire consequences of this incident of flawed policymaking. Finally, implications for future U.S.–Africa relations are drawn.

The Evolution of United States–Ethiopia Relations

Although the United States and Ethiopia have had diplomatic relations since 1903 and concluded treaties of arbitration and conciliation as far back as 1929, a close relationship did not emerge until after the Second World War (Marcus 1983; Spencer 1977). In the aftermath of the Italian fascist occupation of Ethiopia which lasted from 1936 to 1941, the British reinstated Haile Selassie as emperor, and assisted him in administering part of modern-day Ethiopia until 1952. The British role was initially quite extensive, involving military aid and training, economic and technical assistance, as well as a role in the reorganization of Haile Selassie's government. However, after 1943, British influence and involvement in Ethiopia declined rapidly. The emperor systematically cultivated a relationship with the United States, and when the last vestiges of a British presence in Ethiopia disappeared, the United States stepped in as the emperor's main "Big Power" patron. Haile Selassie was anxious that the events of 1936 to 1941—the fascist occupation—not be repeated. On its part, the United States since the early 1940s had coveted a base at Asmara in Eritrea along the Red Sea where it could establish a link in a worldwide radio communications network.

Two agreements were signed in May 1953 to formalize this new relationship, the Mutual Defense Assistance Agreement and the Utilization of Defense Installations within the Empire of Ethiopia. These documents complemented two treaties signed between the countries in 1951 relating to diplomatic and economic cooperation issues. In effect, the United States had agreed to guarantee Ethiopia's security. There was no formal treaty specifying this but there was a written understanding.

By 1975, the total U.S. military assistance to Ethiopia amounted to almost $280 million. In addition, over the same period Ethiopia received $350 million in economic aid in the form of technical assistance, capital goods, and food. This contributed significantly to the military capacity of the Ethiopian state as well as to its efforts at economic development.

With U.S. aid it was more or less guaranteed that the emperor could step up the modernization of his military while at the same time using it as a more effective instrument of local control. Besides receiving arms aid from the United States after 1953, the Ethiopian military also benefited from the presence and activity of a Military Assistance Advisory Group (MAAG) which was established in 1954. The purpose of this group was to work with the Ethiopian military down to the battalion level. By 1970 the total MAAG complement was over 100 persons (Ottaway 1982, 49). American personnel were also involved in officer training at two Ethiopian military academies. In addition, between 1953 and 1976 some 3,978 Ethiopians—more than half of all African soldiers in the same category—were sent to study in the United States at a cost of $22.7 million (USDOD 1981).

The relationship which developed between the United States and Ethiopia is sometimes described as one of dependency, with Ethiopia being dependent on and subservient to the United States This characterization, however, is not wholly accurate. A more apt representation might be one of interdependence. At least at the beginning, each partner got what it wanted and was satisfied with what it got. The United States pursued its own global interests and Ethiopia pursued its aims with more cooperation than coercion or conflict.

American interests in Ethiopia have historically been guided by geopolitical strategic concerns. Between 1953 and 1973 the main purpose for maintaining such close relations with Ethiopia was to insure access to Kagnew Station (Korry 1976; Marcus 1983, passim). The desire to maintain this access forced the United States to become more deeply involved in domestic and regional affairs than strategic planners had ever expected. American policy was centered on keeping Haile Selassie in power and keeping the region relatively stable and free of communism. In this way the strategic interests of the United States came to intersect historically with Haile Selassie's domestic and regional interests. The United States with only occasional reluctance committed arms and other military assistance to the emperor so that he might put down internal upheavals and fend off the irredentist designs of the Somalis. A series of secret agreements between the two governments between 1960 and 1964 resulted in the modernization and dramatic expansion of the Ethiopian military (Newsom 1970).[1] The stated purpose was to prepare Ethiopia's defenses for the Somali threat.

The U.S. government also supplied Ethiopia with counterinsurgency training and on-the-ground advisers in connection with helping suppress the rebellion in Eritrea. The extent of this kind of involvement in Ethiopia's affairs is said to have been minimal, but it is difficult to form an accurate estimate since the U.S. government tried to conceal its role by referring to the advisers as members of "Civic Action Teams" (Bader 1970, 1935).

The scale and character of U.S. military involvement contributed greatly to the development of a low-intensity arms race in the Horn involving the Ethiopians, Somalis, and Eritrean rebels. However, in the pre-Angola era, the U.S. ally, Ethiopia, held the regional balance of power, and U.S. officials, while doing as little as possible, still wanted to do as much as was needed to maintain the status quo.

Despite the closeness of the Ethiopian-U.S. relationship, its permanence was always in doubt. In order for it to continue, each side had to perceive that the benefits outweighed the costs. By 1970, with only eight years left on the Kagnew lease, the United States was beginning to reconsider the necessity of its Ethiopian connection. The Eritrean region had become more unstable by then, and the strategic need for maintaining Kagnew seemed less compelling. The Soviets were now building an Indian Ocean fleet and the Western powers felt that it was necessary to counter that challenge. Strategic planners concluded that this could best be done from naval bases in the Indian Ocean. With this in mind the United States leased the island of Diego Garcia from the British in 1966 and made plans for the construction of a huge naval facility to be completed by 1973.

Kagnew was considered less essential also because advances in satellite communications technology had made radio tracking stations of this kind more or less obsolete. Between 1971 and 1976 the number of U.S. personnel

---

1. In 1963 the total number of Ethiopia's armed forces was between 55,000 and 60,000, but only about 18,000 were in the so-called modern army. The rest were not professional soldiers, but regional conscripts. In comparison, the Somali Army was only about 9,000; at independence in 1960 it was 2,000. See the testimony of David Newsom, Assistant Secretary of State for Africa (1970, 1884–1885).

based at Kagnew was trimmed from over 3,000 to under 40 (Ottaway 1982, 50–53).

By this time it was obvious that the United States perceived that its vital national interests had ceased to mesh with Ethiopia's national and regional interests. This weakened status added to the vulnerability of the faltering imperial state. There was little chance that the United States could have prevented the Ethiopian revolution even if it had resolved to do so. In reality plans had been made to try to deal with whoever succeeded the emperor in hopes that normal relations could continue unbroken (Korry 1976, 37). Little attention was paid to the legacy of U.S. association with Haile Selassie's basically authoritarian regime, or to the kind of society the United States had helped him to build. Each of these factors contributed to the ultimate domestic and regional crises which unfolded after 1975.

National and Regional Realities: The Weight
of History

Haile Selassie ascended the Ethiopian throne in 1930 and quickly gained the reputation of a modernizing autocrat. In the next year, he introduced Ethiopia's first written constitution, which provided for a constitutional monarchy. His basic intention was to strengthen his position vis-à-vis traditional classes. The emperor had inherited a backward, almost medieval empire, the modern form of which was not consolidated until the early 1900s. Serving as regent between 1916 and 1930, Haile Selassie demonstrated that he had two main objectives: to modernize and firmly consolidate the absolutist state, and to have its territorial boundaries accepted as legitimate in the world community.

In order to consolidate his hold over the state, Haile Selassie concentrated on the development of a secularized, competent bureaucracy, a professional army, and a forward-looking indigenous middle class. He initiated efforts to cultivate foreign alliances which could provide him with capital for economic development as well as with defensive arms that were needed not only to protect national borders, but also to maintain domestic order. These initial efforts were halted, however, in 1936 by the invading forces of fascist Italy, and the emperor was driven into exile in Europe.

The war, in retrospect, came almost as a blessing in disguise for the emperor. Before he returned to the throne with the aid of British occupation forces, the Italians had succeeded in disrupting the fabric of traditional Ethiopian society. Traditionally powerful institutions such as the church and landed aristocracy were severely weakened. On his return he was in a better position to introduce new policies designed to secularize and strengthen his authority.

On the diplomatic front, the emperor tried to present the image of being the ruler of a viable and cohesive nation-state. Ethiopia had joined the League of Nations as early as 1923; after the Second World War it became one of the first states to join the United Nations. In 1963 Addis Ababa was designated as the headquarters of the Organization of African Unity (OAU), and several other international and regional institutions also established their offices there. In addition, Haile Selassie constantly used diplomacy to play off one major power against another, always with the aim of emphasizing Ethiopia's sovereignty and consolidating its position in the world. At the same time he tried to build political and economic institutions to help bolster his own authority. The constitution, founded on the principles of constitutional monarchy, provided for quasi-democratic legislative institutions, but in practice the emperor's authority remained absolute. In 1955, a new constitution was adopted to further project Haile Selassie's image, both at home and abroad, as a progressive autocrat. The new constitution called for an elected Chamber of Deputies, to be selected on the basis of universal adult suffrage. Significantly, although electoral competition was allowed, political parties were not. The document also called for a separation of church and state, and established a modern judiciary. In spite of these changes the emperor maintained a strong, absolutist hand. This was the source of growing discontent among the young, educated class.

The emperor's will was allowed to prevail mainly in the political arena as long as the aristocracy was allowed to maintain the most important of its traditional rights and privileges, those relating to land and land use. He had, on several occasions—partly as a result of the urging of foreign aid donors like the United States and Sweden, and partly because he was trying to further consolidate his power—tried to introduce land tax and land reform measures so as to weaken the traditional classes and strengthen his own position. But each time he met with only limited success (Schwab 1972). He never tried to push too hard, especially in the northern parts of the country, for fear that this would lead to widespread political instability. His interest in land reform was never more than half-hearted.

The emperor tried to construct a political economy predominantly based on peasant agricultural production and foreign private investment. The mode of production was peasant based; reforms were mainly intended to improve the state's extractive capacity, rather than to modernize agriculture. Some, mostly foreign and joint-owned, industrial and agricultural plantation activities were introduced during this period, but they were mainly for the purpose of import substitution. The state merely taxed peasant production and supervised and controlled the marketing of such export crops as coffee, hides and skins, and pulses, commodities which made up virtually all of Ethiopia's exports (Gilkes 1975). Elaborate development plans were published between 1953 and 1973, but little real change occurred. Haile Selassie's interest was absorbed by the imperatives of his own survival and that of his absolutist state.

All of this must be considered in terms of the gross inequalities represented in this system on the basis of ethnic affiliation. The modern-day Ethiopian

Empire had been formed simultaneously with the European "Scramble for Africa." Ethiopian emperors used their military might and diplomatic initiative to expand the state and consolidate its hold over peripheral areas in the late nineteenth and early twentieth centuries, incorporating large areas of the south, southeast (including the Ogaden), and the west. At that time, the European powers were establishing their effective control throughout Africa. Italy claimed Ethiopia; the Italians were resoundingly defeated by the forces of Emperor Menelik II, however, when they tried to expand from the Eritrean coast in 1896. Subsequently, the Ethiopian imperial domain was established by treaties with Egypt, Italy, France, and Britain. It included the Ogaden, but not Eritrea, which was annexed in 1962 after a decade of U.N. administration (Markakis 1974; Sherman 1980).

Imperial authority in the newly incorporated areas of the country was maintained by the imperial bureaucracy and military. Not much attention was given to national political integration, and efforts at social and economic development were generally ineffectual. Throughout the last nineteen years of his reign, Haile Selassie exploited his association with the United States to shore up his arbitrary power. The United States did not press him to institute meaningful social, economic, or political reforms. While the United States recognized the dangers inherent in his policies, it simply blinked at the domestic problems which were destined to engulf the imperial throne.

With regard to border problems with Somalia which emerged shortly after Somali's independence, the United States was only interested in deterrence, and not in settlement of the problem by means of negotiation. The same could be said of Ethiopia's struggle to keep Eritrea from seceding.

Whether or not the United States desired to exercise influence over Ethiopia is not the issue. The issue is that by 1974 the association between the two countries was so involved that their fates in the region were inseparable. Ethiopia was viewed both at home and abroad as a U.S. client. The United States, now conscious of the strategic value of Ethiopia as a possible staging ground for the projection of its military power into the Middle East and Persian Gulf, was not as anxious as before to completely abandon Ethiopia. On the line by 1976 were Ethiopia's national and regional interests and America's strategic interests. The crisis caused by the revolution served as a catalyst for a crisis in U.S. foreign policy as well as Ethiopia's regional policy.

The Horn in Crisis

Carter's assumption of the U.S. presidency coincided with the beginning of the most critical phase of the Ethiopian revolution. The military regime that seized power in 1974 was attempting to sketch a program to consolidate its rule amid growing opposition from the civilian left and various other corporate groups, as well as intensified efforts of the Eritrean Liberation Movement. These events caused heated political competition within the ruling committee, the Derg, as well as between and among the Derg and leftist civilian groups like the All Ethiopian Socialist Movement (Meison) and the Ethiopian People's Revolutionary Party (EPRP). These struggles tended to undermine the legitimacy the Derg was trying to build. Initially the Derg allied with the Meison because it expressed a willingness to work with the military in the vanguard of the revolution. By late 1976, the EPRP, calling for a popularly based people's democracy, had declared war on the Derg and its Meison allies. In the autumn of that year it embarked on a systematic terror campaign of urban guerrilla warfare, directing its attacks at high government officials as well as at low-level functionaries who had taken up positions in the newly created Peasant's Associations and Urban Dwellers Associations, *kebeles*. The intention of the EPRP was to demonstrate that the Derg could not rule effectively, and that it had significant civilian opposition.

The Derg's response was to launch in collaboration with the Meison a Red Terror campaign to counter what it called the White Terror of the EPRP. What resulted was massive violations of human rights. I shall return to this point later.

The United States had begun to express concern about violations of human rights in Ethiopia as early as November 1974 when some sixty political prisoners were executed. At that time, Secretary of State Kissinger merely protested, asking that such incidents be halted (Schaufele 1976, 121). Two months later the Eritrean rebels launched heavy attacks on cities in that region, holding them in a virtual state of siege for over a year. By the summer of 1976, the Derg had decided to mount a counteroffensive against rebel positions with a peasant militia of some 160,000 men. By June it had 25,000 men poised on the Eritrean border. They were poorly trained and poorly armed. The Eritrean rebels attacked them before they entered into Eritrea and greatly decimated their forces. The United States then appealed to the Derg to halt its plans to use such a militia in the Eritrean campaign (Sherman 1980, 86–87).

Both the State Department and the Pentagon appeared ready to stand by Ethiopia in this crisis, persuaded that U.S. credibility was at stake. The Ford administration had sought to exercise some moderating leverage on the Derg by dragging its feet on approving the delivery of requested military aid. At the same time it was making plans to deliver $22 million in arms to Ethiopia (Schaufele 1976).

The Derg was desperate. The Americans had hesitated in delivering badly needed military aid since 1975, and with Carter about to take office, there loomed the possibility of a complete cutoff. Ethiopia turned to Turkey, Yugoslavia, China, Vietnam, and Czechoslovakia. It even turned to Libya, striking a deal that in effect guaranteed that Libya would cease to aid Eritrean rebels and give Ethiopia aid instead, if the Ethiopians would allow an anti-Numieri coup to be launched from Ethiopia.

In December of 1976, the Soviet Union signed an agreement with Ethiopia for the delivery of $100 million in military supplies (Gray 1978, 807). At the time Ethiopia appeared to have no intention of completely turning away from the United States, but merely sought to supplement U.S. military aid.

Events in Ethiopia, propelled by their own dynamics, moved on at a dizzying pace. If the United States had ever been in a position to exercise influence over these developments, by January 1977, this was surely impossible. The Derg was in the midst of a bitter power struggle, which ended on February 3, 1977, with Colonel Mengistu Haile Mariam emerging from a bloody palace shootout as the first among "equals." In the next several days there followed a series of bloody encounters involving the Derg, the civilian left, college students, and even elementary and high school students.

During November 1976, President-elect Carter noted his displeasure with the human rights record of the Derg (Funk 1982). Whereas the Ford administration had been reluctant to cut off military aid to Ethiopia, Carter moved swiftly to establish human rights as the centerpiece of his foreign policy. On February 25, 1977, it was announced that because of continued gross violations of human rights by the governments of Ethiopia, Argentina, and Uruguay, U.S. military aid to those countries would be reduced by October 1977. Simultaneously, the United States and other Western countries began to apply economic pressure on Ethiopia (Legum and Lee 1979, 52; Ayele 1981, 22).

In the meantime the Soviet Union moved into the breech, attempting to orchestrate the creation of a Marxist-Leninist federation in the Horn involving Ethiopia, Eritrea, South Yemen, and Somalia. Between March and April 1977 Fidel Castro and Soviet President Podgorny tried to negotiate a settlement of the differences between Ethiopia and Somalia and secure agreement on the federation idea, but to no avail. Siad Barre rejected the notion and prepared secretly for war (Halliday and Molyneux 1981).

These talks coincided with the arrival of the first consignment of Soviet tanks from South Yemen to Ethiopia. A month later more tanks and personnel carriers arrived (Yodfat 1980). These developments were sufficient to allow Mengistu to finally respond to the announced reduction in U.S. military aid two months earlier. In April 1977, he announced that Ethiopia was demanding that the United States close down Kagnew, all MAAG operations, the Naval Medical Research Unit, and the United States Information Service. Also, the personnel of the U.S. embassy and USAID were to be reduced. Mengistu's move came less than a week after Carter is reported to have declared his intentions to move closer to Somalia, in an effort to dislodge the Soviets. He apparently had not entertained the possibility of such a radical move by Ethiopia.

The Soviets continued to supply arms to both Somalia and Ethiopia, while attempting to negotiate a peace between the two sides. The United States and its Western allies stepped up efforts to woo Somalia away from the Soviet Union. The strategy was twofold: (1) to contemplate direct military aid to Somalia, and (2) to encourage indirect aid from third-party countries in the region friendly to the West. Countries like Egypt, Saudi Arabia, and Sudan were encouraged to funnel aid to Somalia, while the United States considered aid requests on its own. These moderate Islamic regimes were themselves concerned about the growing Soviet presence in the region. The United States continued to consider the possibility of direct military aid to Somalia, and on July 26, 1977, it was announced that an agreement had been reached for that purpose. How this accord was reached and under what terms is not clear. The United States claimed that this aid was contingent upon Somalia's rejection of Pan-Somali claims over parts of Djibouti, Ethiopia, and Kenya. The Somalis claimed that through an American doctor, Kevin Cahill, acting as an agent for the U.S. government, the United States had indicated that it had no objection to Somalia's invasion of Ethiopia. They claimed further that the United States had agreed not to resupply Ethiopia if the Somalis invaded, and not to "look askance" if the Somalis themselves asked for military aid (Legum and Lee 1979, 78). This agreement "in principle" was tabled before it could be acted upon because eight days after it was announced, the United States learned that regular Somali troops were fighting alongside guerrillas of the Western Somali Liberation Front in the Ogaden.

The United States denied any complicity in the invasion and suspended further talks on military aid to Somalia until regular troops were withdrawn. Although the Soviet Union continued to supply aid to Somalia after the Ogaden invasion, it began to withdraw its personnel until by September no more than 400 remained out of the more than 1,000 sent (Yodfat 1980, 44). Relations between the two countries deteriorated rapidly, and on November 13, Somalia announced the abrogation of the July 1974 Treaty of Friendship and Cooperation with the Soviet Union. All Soviet military and civilian advisers and technicians were asked to leave, and the USSR relinquished its rights to use Somali bases. In addition, diplomatic relations with Cuba were suspended.

Somali actions were in response to the growing involvement of Cuban troops and advisers and Soviet advisers in Ethiopia. On the evening of November 28, the USSR launched a huge airlift and sealift of arms and materials for Ethiopia (Payton 1979). In a very short time more than $1 billion worth of military equipment was pumped into Ethiopia. In addition, over the next several months more than 11,000 Cuban and 1,000 Soviet military personnel arrived in the country and were dispatched to the Ogaden to help Ethiopian troops halt the Somali advance, which by the end of 1977 had penetrated beyond the Ogaden to the gates of Harar. This aid was decisive in turning the tide in favor of Ethiopia by early 1978.

As a result of the split between Ethiopia and the United States, tension mounted throughout the whole region. Beginning in May, clashes were reported between Sudan and Ethiopia on their common border, and Egypt committed troops to help guard the eastern border of Sudan. Kenya was alarmed first by serious consideration by the United States of supplying arms to Somalia and second by the Somali invasion of Ethiopia. Conservative Arab countries in the region feared rampant Soviet expansion into their domain.

The question arises: What did the Carter policy toward Ethiopia accomplish? There were several obvious short-term and long-term consequences. In the short term, the administration hoped to curb violations of human rights in Ethiopia. In fact, its human rights policy had no apparent effect on conditions in Ethiopia. Human rights violations escalated after February 1977, and by November 1978 an estimated 5,000 young people between the ages of twelve and twenty-five alone had been killed during the Red Terror Campaign. Killings reached a peak between December 1977 and February 1978 when an average of 100 people were killed each night. The government stated that about 200 government officials had been killed (*Amnesty International Index* 1978, 14–15).

Ironically, almost as soon as it realized that its human rights policy toward Ethiopia had backfired, the United States attempted to distance itself from the conflict in the Horn by claiming neutrality. Public charges of human rights violations became more tempered, and efforts were begun to try to reestablish normal relations.

The most outstanding long-term consequence of Carter's flawed policy was the contribution it made to the escalation in the arms race in the Horn. Between 1976 and 1979 Ethiopia's armed forces jumped from 65,000 to more than 250,000 (see Table 9–1).

Somalia's military forces swelled from 31,000 to 54,000 in that same period; Sudan's from 50,000 to 65,000, and Kenya's from 9,000 to 13,000. Military expenditures also skyrocketed. In Ethiopia they more than doubled to $351 million; in Somalia and Sudan they virtually tripled to $92 million and $237 million respectively; and in Kenya there was a fivefold rise in military expenditures to $278 million.

These figures reflected the intense competition among the Big Powers to make sure their clients were adequately prepared. The Soviet Union was the biggest military spender in the Horn, but the United States was striving to be able to meet any future Soviet or Soviet-sponsored threat to its clients with a swift and certain long-range military strike.

The Carter administration set in motion an encirclement strategy by which the United States would try to contain the Soviets by wooing Ethiopia's neighbors with military and economic development aid. On their part, countries like Egypt, Sudan, Kenya, Somalia, and Oman were asked to allow their territories to be used as staging grounds for the U.S. Rapid Deployment Force (RDF), which could be used to project U.S. military power into the Middle East and the Persian Gulf (Jackson 1982). Separate agreements were reached with each country, and in late 1981 Operation Bright Star, a mock RDF exercise, was staged in the region, causing Ethiopia, South Yemen, and Libya to come together in a show of solidarity and jointly resolve to repulse any efforts

TABLE 9–1 Sizes of Armed Forces and Levels of Military Expenditures in Selected Years

YEAR	ETHIOPIA		SOMALIA		SUDAN		KENYA	
	Armed Forces (thousands)	Military Expend. (millions)	Armed Forces (thousands)	Military Expend. (millions)	Armed Forces (thousands)	Military Expend. (millions)	Armed Forces (thousands)	Military Expend. (millions)
1963	55	$ 20	9	$ 4	17	$ 25	15	$ 7
1973	50	44	25	21	35	99	8	39
1975	50	105	30	27	50	109	9	57
1976	65	146	31	28	50	110	9	56
1977	225	186	53	32	50	163	13	106
1978	233	103	54	67	71	231	13	205
1979	250	351	54	92	65	237	13	278

SOURCE: U.S. Arms Control and Disarmament Agency. World Military Expenditures and Arms Transfers 1963–73 and 1970–79 (Washington, D.C., 1973 and 1979).

by the United States or its proxies to intervene in their affairs. The Reagan administration is determined to establish its military credibility, and the Horn appears to be as good a place as any to do so. This posture implies economic assistance programs which seek to reward "friends" handsomely and serve notice to "enemies" in the region that the United States is prepared to use arms to "buy peace" (Hudson 1982). The budget for fiscal year 1983 committed more than $1 billion for the development of the RDF's capabilities. This means the preparation of bases and port facilities in countries friendly to the United States in the Horn and Middle East to accommodate U.S. troops and equipment, should the need arise. Djibouti, Kenya, Somalia, and Sudan were promised almost one-half billion dollars in military and economic development aid for the year (U.S. State Department 1982). The Soviets have continued their heavy investment in military aid to Ethiopia, South Yemen, and Libya.[2]

Evidently the United States intends to pursue a globalist strategy in the Horn. The massive escalation of the regional arms race and the onset of a permanent syndrome of regional tension is regarded as an acceptable price to pay.

The tensions created by the ever-intensifying arms race in the Horn have caused Ethiopia and Somalia to constantly try to outfox each other. Each country sponsors guerrilla campaigns against the other. The consequences have been momentous. Responding to what it considered unquestionable evidence that Ethiopian military support had been provided in the Somali Democratic Salvation Front's invasion of northern Somalia in the summer of 1982, the United States rushed emergency military aid to the Siad Barre regime, and shortly thereafter provided it with the first installment of a promised two-year $40 million military aid package. Egypt and other Arab countries, as well as Italy, followed the U.S. lead with aid of their own. Ethiopia reacted with protest, claiming that even though it had never invaded Somalia and had no intentions of ever doing so, it would have to reexamine its options in view of the U.S. arms shipment to Somalia (*Africa Research Bulletin* 1982).

Conclusion

What lessons can be drawn from this account which might have some implications for U.S.–African relations in the future? First, the key to a successful global policy in a given region is a clearly articulated regionalist perspective: one based on contemporary national and regional realities as well as on an appreciation for the relevance of a country's (and a region's) history in the shaping of contemporary political dynamics. The Ethiopian revolution had been predicted for a long time. The United States should have been better

2. According to the U.S. Defense Department, there are over 2,400 Soviet military advisers in Ethiopia, as well as 550 from East Germany and 5,900 from Cuba. See "From War to Words," *Africa Research Bulletin* (July 1–31, 1982, 6515–6516).

prepared. It could not have prevented the revolution, but it could have attempted to exercise its leverage over Haile Selassie more effectively and at an early date.

Historically, the main U.S. objective in Ethiopia had been to maintain access and a presence in the territory. The sociopolitical and political-economic health of the country was of no more than passing concern to U.S. foreign policymakers. In retrospect, this was a fatal mistake. Domestic and regional conflicts in the Horn between 1976 and 1977 were so intense that they became internationalized. A solution could not be found—as the Carter administration seemed to assume—in simply threatening to end U.S. military support to Ethiopia. Other calculating actors were—as they will be in the future—prepared to make choices of their own, which were bound to be beyond U.S. control. African states like Ethiopia will in the future be guided by their own goals of nationalism or the desire to preserve their territorial integrity. Under such circumstances, ideology is not a primary consideration.

Second, the U.S. should realize that in crisis situations, it must be more prudent in how it applies global policies. It was right for President Carter to draw attention to human rights violations in Ethiopia; but was his approach to dealing with the issue the most appropriate, given other global priorities such as strategic advantage or regional and international peace? If Carter had foreseen that his policy would have little effect on curbing human rights violations, while contributing instead to a massive explosion in the regional arms race, it is doubtful that he would have taken the approach he did to dealing with Ethiopia.

Finally, there is no possible military solution to the problems of the Horn; nor is there any guarantee that the United States will be able to hold this client or that client in check. The states and other domestic social forces currently operating in the Horn have the autonomy to choose patrons; they have the autonomy to set their levels of investment in arms. Given these realities, the best strategy for the United States in the future would be to attempt to ameliorate the crisis. This will not be done by simply providing "friends" with so-called defensive weapons, or by attempting to deter their enemies by shows of U.S. military might. The United States should use its leverage to try to get its clients in the Horn area to negotiate for peace. This could be done most effectively indirectly through third parties. For example, Kenya and Ethiopia have a secure and agreed-upon common border. They are drawn together by their fear of Somali irredentism. The United States could attempt to attract Ethiopia to the bargaining table with Somalia and Sudan through Kenya. It could try to do the same with the Eritrean rebels and Somalia by going through their friends, Egypt, Sudan, and Saudi Arabia, who are linked to them by religious and/or cultural affinity. A negotiated settlement of this multifaceted crisis is the only way to lasting peace and justice in the Horn; and peace with justice in the region is in everyone's national interest, including that of the United States.

REFERENCES

Africa Research Bulletin. 1982. "From War to Words." July.

Amnesty International Index. 1978. "Human Rights Violations in Ethiopia." November.

Ayele, Negussay. 1981. "The Horn of Africa: Revolutionary Developments and Western Relations." *Northeast African Studies* 2, no. 3.

Bader, George W. 1970. "Testimony," in *Hearings before the U.S. Senate Subcommittee on U.S. Security Agreements and Commitments Abroad: U.S. Security Arrangements and Commitments Abroad: Ethiopia*. Washington, D.C.: U.S. Government Printing Office.

Bienen, Henry. 1980. "Perspectives on Soviet Intervention in Africa." *Political Science Quarterly* 95 (Spring):29–42.

Funk, Gerald A. 1982. "Some Observations on Strategic Realities and Ideological Red Herrings on the Horn of Africa." *CIS Africa Notes*, no. 1 (July).

Gilkes, Patrick. 1975. *The Dying Lion*. London: Friedman Publishers.

Gray, Robert D. 1978. "Post-Imperial Ethiopian Foreign Policy: Ethiopian Dependence," in Proceedings of the Fifth International Conference on Ethiopian Studies. Chicago.

Halliday, Fred, and Maxine Molyneux. 1981. *The Ethiopian Revolution*. London: Verso.

Hudson, Michael C. 1982. "Reagan's Policy in Northeast Africa." *Africa Report*, March-April.

Jackson, Henry F. 1982. *From the Congo to Soweto: U.S. Foreign Policy Toward Africa Since 1960*. New York: William Morrow.

Korry, Edward. 1976. "Testimony," in *Hearings: U.S. Senate Subcommittee on African Affairs*. Washington, D.C.: U.S. Government Printing Office.

Legum, Colin, and Bill Lee. 1979. *The Horn of Africa in Continuing Crisis*. New York: Africana.

Marcus, Harold J. 1983. *Ethiopia, Great Britain and the United States 1941–74*. Berkeley: University of California Press.

Markakis, John. 1974. *Ethiopia: Anatomy of a Traditional Polity*. Oxford: Oxford University Press.

Newsom, David. 1970. "Testimony," in *Hearings before the U.S. Senate Subcommittee on U.S. Security Agreements and Commitments Abroad: U.S. Security Arrangements and Commitments Abroad: Ethiopia*. Washington, D.C.: U.S. Government Printing Office.

Ottaway, Marina. 1982. *Soviet and American Influence in the Horn of Africa*. New York: Praeger.

Payton, Gary D. 1979. "The Soviet Ethiopian Liaison: Airlift and Beyond." *Air University Review* 31 (November-December).

Price, Robert. 1978. *U.S. Foreign Policy in Sub-Saharan Africa: National Interest and Global Strategy*. Berkeley, Calif.: Institute of International Studies.

Schaufele, William E., Jr. 1976. "Statement," in *Hearings: U.S. Senate Subcommittee on African Affairs*. Washington, D.C.: U.S. Government Printing Office.

Schwab, Peter. 1972. *Decision-Making in Ethiopia: A Study of the Political Process*. Rutherford, N.J.: Fairleigh Dickinson University Press.

Sherman, Richard. 1980. *Eritrea: The Unfinished Revolution.* New York: Praeger.

Spencer, John H. 1977. *Ethiopia, the Horn of Africa and U.S. Policy.* Cambridge, Mass.: Institute of Foreign Policy Analysis.

USDOD (U.S. Department of Defense). 1981. *Foreign Military Sales, Foreign Military Construction, and Military Assistance as of 1981.* Washington, D.C.

U.S. State Department. 1982. "International Security and Economic Cooperation Program, FY1983." *Special Report No. 99* (March).

Vogelgesan, Sandra. 1978. "What Price Principle?—U.S. Policy on Human Rights." *Foreign Affairs 56*, no. 4 (July).

Yodfat, Aryeh. 1980. "The Soviet Union and the Horn of Africa, Part II." *Northeast African Studies 2*, no. 1.

10

Somalia and the United States, 1977–1983: The New Relationship

DONALD K. PETTERSON

One day in the summer of 1980, I was sitting and talking with Somali President Mohamed Siad Barre in the gazebo outside his quarters where we usually met. Reacting to my latest representation on a particular subject, Siad exasperatedly declared, "You always bring up the Ogaden, Ogaden, Ogaden!" He was exaggerating, but certainly since the time in the late 1970s when the United States government began seriously to work for a new relationship with Somalia, the Ogaden[1] question in all its ramifications, including Cuban troops in Ethiopia, has been the dominant issue confronting the United States in the Horn of Africa and the leitmotif of many of the discussions between representatives of the government of Somalia and the United States.[2]

The Ogaden and U.S. Policy

Other factors also have affected the U.S.–Somali relationship, but I believe that the Ogaden issue and the way the United States handled it offers the best insight into how U.S. policy toward Somalia evolved, the difficulties we have encountered and still face in dealing with Somalia, and the possibilities open to American diplomacy in the Horn in the days ahead.

The stage for U.S. relations with Somalia was set after World War II when the perceived need for a military communications station in Ethiopia cemented close ties between the United States and the regime of Haile Selassie.

1. The *Ogaden* is the term usually employed to describe the eastern part of Ethiopia which has been the focal point of the dispute between Ethiopia and Somalia. Most generally it is applied to the Ogaden and Haud areas of Harerge Province, but at times it has been incorrectly used to include also parts of Bale and Sidamo provinces because of the fighting there between Ethiopians and Somalis.

2. Much of what is related in this paper is drawn from the author's own notes and recollections from his term as ambassador to Somalia from 1978–82.

This friendship deepened in the 1950s and 1960s. The United States also enjoyed excellent relations with Kenya from the time of Kenyan independence in 1963. It followed that Somalia, apparently bent on resorting to arms against Ethiopia and Kenya to achieve its goal of "greater Somalia," was bound to be regarded in somewhat of a bad light by the United States.

In the 1960s the Americans brought the Peace Corps to Somalia and began a fairly substantial economic assistance program. But the overall relationship between the two countries continued to be impaired by the Somali irredentist cause and the leftward tilt of Somalia in its foreign relations (a result, in part, of the close relationship between Ethiopia and the United States). In February 1968, however, when Somali Prime Minister Mohamed Ibrahim Egal paid an official visit to Washington, relations between the United States and Somalia were on the upswing. The State Department believed that Egal and Somali President Abdirashid Shermarke were taking a path of more genuine nonalignment, perhaps heading Somalia in a relatively pro-Western direction. More important, they had moved away from the irredentism of the previous Somali governments. Egal had had talks with the Ethiopians and Kenyans and was looking for American support in achieving peace in the Horn. Unfortunately, the Johnson administration had little to offer him. In Washington, Egal was told that the United States would discreetly support his initiative with his neighbors, but could not assume an active role. Nor would the United States do much in response to a Somali request for more economic aid. Somalia was not one of the nine African countries which the administration had designated as bilateral aid recipients; in fact, the United States was thinking of phasing out its USAID program in Somalia. Despite this less than wholeheartedly enthusiastic welcome to Egal, however, there was a real possibility of an appreciably better relationship between the United States and Somalia.

This changed quickly and markedly after the military takeover in Somalia in October 1969.

The extent to which relations between Mogadishu and Washington had soured by early 1971, just a year later, is illustrated by the belief expressed in the State Department that the United States should seek "to minimize the disruptive capabilities of Somalia and preserve the detente in the Horn of Africa." It was felt that this would, in turn, help to protect the more important interests of the United States in Ethiopia. The view in the State Department was that "an errant Somalia" could create significant difficulties for American interests in the Horn and East Africa.

In the year after the military came to power in Somalia, the Peace Corps program had been terminated by order of the Somali government, five American embassy and USAID officers had been expelled, and most of the U.S. economic assistance program had been halted because of a resumption of Somali-flag shipping to North Vietnam.

Relations between Somalia and the United States remained very strained for several years. In 1976 the Somalis, increasingly disenchanted with the

Soviet Union, expressed a desire for improved relations with Washington, but this came to nothing. Inexorably, though, the profound changes taking place within Ethiopia compelled the United States to alter its relationships with both Ethiopia and Somalia. In 1974, the feudal monarchy of Haile Selassie had been overthrown by the Ethiopian military. In the many months of upheaval that followed, a group of Marxist-oriented officers, dominated by Lt. Colonel Mengistu Haile Mariam, emerged as the rulers of Ethiopia. During this period, U.S.–Ethiopian relations deteriorated. Suspicious of the United States and unhappy about their continued dependence on American military assistance, the revolutionary leadership sought and by the end of 1976 obtained a military aid agreement with the Soviet Union. By the spring of 1977, the United States had suspended the shipment of military materiel to Ethiopia; the Ethiopians had ousted the U.S. Military Assistance Advisory Group and closed the U.S. military's Kagnew communications station and the American Consulate at Asmara; and the Soviets had delivered tanks, armored personnel carriers, and other weapons to Ethiopia.

In its Horn of Africa policy review, the recently elected Carter administration decided in April 1977 to seek to improve relations with Somalia and promote its disengagement from the Soviet Union. The summer rolled around without much visible progress, a reflection of President Siad's caution in cutting loose from the Soviets. Washington believed that Siad was hedging his bets until he had a better picture of both the depth of the Soviet commitment to Ethiopia and the scope of the security assistance the United States and others intended to provide to Somalia. In any event, shortly before the Somalis launched their invasion of the Ogaden in July, the United States had decided that it would begin a military supply relationship with Somalia and had conveyed to Mogadishu an agreement in principle to provide Somalia with arms to defend itself.[3]

With the increase in hostilities and the introduction of regular Somali army units into the Ogaden, Washington quickly backtracked. Secretary of

---

3. From the very beginning, the U.S. intention has been to provide Somalia with an amount of military assistance that would not go beyond helping the Somalis to meet their legitimate defense needs. Both the Carter and Reagan administrations have been mindful of the concerns of Somalia's neighbors and of the U.S. Congress and other interested parties in the United States. Thus it was that of the $65 million allocated for military aid to Somalia for fiscal years 1980, 1981, and 1982, half was for air defense radar and almost all of the remainder for nonlethal items like radios and trucks. No arms were delivered until the summer of 1982, after Ethiopian and Somali dissident forces occupied Balenbale and Goldogob in Somalia. Fearing that the enemy would move farther east and cut the north-south road, the Somali government appealed for and received two emergency airlifts of small arms and ammunition, and 24 armored personnel carriers armed with antitank weapons. These and the aging tanks and other items received from Italy and Egypt have not altered the military balance of power in the Horn, which continues to be vastly in Ethiopia's favor; in fact the military aid to Somalia has barely kept pace with the deterioration of Somalia's armed forces owing to poor maintenance, harsh conditions of operations, and lack of spare parts for Somalia's Soviet-made equipment.

State Vance told President Carter that the United States should not provide Somalia with arms which might assist the Somali military campaign, and that therefore the agreement in principle should not be implemented. A Somali military delegation was informed, in early August, that although President Carter's commitment was still valid, the Somali action in the Ogaden had created a situation which the United States could not ignore. The Somalis were told that under the circumstances, the United States could not send military equipment to Somalia, nor could it authorize third-country transfers of military materiel of U.S. origin. The administration was aware that without international, particularly African, acceptance of Somali control of the Ogaden, implementation of an arms agreement would generate considerable international and domestic criticism.

To demonstrate to the Somalis that the United States continued to desire better relations, however, the administration proceeded with humanitarian and economic assistance.

The U.S. government publicly supported the Organization of African Unity's (OAU) mediation effort, and President Carter privately urged Siad to take advantage of what the OAU was trying to accomplish. Even after the Soviets had begun their massive infusion of arms into Ethiopia, large numbers of Cuban troops had arrived in Ethiopia, and President Siad had ended Somalia's close ties with the Soviet Union, President Carter reaffirmed that the United States could not supply either side with arms as long as the conflict continued. In his foreign policy address of January 19, 1978, he stated: "We have made clear to both sides that we will supply no arms for aggressive purposes. We will not recognize forcible changes in boundaries" (Carter 1979, 121).

There were some in the State Department and the National Security Council who worried about the continuance of the agreement in principle and what they were sure was an implication that once the tide of battle turned against the Somalis and Somalia was under attack, the United States would send arms. They believed that any arms shipments to Somalia under any circumstances would only exacerbate the Horn problem. Nonetheless, the agreement in principle was maintained. Since it produced no arms for Somalia, however, the Somalis began what turned out to be a long series of complaints which in essence charged that the United States was not nearly firmly enough opposed to Soviet intervention in the Horn.

The U.S. hope for a negotiated settlement was dampened in early 1978 by the very successful Ethiopian counterattack, which devastated the Somali army and apparently ended any possible inclination of the Ethiopians to negotiate. In talks with the Soviets at this time, the Americans found them uninterested in working together to promote a lasting settlement. It soon became clear that they were motivated primarily by a determination to preserve and enhance their own influence in the Horn. Fortunately for Somalia, the Soviets saw their interests best served by restraining the Ethiopians from invading Somalia.

Faced with the radically changing military situation in the Ogaden, President Carter considered, with other leaders like Egypt's Anwar Sadat and France's Valéry Giscard d'Estaing, what still might be done to promote a peaceful resolution of the Somali-Ethiopian conflict. In an exchange of messages in early February, for example, Carter and Giscard agreed that there should be a conference of interested states in the region which would lead to an OAU initiative to expedite Somali withdrawal from the Ogaden in return for the departure of Soviet and Cuban military forces from Ethiopia. Among these and other proposed measures which did not produce the desired result was agreement by the two presidents that countries friendly to Somalia should consult regarding a supply of "appropriate military equipment" to Somalia.

The arms supply question was shelved momentarily as the administration focused on trying to get a Somali withdrawal, Soviet-Cuban disengagement, and a negotiated settlement in the OAU context. But concern about arms to Somalia persisted. State Department officials, for example, strongly advised Secretary Vance that military inducements to bring about a withdrawal of Somali forces from the Ogaden should be used only as a last resort.

Nevertheless, after Somali units, as such, were removed from the Ogaden, Assistant Secretary of State Richard Moose went to Mogadishu in March to confer with Siad about U.S. assistance to Somalia. After lengthy discussions, they reached an understanding that no U.S. military aid would be forthcoming unless Somalia gave formal assurances it would refrain from the use of force against any other country and would use U.S.–provided military equipment for defensive purposes only and solely within Somali territory. These assurances were given on April 23, but further consultations with Siad on U.S. defensive arms were put in abeyance in July following intelligence information of growing covert Somali military support for the Western Somali Liberation Front (WSLF). Clearly, the Somalis were not living up to the spirit, or even, as became apparent later, the letter of their assurances.

I arrived in Mogadishu in November 1978, at about the time the Ethiopians started conducting a prolonged series of air raids on Somali towns and villages in the vicinity of the border. No sooner had I presented my credentials than the Somali government began appealing for the United States to do something to end the Ethiopian attacks and to reconsider the decision about arms for Somalia. When Washington did not respond in the way they were hoping for, the Somalis professed that the United States and the West were indifferent to what the Soviets and Cubans were doing in the Horn. In their arguments, they pointed to what they characterized as the threat of Soviet expansionism in the region, the need for greater U.S. resolve to deter Soviet aims, the desire of Somalia for an extremely close relationship with the United States, and the justice of the cause of western Somali freedom-fighters. They asked us to separate the Ogaden problem from the question of U.S.– Somali relations. In response I reiterated our position that the U.S. government could not give any military assistance to Somalia as long as the Somali army was directly involved militarily in the Ogaden. I described the international and U.S. domestic factors upon which our policy was based, including our need to respect the OAU's position on the Horn conflict.

During the balance of 1979, a considerable number of the many discussions in Mogadishu with high-level Somali officials took the form of a Somali request for help on an urgent basis because of repeated Ethiopian raids on Somali border towns, an American response that there could be no U.S. military aid while the Somali army was in the Ogaden, a Somali denial that it was, and an American insistence that the U.S. government knew beyond the shadow of doubt that indeed it was.

Throughout this time, many influential Somalis held the belief that Ethiopia still could fall apart, especially if military pressure were maintained by the Somalis in the Ogaden, as well as by the Eritrean, Tigrean, and Oromo guerrillas, all of whom were conducting military operations against the central government. These Somalis thought their goal of gaining control of the Ogaden by military means was still achievable. They said they could not fathom why the United States could not see that persistent guerrilla activity would create enormous difficulties for the Soviets. Further, they did not believe a negotiated solution was attainable; an Ethiopian offer of autonomy for the Ogaden, in the unlikely event one were made, would be unacceptable, they said, because they could not trust the Ethiopians. Thus, short of full self-determination, the conflict would go on.

U.S. Objectives

The U.S. government's continued concern in 1978 and 1979 about Siad's Ogaden policy stemmed from American interests in Somalia, which were largely geopolitical and derivative in nature. We wanted to see an end to the instability and violence in the Horn which, in addition to causing widespread human suffering, provided the Soviet Union and Cuba with opportunities for intervention and expanded influence. We wanted to act in ways consistent with OAU tenets and not to damage our relations with other African countries, Kenya for example. We also had to consider indications from some of the moderate Arabs that the United States should take measures to deter the Soviets. And we wanted to strengthen Somalia's ties with the West.

Humanitarianism was another important element in American thinking and actions with regard to Somalia. The United States responded more quickly than most donors and for a long time more generously than all in providing emergency aid to the hundreds of thousands of refugees who streamed into Somalia from the Ogaden and from Bale and Sidamo provinces. For a fleeting moment, the plight of the refugees caught the attention of a fairly large segment of the American public. For a sustained period it has elicited considerable money and food from the U.S. government; and it has added to the urgency to find a way to end the warfare between Somali and Ethiopian forces.

The Access Agreement

The Carter administration, impelled by the crises in Iran and Afghanistan, decided in December 1979 to seek military access to Somali, Kenyan, and Omani ports and airfields. Regional (in a very broad usage of the word) considerations loomed very large now as a determinant of U.S.–Somali relations. But the Ogaden issue did not vanish as a factor in American policy; U.S. concern about Somali involvement there was not overridden by the desire for a signed access agreement. On the eve of the first round of access negotiations, in fact, the United States was continuing to state its concern about the Ogaden. For example, in a meeting in mid-October, on instructions from Washington I told President Siad that because of the Somali government's military involvement in the Ogaden, the United States would not change its decision on military assistance.

In late December, a team from Washington came to Mogadishu to express to the Siad government the U.S. interest in obtaining access to Somali facilities and to lay the groundwork for subsequent negotiations. In the talks over the next few months, U.S. concern about the Ogaden was restated and our policy on arms reiterated. Nonetheless, for a time the talks went well. By the late spring of 1980, however, the access negotiations had almost broken down. Because of an exaggerated sense of the importance of Somalia to the United States, the Somalis had gone much too far in trying to extract the maximum amount of U.S. economic and military assistance in return for American use of Somali ports and airfields. This and an increasing realization of the potential risks involved in much closer ties with Somalia convinced some officials in Washington that the United States should back away from the plan to obtain access to Somali facilities. It was evident that some of the advocates of an access agreement had, in the crisis atmosphere of late 1979, rushed to push for an agreement with Somalia without first carefully weighing the full consequences of such a move. Fear in Washington in mid–1980 that the Ethiopians were about to invade northern Somalia, coupled with the Somali bargaining-ploy miscalculation, the persistent Ogaden problem, and the fact that with access to Omani and Kenyan facilities assured, the Somali facilities became less important to the United States—all these factors resulted in a cooling of Washington's ardor for an agreement.

This was a relief to those in the administration who from the very beginning had only reluctantly gone along with President Carter's decision for the United States to seek access to Somali facilities. There were very strong differences about our Somalia policy between the African Affairs Bureau and the Political Military Affairs Bureau in the State Department and also between State and the National Security Council. Those who believed the United

States would be much better off without an agreement were influenced by their strong distrust of Siad, their belief that Ethiopia meant much more to the United States than did Somalia and that a military relationship with Somalia would finish any chance of resuming closer ties with Ethiopia, and their fear that the United States would get entangled in an African conflict (and be on the wrong side).

As it happened, the Ethiopian invasion of northern Somalia did not take place that summer, and the feeling that the risks were too high began to fade in the minds of those who finally prevailed in the decision-making process. Moreover, the Siad government, realizing that Washington was losing interest, completely changed its bargaining tactics. In late July 1980, the Somalis let us know they were willing to accept the amount of Foreign Military Sales (FMS) credits and economic support funds contained in our original offer. Anxious not to let closer ties with the United States slip away, the Somalis wanted to sign the access agreement as soon as possible. This was done on August 22.

But it came close to being undone. Before the agreement had been signed, the administration was satisfied, based on available intelligence information, that Somali army units were no longer operating in the Ogaden. The ink on the agreement was barely dry when Washington learned that this no longer was so. Congress was duly notified of this development, and in short order the African subcommittee of the House Foreign Affairs Committee and the Foreign Operations subcommittee of the House Appropriations Committee both voted to oppose any FMS credits until the administration could give assurances that the Somali regular units were out of the Ogaden. Before long, increasingly successful Ethiopian military operations and U.S. insistence that the Somali army had to remove all of its regular forces from the Ogaden brought about the Somali withdrawal, and by the end of the year the administration was able to give the required assurance to the Congress.

The Ogaden in Both Regional and Global Contexts

The Siad government's Ogaden policy continues, nevertheless, to be a troubling element in the relationship between Somalia and the United States. It is abundantly clear that there can be no end to the instability and tension along the Somali-Ethiopian border and in the adjacent territories of both countries as long as any Somali-supported forces are engaged in military activity in the Ogaden. It is equally clear that without an end to the fighting, Somalia's security will remain threatened, U.S. interests will be in jeopardy, Somalia will be unable to progress economically, and the refugee problem will be perpetuated. In short, U.S. goals and objectives with regard to the Horn cannot be achieved while the WSLF, supported by Somalia, continues to fight in the Ogaden. Consequently the United States cannot ignore and indeed has not been ignoring the need to find a way to end the violence and lower the tension between Somalia and Ethiopia. As of late 1983, the accent necessarily was on getting the Ethiopian forces which seized Somali territory in July 1982 to relinquish it and withdraw. Concurrently, however, the problem of Somalia's involvement in the Ogaden continued to have to be addressed.

As much as anywhere else in the continent, in the Horn of Africa U.S. policy is heavily influenced by East-West considerations. The Ogaden issue, because it is a matter of importance to African states, would have had some bearing on U.S. policy toward Somalia even if the Soviet Union had not assumed its prominent role in the area, if thousands of Cuban troops had not been stationed in Ethiopia, or if developments in the so-called arc of crisis had not taken the turn they did at the close of the 1970s and since. However, the OAU was only fitfully engaged in trying to resolve the Somali-Ethiopian dispute, and had it not been for the injection of great power rivalry into the Horn, neither the Ogaden nor any other current aspect of Somalia, for that matter, would have figured as prominently as it has in U.S. concerns and interests in Africa. The reality of Soviet ambitions and actions is something that neither the Ford, nor the Carter, nor the Reagan administration could ignore.

Other Determinants of U.S. Policy:
Siad and His Internal Policies

Personalismo may be a term coined for the politics of Latin America, but the concept is very much applicable to Africa. Certainly this is true of Somalia. Mohamed Siad Barre rules Somalia, and both his personality and his authoritarian style of rule have affected the course of the development of U.S.–Somali relations. The man who opted for a special relationship with the Soviet Union fourteen years ago and joined the militant opponents of the United States could not but be regarded at the time with some hostility by American policymakers, and then with suspicion when he apparently changed his spots and began asking for U.S. help. Furthermore, many believed that Siad's reputation for deviousness was well earned; his less than truthful protestations about the involvement of Somali regulars in the Ogaden added to the feeling in Washington that he could not be trusted. The combination of Siad's personality, his past policies, and the human rights record of his government have had an influence on the Carter and Reagan administrations, and have contributed to the opposition in Congress, certainly among liberals, to the access agreement and especially to security assistance for Somalia.

There is another side to Siad which the United States has had to take into consideration as it has developed its Somalia policy over these past few years. Mohamed Siad Barre has strengths as a leader which have enabled him to stay in power for over fourteen years. As any Somali knows, he is a shrewd and extremely capable politician. He does, as he says, know his people. Siad is the man with whom perforce the U.S. government has had to deal, and in all likelihood, barring the unforeseen, the man with whom it and other governments and international organizations with diplomatic missions in Mogadishu are going to continue to deal. During the four years I was in Somalia, I heard many predictions of Siad's imminent political demise. These ignored his strengths, the lack of cohesion among his opponents, and the fact that within Somalia in recent years no person or faction had emerged as a realistic alternative to him.

Looking at Somalia, let us bear in mind that all things are relative, and in the sphere of human rights the Siad government does not compare all that unfavorably with many other Third World governments. Consequently, although Siad's internal security and political freedoms policies have been a constraint on the kind and extent of the relationship that has evolved between the United States and Somalia, they never deterred the U.S. government from pursuing first closer ties and later the access agreement. Nor have they been such as to stimulate vehement opposition in this country to what the current and previous administrations have set out to accomplish with respect to Somalia and the Horn of Africa.

From the beginning, when the United States reinstituted an economic-development assistance program with Somalia in 1978, American officials have worked together with the Somalis to devise and implement aid projects. At first the extant economic system presented no serious problems for the United States. However, Somalia's inefficient and wasteful excessive government controls over the economy became an impediment to the achievement of the developmental goals the United States and the Somalis had formulated. As a result, the American Embassy and USAID began to pump for changes in the Somali government's economic policies. There were those in the Somali ruling establishment who resisted any departure from Somali socialism. Some were motivated by ideology, others simply were making a lot of money and wanted no change which could endanger their preferred status. There were others in the government, however, who advocated moving toward more private enterprise. Rigid adherence by Siad to the economic system he had fostered would have caused increasingly serious problems in the U.S.–Somali relationship, especially after the advent of the Reagan administration, which attaches greater importance in its foreign relations to the desirability of the free-market economic system. Such problems never materialized, however, because beginning in 1981 Siad gave his stamp of approval to changes in the managing of Somalia's economy, including some measures favoring less state involvement. He was responding to American encouragement, to recommendations from within his own government and from the Saudis, and to conditions laid down by the IMF. In addition, and probably most important, he was influenced by the obvious failure of Somalia's brand of socialism and the deplorable state of the Somali economy.

Conclusion

Siad's domestic policies were of some significance in shaping U.S. decisions regarding Somalia. But far, far more important were strategic considerations growing out of the mutual distrust, fear, and competition that characterize U.S.–Soviet relations. This was the main prism through which we came to view the Horn of Africa. Our past association with Ethiopia and distrust of the Somalis, the Vietnam experience and fear of military involvement in remote places of marginal importance to vital U.S. interests, and our support for the OAU position on territorial boundaries deeply affected how we dealt with the Ogaden problem itself. With regard to the broader issue of instability in the Horn and U.S. involvement there, these imperatives came to be to some degree overshadowed by our determination to counter Soviet objectives in the Horn and southwest Asia, and to keep oil flowing from the Persian Gulf to Europe and North America.

The United States desires to maintain access to the airfields and ports of Berbera and Mogadishu. We want to do whatever we can to stop the fighting between Somalia and Ethiopia,[4] and thereby to reduce the terrible human cost, including the misery of the refugees, produced by the conflict. We have indicated that to both Ethiopia and Somalia. The obstacles to achieving a cease-fire are formidable, but at least there now finally is a realization within the Somali government that a military solution is out of the question and that at some point Somalia and Ethiopia must sit down together and try to work out their differences.

We want to see Cuban troops depart from Ethiopia and Soviet influence diminish. We hope to see a further improvement in relations between Somalia and Kenya. We want to see greater liberalization of the Somali economy and progress toward political reconciliation. Our association with Somalia manifestly presents us with problems, but at the same time it also presents us with an opportunity to enhance our influence and to use it to try to realize the objectives I have described. To do this, the United States must continue to be engaged in the Horn, preferably with both sides to the Somali-Ethiopian dispute, if that is at all possible. As regards Somalia, this will of necessity require further allocation of U.S. resources for economic developmental and humanitarian aid, and, for the time being, continuation of a modest security assistance program to help strengthen Somalia's ability to defend itself.

REFERENCE

Carter, Jimmy. 1979. *Public Papers of the Presidents of the United States. Jimmy Carter. Book 1.* Washington, D.C.: U.S. Government Printing Office.

4. The long-term historical-legal dispute over the Ogaden will be extremely difficult to resolve and no doubt will involve a protracted period of negotiations. For now, the focus must be on what might be attainable sooner—a cease-fire.

PART III

Zaire and Saharan Africa

The chapters in Part III relate to a disparate group of American allies in Africa. They illustrate the primacy of geopolitical considerations in the conduct of American policy toward Africa. In these cases, African-centered values, such as local autonomy, economic development, and political democracy, have weighed lightly in the calculations of American policymakers by comparison with their perceived geopolitical assets for competition with the Soviet Union.

Two chapters on American policy toward Zaire feature the remarkable career of President Mobutu Sese Seko, whose autocratic credentials are proverbial in postcolonial Africa. His immense personal wealth, reported by congressional investigators to include a "fortune in foreign exchange alone [that] is widely estimated to be in the billions of dollars" (Committee on Foreign Affairs 1984,28) in addition to vast holdings of property in Zaire, poses a modern test for the classical defense of rich and business-minded despots. The eighteenth-century French physiocrats favored the acquisition by kings of extensive property holdings on the ground that such interests and the preoccupations to which they give rise would serve to bridle and curb the tyrannical inclinations of sovereign rulers (Hirschman 1977, 70, 96–99). Who can say that the citizens of Zaire would not be worse off under a more purely political despot whose "passionate excesses" were not diverted by an insatiable lust for personal wealth? Are the Mobutists in Washington latter-day physiocrats?

In Chad, a civil war that has torn a nation of questionable identity for nearly two decades is watched with wary eyes by France, the Soviet Union, and the United States. These external powers become aroused and snarl whenever one of them, acting through a surrogate, appears to gain the upper hand. The available surrogates themselves include Chadian factions and neighboring states, principally Libya and the Sudan, neither of whom will countenance the emergence in Chad of a government which favors the other in preference to itself. The United States was aligned with the embattled regime of President Jafaar al-Numeiri in the Sudan. Christian separatists in the southern Sudan had resumed guerrilla warfare in response to centralizing measures that threatened southern regional autonomy. Numeiri had undertaken to construct a fundamentalist Islamic state, enforcing Islamic law against wanton crime and dissidence alike. His regime was overthrown by a military coup in April 1985. Early signs indicate modification of Numeiri's extreme pro-American orientation. Meanwhile, the intractable conflict in Chad persists against a backdrop of drought-related famine that has begun to resemble the tragedy in Ethiopia.

In northwestern Africa, the United States is aligned with the quasi-constitutionalist regime of King Hassan II of Morocco. Hence the United States has given diplomatic support and military assistance to Morocco in its decade-long war of annexation against the independence movement of Western (formerly Spanish) Sahara—Polisario. However, the likelihood of a military solution to the conflict is minimal. Morocco controls valuable phosphate mines and most of the settled population of the territory within "sand walls" that have been equipped with electronic detection devices and stretch for more than 800 miles from Algeria to the Atlantic Ocean. Beyond the walls, motorized guerrillas roam the desert at will.

As in the case of Chad, American initiatives for peace have been muted or suppressed in deference to the sensibilities of a geopolitical ally. Meanwhile, serious proposals for political compromise have emanated from Algeria, Polisario's patron state. Counterinsurgency warfare is a dangerous weapon, known to backfire when soldiers and citizens come to the end of their patience with costly, inconclusive, and demoralizing exertions on behalf of imperial ambitions. Should that fate befall the Moroccan monarchy, the United States would be out on a limb, as it was in 1974, when enlightened soldiers deposed the imperial dictatorship of Portugal.

REFERENCES

Committee on Foreign Affairs. 1984. U.S. House of Representatives. *The Impact of U.S. Foreign Policy on Seven African Countries.* Washington, D.C.: U.S. Government Printing Office.

Hirschman, Albert O. 1977. *The Passions and the Interests.* Princeton: Princeton University Press.

11

The Zairian Crisis and American Foreign Policy

CRAWFORD YOUNG

Zaïre as a title for epic tragedy first became familiar to European salons 250 years ago, with the presentation of the Voltaire play of that name. In this drama, Zaïre is a lovely slave maiden unaware of her noble antecedents, in bondage to the Saracen king of Jerusalem. She willingly submits to her fate, all the more when her master declares his love for her. This idyll is disrupted by the appearance of Zaïre's brother, bearing her ransom. Torn between the discovery of her own birthright and her new bondage of affection to the king, Zaïre hesitates. Her master, mistaking her brother for a rival lover, murders Zaïre in a jealous rage, then takes his own life on discovering his error (Roberts 1979).

The curiously prophetic ring of this plot as metaphor for Zairian-American relations requires no elaboration. Probably Reagan and Mobutu would both chafe at their symbolic transformation into Saracen prince and ravishing slave maiden respectively. The imagery is captivating nonetheless.

Circumstance has indeed produced a close and long-standing linkage between Zaire and the United States. The sudden and unexpected surge to independence in 1960 triggered improvised American plans to make the Congo a showcase for its newly launched African aid program. When "crisis" and "chaos" intervened, the United States became the principal force underpinning the U.N. operation, and the primary external patron of struggling Kinshasa regimes. The 1965 Mobutu coup which swept away the First Republic occurred with American blessing (to put the matter modestly). Mobutu's quest for personal, centralized authoritarianism enjoyed unstinting American backing, and the United States basked with Mobutu in the brief sunlight of his triumphant hegemony at the beginning of the 1970s. The decade of decline since 1973 has been punctuated by occasional episodes of tension, with longer periods of ineffectual and sometimes despairing American solicitude for the ailing client.

Map 4.   *Zaire*

A short decade ago, almost no one recognized that Zaire was teetering upon the precipice of a crisis so deep that no upward pathway is remotely within view. From the summit of veneration as world-historical figure and national success story to the abyss of general derision as paradigmatic case of venality and failure, the fall was far and fast. The once plausible claims of a rendezvous with abundance in the 1980s became a grim jest. Our examination of Zairian-American relations will focus on this decade of crisis. The stage must first be set by a brief review of the 1960–65 period.

American Involvement in Zaire in the Sixties

The circumstances of Zairian independence brought overwhelming American involvement within days of the transfer of sovereignty. The Belgian *pari congolais,* a formula for transfer of power in the political organs (ministers, parliamentarians) while Belgian personnel continued to run the administration and army, foundered within five days. With Belgium utterly discredited internationally and within Zaire, Zairian leaders, desperate at the prospective disintegration of their country, appealed in all directions for help. Within a few days, such pleas for intervention and assistance went to the United States, the United Nations, and the Soviet Union.

Cold war tensions were high, and American policy thought was pervaded by the specter of "Soviet expansion." Castro was moving steadily toward Soviet alignment, the Sino-Soviet split was not yet fully apparent, the Berlin issue was at fever pitch, and John Kennedy was campaigning for president on the (false) claim that a "missile gap" existed. From the Washington perspective, the greatest danger in the Congo crisis was the emergence of a power vacuum in which the mercurial and unpredictable Zairian prime minister, Patrice Lumumba, would invite a Soviet takeover.

The United States intervened vigorously on two fronts. The Zairian appeal for American troops was declined, in favor of recourse to the United Nations. At the same time, the United States escalated its diplomatic and intelligence action to construct a coalition of Zairian leaders and factions hostile to Communist penetration and Soviet guidance.

On the United Nations front, the United States counted upon its ability to mount a coalition of Western and moderate Third World states in the governing institutions of the United Nations (the General Assembly and especially the Security Council) to constitute an international military force with mandates allowing it to "hold the ring" and thus preempt direct Soviet intervention, while avoiding its becoming an instrument for power consolidation of the most radical elements in the confused nationalism of 1960. By late July 1960, a hastily assembled U.N. force comprised the dominant military factor in the country, and it sealed off Zaire from bilateral armed intervention. The United Nations was by no means entirely at American bidding, and U.S. aims had to be tailored to win the support or at least acquiescence of such key Afro-

Asian states as Ghana, Tunisia, and India. However, American influence remained strong at all levels of the U.N. machinery, and additional leverage derived from the American role as primary paymaster for the Congo operation (about $100 million per year).

With the United Nations providing an umbrella, American diplomacy moved aggressively to induce a stabilization of the political situation by some formula which would minimize Soviet influence. In the months before the sudden 1960 independence, various external forces—public and private—were busy recruiting a clientèle, especially among the Congolese studying abroad. Political notables attracted—sought or unsought—networks of foreign advisers, a number of whom had their own intelligence or mercantile connections. The CIA was one active participant in this game of building access points to the Zairian political arena.

By mid-August 1960, the United States became convinced that Lumumba was unreliable, and an instrument of Soviet policy. This conviction is recorded in the crucial August 18 dispatch from CIA station chief Lawrence Devlin:

> Embassy and Station believe Congo experience classic Communist takeover Government.... Whether or not Lumumba actually Commie or just playing Commie game to assist his solidifying power, anti-west forces rapidly increasing power Congo and there may be little time left in which take action to avoid another Cuba. (Weissman 1978)

Through a combination of Zairian opposition, CIA stimulus, and U.N. acquiescence, Lumumba was ousted as prime minister by President Joseph Kasavubu on September 5, 1960. This ill-planned operation did not include clear provision for an alternative government, and led nine days later to the proclamation by Army Chief of Staff Mobutu that both Kasavubu and Lumumba were "neutralized," and that an interim "College of Commissioners" was installed. With Kasavubu's residual constitutionality as president covering this undertaking and providing a legal basis for U.N. cooperation with the new power-holders, an anti-Lumumba regime slowly consolidated a relative grasp on authority in the capital. Key members of the new team were in close contact with the American embassy, beginning with Mobutu himself—with whom Devlin had established a fruitful relationship in Brussels several months before independence.

Space precludes a recapitulation of the complex sequence of events through which a constitutionally legalized regime, with Cyrille Adoula as premier, emerged in August 1961. Léopoldville (later called Kinshasa) only slowly reestablished a precarious authority over the entire country; this was particularly true of the eastern regions, where Lumumbism was strong, and the breakaway province of Katanga, the secession of which was nullified by U.N. military action in January 1963. For our present purposes, the decisive pattern established was an enduring relationship of patronage and sponsorship by the United States for the successive incumbents in Kinshasa. This protective linkage lies at the root of durable perceptions in Zaire and abroad that, for better or for worse, the configuration of power in Kinshasa was an American design, if not imposition. In American policy circles, it created an enduring sense of "responsibility" for Zairian stability and development.

Within the United States, the dénouement of the Congo crisis was portrayed as a major defeat for the Soviet Union. This view appears to have been shared in Moscow, which failed to project its power effectively in support of revolutionary forces. As a result of the perception by the politically victorious Zairian coalition that its adversaries had enjoyed Soviet backing, however, anti-Sovietism became entrenched as a constant in Zairian diplomacy. No Zairian head of state or prime minister has ever paid a state visit to Moscow—though most other significant countries in the world have been thus honored. On virtually every important occasion of major challenge to the regime, the Soviet Union or its allies have been charged with responsibility (the 1964–65 rebellions, 1969 and 1971 student disturbances, and 1977 and 1978 Shaba invasions). Further reinforcing the anti-Soviet theme in Zairian diplomacy was the opening to China with the spectacular Mobutu state visit to Beijing in January 1973.

Other noteworthy milestones in the deepening American commitment to Zaire are found in Washington's response to the 1964–65 rebellions, the presidential contest between Moise Tshombe and Kasavubu in 1965, and the mercenary revolts in 1966 and 1967. Through intelligence channels, the United States provided important military succor to the Zairian armed forces, which in July 1964 were on the verge of disintegration and panic before insurgent advances. In 1965, the American embassy was in close touch with Mobutu in the weeks leading up to his November coup. Historical evidence currently available does not permit one to go beyond the conclusion by Weissman (1978, 394) that the CIA "was involved" in the Mobutu takeover. Whatever the suppressed details may be, the critical point is the belief in Zaire and elsewhere that the United States was godfather to the Second Republic. In 1967, the United States supplied three C–130s and support personnel to buttress the airlift capacity of the Zairian armed forces in their eventually successful campaign against mutinied mercenary and former Katanga gendarme units. This last concrete gesture produced a barrage of congressional criticism, and led President Johnson to declare that America "would not again get so involved in Africa except out of the most overwhelming necessity" (Lake 1976, 120).

Another episode with enduring emotional impact was American complicity in the assassination of Lumumba in January 1961. It is not clear that the CIA actually participated in the final murder, but its involvement in a series of unsuccessful attempts to remove him during fall 1960 is amply documented

(U.S. Congress 1975). Though softened by time, the shadow of this tragedy lingers yet upon the political landscape.

In the deepening of the Zairian-American relationship in the first decade of independence it is worth remarking that the determinants were almost exclusively political. The diplomatic and intelligence community pursued a policy aimed at consolidating the power of a "moderate" regime, and excluding Soviet (and initially Chinese) influence, unconstrained by pressures from important economic interests. Thus from the outset American policy firmly opposed the Katanga secession; the political importance of Zaire as a whole far outweighed the pleas of anticommunist solidarity by the Katanga regime, and concern for the mining interests—despite some small, indirect U.S. holdings—played no part at all. A feeble "Katanga lobby" appeared on the political right, but it had no significant backing from Wall Street. The "strategic minerals" argument that surfaced in the late 1970s had yet to make its appearance. Other small American interests in Zaire—notably in Forminière—had no perceptible impact. Probably the most concrete American interest group—outside the purely political realm—was the substantial American Protestant missionary population. They were above all preoccupied with the security of their personnel and restoration of sufficient order to permit continuation of their labors. Most were frightened and offended by the aggressiveness of the political language of Lumumbism, and thus wholeheartedly supported official promotion of "moderate" authority in Kinshasa.

U.S. Policy toward Zaire during the Mobutu Era

The texture of the relationship changed in several ways during the short-lived epoch of triumphant Mobutism from 1969 to 1973. In the early period of his reign, Mobutu remained receptive to detailed advice, both from his close political associates from First Republic days, and from trusted external sources—American, Belgian, French. Apparently he continued to draw a CIA retainer until about 1969 (Weissman 1978, 394). By the end of the 1960s, those dealing with Mobutu had to disguise their counsel with sycophantic praise; increasingly self-confident, and obsessively susceptible to perceived affronts to his dignity, the president was no longer so malleable as in the early 1960s.

By this time, the regime had also become much less dependent on external aid. Large numbers of Zairians were returning from the overseas universities, and growing cohorts graduated from the Zairian universities; the days of acute shortages of formally qualified personnel in virtually every field were over. The 1967 economic stabilization plan had brought inflation and public finances for the first time under relative control. The currency was convertible, foreign exchange accounts in balance, and the heavy colonial debt incurred in the final Belgian years shed by inflation and negotiation.

Symptomatic of the changing times was the style and role of Sheldon Vance, the American ambassador during the 1969–73 period. He developed finely honed skills in catering to Mobutu's sensitivities, maintaining access through arm-stroking rather than paternal advice. Much of his energy was devoted to serving as spokesman in Washington for Mobutu and salesman for Zaire. He believed that the Second Republic was a major showcase for American assistance; Zaire was no longer a dependent liability, but a potential regional leader, with the size and power to serve as a gendarme for Central Africa. He earnestly courted the financial and multinational milieux, offering apparently convincing arguments concerning the investment opportunities in Zaire. With vast Zairian mineral wealth, impressive energy and agricultural potential, and a stable government in healthy financial condition, Vance had a plausible brief.

During these years the Zairian-American relationship acquired an important economic dimension. Extensive lending occurred from international syndicates of banks, with several large American banks (Citibank in particular) leading the way. The most visible investment project was an American-led consortium (though American equity was only 30 percent), which won a heated bidding contest for access to some exceptionally rich copper ore deposits, organized by Maurice Tempelsman, scion of an Antwerp diamond merchant who had transferred his operations to New York. A confidant and patron of Mobutu since 1959, Tempelsman was also a generous political contributor to American candidates of both major parties. His consortium, Société Minière du Tenge-Fungurume (SMTF), promised an investment of $250 million. In fact, SMTF never really came into production; it was mothballed after much of the initial capital was sunk in 1976, because of the poor copper price prospects.

In both the natural resource and manufacturing fields, there was at this juncture the appearance of a truly massive investment inflow. Ambassador Andrew Young in 1979 claimed that the United States had nearly $2 billion invested in Zaire, a figure that was widely bandied about. Actually, the total real investment was little more than 10 percent of that figure (Pachter 1982).

Gulf signed a thirty-year offshore oil agreement with 50 percent equity in 1973; production began in 1975, and peaked at about 26,000 barrels per day the following year. The illusion of much greater resource investment was fostered by reports and rumors of exploratory ventures: Texaco and Exxon oil prospecting in potentially attractive areas of the central basin; Union Carbide seeking titanium and other rare metals in the Kivu area; Bethlehem Steel participating in a Union Minière consortium bidding against the Tempelsman combine for Shaba mineral concessions; Kaiser and Reynold Aluminum considering aluminum smelters on the coast to use power from the Inga Dam. None of these investments materialized.

Several small plants were created by major American corporations. The largest was a tire factory established by Goodyear, representing a $20 million investment (though claimed by Mobutu as ultimately worth $80 million when hypothetical future rubber plantation development was added). The Goodyear plant has employed 400 to 450 workers since it came on line in the early 1970s; much of its materials were imported, and the economic crisis crippled its operations by making foreign exchange for these inputs difficult to obtain. Goodyear would prefer to close the plant, which operates at less than 20 percent of capacity, but has been under strong embassy as well as Zairian pressure to keep limping along (Pachter 1982). Continental Grain opened a flour mill in Matadi, the operations of which are in good part assured by PL 480 wheat, and profitable markets guaranteed by the massive shift of taste preference in Kinshasa to wheat-based (rather than manioc-based) bread. The start-up costs for Continental Grain were only $8.5 million, of which 72 percent were bank and supplier credits. In addition, there was a small General Motors assembly plant in Kinshasa (the one once announced by Ford never materialized), a bottle cap factory in Lubumbashi owned by Crown Cork, and a few other small undertakings.

Aside from bank loans, by far the biggest American economic involvement has been in the form of contracted services, which tended in the official imagination to be assimilated to "investment"—a phenomenon Benoit Verhaegen (1978) has labeled "technological imperialism." Because the profit occurs on the transaction, and does not depend on the long-term viability of the economic activity, the risk is shifted to Zairian political society, and the benefits divided by the foreign corporation and Zairian political leaders who collect lucrative rents on the contracts. The hordes of corporate salesmen who crowded the lobby of the Inter-Continental Hotel in the early 1970s were primarily attracted by the scent of enormous public sector contracts and equipment sales. McDonnell-Douglas sold two DC–10s to Air Zaire (Eximbank financed, lubricated—allegedly—by a $600,000 commission to Bank of Zaire Director Sambwa Pida)(Pachter 1982, 14). Westinghouse peddled generators ($160 million) for the second stage of the Inga Dam. ITT-Bell and Pan-American scooped up management contracts for two of the most notoriously unreliable public services, the telephone system, and the national airline, Air Zaire.

The serried ranks of buccaneering contract-peddlers had hopes of other giant state projects which largely aborted: a new port at Banana, estimated by 1980 as likely to cost close to $1 billion; an extension of the rail net from Luebo to Kinshasa, and Matadi to Banana, that would probably cost a similar sum in contemporary dollars; other transportation infrastructure, and much more. The one that did get sold, a "white dinosaur" of epic dimensions, was the Inga-Shaba direct-current 1,800-kilometer power transmission line. Its initially estimated cost of $250 million ballooned during construction to roughly $1 billion; its initial completion target date of 1976 was missed by six years. In the interim, Gécamines expansion plans stalled and SMTF was moth-balled, removing from the picture its projected consumers. Its technology was unproven, and its operating and maintenance costs had been greatly underestimated. Rather than delivering cheap and abundant power for energy-intensive smelting operations, it provided exceptionally expensive power (70–80 mills, as compared to 4–6 paid by Kaiser to the Volta Dam Authority in Ghana) which no one needed. It began operating in mid–1982 and had to be closed down for several months by early 1983; Zaire lacked the technological capacity to keep it running, and the expensive hard-currency costs of hiring a foreign contractor to manage it (perhaps $30 million annually) are a heavy drain (Huybrechts et al. 1981; Willame 1981).

Responsibility for this colossal miscalculation does not rest upon the Mobutu regime alone. The project was actively promoted by the private interests tied to the SMTF enterprise; once its political attractiveness to Zaire became evident, the American embassy as well gave it strong support—partly to ensure that the prime contractor was American. Morrison-Knudsen did emerge victorious in a heated competition for this rich prize. While this Idaho-based international contracting corporation had received negative publicity on the project, and perhaps has incurred losses on the final stages of the construction, it also collected substantial management fees, and was provided a laboratory for the perfection of relatively untested power transmission techniques.

This deepening American involvement in the crucial economic choices of the Mobutu regime had important consequences. As partner in the elaboration of a development strategy that proved catastrophically wrong, the United States acquired responsibilities that could not easily be shed. In subtle yet vital ways, these strands of involvement intertwined with the earlier bonds forged in the American engagement in the 1960 crisis, then in the initial power seizure by the Mobutu regime. When Zaire became a disaster area in the late 1970s, the United States inherited its share of the blame, and an inescapable obligation to participate in the salvage efforts.

An interlude of relative tension ruffled American-Zairian relations in the 1973–75 period. With the departure of Ambassador Vance in late 1973, Mobutu lost an influential advocate. His successor, Deane Hinton (subsequently ambassador in El Salvador), was by personal disposition and departmental instructions less inclined to cultivate the degree of deferential intimacy with Mobutu that Vance enjoyed. Mobutu nursed grandiose ambitions of African leadership, and needed to distance himself from American patronage. He used the occasion of a U.N. speech on October 4, 1973, to proclaim his rupture with Israel (two days before the Yom Kippur War), triggering an African chain reaction—and greatly angering Secretary of State Henry Kissinger, who in general took little note of Mobutu (mentioning him only once in the first two volumes of his memoirs). The U.S. embassy at Kinshasa was dazed by the shrillness of regime pronouncements, and the scope of its seizure of foreign assets in the "Zairianization," "radicalization," and corollary measures (though almost no American property, except petroleum distribution networks, was affected). In January 1975, Mobutu used the forum of an African-American Institute conference to accuse then Assistant Secretary of State for African Affairs Nathaniel Davis of being an architect of destabilization, and later that year forced the withdrawal of Ambassador Hinton (he had earlier used the persona non grata device to rid himself of Ambassador McMurtrie Godley in 1966, deemed too close to former premier Tshombe). In June 1975, he accused the CIA of fomenting a military coup against him, and even planning his "physical liquidation."

Parallel interests in Washington and Kinshasa in thwarting the triumph of the *Movimento Popular de Libertação de Angola* (MPLA) in the Angolan civil war rapidly healed the breach. By August 1975, Zairian units were already committed across the border, with CIA operatives in liaison with them (Stockwell 1978). Vance was urgently dispatched on a fence-mending mission, and Zaire was assigned a ranking ambassador more to Mobutu's taste, Richard Cutler. The shared humiliation at the fiasco of their efforts, and the common stigma attached to their collaboration with South Africa in the anti-MPLA struggle also contributed to the restoration of closer links. Angola hopelessly tarnished Mobutu's bid for African leadership. With the exposure of South African and CIA military involvement in the Angolan civil war, the OAU consensus shifted from support for a coalition of the three major Angolan insurgent groups to backing of the MPLA and acceptance of the decisive Soviet-Cuban intervention in its support. Zairian standing in Africa was further compromised by Mobutu's support for Cabindan separatists. This outcome all but eliminated the Third World alternative for Zairian diplomacy; Mobutu had little option but to return to his American dependent partnership, attenuated by his courting French patronage as well.

The deepening economic crisis by 1975 was pushing in the same direction. By late 1975, it was clear that Zaire was bankrupt. Rescheduling negotiations with both public and private creditors was imperative. Mobutu initially hoped to secure these facilities on the strength of his past political partnership, without recourse to the irritating scrutiny and supervision of the IMF, but this was out of the question for both public and private creditors. In March 1976, an initial agreement was reached with the IMF on a "stabilization program," which paved the way for June and November 1976 rescheduling accords. Among the conditions was a rollback of the Zairianization and radicalization measures; the expropriated enterprises affected were by this time mostly in a sorry shambles, and "retrocession" encountered little internal opposition, except from a handful of the Zairian beneficiaries of the asset distribution.

The fragility of the Zairian political system was exposed in March 1977, when a few thousand lightly armed Zairian exiled insurgents invaded Shaba from Angolan bases. The Zairian security forces seemed unable to stem their advance, and for a brief moment the regime appeared on the verge of panic and dissolution. The immediate military threat was ended through airborne intervention of Moroccan troops, with active French logistical assistance, and more distant and ambivalent American backing. The new Carter administration Africanist team was in the process of reconsidering its African priorities, and was disposed to downgrade Mobutu from his earlier status as regional point of support for American policy. The American response was accurately described by interim Assistant Secretary of State for African Affairs William Schaufele as "limited and measured."

A second invasion effort in 1978, which actually captured the key mining center of Kolwezi, brought a swifter and more direct Western reaction. On the debatable ground that the lives of the substantial expatriate community were endangered, French Foreign Legion and Belgian paratroop units landed in Kolwezi to rout the insurgents, who lacked both military strategy and political program. The massive Soviet-Cuban involvement in Ethiopia intervened between Shaba I and Shaba II, producing a more anti-Soviet psychosis in Washington, and a greater disposition to see the hand of Havana and Moscow in African events. This mood produced more direct and active American support for the military measures to crush the insurgents.

Reform Efforts

By 1977, the initial illusions that the Zairian crisis was merely a short-term downturn which could be bridged with stop-gap assistance began to dissipate. A strategy emerged in Washington for pursuing "reform" simultaneously in the political and economic realm. Politically, Mobutu was encouraged to mitigate personalist autocracy by creating a prime minister post, and by "opening up" a space for political dialogue through giving more latitude for the national legislature to debate issues of public policy. Economically, Zaire would receive aid and support in dealings with its restless creditors, in return for cooperating with the IMF, and accepting expatriate advisers and monitors at key points in the flow channels of public resources (central bank, finance ministry, customs service).

Mobutu, who by this time had developed impressive skills in the diplomacy of dependency, apparently accepted the "reform" proposals, and indeed seemed to extend their scope farther than had been anticipated. He announced that a majority of the Popular Movement of the Revolution (MPR) Political Bureau seats would be thrown open to election, as well as all parliamentary seats and urban councils. A respected intellectual, Mpinga Kasenda, was named as prime minister. Mobutu went well beyond the Tanzanian single party election formula, permitting unlimited numbers of candidates for each seat—thus drawing into the race an average of ten contestants for each vacancy. Though it was soon apparent that Prime Minister Mpinga was utterly without power or influence, the elections themselves provided months of public distraction, and until 1980, parliamentarians were permitted to embarrass ministers with "interpellations." It was during this period that a parliamentary commission extracted information from the Bank of Zaire concerning the $150 million diversion of foreign exchange by the Mobutu family, publicly revealed by defected ex-premier Nguza Karl-i-Bond in September 1981 (U.S. Congress 1981).

An international team of "plumbers" arrived about this time to seal the leaks in the financial system. Most prominent among them was Erwin Blumenthal, a West German central banker who quickly earned the nickname "Bula Matari" for his energetic efforts to combat illicit foreign exchange transactions by leading regime dignitaries. For a brief moment, Blumenthal seemed to have some success; within less than two years, he abandoned the mission in utter despair, and in 1982 recorded the failure of his mission in an explosive report apparently leaked by Mobutu himself to discredit leading Belgian figures allegedly compromised financially in Zairian dealings. "There was and there is yet," wrote Blumenthal, "a single major obstacle which annihilates all prospects of recovery: the CORRUPTION of the ruling group" (Info Zaire 1982, 9).

During 1977–1978, the "reform" campaign enjoyed some credibility; on the American side, it was vigorously pursued by Ambassador Cutler, and in Washington by an old Zaire hand, then Deputy Assistant Secretary of State for African Affairs Lannon Walker. In early 1979, in Senate hearings on additional Eximbank funding of the latest Inga-Shaba cost overrun, Walker was able to claim headway on several fronts:

> Since mid–1977, Zaire has been engaged in the first steps of a long process of liberalizing its political system and has begun to decentralize authority and responsibility. Elections have been held at the levels of the urban zone, the national legislature and the party and the party political bureau. President Mobutu has instituted the office of Prime Minister and named the able ex-president of the national Legislative Council to fill it. The Legislative Council itself has shown encouraging signs of activity and independence.

Walker cited headway on human rights, diplomatic reconciliations with Angola, and reorganization of the armed forces. He claimed that "significant progress has been made on economic reform in support of economic recovery." Though Walker conceded that overall progress on reform was mixed, he found "the outlook nonetheless encouraging" (U.S. Congress 1979).

Conviction on this front was waning, however. When Thomas Oakley took over as ambassador to Kinshasa in 1979, he concluded that political change was unlikely, but that U.S. influence could still be brought to bear on economic matters. There was indeed a short-lived improvement in 1980.

Copper prices recovered from their 1975 nadir to 90 cents a pound in 1979, and 99 cents in 1980, appearing to confirm the perennially optimistic prognostics in official Washington. (They fell back to 79 cents in 1981, and 68 cents in 1982) (Pachter 1982). Blumenthal attributes the 1980 recovery to Mobutu's absence from the country most of the year, permitting the then prime minister (Nguza), the finance ministry, and central bank officials to work without interference (Info Zaire 1982, 6). The window of recovery in 1980 permitted a major $912 million SDR (special drawing rights) IMF financing agreement in 1981.

By 1982, illusions of economic reform were again shattered. Zaire was hopelessly out of compliance with its engagements to the IMF, and the dilapidation of public resources continued unabated. This led by early 1982 to a suspension by the IMF of further advances, and a new impasse with external creditors. Now, however, the Zaire debt question was eclipsed by the vastly more important Latin American crises.

The advent of the Reagan administration offered a new opening to the Mobutu regime in its ceaseless search for external assistance: the concept of anti-Soviet "strategic consensus" as a passe-partout foreign policy guide by Secretary of State Alexander Haig. Various personalities associated with the Reagan foreign policy team were on record during the campaign with statements sympathetic to Mobutu as an embattled pro-Western leader. Kenneth Adelman had written a dissertation on Zaire which compared the MPR to other major religions in Zaire. He had also publicly called for greater understanding of Zaire's difficulties (Adelman 1975), as had Assistant Secretary of State Chester Crocker. Mobutu's anti-Soviet credentials were excellent. In addition, Zaire had won a seat on the U.N. Security Council, where its voting behavior could not fail to win the admiration of Ambassador Jeane Kirkpatrick.

By this time, however, skepticism about Zaire under Mobutu's stewardship had become so widespread that sources of additional assistance became difficult to find. Increases in military and security assistance were recommended by the administration, but "selling Zaire" on Capitol Hill had become almost impossible. A constant barrage of unflattering information came to light. Mobutu spent at least $2 million in 1982 taking an entourage of ninety-three, many of them close relatives in mourning for recently deceased senior kinsman (and vintage embezzler) Litho Maboti, to Disney World in Florida, aboard a chartered aircraft. A harshly critical Senate staff report in 1982 recited many instances of Mobutu regime corruption, and concluded that "it is widely accepted that he has managed to amass a legendary personal fortune at the nation's expense" (U.S. Congress 1982, 1). Word of the contents of this report led Mobutu to announce melodramatically in May 1982 that he was refusing additional American aid, a threat that quietly vanished from the record. Mobutu's hopes were momentarily revived during 1982 by official visits by Ambassador Kirkpatrick and Vice President Bush, both of whom were evidently charmed into issuing statements calling for reinforced aid for Zaire. One may doubt whether these ill-considered statements will have any real impact. They certainly do not reflect the views of the working-level diplomatic bureaucracy.

The Present Impasse

What shall we conclude about the nature of American interests in Zaire? They were essentially political in origin, and they remain predominantly so. The large-scale involvement in Zairian affairs had its genesis in the 1960 crisis, and a series of landmark episodes served to deepen and institutionalize it (the rebellions and American involvement in the takeover and consolidation of the Mobutu regime). There is probably no country in Africa where CIA action has been so extensive; retired former Kinshasa state chief Devlin, in recent years a well-remunerated representative of Tempelsman in Kinshasa, continues to offer Mobutu a direct channel to Washington outside the diplomatic hierarchy. The heavy burden of the past, the pervasive sense of American responsibility for Zaire, its regime, and some of its worst errors (Angola, Inga-Shaba), make the option of disengagement difficult of execution.

The economic interests, overall, are relatively small, and have not increased in recent years. Amoco Minerals has bailed out of the SMTF combine, leaving no significant American participation (except the 2 percent allocated to Tempelsman). The age of the giant development contract is over; Morrison-Knudsen has finished Inga-Shaba, Westinghouse has installed its turbines, and Pan-American has withdrawn from its Air Zaire management services. There remain only the banks holding the Zaire debt. This was syndicated over a large number of institutions; the most deeply involved was Citibank, which according to one of its vice presidents, has no more than $30 million of its own funds that are not publicly guaranteed in one way or another. There were fears in 1975, in the wake of the failures of the Franklin Bank and United States Bank of San Diego, that a Zairian default might cause turbulence among some major banks. These anxieties with relation to Zaire no longer count for very much; the Zairian debt is a very small part of a much larger picture.

In the late 1970s, a debate emerged over the issue of access to strategic minerals. Zaire is the major supplier of industrial diamonds and cobalt on the international markets. The 1980 Santini Report argued the dependence of Western economies on the continued supply of a series of strategic minerals found in southern Africa (U.S. Congress 1980). However, other analysts cast doubt on alarmists' forecasts of possible interruption of supply (Pachter 1982). No Zairian regime, whatever its political complexion, could afford to deny itself the foreign exchange that sales of these commodities provide; nor does the Soviet Union provide an alternative market. The one scenario which might bring disruption of supply of these minerals would be prolonged civil strife—improbable, but not impossible.

One final aspect of the American-Zairian relationship deserving brief mention lies in the military sphere. One of the constants of the Mobutu era has been simultaneous processes of "reform" of the military, and its undermining by politically motivated purges. The 1982 Senate staff report noted this paradox:

> As bad as the military situation may be, some critics have concluded that Mobutu deliberately seeks to frustrate real improvement or even to make it worse. In this view, Mobutu believes that strength at the top is best preserved by perpetuating weakness at the bottom. Thus, as with his cabinet, Mobutu has a benign view of corruption and engages in regular military personnel shifts and sackings. (U.S. Congress 1982, 4)

Since Shaba II, two units (the 21st and 31st brigades) have been reorganized with Belgian and French advisers, respectively; these units are more reliable than the others, and provide an ultimate guarantee to the regime. As the same report observes, "foreign military intervention for Mobutu remains more prestigious and reliable, less expensive, and far less challenging to his leadership than a well commanded and organized military program within Zaire. . . . Conspicuous evidence of Western support has a symbolic value which far exceeds the actual number of foreign personnel involved" (U.S. Congress 1982, 5). In an incisive paper, Michael Shafer (1982) argued that American military assistance to Zaire had been essentially symbolic. From 1971 to 1981, American military aid to Zaire totaled $64 million, more than half of which was spent on seven C–130s and 30 Cessnas. Much of the rest was spent in a losing struggle to keep these aircraft in the air. No more than three of the C–130s now fly; two crashed on smuggling runs, one is used as a presidential aircraft, and one is apparently primarily assigned to airlifting cobalt to Belgium for Mobutu's personal account (Shafer 1982). The sole importance of this aid is the impression it fosters, especially within Zaire, that Mobutu enjoys the backing of powerful external patrons.

In sum, American relations with Zaire are at an impasse. The United States has undeniable responsibilities in Zaire, but a formula for constructively fulfilling them eludes analysis. Hope for reform of the present regime is impossible to sustain. Mobutu, meanwhile, turns the very weakness of the regime and decay of the state into assets for his own survival. These basic facts serve to foster the credibility of the "Mobutu or chaos" argument, which has—so far—always brought enough Western support in the face of any serious challenge to sustain the regime. By repressing, dividing, and coopting potential opposition, the regime succeeds in preserving near total uncertainty abroad as to the shape of an alternative political formula, or how it might come into existence. This leaves ample play for the diplomatic community—by instinct and training disposed to short-term risk aversion—to prefer a hopeless present to an unknowable future. Thus, the Mobutu regime can still extract reluctant, limited, but sufficient backing when mortal peril arises. The crisis—insoluble—continues.

REFERENCES

Adelman, Kenneth Lee. 1975. *The Influence of Religion on National Integration in Zaire.* Doctoral dissertation, Georgetown University.

Huybrechts, Andre et al. 1981. *Du Congo au Zaïre 1960–1980.* Brussels: Centre de Recherche et d'Information Socio-Politiques.

Info Zaire. 1982. *Le rapport Blumenthal & Annexes.* Brussels.

Lake, Anthony. 1976. *The "Tar-Baby" Option: American Policy Toward Southern Rhodesia.* New York: Columbia University Press.

Pachter, Elise. 1982. "The Economic Component of U.S.–Zaire Relations." Paper presented at the 25th Annual Meetings of the African Studies Association. November. Washington, D.C.

Roberts, Allen F. 1979. "'The Ransom of Ill-Starred Zaire': Plunder, Politics, and Poverty in the OTRAG Concession," pp. 213–236 in Guy Gran, ed. *Zaire: The Political Economy of Underdevelopment.* New York: Praeger.

Shafer, Michael. 1982. "United States Military Assistance to Zaire." Paper presented at the 25th Annual Meetings of the African Studies Association. November. Washington, D.C.

Stockwell, John. 1978. *In Search of Enemies.* New York: W. W. Norton.

U.S. Congress. 1975. *Interim Report: Alleged Assassination Plots Involving Foreign Leaders.* Senate, Select Committee to Study Governmental Operations with Respect to Intelligence Activities, 94th Congress, 1st Session, November 20.

———. 1979. *U.S. Bank Loans to Zaire.* Senate, Committee on Banking, Housing, and Urban Affairs, Subcommittee on International Finance, Hearing, 96th Congress, 1st Session, May 24.

———. 1980. *Sub-Saharan Africa: Its Role in Critical Mineral Needs of the Western World.* House of Representatives, 96th Congress, 2nd Session, July.

———. 1981. *Political and Economic Situation in Zaire—Fall 1981.* House of Representatives, Committee on Foreign Affairs, Subcommittee on Africa, Hearing, 97th Congress, 1st Session, September 15.

———. 1982. *Zaire.* Senate, Committee on Foreign Relations, Staff Report, 97th Congress, 2nd Session, July.

Verhaegen, Benoit. 1978. "Universities, Social Classes, and Economic-Dependency." Paper presented at the Conference on the African University and Development. August. Bellagio, Italy.

Weissman, Stephen. 1978. "The CIA and U.S. Policy in Zaire and Angola," pp. 381–432 in René Lemarchand, ed. *American Policy in Southern Africa.* Washington, D.C.: University Press of America.

Willame, Jean-Claude. 1981. "Le saga d'Inga." *Cahiers du CEDAF,* 5–6.

12

United States Policy
toward Zaire

NZONGOLA-NTALAJA

This study of U.S. involvement in Zairian affairs deals with determinants as well as effects. It attempts to show that given the overriding American objective to counter or preempt Soviet influence in central and southern Africa, U.S. involvement in Zaire is a major factor of the continuing crisis of the Zairian state and society. To illustrate this point, the paper analyzes U.S. policy in each of the two major periods of postcolonial Zairian history: (1) 1960–65, the period of the "Congo Crisis," and (2) 1965 to the present, the period of the Mobutu regime.[1]

The United States and the Congo Crisis, 1960–65

What became known as the "Congo Crisis" was a period of instability and civil war that began with the mutiny of the armed forces on July 5, 1960, five days after the proclamation of independence. It all started with General Emile Janssens, commander of the *Force Publique*, the colonial army, who had been kept at his post by the new government of independent Congo. Speaking to soldiers assembled at the main army camp in Léopoldville on July 4, he told them that there would be no changes in the army as a result of independence. At this time, there was not a single Congolese above the rank of warrant officer (*adjudant*), and the general was fully aware of the widespread feeling of betrayal among soldiers, who felt that they were being denied a fair share of the fruits of independence.

1. For reasons of historical authenticity, the name of the country and all place names are retained as they were known during the particular period discussed in the text. The country's name was changed on October 27, 1971, from "Congo" to "Zaire." The current names of the cities and provinces mentioned in the text are given here in parentheses: Leopoldville (Kinshasa), Katanga (Shaba), South Kasai (now part of Eastern Kasai), Bakwanga (Mbuji-Mayi), Stanleyville (Kisangani), Thysville (Mbanza-Ngungu), Elisabethville (Lubumbashi), Paulis (Isiro), Kongo Central (Bas-Zaire). Lovanium University is now the University of Kinshasa.

The mutineers demanded promotions, salary increases, and the dismissal of all Belgian officers. As the mutiny began to spread all over the country, President Joseph Kasa-Vubu and Prime Minister Patrice Lumumba made several trips into the interior with the hope of restoring law and order. They also considered several options with regard to foreign military assistance in order to achieve this goal. These included U.S. military assistance, which was in fact requested without Lumumba's knowledge by the supposedly "communist" Deputy Prime Minister Antoine Gizenga.

The situation changed for the worse on July 10, with the intervention of Belgian troops. The officially stated goal of this unilateral intervention was the protection of European lives and property. But the first concrete results of the Belgian aggression were the secession of the mineral-rich province of Katanga, which was made possible by the Belgian military occupation of all the strategic locations within the province, and the killing of a large number of innocent citizens at Matadi. The secession was proclaimed on July 11, one day after the Belgian intervention.

On July 12, Lumumba and Kasa-Vubu appealed to the United Nations for help, requesting the dispatch of U.N. troops to protect the country from external aggression and to restore its territorial integrity. This request for U.N. intervention reinforced an earlier initiative by U.S. Ambassador Clare Timberlake, who since July 10 was already advocating the presence of U.N. troops as the best way of protecting Western interests, and who hoped at the very least to place the Belgian intervention under a U.N. umbrella (Kalb 1982, 7). This idea of a U.N. umbrella or cover for Western or specifically U.S. interests became an integral part of U.S. policy in the Congo.

The task of using the U.N. umbrella for purposes of promoting Western interests was greatly facilitated by the fact that nearly all the top U.N. officials with responsibility for Congo matters shared a common cold war outlook with U.S. policymakers and saw their mission in the Congo as that of preserving the existing balance of forces in the world. U.N. Secretary General Dag Hammarskjöld is said to have "believed that the West had a sacred mission toward Africa in general, and especially the Congo" (Kanza 1972, 220). There was a commonality of views between Hammarskjöld and his chief collaborators on Congo matters—Under Secretary General Ralph Bunche, U.N. Congo Force Commander General Carl von Horn, and Hammarskjöld's assistants Brian Urquhart and Andrew Cordier—on the one hand, and U.S. officials, on the other, concerning Lumumba, whom they all distrusted, and on what needed to be done to preserve Western interests in the Congo (Kalb 1982, 17–35).

That the secretary general was thoroughly biased in this regard can be ascertained from the rather complimentary assessment of his record by the Indian diplomat Rajeshwar Dayal (1976), who replaced Bunche as Hammarskjöld's representative in the Congo in September 1960. Dayal (1976, 308) reports that Hammarskjöld "had little respect for the Soviet [U.N.]

Under-Secretary, G. P. Arkadiev, and though Arkadiev's functions were political, he was rather pointedly excluded from participation in the Congo discussions." Dayal does not tell us why a senior U.N. political affairs official was so excluded by a man he claims was committed to the philosophy of nonalignment. The exclusion was the more significant in view of the fact that these "Congo discussions" in the U.N. Secretariat were a major responsibility for Hammarskjöld's American aides Ralph Bunche and Andrew Cordier. Did Hammarskjöld believe that Arkadiev was a faithful servant of Soviet interests, while the Americans were, like him, true international civil servants with no attachment, sentimental or other, to U.S. interests?

Subsequent events were to show that U.N. objectives as understood by Hammarskjöld were compatible with U.S. objectives in the Congo. Like Hammarskjöld, the U.S. government had no intention of collaborating with the legally constituted government of Lumumba to resolve the crisis. U.S. officials in Léopoldville were doing their best to undermine and subvert this government (U.S. Congress, Senate 1975, 13–70). When Hammarskjöld's trusted aide Andrew Cordier became the acting head of the U.N. Congo mission between Bunche's departure on August 28 and Dayal's arrival on September 8, 1960, there was no doubt as to the fact that the United Nations had become a simple instrument of U.S. policy in the Congo. Cordier and Timberlake worked hand in hand to implement U.S. policy objectives. Acting as a viceroy, the "cold warrior" Cordier helped engineer and execute the illegal overthrow of Lumumba from power, beginning with the Kasa-Vubu coup of September 5.

Since U.N. officials were wittingly or unwittingly serving Western interests in the Congo, their interpretation of their mandate was diametrically opposed to Lumumba's interpretation. The Congolese prime minister was under the impression that U.N. troops were in his country to obtain the evacuation of Belgian troops, who were concentrated in Katanga, and to end this province's secession. U.N. officials, on the other hand, emphasized their law-and-order functions, and placed a greater value on the restoration of the economic and social infrastructure of the country than on confrontation with Moise Tshombe and the Belgians in Katanga. For U.N. and U.S. officials, the question of the Katanga secession was to be resolved on terms favorable to Belgian and Western interests in the Congo, and after Lumumba and his followers were no longer a threat to the ambitions of the pro-Western moderate leaders.

The secession of Katanga was the single most important issue in Lumumba's dispute with the United Nations, and one that contributed to his demise. Because of U.N. reluctance to act, Lumumba felt compelled to seek military assistance elsewhere, and he obtained some help from the Soviet Union. This, in the eyes of U.S. policymakers, was his capital offense.

Both U.S. and U.N. officials raised such a fuss about Soviet planes, trucks, and supplies that it was largely forgotten that the first shipment of these items had come as part of the Soviet contribution to the U.N. operation, which included the ferrying of Ghanaian troops to the Congo (Kalb 1982, 57–58). Moreover, as the Soviet government argued in a note to the U.N. Secretary General, "the sending by the Soviet Union of help to the government of the Republic of the Congo—in the form of civil aircraft and motor vehicles—was not contrary to the terms of the resolutions of July 14 and 22, 1960, since the said resolutions set no limit on the right of the government to ask for or be given direct bilateral aid" (quoted in Kanza 1972, 282).

When told of U.S. concern over the arrival of Soviet planes in Stanleyville on August 31, 1960, Hammarskjöld is said to have reassured the Americans "that he had given strict orders not to permit any 'unauthorized landings' by Soviet planes transporting Lumumba's troops to Katanga" (Kalb 1982, 69). This is a good example of how U.N. interference in the internal affairs of the Congo was part of the U.S. strategy of indirect intervention. In this particular case of Soviet assistance to Lumumba, U.N. actions were also part of a wider propaganda campaign in the West to convince world public opinion that Lumumba was bringing communism into the heart of Africa. As Kanza (1972, 284) points out, this propaganda campaign "was part of the necessary psychological preparation for a major diplomatic coup in the Congo, a coup inspired and supported by the Western powers." For this coup to succeed, the support of the U.N. Secretariat was indispensable.

By September 1, troops of the Congolese National Army (ANC) had successfully invaded the secessionist province of South Kasai and were advancing toward Katanga. Frightened by reports of the boldness of these ANC troops, the secessionist leaders Tshombe and South Kasai's Albert Kalonji appealed to Kasa-Vubu, their federalist ally, to stop Lumumba's antisecessionist drive.

Two critical factors gave Kasa-Vubu the impetus he needed to make his move against Lumumba. The first was that the ANC military action in South Kasai had resulted in the massacre of innocent civilians in several locations, notably at Bakwanga and at Kasengulu, near Tshilenge. Hammarskjöld immediately exploited these unfortunate killings by describing them as constituting an "act of genocide" against a people, the Kasai Baluba. Kasa-Vubu blamed Lumumba for the incidents, while sparing Joseph-Désiré Mobutu, the ANC chief of staff, and the officers who commanded the invading force.

The second factor was the presence in Léopoldville of Andrew Cordier, who "arranged things in favor of Kasavubu and the interests of the West" (Kanza 1972, 301). Cordier threw the weight and prestige of the United Nations behind the Western demand that Kasa-Vubu dismiss Lumumba. Such an act was clearly beyond Kasa-Vubu's limited constitutional powers as a ceremonial head of state. By dismissing Lumumba illegally, Kasa-Vubu created a constitutional crisis for the young republic, as the parliament complicated matters by rejecting his decision and by overwhelmingly reaffirming its confidence in Lumumba.

There were only two ways of resolving the constitutional crisis: either by reconciling Lumumba and Kasa-Vubu or by forcibly removing one of them from the political scene. Diplomats from a number of African countries and U.N. envoy Dayal chose the first option, but failed. The path of reconciliation had already been made into an obstacle course by the good works of Andrew Cordier, the U.S. embassy in Léopoldville, Kasa-Vubu's Belgian advisers, and Colonel Mobutu's CIA and U.N. friends—namely, CIA Station Chief Lawrence Devlin, U.N. Commander von Horn, and his deputy, General Ben Hammou Kettani of Morocco.

Since Lumumba continued to be recognized as the legitimate head of government by the parliament, Kasa-Vubu adjourned the latter on September 14, without having consulted with the Council of Ministers or the leaders of the House and the Senate. On the same day, Colonel Mobutu staged a coup d'état, with the help of General Kettani. Although Mobutu announced the "neutralization" of both Kasa-Vubu and Lumumba, U.N. and U.S. officials did their best to ensure that only Lumumba would be effectively "neutralized." Kasa-Vubu was needed to provide some semblance of legality. He was thus able to formally swear in the College of Commissioners, the group of university graduates and students that Mobutu set up to act as a government after his coup d'état, and his delegation to the U.N. General Assembly won the credentials battle over the rival delegation representing the Lumumba government.

Having succeeded in removing Lumumba from power, the anti-Lumumba alliance of U.N. officials, U.S. diplomats, and Congolese moderates was now preoccupied with how to prevent his return to power. Timberlake, the U.S. ambassador in Léopoldville, was totally obsessed with this question, and sought U.N. approval for Lumumba's arrest. More elegant and diplomatic than Timberlake, Hammarskjöld played for time, so as "not to create the impression that he was 'out to get Lumumba'" (Kalb 1982, 137). Thus, when Lumumba was actually arrested by Mobutu's troops, Hammarskjöld pretended in a statement to the Security Council on December 10, 1960, that the United Nations could not do anything for him since his arrest warrant was signed, or at least approved, by the chief of state (Nkrumah 1967, 91–92).

Even in jail, Lumumba continued to represent a threat to the moderate leadership in Léopoldville and to its Western backers. Both the moderates and U.S. policymakers were convinced that he had to be physically eliminated. By this time, Lumumba had already become a target of a CIA assassination plot. The order to assassinate him was given by President Dwight D. Eisenhower at a National Security Council meeting on August 18, 1960, in Washington (Kalb 1982, 50–55). The only problem was to find the best way of doing it, a way which would ensure that the act itself could not be traced back to the United States.

Whereas U.S. officials in Léopoldville sought to achieve this goal through Lumumba's Congolese enemies, an overanxious boss at CIA headquarters ordered the CIA's top scientist to develop a deadly poison with which to kill

Lumumba. The cobra venom prepared for this purpose by Sidney Gottlieb did not find its way into Lumumba's food or toothpaste, as intended. But the CIA did encourage and support, both morally and materially, the Congolese leaders who conspired to kill Lumumba. The CIA's responsibility in Lumumba's murder is well established; it cannot be denied, or even obscured, as the Church Committee reports attempt to do (Weissman 1978).

By January 1961, the Lumumbist government headed by Deputy Prime Minister Gizenga in Stanleyville began expanding its control and authority in the eastern part of the republic and thus encouraged Lumumba's followers all over the country to continue the struggle for genuine independence, national unity, and territorial integrity. The U.S. embassy was greatly displeased with the course of events and preoccupied by rumors of a pro-Lumumba coup d'état in Léopoldville. Added to all this was the Congolese authorities' fear that Lumumba might be set free by the soldiers guarding him in Thysville. Kasa-Vubu, Mobutu, Foreign Minister Justin Bomboko, and their allies decided to transfer Lumumba to Elisabethville on January 17, 1961. He was murdered on the same day by the authorities of the secessionist province of Katanga.

Just as they worked together to eliminate Lumumba politically and physically, the Americans and their Congolese allies worked hard during the next seven months to determine and install his successor. The main objective now was to prevent Gizenga or any other prominent Lumumbist from becoming head of government. Everything had to be done to make sure that the radical nationalists would not control or dominate parliament and the government. Under U.N. auspices, the parliament was convened on the campus of Lovanium University. The outcome was never in doubt, as those external forces controlling the situation had decided that Cyrille Adoula was the best choice for the post of prime minister. U.S. officials have described the entire process as "really a U.S. operation but using outstanding U.N. personalities" (quoted in Weissman 1974, 147).

According to Stephen Weissman (1974, 208), the American government "not only supported Adoula; it was, in many different ways, part of his government." Having outmaneuvered the Lumumbists at Lovanium, Adoula's tutors and advisers sought to diminish their influence in the new government before dismissing them. Most of the important Lumumbists were eliminated from the political scene by October 1963. Some of them went into exile across the river in Brazzaville, where a revolution had replaced the conservative government of Abbé Fulbert Youlou with a more progressive leadership. It was in Brazzaville that a number of Lumumbists founded the *Conseil National de Libération* (CNL) to spearhead their struggle to regain power.

The pattern of U.S. involvement in Congolese affairs changed in 1964, with the departure of the U.N. force from the country on June 30. Without the U.N. umbrella, the United States had to find another way of influencing the course of events in the Congo. Since a heavy American presence was excluded from the very beginning, the most appropriate strategy was that of multilateral Western involvement underwritten by the United States, with Belgium playing a leading role in coordinating the involvement and supplying the necessary personnel for its success. Given its vital interests in the Congo, its colonial experience, and its familiarity with the country and its leaders, Belgium was perfectly suited to play this role. The nomination of Tshombe as prime minister in July 1964 and the U.S.–Belgian military intervention at Stanleyville and Paulis on November 24, 1964, were the first concrete manifestations of this multilateral strategy, whose major partners today are the United States, France, and Belgium.

For the moderate Congolese leaders, the departure of the U.N. force increased their dependence on the United States and Belgium. A consequence of this dependence was the inability of both the Adoula and Tshombe governments to resolve the conflict which opposed them to the radical nationalists, the heirs of Patrice Lumumba. The Adoula government was unable to achieve a lasting reconciliation because it was basically a puppet government, taking its directives from the U.S. embassy in Léopoldville and responsive to the pressures exerted on it by General Mobutu and his Binza Group.[2] This was a politically powerful clique supported by the CIA through Devlin, the principal members of which controlled the key organs of the central government machinery closely linked to external sources of assistance and pressure: the military (Mobutu), the security police (Victor Nendaka), internal affairs (Damien Kandolo), the central bank (Albert Ndele), and foreign affairs (Bomboko).

To protect Western interests and save the moderates, the United States and Belgium had to step in more forcefully to fill the "internal security gap" created by the departure of the U.N. force, in the midst of popular insurrections for a "second independence." For ordinary people, independence was meaningless without a better standard of living. The politicians had failed to honor their promises for a better life, lived in much greater luxury than their European predecessors, and used violence and arbitrary force against the people. These insurrections were therefore a revolutionary attempt to end injustice and the new social order favorable to the neocolonial ruling class at the expense of ordinary people.

The Lumumbists assumed the leadership of the "second independence" movement by organizing the armed struggle in Kwilu and in the east. They sought and obtained support from the socialist countries, mainly from the People's Republic of China, and from a number of African countries, includ-

2. After his fall from power, Adoula seems to have acknowledged in a letter to Ghanaian President Kwame Nkrumah that he was not free to make his own decisions on sensitive issues (Nkrumah 1967, 276).

ing Egypt, Ghana, Congo-Brazzaville, Burundi, and Sudan. Like Lumumba, they were accused of being communists or agents of Chinese communism.

In order to fight them, the United States and Belgium prevailed upon Kasa-Vubu and Mobutu to accept Tshombe as prime minister in view of the proven ability of the military forces at his disposal: his former secessionist army of gendarmes and white mercenaries, then stationed in Angola. The situation became critical shortly after Tshombe assumed office, as the Lumumbists received more support at home and abroad in their struggle against a man who was seen as a traitor all over Africa. The CNL took control of Stanleyville on August 4, 1964, and proclaimed a people's republic. By this time, nearly one-half of the nation's territory was under Lumumbist control.

As in the case of the dispute between Kasa-Vubu and Lumumba, the United States and its allies did everything possible to undermine African diplomatic efforts to resolve the crisis by negotiations. The U.S. government under President Lyndon B. Johnson had already started to intervene unilaterally during the month of June (Nkrumah 1967, 253). U.S. transport planes were sent to assist the Congolese government, and U.S. paratroopers followed to protect these planes and other U.S. property in the Congo. In addition to military transport aircraft, the United States provided Léopoldville with a small air force operated by the CIA with anti-Castro Cubans. The CIA Congo air force was registered in Liechtenstein as Western International Ground Maintenance Organization (WIGMO).

Using a humanitarian pretext, and one that smacked of racism, President Johnson sent U.S. planes to drop Belgian paratroopers on Stanleyville and Paulis on November 24 with the expressed aim of rescuing whites from the conflict area. However, the real purpose of this intervention was to pave the way for the recapture of those cities by the Congolese government. Thus, with military and financial support from the United States, Belgium, Israel, and others, Tshombe used his gendarmes and mercenaries to defeat the CNL regime and its army, and thus succeeded where Mobutu's army had been profoundly humiliated. Although the CNL regime was overthrown, popular resistance continued in the countryside, and thus necessitated the retention of white mercenaries in the country until 1967.

The inability of the neocolonial state to come to grips with this popular resistance intensified the political rivalries within the moderate leadership headed by Tshombe, Mobutu, and Kasa-Vubu. In spite of his victory over the CNL and the moderate improvement in the country's economic situation under his rule, Tshombe had failed to end the political crisis. Mobutu took advantage of this failure to make his second dramatic appearance on the political scene on November 24, 1965, this time to assume the reigns of power as head of state. His coup d'état was supported by the U.S. government, which saw it as being necessary for putting an end to political instability in the Congo. The fact that Mobutu undermined the democratic process, as he and

Kasa-Vubu had done with U.S. encouragement and support in 1960, was of no concern to Washington.

The United States and the Mobutu Regime, 1965–83

U.S. policy since 1965 has consisted of an unswerving support for Mobutu, his corrupt, arbitrary, and dictatorial rule notwithstanding. The support is based on at least three premises: (1) that a vast and multiethnic country like Zaire needs a "strong man" whose iron rule would help maintain stability and thereby safeguard Western interests; (2) that the United States ought to support its loyal friends, regardless of their behavior; and (3) that Zaire under a pro-Western government can play a gendarme role in the region as a whole.

The first premise is grounded in both the cold war mythology concerning communist infiltration and subversion, and the evolutionist perspective of Western images of the Third World in general and Africa in particular. The vision of a Zaire torn asunder by ethnic rivalries and thereby exposed to all sorts of external intervention in the absence of a strong central rule emerges with a surprising consistency from statements made by African policy specialists in the U.S. government in the last twenty years. Two examples will suffice to demonstrate this point. G. Mennen Williams, assistant secretary of state for African affairs in the Kennedy and Johnson administrations, saw "tribalism" as "a prime cause for the lack of national unity" and the U.S. role in Zaire as that of preventing "extremist infiltration" and making sure "that the Congolese and not Communists control the Congo" (Williams 1965, 13). Fourteen years later, the then head of the State Department's Africa Bureau, Richard M. Moose, stated at a congressional hearing that the "breakdown of existing patterns" in Zaire could very well result in a communist takeover, as "those people usually get their act together before other people do, and they stand to benefit in the first instance" (U.S. Congress, House 1979, 440).

U.S. policymaking with regard to Zaire seems to follow Williams's naive and ahistorical view of ethnicity as a matter of primordial identity as a function of "tribal loyalties and ancient enmities." The implication one gets from such a view is that these ancient enmities were kept in check by the colonialists through force, and can therefore be kept from tearing the country apart by the authoritarian rule of a "strong man." Ethnic competition in Africa is seen as being different from ethnic politics in the United States, Belgium, or other multiethnic societies in Europe and America.

The evolutionist bias informing this view was shared by both conservative and liberal policymakers in Washington, and continues to underlie much of the discussion concerning African politics in the American news media. According to Madeleine Kalb (1982, 220–221), U.S. Ambassador Timberlake portrayed the Congo as "an extremely primitive country with no tradition of democracy" to President John F. Kennedy and to the Senate Foreign Relations Committee on February 4 and 6, 1961, respectively, and "found the President receptive and many of the senators even more so." More sophisticated than Timberlake and Williams, today's policymakers still find it convenient to play on the U.S. lawmakers' fear of instability and communist subversion in order to rationalize their support for Mobutu.

For these policymakers, the question of Zaire's future seems to be reduced to a fateful dichotomy, "Mobutu or chaos!" In reality, real chaos and institutional paralysis are more evident today than during the days of the Congo crisis. In spite of the civil war and bickering among politicians, the state machinery continued to run in those areas not seriously affected by armed conflict. Records were kept, social services were provided without too much trouble for ordinary citizens, and corruption was not institutionalized. The quality of administrative services was remarkably high in a number of provinces with a dynamic government and an adequate level of resources, notably in Kongo Central and in South Kasai.

Under Mobutu, on the other hand, the effective abolition of representative institutions at the central, regional, and local levels has denied ordinary people an adequate means of applying pressure on the ruling class through elections. The basically rubber-stamp parliament established in 1970 and the new but powerless municipal and regional councils are stifled by the monopoly of power held by Mobutu, and cannot really be said to be a veritable expression of the will of the people.

Moreover, Mobutu's constantly reshuffled government is responsible for an administration that cannot administer. Lacking the most elementary demographic and other statistical data due to the poor quality of record-keeping, the Zairian public administration usually works with fictitious data. Economic regulation is at best limited to the selling of various business licenses, the privileged groups whose activities and businesses often endanger public health and safety being able to frustrate basic law enforcement. The rich and the powerful use their might to evade taxes while the poor and the powerless suffer a state of permanent insecurity due to the arbitrary nature of revenue collection at the local level and to all kinds of extortion by soldiers and other state agents. Given the insufficient revenues available to municipal and national field services together with mismanagement and generalized corruption, the system as a whole is incapable of providing for the welfare of the population. Mobutu's Zaire never fails to bare the primacy of its exploitive and repressive functions.

In this light, the pertinent question with regard to instability and chaos is, Stability for whom? Who stands to gain and who stands to lose in the eventuality of Mobutu's demise? The answer for the United States, as suggested by Professor Crawford Young in a *Foreign Affairs* article on the Zairian crisis (Young 1978, 184), is that the stability of Mobutu's Zaire is good for the credibility of the United States and the West with respect to their moral commitment to their friends and allies. According to Young, identification with the West is likely to be perceived by Africans as a prescription for disaster if the United States and the West were to abandon Mobutu Sese Seko.

This is a perfect statement of the second premise on which U.S. policy toward Zaire is based. Young's position was strongly endorsed as being compatible with U.S. policy at a Senate hearing by Lannon Walker, deputy assistant secretary of state for African affairs in the Carter and Reagan administrations (U.S. Congress, Senate 1979, 29). In the political calculations of U.S. policymakers, the fact that President Mobutu may be guilty of blatant corruption and gross violations of human rights to the detriment of the people of Zaire is of no real importance. What matters the most is that he has been a friend of long standing and an ally of the United States since his esteemed collaboration in the CIA effort to eliminate Lumumba, and for which he was personally congratulated by President Kennedy in the White House rose garden on May 31, 1963 (Kalb 1982, 372).

Finally, U.S. support for Mobutu is based on Zaire's potential as a regional gendarme for the United States and the West in central and southern Africa. Zaire is one of the few countries that are suitable for this role in the region, given its economic and strategic importance and the fact that it shares common borders with nine other countries. Within the framework of neocolonialism, the main objective of this gendarme role is to preserve the existing balance of forces in the world by suppressing revolutionary movements likely to threaten Western economic and strategic interests. This objective coincided with the basic goal of the Mobutu regime since 1966, namely, to reinforce its bargaining power vis-à-vis foreign monopoly capital in order to provide the Zairian bourgeoisie a solid economic base (Peemans 1975, 163).

This convergence of the interests of the Western powers and those of the Zairian bourgeoisie explains the willingness of the Mobutu regime to act as a gendarme in central and southern Africa. Bolstered with American C–130 transport aircraft and other military equipment, Zairian troops intervened in Burundi in 1972 and in the Central African Empire in 1979 to help unpopular regimes suppress civil disturbances. These simple police actions were merely dress rehearsals for the more internationally significant performances of the gendarme duty, those which involve a struggle against individuals or political movements perceived as a threat to Western interests in Africa. Such interventions occurred in Angola in 1975–76 and twice in Chad, in 1981 and 1983.

I have argued elsewhere (Nzongola 1982, 91–103) that far from being a simple execution of American directives by the Mobutu regime, Zaire's intervention in the Angolan civil war was primarily related to Mobutu's struggle for survival, in the face of the political challenge posed to his regime by the victory of the People's Movement for the Liberation of Angola (MPLA) in Luanda. The desire to confront this challenge head on coincided with the foreign policy objectives of the United States with regard to both Zaire and Angola.

Thus, in striving to crush the MPLA and to advance the cause of the pro-Western groups in Angola, the Mobutu regime was attempting to defend its own class interests as well as to discharge its obligations as a junior partner of U.S. imperialism in Africa. Needless to say, the Angolan intervention cannot be fully understood without reference to the higher economic and strategic stakes involved for the West in southern Africa. It is these stakes which account for the involvement of the racist state of South Africa in the military aggression against the People's Republic of Angola.

In the case of Chad, the civil war had been internationalized by the interference of neighboring countries and their external allies in Chadian domestic affairs. For the West, the most dangerous development was the involvement of Libyan troops, who intervened at the request of the transitional government of President Goukouni Oueddei in December 1980. In 1981, Zaire was the first African country to rush its troops to Ndjamena as part of the OAU peacekeeping force sent to replace the Libyans.

That Mobutu and his U.S., Egyptian, and Sudanese allies were supportive of Hissène Habré was demonstrated by the ease with which Habré was able to overthrow the Goukouni government. A peacekeeping force whose mandate was to stop rival factions from fighting one another allowed Habré's army to march all the way from the Sudanese border to Ndjamena, under the pretext that the OAU force could not interfere in the internal affairs of Chad. Those who used this argument had conveniently forgotten their virulent opposition to the presence of Libyan troops, invited by the legitimate government. Habré's triumph was a victory for the United States, which had provided him with weapons and other military supplies through Egypt, Sudan, and Zaire.[3] Mobutu's gendarme role and his pro-Habré sympathies were further confirmed by his second military intervention in 1983.

Along with the suppression of progressive forces domestically, these interventions show how well Mobutu has faithfully met his obligations to the United States with respect to the protection and promotion of Western interests in Zaire and in the region. In return, he has greatly benefited from U.S. support, in spite of the frequent criticism in Congress of his human rights record, economic mismanagement, and corruption. Whatever the level of economic and military assistance might be in a given year, Mobutu knows well that when the chips are down, U.S. support will be forthcoming. Thus, in 1977 and 1978, the United States joined France and Belgium to rescue him from disaster after the invasion of Shaba province by the National Front for the Liberation of the Congo (FLNC). Since 1976, the United States has been a major participant in the generally unsuccessful international effort to stabi-

3. Data on the Chadian situation were obtained from the following magazines and newspapers: *Africa News*, *Africa Now* (London), *Africa Report*, *Afrique-Asie* (Paris), *Le Monde* (Paris), *New York Times*, *Washington Post*, *West Africa* (London).

lize the Zairian economy and to enable it to meet its debt and other obligations toward the international capitalist system.

Conclusion

The strategic and economic interests of the West in central and southern Africa seem to dictate the necessity of keeping Zaire under strong Western control. Thus, efforts at collective Western neocolonialism began right after independence, with the United States eventually replacing Belgium as the major arbiter of the country's destiny. These efforts have continued ever since, and include military, economic, and technical assistance to every moderate leader (Adoula, Tshombe, Mobutu), in addition to the elimination of Lumumba, the suppression of Lumumbist-led insurrections in the 1960s, and the more recent interventions during the Shaba wars of 1977 and 1978.

U.S. and Western involvement in Zairian affairs has not only undermined the process of institution-building, it has also had the effect of prolonging the crisis of the Zairian state and society. That crisis will continue as long as the United States and its Western allies persist in viewing Zairian affairs in terms of the East-West confrontation. The only foundation of political stability and long-term economic health for Zaire is respect for human rights, including the democratic right of the people of Zaire to choose their own leaders. This is a right that they have lost since 1965, thanks to U.S. support for Mobutu's dictatorship.

REFERENCES

Dayal, Rajeshwar. 1976. *Mission for Hammarskjöld: The Congo Crisis.* Princeton: Princeton University Press.

Kalb, Madeleine G. 1982. *The Congo Cables: The Cold War in Africa—From Eisenhower to Kennedy.* New York: Macmillan.

Kanza, Thomas. 1972. *Conflict in the Congo: The Rise and Fall of Lumumba.* Baltimore: Penguin Books.

Nkrumah, Kwame. 1967. *Challenge of the Congo.* New York: International Publishers.

Nzongola-Ntalaja. 1982. *Class Struggles and National Liberation in Africa: Essays on the Political Economy of Neocolonialism.* Roxbury, Mass.: Omenana.

Peemans, Jean-Philippe. 1975. "The Social and Economic Development of Zaire since Independence: An Historical Outline." *African Affairs* 74, no. 295 (April): 148–179.

U.S. Congress, House. 1979. *Foreign Assistance Legislation for Fiscal Years 1980–81,* Part 6: "Economic and Military Assistance Programs in Africa." Hearings Before the Subcommittee on Africa of the Committee on Foreign Affairs, 96th Congress, 1st Session, February and March.

U.S. Congress, Senate. 1975. *Interim Report: Alleged Assassination Plots Involving Foreign Leaders,* by the Select Committee to Study Government Operations with Respect to Intelligence Activities, 94th Congress, 1st Session, November 20.

———. 1979. *U.S. Loans to Zaire.* Hearing Before the Subcommittee on International Finance of the Committee on Banking, Housing, and Urban Affairs, 96th Congress, 1st Session, May 24.

Weissman, Stephen R. 1974. *American Foreign Policy in the Congo 1960–1964.* Ithaca, N.Y.: Cornell University Press.

———. 1978. "The CIA and U.S. Policy in Zaire and Angola," pp. 381–432 in René Lemarchand, ed. *American Policy in Southern Africa.* Washington, D.C.: University Press of America.

Williams, G. Mennen. 1965. "U.S. Objectives in the Congo 1960–65." *Africa Report* 10, no. 8 (August):12–20.

Young, Crawford. 1978. "Zaire: The Unending Crisis." *Foreign Affairs* 57, no. 1 (Fall):169–185.

13

The Crisis in Chad

RENÉ LEMARCHAND

In July and August 1983, Chad, until then hardly a household name, entered the consciousness of the American public with a vengeance. What gave this little known legacy of French colonial rule instant prominence in the media was the quasi-pathological concern of the Reagan administration over the renewed intervention of Libyan forces in the maelstrom of factional strife which has plagued the Chadian state, such as it is, almost from its birth. In a matter of days the oasis town of Faya-Largeau became the focal point of an international crisis which saw the United States and Libya edging toward yet another confrontation, revealed basic differences between France and the United States in their respective assessments of the Libyan threat, and in the end prompted the French to engage in the largest military intervention in Africa since the Algerian war.

If it is difficult to visualize the vast camel market of Faya-Largeau as a major stake in the Chadian poker game, the irony goes far beyond the boundaries of this improbable state. After years of fruitless efforts aimed at breaking the back of the northern rebellion, France found itself more heavily committed than ever on behalf of the ex-rebel-turned-president, Hissène Habré, and the initiative for this latest experiment in counterinsurgency came from none other than François Mitterrand, who in the 1960s and 1970s went on record as the most vocal and consistent critic of "military adventurism" in Chad. Moreover, in backing Habré the French made a decision that ran directly counter to the political formula adopted by Mitterrand in the fall of 1981 and which in effect gave France's accolade to Goukouni Oueddei.

Through its contradictions and bizarre outcomes the crisis in Chad brings into focus some major dilemmas confronting U.S. policies in Africa. For one thing it raises the perennial question of whether America's choice of allies, in Chad as elsewhere, should solely or very largely be determined by the

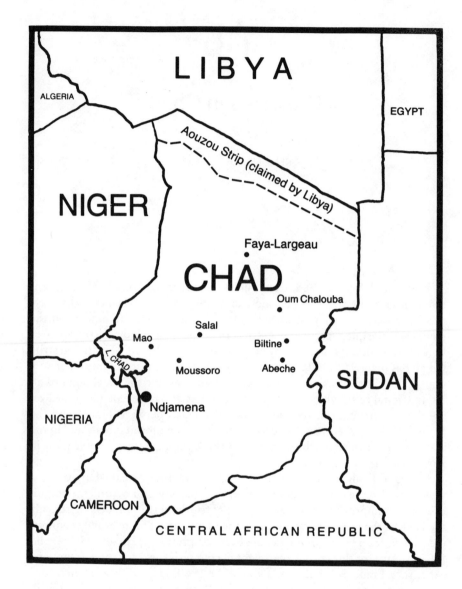

Map 5. Chad

strength of their opposition to its perceived enemies, Libyan, Cuban, or Soviet; or, to put it differently, whether the assumption that "the enemies of our enemies are our friends" can provide an adequate basis for discriminating between friend and foe. The obsessive concern of the United States with what it perceives to be Moscow's proxies in Africa—the Libyans in Chad, the Cubans in Angola—matched as it is by a surprising disregard or plain ignorance of the internal dynamics of African politics, is not only a major handicap in selecting "friends"; it also impels one to wonder how one might conceivably translate the short-run tactical advantages gained from supporting a friendly warlord into a long-term investment in political stability. Nowhere, save in Lebanon, is this dilemma more palpable than in Chad. What is reasonably clear is that the divergent sets of perceptions shared by the participants in the crisis, most notably France and the United States, have seriously complicated the process of crisis management. The obvious reluctance of the Mitterrand government to play a role that might appear to be taken from an American script raises the more global question of how much leverage the United States can hope to exercise on its European allies in the pursuit of its geopolitical interests on the continent.

Anatomy of a Basket Case

Only by legal fiction or diplomatic courtesy can Chad be described as a state. After eighteen years of civil strife, half of its national territory is under the control of Libyan-backed insurgents; its jurisdiction within the other half is severely contested, with a situation of chronic anarchy prevailing in some of the southern prefectures; the capacity of its political institutions to maintain order and execute policy is virtually nonexistent beyond the perimeter of the capital city and a few major towns. No other state in Africa, with the exception of Uganda, is so thoroughly lacking in even the most elementary attributes of statehood. None is more vulnerable to the twin dangers of foreign penetration and foreign-linked factionalism.[1]

Chad's inherent fractiousness is not reducible to any single set of circumstances. Its roots lie in part in the sheer diversity of ethnocultural aggregates comprised within its boundaries, in part in the very superficial impact of French colonial rule beyond the country's southern tier, and in part in the complex interactions brought to light after independence between various domestic groups and factions on the one hand, and their wider geopolitical environment on the other.

1. Nothing is more revealing of the general impotence of the Chadian polity than the astonishing news that "a special tax-exempt fund has been set up to help the members of the Chad Mission to the U.N. to buy food and pay rent. About $15,000 has already been pledged by corporations and individuals to alleviate the plight of the diplomats.... The contributions will be channeled through the Phelps-Stokes Fund, an educational foundation specializing in African countries" (New York Times, October 22, 1983). Whether this unprecedented rescue operation will produce yet another form of foreign-linked factionalism remains unclear.

Individual and collective identifications in Chad cover a remarkably wide spectrum of reference points, some pertaining to religious affiliations, others to regional ties, others to distinctive ethnocultural aggregates within a given region or to subcultural or personal loyalties within a given ethnic group (Lemarchand 1981). At each successive phase of Chadian political history collective identities have tended to shift from one level of differentiation to another, partly in response to specific political events, partly as a result of the calculations of political entrepreneurs or self-appointed warlords.

In the years immediately following independence, from 1960 to 1975, the fundamental line of cleavage was between the predominantly Islamized north and the Christianized, Sara-dominated south. Until the fall of President François Tombalbaye in April 1975, and for some time thereafter, the Chadian state was largely the monopoly of Sara elements, and Sara dominance the most powerful source of cohesion among the Muslim insurgents affiliated to the *Front de Libération National Tchadien* (Frolinat). Founded in 1966 by Ibrahim Abatcha, the Frolinat was from the very beginning plagued by internal divisions. Precisely when the hold of Sara elements on the apparatus of the state began to falter, factional splits developed within the Frolinat which tended to reflect the divisive pull of its several ethnic components.

By 1975 the north-south dialectic had given way to a more complex pattern of ethnic conflict. Coinciding with a struggle for power in Ndjamena among Sara elements, a bitter rivalry emerged among the insurgents between Arabs and Tubus followed almost immediately by an even deeper and long-lasting feud between two different segments of the Tubu cluster, one led by Hissène Habré, and the other by Goukouni Oueddei, the younger son of the paramount chief of the Tubu (the so-called Derdei), Oueddei Kefedemi.[2] Although Habré and Goukouni remain to this day the leading protagonists in the Chadian drama, they are by no means the only actors in the cast. By 1979 no less than eleven factions had emerged in the political arena. Meanwhile the once seemingly homogeneous south showed an alarming vulnerability to factional splits. Today there are possibly as many Sara fighting on Habré's side as there are on Goukouni Oueddei's.[3]

2. Underlying the Habré-Goukouni feud are significant cultural and linguistic differences, reinforced by contrasting historical experiences, between their respective groups of origin, i.e., the Teda (Goukouni) and the Daza (Habré). The former, located in the Tibesti, in and around Bardai, Aouzou, and Zouar, have strong cultural and historical affinities with the populations of southern Libya; the Daza, on the other hand, are found primarily in the Borkou and Ennedi regions, especially in the vicinity of Faya-Largeau and Ounianga Kebir, and their trade links have been in the direction of Biltine and Abeche rather than with Libya. The Teda have been Islamized via the Senussiya, and when the French moved into the area many found refuge in Libya; the Daza came in contact with Islam through Arab traders and "holy men" from the Sudan and Egypt (d'Arbaumont 1954; Chapelle 1957).

3. Inasmuch as these labels have any meaning given the extreme fluidity of factional alignments, three principal factions are currently fighting on Goukouni's side: (1) the remnants of Goukouni's own *Forces Armées Populaires* (FAP), (2) Rakhis Manani's *Conseil Démocratique*

First Islam, then ethnicity, then intra-ethnic factionalism: these different levels of identification correspond to specific moments in the process of polarization that has characterized Chadian politics. These mutations are by no means unique to Chad; what makes Chad a special case is the extent to which factions, that is, "politically oriented quasi-groups whose members are recruited on diverse social principles by a leader" (Bujra 1973, 133), have tended to dominate the political process.

The prevalence of factionalism in Chadian politics must be seen in the light of the segmentary organization of northern societies, most notably Arabs and Tubus. In these societies power is widely diffused; relations among different segments, clans, subclans, or kinship groups, exhibit considerable fluidity, because "there is no center at which the means of cohesion are concentrated and which can impose its will on other groups" (Gellner 1973, 4). Oppositions and alliances are constantly recalculated, prompting some observers to describe such segmentary systems as "anarchic." These dispositions are especially marked among the Tubu: "The principle of freedom raised almost to the level of anarchy is so deeply rooted in the Teda philosophy of life that many families refuse to acknowledge anyone as their chief, while individuals frequently dispute the authority even of their own family headmen" (Briggs 1960, 170). What has been referred to as "the centrifugal nature of the Teda clan structure and the resulting tendency toward extreme fragmentation" (Briggs 1960, 170) applies equally well to the Arabs.

If only by omission, French policies have largely contributed to the persistence of faction-based segmentation as a mode of social organization. The vast stretch of territory known as the BET (Borku-Ennedi-Tibesti) prefecture, the traditional habitat of the Tubus, never had the benefit of a civilian administration, and for five years after independence French troops continued to administer the area from a few isolated posts like Faya-Largeau and Bardai. "Not until 1960 were parts of the huge prefecture fully charted or explored; the taciturn Tubus who avoided contact with the French were largely left alone, as were many of the nomadic Arab clans and other groups in Kanem and Biltine" (Decalo 1980, 495). Neglect of the north by the French colonial state, made even more conspicuous by the concentration of socioeconomic development in the south, is certainly a major element in the background of the north-south conflict in the years following independence. But it also explains the continued vitality of traditional segmentary structures

---

Révolutionnaire (CDR), formerly led by Acheikh Ibn Oumar and the late Ahmed Acyl; (3) and a splinter group of the Sara-dominated *Forces Armées Tchadiennes* (FAT), led by Abd-el-Kader Kamougue. The latter's decision to cast his lot with Goukouni was partly motivated by the pro-Habré stance of his immediate rival and Sara kinsman, Lieutenant Batinda Rodai. Kamougue and Rodai belong to different subgroups of the Sara cluster, the former to the Mbaye and the latter to the Nar (who claim, along with the Madjingaye, the status of "true Sara").

among northern societies. At no point in the history of the rebellion did the north-south conflict crystallize to the point of superseding the internal divisions inherent in the social structure of the Islamized north.

As the incipient forces of factionalism played themselves out on the broader canvas of international politics, numerous though seldom permanent links developed between various opposition leaders and their external environment. Domestic factionalism quickly ramified into foreign-linked factionalism. The presence of "privileged sanctuaries" in neighboring states gave a decisive impetus to the process of fragmentation within the rebellion. Not only were resources made available to groups of insurgents which left to themselves stood little chance of survival; more important still, the multiplicity of such sanctuaries—first the Central African Republic, then the Sudan and Egypt, and finally Algeria and Libya—together with the cross-pressures emanating from their diverse political settings, contributed in no small way to the proliferation of factional splits.

The key to an understanding of factional processes is that "they are in a dialectical relationship with other social and political processes going on both within and outside the community being studied" (Bujra 1973, 133). In the case of Chad this dialectical relationship is traceable to Tombalbaye's decision in 1962 to ban all political parties except his own, causing several key figures of the *Union Nationale Tchadienne* (UNT), the precursor of the Frolinat, to seek asylum in the Central African Republic and the Sudan (Buijtenhuijs 1978, 110; Thompson and Adloff 1981, 51). Another turning point was the so-called October 1964 revolution in the Sudan, which brought to power a government openly supportive of national liberation movements, thus offering a major operational base to the exiled leadership of the UNT. It was at Nyala in the southwestern Sudan, on June 22, 1966, that the late Ibrahim Abatcha (killed in action in 1968) organized the historic conference from which emerged the Frolinat (Buijtenhuijs 1978, 121). The third and by far the most significant event in the history of the rebellion was the 1969 coup in Libya. With the opening of the Libyan sanctuary and the growing involvement of Qadhafi in the internal politics of the Abatcha succession, the center of gravity of the insurrection shifted to the BET, greatly accelerating the recruitment of Tubu elements into the fold of the Frolinat, and at the same time creating the conditions for a bitter rivalry between the external (Libyan-based) and predominantly Arab leadership of the movement and its operational Tubu-led "armies" on the ground, and ultimately between the Habré and Goukouni factions.

A full treatment of the many-sided rivalries that have accompanied the "war of Abatcha's succession" lies beyond the scope of this chapter. Suffice it to note that in this complex intramural struggle Qadhafi played a decisive role, never missing an opportunity to play one faction off against another in order to advance his own strategic objectives. His strategy and tactics have remained remarkably constant; only the methods have changed. His overriding long-term objective is to convert Chad into a Libyan sphere of influence; his tactics are disarmingly simple: to reward his obedient clients for their willingness to accept Libyan hegemony, and penalize the recalcitrant. In so doing, however, Qadhafi overplayed his hand, turning his former ally, Habré, into his bitterest enemy. It is worth noting in this connection that, unlike Goukouni, Habré has consistently denounced the Libyan claim to Aouzou (as well as the historic precedent behind it).[4] The annexation of the Aouzou strip in 1973 must be seen as only the first step in a global strategy aiming at merging Chad and Libya into the framework of a greater *Jamahiriya* (State of the Masses.)

What has become dramatically clear since 1980 is that Qadhafi is no longer content to supply Goukouni with cash, training facilities, and a secure sanctuary; the new element in the power equation is Qadhafi's ability to project his logistical and military capabilities into Chad on a very substantial scale. As we shall see, this is what enabled Goukouni to emerge victorious from his trial of strength with Habré during the battle of Ndjamena in December 1980; today this factor lies at the heart of the Chadian crisis.

The Politics of Foreign-Linked Factionalism

Looked at from a broader perspective the Libyan connection calls to mind an analogy: while the French are doing for the Habré government what the Cubans are doing for the government of Angola, Libya is engaged in subversive operations in northern Chad not unlike those performed by South Africa on behalf of the Savimbi rebels in southern Angola. The critical difference between Chad and Angola revolves around the issue of legitimacy. Which of the two principal warlords in Chad has the stronger claim to legitimacy is open to debate. While Habré now enjoys the backing of the majority of the Organization of African Unity (OAU), until June 1982 it was Goukouni who, as head of the Transitional National Union Government (GUNT), had the blessings of the OAU. So unequivocal was the support of the OAU for Goukouni that it proceeded, at great cost, to dispatch an inter-African peacekeeping force to Chad in January 1982 to protect him against the onslaughts of Habré's "rebel" forces. As we now realize, this protective measure proved illusory, and by June 1982 Habré had successfully fought his way back into

---

4. Covering approximately 37,000 square miles along the Chadian-Libyan border, the Aouzou strip was formally ceded by France to Italy through the Rome treaty of January 7, 1935, following the Laval-Mussolini accords. The treaty, however, was never ratified, and thus remained a dead letter (Lanne 1982). Qadhafi's claim to Aouzou, and indeed to the whole of the BET, goes back to precolonial times and is based on what he referred to in 1981 as "a very old historical interaction between the Libyan and Chadian people and the Arab nation" (Legum 1982, A 41). On this point, as anyone familiar with the history of the Senussiya brotherhood will readily concede, Qadhafi's case has some degree of validity.

power. Given the extreme instability of the political arena, and the weather-vane quality of the OAU accolade as a source of legitimacy, it is hardly surprising that to this day no single candidate can effectively press his claim as the recognized spokesman of Chadian interests.

In these conditions foreign-linked factionalism resembles nothing so much as a game of musical chairs. There is indeed a curious symmetry in the repetitive and so far inconclusive involvement of France and Libya on behalf of their respective clients. While currently confronting each other by proxy on each side of the fifteenth parallel, they have exchanged partners so many times that no single faction can claim to have received political or military support exclusively from France or Libya. Such is the irony of international clientelism in Chad that every faction or government, including the Tombalbaye government, has had at one time or another, though seldom simultaneously, either France or Libya as its external patron.

In the past, France and Libya have been willing to withdraw their troops when asked to do so by their respective clients, and in each case with disastrous consequences for their henceforth unprotected protégés. It was at the request of the Malloum government in 1975 that Giscard recalled the French military contingent and evacuated the land/air base in Ndjamena, which in effect cleared the way for Habré and Goukouni on their march to the capital. Likewise when Goukouni asked the Libyans to withdraw their troops in November 1981, he did so at his own peril:[5] seven months later Habré had overthrown Goukouni and taken Ndjamena by storm while the OAU peace-keeping force assumed the role of a passive onlooker.

Between 1975 and 1981 the Chadian political landscape underwent rapid and spectacular alterations, transforming the capital city into a killing ground, first between northerners and southerners, and, beginning in March 1979, between the Goukouni and Habré factions. By insisting on the withdrawal of French troops and guns in 1975 (only to bring them back on a reduced scale in 1978) Malloum sealed his fate. Once the protective shield of the French forces was removed from the Chadian cauldron the Frolinat armies took full advantage of Libyan support to consolidate their position on the

---

5. Goukouni's decision to request a Libyan withdrawal was motivated in part by his expectation that "an effective OAU-endorsed peace-keeping force, with U.S. and French logistical and financial support . . . [would] substitute for the Libyans in preserving domestic order" (Yost 1983, 977), in part by his realization that an OAU military presence would be infinitely preferable to being held hostage, as it were, by Libya (Legum 1982, A 40), and finally by the strong diplomatic pressures exercised by the Mitterrand government in favor of such an arrangement. As has been noted, "Mitterrand's policy differed from his predecessor's by renewing bilateral relations with the GUNT, supporting OAU peacekeeping efforts more vigorously, and adopting a more conciliatory approach to Libya. In the view of the Mitterrand government, the solution to the Chad question was to stabilize the authority of Goukouni's GUNT so that less need for Libyan support would be perceived" (Yost 1983, 977).

ground and begin their march on Ndjamena. In 1977 Bardai and Zouar fell into Goukouni's hands; then came the capture of Faya-Largeau in February 1978, along with the surrender of 2,500 government troops, approximately one-fourth of Malloum's armed forces. At this point the search for accommodation seemed the only realistic option for Malloum, and in August 1978 the first of many abortive attempts at national reconciliation led to a lame compromise whereby Malloum would act as president and Habré as prime minister in a government in which north and south were evenly represented.

The arrangement, which had received the unofficial backing of the French, led to a total deadlock. The way out of the impasse came in February 1979 through a trial of strength between Habré's *Forces Armées du Nord* (FAN) and what was left of Malloum's national army. Overwhelmed by Habré's battle-hardened Tubus, and with the French adopting a posture of neutrality, Malloum's troops under the command of Lieutenant Colonel Abd-el-Kader Kamougue withdrew from Ndjamena to the south, leaving hundreds of Sara civilians at the mercy of Habré's men. Thus ended the first battle of Ndjamena.

With the defeat of Malloum's army and the de facto secession of the south the parameters of conflict shifted abruptly from a north-south confrontation to a deadly struggle between Habré's FAN and Goukouni's *Forces Armées Populaires* (FAP). Almost exactly a year after the first battle of Ndjamena an even more savage eruption of violence took place in the capital between FAN and FAP. By then Habré was formally cast in the role of minister of national defense in a GUNT headed by Goukouni as president, in conformity with the arrangement reached at the first Kano conference. Once again the compromise proved short-lived. By May 1980 the death toll had reached 2,000. Months of vicious fighting followed. As the "war of position" dragged on, and with the French out of the picture, Libya threw the full force of its military arsenal behind Goukouni. Late on December 14 Qadhafi's Islamic Legion, assisted by Soviet-supplied T–54 and T–55 tanks, multiple rocket launchers, and 81mm mortars, marched into Ndjamena.

The next phase in the Chadian imbroglio begins with the abortive Libyan-Chadian merger in January 1981 and comes to a close in June 1982, with the triumphant return of Habré to Ndjamena, following the routing of Goukouni's FAP and its various armed *groupuscules*. Three crucially important developments took place during this period: (1) acting at the request of Goukouni, in November 1981, Qadhafi ordered his troops out of Chad; (2) to fill the vacuum created by the Libyan pull-out an OAU-sponsored inter-African peace-keeping force of approximately 3,000 men was sent to Chad in early 1982; (3) despite the deployment of the OAU peace-keeping force Goukouni's position on the ground (as well as his political credibility at home and abroad) rapidly deteriorated in the face of the seemingly miraculous resurrection of Habré's military power.

Central to an understanding of these and subsequent developments are the radically divergent positions of the French and American governments on how to deal with the Libyans. Although both were in agreement on the desirability of a Libyan pull-out there were sharp differences of opinion as to how this could best be accomplished. For Mitterrand the essence of the dilemma in 1981 was to persuade Goukouni to request a Libyan withdrawal in return for a substantial aid package accompanied by the rapid deployment of an inter-African *cordon sanitaire*. Washington's reception to this strategy was extremely cool, even when it appeared to succeed. For the Reagan administration the prospects of detaching Goukouni from his Libyan patron seemed unrealistic from the start, a view apparently shared by Giscard prior to his defeat by the Socialists; instead every effort was made to prop up Habré through covert military and financial assistance, pending the moment when he could be safely unleashed against Goukouni. Through an elaborate network of intermediaries running from Cairo to Khartoum, the CIA in early 1981 proceeded to funnel important quantities of cash, armaments, and vehicles into Habré's hands, thereby jeopardizing the chances of success of the OAU peace-keeping operation before it even materialized. As one acute observer put it, "for most of 1981 the Reagan campaign's covert aid to the Habré guerrillas undermined the one test that the French, the Libyans, the OAU and Goukouni's government had agreed on—the establishment of a peace-keeping force" (Wright 1982, 34). This, however, did not prevent the Reagan administration from giving lip service, as well as $12 million worth of logistical assistance, to the OAU peace-keeping force.

The collapse of the Goukouni regime in June 1982 had far-reaching implications: it dealt a severe blow to French policies in Chad, spelled the defeat of the formula advocated by the OAU Committee on Chad, and exposed the utter impotence of the OAU peace-keeping force on the ground. For this triple defeat the Reagan administration could claim much of the credit.

On the other hand, the series of victories scored by Habré against the GUNT forces testified once again to his remarkable skill and physical courage as a guerrilla fighter and further demonstrated the sheer ineptitude of Goukouni as a statesman and politician. As much as Goukouni's refusal to heed the call of the OAU for a negotiated solution in February 1982, Habré's military success was a decisive factor behind the OAU's subsequent decision to grant him political recognition. By then even the French were willing to recognize Habré as Chad's sole legitimate ruler.

The Dynamics of Escalation
What Habré had managed to accomplish with covert U.S. aid Goukouni was now determined to do with Qadhafi's military backing, thus paving the way for a reenactment of the 1980 Libyan intervention.

Despite appearances to the contrary the second Libyan intervention (1983) differs from the first (1980) in one fundamental respect: when Libya first moved into Chad it was at the request of the GUNT, to bring to an end Habré's dissidence; the 1983 intervention, on the other hand, was clearly directed against a government which enjoyed the official recognition of the vast majority of the OAU. It was the repeated failure of Qadhafi to gain for his client the recognition of the OAU, first at the Tripoli summits in 1982 and then at Addis Ababa in 1983, which convinced him that force was indeed the only alternative to diplomacy.

The timing of the 1983 intervention confirms this interpretation. It was shortly after the Addis summit, on June 23, that Goukouni's Libyan-backed forces launched their first major attack on Faya-Largeau. The assault lasted twenty-four hours and involved anywhere from 1,500 to 2,500 "rebels" assisted by an estimated 2,000-strong mobile column consisting of Libyan regulars and elements of the Islamic Legion equipped with B–12 and B–13 multiple rocket launchers and SAM–7 surface-to-air missiles. On June 24, Habré's troops fell back before the massive firepower of the insurgents who quickly pushed their way into the southeast, scoring one victory after another. On July 8, the strategic border town of Abeche fell into their hands. Almost immediately Habré launched a brilliant counteroffensive. Realizing the vulnerabilities of his opponent's forces, now hundreds of miles from their lines of supply, he struck back on July 12. Abeche, Biltine, Kalait, and Oum Chalouba were recaptured in a matter of days, and on July 31, against heavy odds, the FAN successfully fought their way back into Faya-Largeau. Once again Habré had proven himself a master at the art of desert blitzkrieg.

As Habré's fortunes ebbed and flowed on the battlefield, the spotlight suddenly shifted to the diplomatic front where intensive efforts were being made to boost his military capabilities. At first a consensus of sorts appeared to emerge among France, the United States, and Zaire in their attempt to organize a rescue operation. Shortly after the fall of Faya-Largeau, on June 28, Mitterrand agreed to an emergency aid package, and by mid-July 400 tons of military supplies, including antitank weapons and surface-to-surface rockets, were flown to Ndjamena. On July 10, Reagan authorized $10 million in emergency military aid to Chad, adding an extra $15 million on August 5. By then two AWACS electronic surveillance planes were on the scene, and a handful of military advisers had arrived. Meanwhile some 1,800 Zairian paratroopers, accompanied by three Mirage aircraft, arrived in Ndjamena. Mobutu's visit to Washington on August 3 brought to light total agreement between him and Reagan on their condemnation of Libya. On this occasion Reagan paid public homage to "America's faithful friend for 20 years" for his "courage" in sending troops to Chad.

Very different were the signals sent out to Mitterrand. The very modest role which the French at first intended to play in Chad became a matter of growing concern in Washington. French insistence that the 1976 *accord de coopération* did not commit them to send troops to Chad came out loud and clear from the lips of the official Elysée spokesman, Max Gallo, on July 7: "There are no French soldiers in Chad, and there will be none" (*Sun* [Washington], July 8, 1983). As Habré's position in Faya-Largeau came under increasing threats Washington renewed its pressure on Mitterrand to persuade him to assume a more active role. Such was the intended purpose of the visit by Reagan's special envoy, Vernon Walters, to Mitterrand's residence in Latche on August 6. For Walters a French air strike against rebel-held positions, supported by American F–15 fighter escorts and AWACS planes, was the only sensible strategy; continued French inaction, on the other hand, raised the possibility of Faya-Largeau once again passing into Goukouni's hands, this time for good. Mitterrand remained adamant.

The crunch came on August 10 when a massive assault against Faya-Largeau delivered the oasis back into Goukouni's hands. Against the heavy pounding by Libyan artillery and the bombing raids of MIG–23 and SU–22 fighter-bombers, Habré's desert warriors caved in. One-third of his troops, that is, about 1,000, were killed or captured during the assault; the rest, including his minister of foreign affairs, Idriss Miskine, and chief of staff, Idriss Debi, miraculously escaped only moments before the oasis fell.

Precisely when the town was about to fall, on August 9, the French ambassador to Ndjamena, Claude Soubeste, informed Habré that Mitterrand had finally agreed to send in French paratroopers and air support. Operation Sting-Ray was underway. Before the first batch of a total of 3,000 paratroopers had even set foot in Ndjamena a totally new situation developed on the ground. As Habré's troops fell back some 200 miles to the south, the Libyans dug in. Dislodging Goukouni's Libyan-backed forces from Faya-Largeau now appeared well beyond the capacity of Habré's FAN, and indeed beyond the will of the French. As Habré took up defensive positions on a line running from Abeche in the east to Salal, Moussoro, and Mao in the west, and as Libyan troops, tanks, and artillery consolidated their hold on the northern half of the country, the military stand-off inevitably led to a de facto partition of the country.

Sting-Ray brought to an end a process of escalation in which diplomatic pressures and counterpressures played a crucial role in shaping the outcome of the struggle on the ground. French reluctance to intervene on Habré's side at a time when such intervention could have turned the tide must have had a determining effect on the Libyan decision to move ahead. U.S. pressures, on the other hand, appear to have been equally instrumental in prompting the French to procrastinate. In the end Sting-Ray was not so much a belated recognition of the wisdom of the American position as it was an eleventh-hour effort on the part of Mitterrand to avoid losing credibility with the majority of French-speaking African states.

France and the United States:
Cross-Current Diplomacy

Acting on the strength of his previous and successful attempt to exercise diplomatic leverage on Qadhafi, Mitterrand at first opted for a negotiated solution with Libya. Hence his decision to send his trusted and long-time friend, Roland Dumas, on a diplomatic mission to Tripoli in early August. The fall of Faya-Largeau, on August 10, shot that calculation to bits, while at the same time providing the justification for operation Sting-Ray.

Until then French caution in countering the Libyan threat stemmed from several considerations. First and foremost were the perceived failings of previous French interventions in Chad, and Mitterrand's personal conviction that military solutions were not likely to bring about political stability. Second, military intervention seemed ruled out from the outset by the very nature of Mitterrand's declared policy on Chad, based on an explicit commitment to the OAU as the only legitimate forum for defining and implementing a solution to the Chadian crisis. Third, the economic costs of military involvement seemed hardly worth the gamble: quite aside from the fact that, militarily, the success of a "punctual" strike against Libyan forces was by no means a foregone conclusion given the operational limitations of French interventionary forces (Yost 1983, 990),[6] economically, the resulting loss of the Libyan market could only hurt French business interests, and this at a time when the French economy could hardly sustain further setbacks.[7] Moreover, "any military intervention would raise difficulties for President Mitterrand in his

6. This, however, is not the opinion of the French military authorities interviewed by this writer: according to Generals Edouard Cortadellas and Jean-Louis Delayen, both of whom saw active duty in Chad, there is little doubt that the kind of military intervention suggested by the United States prior to the fall of Faya-Largeau would have achieved its intended objective (personal communication from Cortadellas, October 1, 1983; interview with Delayen, October 28, 1983). A very different assessment was voiced by Mitterrand in his interview with Jacques Amalric and Eric Rouleau on August 25, 1983: "To bombard and strafe Aouzou, the roads leading into Faya and Faya itself, eventually wage an air battle a thousand kilometers and more away from Ndjamena, in short get involved in a war and forget about the rest: the impression I get in the light of many commentaries is that we were being invited to take a walk in the countryside. Well! Let me say that it is to show considerable contempt for the people of this region to think that they would run away at the first ranging shot. . . ." (*Le Monde,* October 26, 1983).

7. An awareness of the scale of French economic interests in Libya, along with the presence of some 2,500 French citizens, is crucial to an understanding of Mitterrand's determination to avoid a direct confrontation with Libya. About fifty French enterprises are currently doing business with Libya, including Thompson, Peugeot, Renault, Airbus Industrie, and Dassault. French exports to Libya amounted to 6 billion francs in 1981, but dropped to 2.7 billion in 1982. In that year France bought 3.9 billion francs of Libyan oil. Ironically, the overwhelming proportion of French sales to Libya is in the form of military aircraft and missiles. Since 1970, 116 Mirage III and 32 Mirage Fl, 40 Alouette III and 8 Super-Frelon helicopters, 90 launching pads for anti-aircraft Crotale missiles, and an undisclosed number of air-to-air 530 Magic missiles were sold to Libya (*Nouvel Observateur,* August 26–September 1, 1983, p. 24).

own Socialist party" (Yost 1983, 990), and particularly so if such intervention were to be seen as a concession to U.S. pressures. In fact the mere prospect of a military intervention caused bitter disagreements within Mitterrand's cabinet long before operation Sting-Ray even materialized.[8]

Habré's previous record as a "rebel" might be viewed as yet another reason why Mitterrand showed so little enthusiasm for an intervention on his behalf. As the man who engineered the kidnapping of Françoise Claustre in 1974, and who subsequently ordered the execution of Major Pierre Galopin on April 4, 1975 (Thompson and Adloff 1981, 85), Habré would never win a popularity contest among the French; yet for no other reason than that of state, Mitterrand, like Giscard before him, was willing to forget and forgive. What finally provoked his presidential anger, however, and caused him to further temporize (even though preparations were already under way for a possible military intervention) was Habré's undiplomatic characterization of Mitterrand's advisers during his press conference of August 6: "Those poor imbeciles who know nothing about Africa. . . ." This, according to a reliable source, "was one of the reasons why Mitterrand rejected Hernu's proposition (on August 7) to launch an air strike on Faya" (Soudan 1983, 47).

A more compelling reason has to do with the mounting pressures from Washington—beginning with the "Dear François" letters from Ronald Reagan and culminating in Vernon Walters' impromptu visit to Latche on August 6 (Soudan 1983, 46)—to induce Mitterrand to strike against the Libyans. Quite aside from the intrinsic merits of the American case, the sheer forcefulness with which it was pressed upon the Elysée was enough to raise fears in Mitterrand's mind that a French intervention, at the time and place advocated by the White House, would be perceived as being dictated by Washington. That such a response would generate considerable criticisms from Third World countries in general, Libya in particular, and most importantly within his own Socialist Party, not to mention the Communists, seemed patently clear. Resisting American pressures had long been an article of faith among hard-liners within the Socialist Party; it was now seen by Mitterrand as a condition of his political credibility at home and abroad.

American perceptions of the Chadian crisis developed within a radically different framework, and in response to very different preoccupations. From the outset there was total unanimity among Reagan's advisers about the need to contain and punish Qadhafi's adventurism in Chad. Seen by some as the

8. While the Quai d'Orsay stuck to a noninterventionist position—reflecting the views of Claude Cheysson, minister for external affairs, and Guy Georgy, ex-ambassador to Libya, now serving as ambassador to Algeria and widely regarded as the spokesman of the "Libyan lobby"—others, such as Christian Nucci, minister of cooperation and development, Charles Hernu, minister of defense, and Guy Penne, Mitterrand's personal adviser for African Affairs, were said to be generally receptive to the American position. The pros and cons of intervention were aired in the course of a *conseil de crise* held at the Elysée on August 5 (Soudan 1983, 47).

Trojan horse of Soviet communism in Africa, Libya's reentry into Chad carried ominous implications. Not only would Egypt and the Sudan be directly exposed to the contamination of Qadhafi's imperial designs, with the Soviets and the East Germans acting as vectors of Libyan subversion, but ultimately most of Chad's neighbors, including Nigeria, were visualized as falling dominoes. Chad as such was not the issue; at stake was the stability of Chad's neighbors. In this Dullesian scenario very little room was left for accommodation and compromise. Reagan's handling of the Chadian crisis fits into the general pattern recently described by Arthur Schlesinger (1983, 7): "By construing every local mess as a test of global will, ideology raises stakes in situations that cannot be easily controlled and threatens to transmute limited into unlimited conflicts. Moreover, ideology, if pursued to the end, excludes the thought of accommodation or coexistence."

Accommodation, on the other hand, was clearly uppermost in Mitterrand's mind, at least until the fall of Faya on August 10. By then, however, the costs of compromise were all too evident. Losing credibility among Francophone states for what many felt was a policy of appeasement in the face of Libyan blackmail was far too heavy a price to pay for placating the "Libyan lobby" and hard-liners within the cabinet. The Ivory Coast, Senegal, and Zaire played a decisive role in driving home to Mitterrand the anxieties of most Francophone states (with the notable exceptions of Benin and the Congo) over Qadhafi's "adventurism" and, as far as Zaire and Senegal were concerned, their readiness to turn to Washington as an alternative source of support. As African pressures mounted, the fall of Faya-Largeau made dramatically clear the bankruptcy of previous attempts at accommodation with Libya; such, also, was the implication of the Sankara coup in Upper Volta (now called Burkina Faso) on August 4, which gave Mitterrand an additional opportunity to take the full measure of the Libyan menace. At long last on August 10, Mitterrand crossed the Rubicon. In so doing, as has been noted, "he chose to lose his virginity rather than his credibility" (*West Africa,* August 22, 1983).

Reflecting on the contrasting responses of Paris and Washington to the Chadian crisis Piero Gleijeses (1983) offers the following assessment of their respective merits:

> The skill and flexibility demonstrated by President François Mitterrand in response to developments in Chad contrasts with the Reagan administration's myopia and intransigence. French policy has reflected a deeper understanding of Chad and a desire to limit Paris's conflict with Colonel Muammar el-Qaddafi. Washington seeks to "punish" the Libyan leader and neglects the Chadian dimension of the war.

Tempting as it is, in retrospect, to credit the author of these lines with prophetic insights—and French diplomacy with the merits that he found to be so conspicuously lacking in the "myopia and intransigeance" of the Reagan administration—a closer look at French diplomacy and Libyan behavior since 1983 suggests a far more cautious appraisal.

Although the Chadian crisis has yet to find its denouement, there is no gainsaying the significance of the Franco-Libyan mutual withdrawal agreement of September 16, 1984; whether this breakthrough in the military stalemate can also be viewed as a diplomatic victory for the French is highly questionable.

In anticipation of what the joint Franco-Libyan communiqué termed "the complete, mutual and simultaneous withdrawal of French and Libyan troops from Chad," some observers concluded—all too prematurely—that French efforts to move the Libyans from their position of intransigeance to one of accommodation had finally paid off. Not only had Mitterrand met the immediate objectives he had initially set for himself—namely, avoiding a direct confrontation with Qadhafi while at the same time displaying enough military strength on the ground to prevent a Libyan takeover of the capital—but the ultimate goal of restoring Chadian sovereignty over its national territory was now on the verge of becoming a reality. Subsequent developments proved this assessment to be unduly optimistic, however, for if the short-term objectives of French intervention have indeed been met, the more fundamental goal of French diplomacy (the restoration of Chadian sovereignty) remains as much a mirage today as it was prior to the signature of the Tripoli accord.

As is now patently clear, Qadhafi's unwillingness to honor his obligations under the terms of the mutual withdrawal agreement, along with the reluctance of the Mitterrand government to concede diplomatic failure, have done little to bridge the gap between the French and U.S. positions on how to deal with Libya, or for that matter to improve French credibility with the Chadian authorities. American disclosures of what came to be seen as a Libyan ruse were not the least of the irritants that have contributed to sharpening the tensions between Paris and Washington. Disputing the terms of a Franco-Libyan communiqué on November 10 that France and Libya had completed their agreed pullout, the U.S. State Department claimed on November 14 that "a substantial number" of Libyan troops were still on the ground. American claims were at first rejected by the Mitterrand government, but as U.S. intelligence reports showed otherwise, and following an impromptu meeting of Mitterrand with Colonel Qadhafi in Crete on November 15, the Elysée reluctantly admitted the continuing presence of Libyan troops in northern Chad. Further adding to French discomfiture, a report from the French National Defense Secretariat (a government advisory body on military affairs) revealed on November 20 that an estimated 3,000 Libyan troops with heavy equipment remained in Chad, and not the 1,000 men that Mitterrand claimed on his return from Crete. Irrefutable proof of Libyan insincerity failed to move the French government any closer to the American position; while acknowledging "great disappointment" that Libya had not pulled out all its troops, on the occasion of his visit to Washington on November 20 Cheysson reiterated the basic French argument that U.S. policy toward Libya was fundamentally mistaken. Trying to put the best possible face on what many perceived as a major foreign policy blunder, French Foreign Minister Claude Cheysson added: "Colonel Qadhafi is, I may say, a fact; he is there ... to ignore him would be a political mistake. We want to have with Libya normal relations" (*New York Times,* November 21, 1984). The logic of the American alternative, by contrast, could lead to military action against Libya that "no one would recommend." Or, to put it in plain language, the political and military costs of sanctions against Libya far exceed the benefits that France might expect from such sanctions. This, rather than Qadhafi, is the basic "fact" behind France's pull-out from Chad, a fact which did not go unnoticed in Ndjamena.

Nowhere is the disillusion over French policies more apparent than in Ndjamena. Habré's anger over the Franco-Libyan agreement, concluded without prior consultation with the Chadian government, has been compounded by France's unwillingness at first to recognize that Qadhafi had not kept his word and its subsequent reluctance to apply sanctions. For Habré the Libyans have merely redrawn their defense perimeter further north, without any substantial scaling down of their ground forces. Hence the withdrawal of French troops appears palpably inconsistent with the operating principle which, according to Cheysson, would serve as the basis of French policy in Chad: "If they stay, we stay; if they leave, we leave."

Faced with mounting criticisms of his Chadian policies at home and abroad, Mitterrand confronts a difficult choice: either to redeploy his troops along the sixteenth parallel and run the risk of another military escalation, or accept the status quo in hopes that Qadhafi will eventually keep his promise to withdraw. The latter appears the only viable option for the time being. Short of a massive reentry of Libyan troops in the region immediately north of the sixteenth parallel, a redeployment of French troops in Chad appears most unlikely.

Meanwhile the Sisyphean task of restoring a measure of stability to the Chadian polity appears more futile than ever. French policies have now come full circle. After completing their third military withdrawal since 1975, and after lending their grudging support to almost every contestant, from the late Tombalbaye to Malloum, from Malloum to Goukouni, and from Goukouni to Habré, the French are back to square one, desperately trying to shore up a client state on the shifting sands of factionalism and civil strife. *Plus ça change, plus c'est la même chose.*

REFERENCES

Briggs, Lloyd. 1960. *Tribes of the Sahara.* Cambridge, Mass.: Harvard University Press.

Buijtenhuijs, Robert. 1978. *Le Frolinat et les Révoltes Populaires.* Paris: Mouton.

Bujra, Janet. 1973. "The Dynamics of Political Action: A New Look at Factionalism." *American Anthropologist* 75, no. 1:132–152.

Chapelle, Jean. 1957. *Nomades Noirs du Sahara.* Paris: Plon.

D'Arbaumont, Jean. 1954. "Le Tibesti et le Domaine Teda-Daza." *Bulletin de l'IFAN* (Dakar) 16, nos. 3–4:255–306.

Decalo, Samuel. 1980. "Chad: The Roots of Center-Periphery Strife." *African Affairs* 79, no. 317 (October):491–509.

Gellner, Ernest. 1973. "Introduction to Nomadism," pp. 1–9 in Cynthia Nelson, ed. *The Desert and the Sown.* Berkeley: University of California Press.

Gleijeses, Piero. 1983. "French Skill in Chad." *New York Times,* August 29.

Lanne, Bernard. 1982. *Tchad-Libye: La Querelle des Frontières.* Paris: Karthala.

Legum, Colin. 1982. "The Crisis over Chad," pp. A35–A46 in *Africa Contemporary Record 1980–81,* vol. 12. New York: Africana Publishing Co.

Lemarchand, René. 1981. "Chad: The Roots of Chaos." *Current History* 80, no. 470 (December):414–436.

Le Monde. 1983. June 25; October 26.

New York Times. October 22, 1983; November 21, 1984.

Nouvel Observateur. August 26–September 1, 1983.

Schlesinger, Arthur. 1983. "Foreign Policy and the American Character." *Foreign Affairs* 62, no. 1 (Winter):1–16.

Soudan, François. 1983. "Tchad: Ce que Mitterrand n'a pas dit." *Jeune Afrique,* no. 1183. September 7.

Sun (Washington). July 8, 1983.

Thompson, Virginia, and Richard Adloff. 1981. *Conflict in Chad.* Berkeley: University of California, International Studies.

West Africa. 1983. August 22; October 10.

Wright, Claudia. 1982. "Libya and the West: Headlong into Confrontation?" *International Affairs* 88, no. 1 (Winter):13–41.

Yost, David S. 1983. "French Policy in Chad: The Libyan Challenge." *Orbis* 21, no. 1 (Winter):965–997.

14

At Odds with Self-Determination: The United States and Western Sahara

TONY HODGES

For almost a decade, a bitter and seemingly intractable war has been fought for control of Western Sahara, a bleak but phosphate-rich territory bordering the Atlantic, to the immediate south of Morocco. Although it has received only sporadic coverage in the American press, this conflict raises issues of great import for the Maghreb, for Africa, and for the international community at large, including the United States. In the Maghreb, it has compounded the grave financial difficulties facing Morocco, thereby undermining the stability of the pro-Western regime of King Hassan II. It has severely strained relations between Morocco and its powerful Maghrebi neighbor, Algeria. As an inter-African conflict, the Saharan war has become a major challenge for the Organization of African Unity (OAU). For the United States, France, and other Western powers, wider strategic issues are at stake, since the continuation of the war could culminate in radical political change within Morocco.

At issue also is the cardinal principle of the contemporary philosophy of decolonization—the right of self-determination—for this war was spawned by the unusual and much criticized way in which Spain, which first laid claim to Western Sahara in 1884, "decolonized" it in 1975–76 without reference to the wishes of its indigenous inhabitants. In effect, it was simply handed over, without popular sanction, to its northern and southern neighbors, Morocco and Mauritania, which had long-standing territorial claims to the area. Moroccan and Mauritanian troops entered the colony, as the Spanish withdrew, during a brief transitional period of tripartite administration, between November 1975 and February 1976. The Spanish flag was pulled down for the last time on February 26, and the following April the territory was formally partitioned, Morocco receiving 68,340 square miles in the north and Mauritania 34,750 square miles in the south.

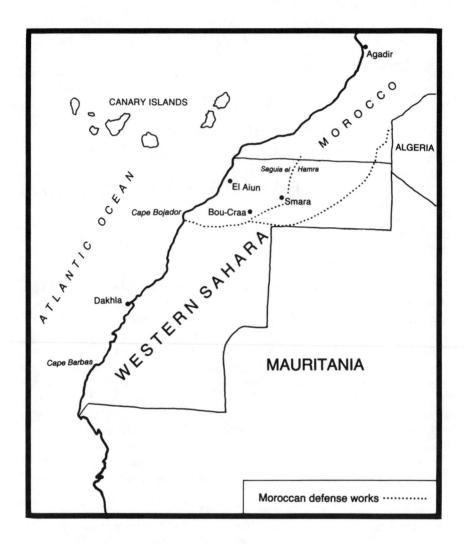

Map 6. Western Sahara

The local population was never genuinely consulted, despite the fact that, on the very eve of these events, the International Court of Justice at The Hague, in an advisory opinion on the territory, had upheld the primacy of "the principle of self-determination through the free and genuine expression of the will of the peoples of the Territory" (International Court of Justice 1975, 68). Indeed, the U.N. General Assembly had been urging Spain since 1966 to organize a referendum on the territory's future. It was never held. If it had been there seems little doubt that it would have resulted in a large majority for independence. A U.N. mission of inquiry, which had toured the country in May 1975, had come away convinced that "there was an overwhelming consensus among Saharans within the territory in favour of independence and opposing integration with any neighbouring country" (Report . . . 1975, 59). It had also been struck by the widespread support for the *Frente Popular para la Liberación de Saguia el-Hamra y Río de Oro,* the pro-independence movement commonly known by its acronym, Polisario, which had been founded two years earlier and had been staging small hit-and-run raids against the Spanish.

However, King Hassan and his Mauritanian ally, President Mokhtar Ould Daddah, underestimated the Saharawis' determination to resist annexation — and Algeria's determination to give them the wherewithal to do so. Tens of thousands of Saharawis fled to Algeria, and on February 27, 1976, Polisario proclaimed the birth of an independent Saharan Arab Democratic Republic (SADR), which has since been recognized by sixty states, including thirty in Africa, and in 1982 gained controversial admission to the OAU.[1] In July 1978, President Ould Daddah was deposed by his war-weary army, and a year later, in August 1979, Mauritania signed a peace treaty with Polisario, formally renouncing its claim to Western Saharan territory. This prompted King Hassan to annex the erstwhile Mauritanian sector of Western Sahara too.

Since then, the war has dragged on, without any real sign of resolution in the near future. Under a gradual retrenchment policy, carried out in 1979–81, the Moroccan *Forces Armées Royales* (FAR) pulled back to two strategic enclaves near the coast. A continuous defense line, known as the "wall," was

1. The SADR's admission to the OAU in February 1982 was contested by a minority of African states. Boycotts, occasioned by disputes over the SADR's membership, the representation of strife-torn Chad, and the scheduling of the 1982 OAU summit in Libya deprived the OAU of the required two-thirds quorum for its ministerial and summit conferences, with the result that no summit could be held in 1982. It took a change in venue and a decision by the SADR to stay away for a summit finally to be held, in Addis Ababa, Ethiopia, in June 1983. Thereafter, Morocco steadily lost diplomatic ground in the OAU, due principally to King Hassan's refusal to hold OAU-sponsored talks with Polisario, as well as disquiet among African "moderates" over Morocco's "treaty of union" with Libya in August 1984 and a widespread desire on the part of African leaders to avoid further rows on the SADR's OAU membership that could detract from the OAU's need to focus attention on the continent's grave economic problems. At the OAU summit in Addis Ababa in November 1984 the SADR took its seat almost unchallenged, with only Zaire following Morocco in a protest walkout.

built in the northwest to secure the largest of these enclaves, the so-called useful triangle, which includes the phosphate mines at Bou-Craa and the two main Western Saharan towns, El-Ayoun (the old Spanish capital) and Smara. The other, much smaller enclave was farther south, around the coastal settlement of Dakhla. Since then Morocco has reinforced its army in Western Sahara to over 100,000 men and extended its enclaves by building new defense lines. By early 1985 Morocco controlled just over one-third of the territory's land area. Polisario, meanwhile, has evolved into a semi-conventional army, and in October 1984 it launched a major new campaign, entitled the Greater Maghreb Offensive, resulting in some of the fiercest fighting of the war. Meanwhile, little if any real progress has been made toward resolving the conflict diplomatically. In June 1983, at its Addis Ababa summit, the OAU drew up a peace plan, which hinged on Morocco and Polisario negotiating a cease-fire so that a referendum could be held by the end of the year. However, Morocco refused to talk to the guerrillas. The OAU's deadline for the referendum passed by, therefore, without even any progress toward achieving a cease-fire.

Polisario claimed that Morocco's refusal to negotiate was ultimately attributable to the generous arms supplies provided to the FAR by the Western powers, in particular the United States and France. This military assistance, the Saharawi nationalists argued, had encouraged King Hassan to believe that he could win a military victory—an illusion which served only to prolong a war of attrition that was sapping the Moroccan economy and the stability of the very regime the West hoped to safeguard. What, in fact, has been the policy approach taken by the United States to this African conflict, under the successive administrations of Presidents Ford, Carter, and Reagan? What are the principal strategic considerations that have influenced U.S. policy? How much military support has the United States given Morocco? And what has been, or might yet be, the outcome of U.S. policy?

The Importance of Morocco

It is a paradox that U.S. policy on the Saharan war has never really been motivated by strong views on the future of Western Sahara itself. The territory is of minimal importance to the United States. Economically, Western Sahara has large deposits of phosphates, but that resource is of no interest to the United States, which is the largest phosphate producer in the world and a net exporter of the mineral. Nor is the United States interested in denying the USSR access to this phosphate wealth. The USSR is the world's second largest phosphate producer and, insofar as it needs to supplement its own supplies, has been able to do so without difficulty from Morocco, the third largest producer and by far the largest exporter.

It has sometimes been suggested that, as a ministate, an independent Western Sahara would be unviable and thus might quickly fall under the influence of outside powers, such as the USSR or Libya, and become a source of regional instability. However, there is little basis for such hypotheses. First, Western Sahara would be no more a ministate than many existing African countries with which the United States has generally cordial relations. It would really only be small in terms of population—and, even in those terms, it would not be the smallest of African states. A census conducted by Spain in 1974 recorded a total population of 95,019, of whom 73,497 were Saharawis. However, this census missed part of the still nomadic population, and it also took no account of the large number of Saharawis (probably an absolute majority of the whole Saharawi population) who had settled in neighboring countries during the last decade and a half of Spanish rule. Many of these Saharawis from northern Mauritania, southern Morocco, and southwestern Algeria have since joined Polisario and could be expected to settle in Western Sahara once it achieved independence. Thus, taking also into account the population growth during the decade since 1974, it is not unreasonable to project that an independent Western Sahara would have a population of at least 150,000 and perhaps as high as 225,000 (Hodges 1984, 131–132). This would still be small, but it does not mean that Western Sahara would be unviable as an independent state. By virtue of its large phosphate resources (there are 1.7 billion tons of high-grade ore at Bou-Craa alone), it would enjoy one of the highest levels of per capita income on the African continent.[2]

There is likewise little evidence that Polisario would constitute a threat to the governments of neighboring states if Western Sahara gained independence. "Our fight is a liberation war, for national independence, and is not intended to overthrow foreign regimes," declared the General National Program adopted by Polisario's fourth congress in September 1978 (Polisario Front 1978). Polisario has never espoused Marxist principles, even verbally, and, as a proudly nationalist movement, it would be most unlikely to end up beholden to any foreign power after successfully concluding its long and difficult struggle for independence.

It is Morocco, rather than Western Sahara itself, which matters to the West. U.S. policymakers have been interested primarily in the implications of the Saharan war for the stability of the Hassan regime, which has long been valued in Washington as an important ally.

Morocco lies astride the entrance to the Mediterranean, one of the most strategic waterways in the world. Morocco's excellent deepwater ports have always welcomed U.S. warships, and until 1963, the Strategic Air Command

---

2. Spanish officials informed the U.N. mission which visited Western Sahara in 1975 that, when phosphate production reached 10 million tons a year, as planned by Spain, per capita income would be comparable to that in many Western European countries.

had bases in Morocco. After the latter's closure, the U.S. Navy retained communications facilities in Morocco until 1978, when they were no longer required. More recently, the United States has acquired transit facilities in Morocco for the Rapid Deployment Force (RDF), the special force readied for emergency intervention in the Middle East. Agreed to in principle during a visit by President Reagan's first secretary of state, Alexander Haig, to Marrakesh in February 1982, these transit rights were formalized the following May when King Hassan visited Washington and a secret military agreement was signed by Haig and the Moroccan foreign minister, M'Hammed Boucetta. Valid for an initial six years, the agreement gave the RDF access to two Moroccan air bases, complementing the facilities it had already been granted in Egypt, Somalia, and Oman. "Morocco happens to be properly situated," commented a Pentagon official at the time. "Morocco to Egypt is a good hop" (Interview 1982).

King Hassan's importance to U.S. administrations has gone far beyond these logistical considerations, however. The king has always been regarded in Washington as a "moderate" in the Arab world who has opposed the more militant opponents of Israel. He has kept open discreet lines of communication with several influential Israeli politicians, and he supported the initial stages of the detente between Egypt and Israel in 1977–78. He lauded the late President Anwar Sadat for "his courageous initiative" in flying to Jerusalem in November 1977 and welcomed him to Morocco immediately after the Camp David Accords in September 1978. The king did later join the Arab boycott of Egypt, but the Carter administration recognized that this was a purely pragmatic move, designed to ensure the continued flow of vital Saudi financial aid to Morocco. Hassan was later able to boost his stature in the Arab world— and thus also his diplomatic leverage in the West—by assuming the chairmanship of the Al-Qods (Jerusalem) Committee set up at an Islamic conference in Fez in May 1979, and by hosting the Arab League summit in Fez in September 1982 at which a new blueprint for a comprehensive Middle East settlement was adopted, and by presiding over the Islamic summit in Casablanca in January 1984, at which Egypt was welcomed back into the Islamic Conference Organization. There was concern in Washington over King Hassan's decision to sign a unity treaty with Libya in August 1984, but U.S. officials recognized that Morocco hoped thereby to end Libyan support for Polisario, while there was considerable skepticism that a pact between such ideological opposites could last any longer than Colonel Qadhafi's earlier ill-fated "marriages" with Arab and African states.

U.S. administrations have also been impressed by King Hassan's readiness to act as a regional gendarme in defense of Western interests in Africa. On two occasions, in April 1977 and May 1978, the king sent 1,500 Moroccan troops to Zaire to help President Mobutu Sese Seko defeat the Angolan-backed rebels who had seized control of parts of the mineral-rich province of

Shaba. In addition, Morocco has tended to align with the United States in votes at the United Nations and has been particularly vocal in its condemnation of Soviet actions in Afghanistan.

The loss of such an ally would be a serious setback for the U.S. government, or would at least entail serious risks, for there is no guarantee that King Hassan's successor would retain Morocco's close ties with Washington. It is on the conflict in the Sahara, moreover, that the king's fortunes largely hinge. The "recovery of the Moroccan Sahara" has been a dominant issue in Moroccan politics since 1974. The evolution of the conflict in the desert not only has major implications for the Moroccan economy, but also for the king's prestige and his relations with the FAR, the one force in Moroccan society with the power to depose him, and so his fate may well be inextricably linked with the war's ultimate outcome.

Kissinger and the Madrid Accords

The Madrid Accords of November 14, 1975, by which Spain agreed to transfer its administrative powers in Western Sahara to Morocco and Mauritania, marked a radical shift in Spanish policy. In July 1974, following the coup in Lisbon the previous April which paved the way for the decolonization of Portugal's African empire, the Franco regime had announced plans for internal self-government in Western Sahara, and a month later it had announced plans to hold a referendum, which was expected to result in independence. To thwart these plans, King Hassan massed thousands of troops on the Western Saharan border, harassed Spanish fishing boats off the Moroccan coast, revived dormant claims to the Spanish-ruled enclaves of Ceuta and Melilla on Morocco's Mediterranean coast, sent guerrilla groups into Western Sahara, and in a crowning act of defiance massed 350,000 of his subjects on the Western Saharan border to stage a "Green March," named after the holy color of Islam, into the Spanish colony. By launching a patriotic-cum-religious crusade for the liberation of Morocco's "amputated" Saharan provinces, the king aroused enormous enthusiasm among the Moroccan masses, greatly increasing his popularity. He also outmaneuvered the Moroccan opposition parties, all of which supported the claim to Western Sahara (and had previously criticized his government for not taking sufficiently strong action against Spain), and provided a noble—and conveniently distant—mission for the FAR, which had twice attempted coups against him, in 1971 and 1972. In short, the Western Saharan crusade enabled the king to recover politically from the crises which had rocked his regime in the early 1970s.

Henry Kissinger, who was President Ford's secretary of state at the time, recognized this, and also knew that if the crusade failed to attain its objectives after the venting of so much passion, the king would be publicly humiliated and face a potentially dangerous resurgence of domestic opposition. The Ford administration was also concerned that a direct confrontation between Spain and Morocco would endanger the transition to a stable new post-Francoist order in Spain. General Franco, who was eighty-two, fell ill in October 1975 and lay unconscious in a coma at the height of the crisis in Spanish-Moroccan relations. He died on November 20, six days after the signing of the Madrid Accords. Washington feared that the caudillo's death might trigger the kind of turmoil that had gripped Portugal since April 1974. This was not a time, in Kissinger's view, for foreign adventures. There was a military consideration too. The political upheaval in Portugal threatened the U.S. base rights at Lajes in the Azores, which had proved invaluable to the U.S. Air Force as a refueling stop for its emergency airlift to Israel during the 1973 Arab-Israeli war, and so gave added importance to the four huge U.S. bases built in Spain since 1955 at a cost of more than $450 million. Their lease was being renegotiated at the time, and was eventually renewed in January 1976 in return for $1 billion in U.S. aid and the sale of seventy-two F–16 aircraft to the Spanish Air Force (*Defense Monitor* 1976; Ware 1975).

Details of the diplomatic exchanges between Washington, Rabat, and Madrid about Western Sahara during 1975 have never been made public, but King Hassan spoke on October 27, 1975, of the United States being "sandwiched" between Morocco and Spain and encouraging its two allies "to consider a peaceful solution through dialogue" (Hassan II, 1975). Alfred Atherton, one of Kissinger's assistant secretaries of state, had visited Morocco to meet the king on October 22, and the deputy director of the CIA, General Vernon Walters, had gone to Madrid to put American views on the Saharan crisis to Spanish leaders.[3] It would be far-fetched to suggest that the United States mediated between Spain and Morocco, or, as Lieutenant Colonel Luis Rodríguez de Viguri, the last secretary-general of the Spanish colonial administration in Western Sahara, has since claimed, that the United States put pressure on Madrid to succumb to Morocco (*El País* 1978). Prince Juan Carlos, who assumed the functions of head of state on October 30, as Franco lay in his coma, and Carlos Arias Navarro, the prime minister, had good reason, in view of the delicacy of the political situation in Spain itself, to cool the dispute with Morocco, which risked getting out of hand and leading to war. However, the United States did work behind the scenes in the U.N. Security Council to tone down its resolutions condemning the Green March, and it was satisfied that the final outcome of the crisis, the Madrid Accords, both averted a head-on confrontation between Spain and Morocco and allowed King Hassan to boast a great victory to his enthusiastic subjects (Franck 1976, 694–721). On December 10, 1975, the United States accordingly ab-

3. In an interview with an *Africa News* correspondent, General Walters declined to disclose the precise nature of his mission. "It would look like the King of Morocco and the King of Spain are pawns of the U.S., and that wouldn't be in anybody's interest," he said. Prince Juan Carlos had assumed the functions of Spanish head of state on October 30, as Franco lay in a coma (*Africa News* November 2, 1979).

stained in the U.N. General Assembly on an Algerian-backed resolution (3458A) reaffirming the United Nations' traditional calls for a referendum and voted instead for a rival resolution (3458B), backed by Morocco, because, as a State Department official later explained, "it took note of the Madrid Agreement, which we believed at the time offered the best basis for an eventual peaceful settlement" (Veliotes 1977, 39).

Meanwhile, the United States had been giving Morocco help of a more material nature. Since 1974, U.S. experts had been drawing up a rearmament program for the FAR, and, as a result, Foreign Military Sales (FMS) agreements signed by the U.S. government with Morocco soared from $8.2 million in Fiscal Year (FY) 1974 to $242 million in FY1975. The official explanation in Washington was that the FAR needed rearmament to defend Morocco in the event of a war with Algeria—although it was quite evident that the likely spark for such a war, if it broke out, would have been Morocco's designs on Western Sahara, for which military preparations had been underway since July 1974. When King Hassan discovered, after the Madrid Accords, that the war with Polisario might be long and costly or escalate into a head-on confrontation with Algeria, he sent a former premier, Karim Lamrani, to meet with Kissinger in Washington on January 29, 1976. Two weeks later Kissinger informed Congress that Morocco would be sold a squadron of twenty-four Northrop F–5 aircraft for $120 million, along with $36 million worth of armored vehicles.[4] Moreover, special steps were taken to rush equipment to Morocco and Mauritania in 1975–76. The State Department gave approval for numerous transfers of U.S. arms, including F–5 aircraft, from Iran and Jordan (New York Times, May 23, 1976; U.S. House of Representatives 1978). Thus, while the Ford administration did not give formal recognition to the Moroccan claim of sovereignty over Western Sahara, it gave tangible support to Morocco's attempt to secure control of the territory.

Carter's Temporary Arms Sale Curbs

The delivery of arms to Morocco was not without its problems for Washington, however. By the time the Carter administration took office, in January 1977, it could no longer be casually assumed that Morocco and Mauritania would soon defeat Polisario and secure undisputed control of Western Sahara. The supply of U.S. arms to Morocco, for use in the Saharan war, risked damaging U.S. relations with Algeria, which, as a major oil and gas producer, was an important commercial partner of the United States, and as a particularly influential force in the nonaligned movement, was targeted for conscious cultivation by President Carter, who aspired to improve U.S. relations with the Third World.[5] Besides, the fact that the United States did not

4. In fact, Morocco ended up buying Mirage F–1 aircraft from France instead.

5. Carter appointed Ulric Haynes, a close associate of Andrew Young, as his ambassador to Algeria.

recognize Moroccan sovereignty in Western Sahara meant that U.S.–supplied arms were being used there in violation of both the U.S. Arms Export Control Act and a U.S.–Moroccan agreement signed in 1960 which barred the use of U.S. arms by Morocco for nondefensive purposes beyond its recognized borders. Furthermore, the use of U.S. arms against Polisario identified the United States with what looked, especially in African eyes, like a particularly brazen case of territorial annexationism and disregard for the right of self-determination. Questions about Morocco's use of U.S.–supplied weaponry in the desert war surfaced in Congress in October 1977, when, for the first time, a hearing on the Western Saharan problem was held by the House of Representatives' subcommittees on Africa and International Organizations (U.S. House of Representatives, 1977). Then, in a letter sent to President Carter on February 8, 1978, the chairman of the Senate's Subcommittee on Africa, Senator Dick Clark of Iowa, argued that the sale of arms to Morocco "for pursuit of a conflict of questionable legitimacy" associated the United States with "an effort by Morocco to suppress what many African states perceive to be a war for self-determination," and risked "escalating the war far beyond the local conflict it is at the moment, possibly triggering a greater Soviet response in support of Algeria."

The same month, the Carter administration decided to reject a Moroccan request to purchase twenty-four OV–10 "Broncos," low-flying aircraft used for counterinsurgency operations during the Vietnam War, and twenty-four Bell Cobra helicopter gunships, and it asked the Moroccan government to stop using its Northrop F–5 aircraft in Western Sahara. This was not a total military sales ban, however. In February 1979, the State Department approved the sale of six Chinook CH–47 helicopters, and a month later $3 million worth of ammunition for F–5s and $2.4 million worth of spare parts for F–5s and C–130 Hercules transport planes were delivered to Morocco, even though Morocco had refused to stop using its F–5s in Western Sahara. The following May, the State Department approved a proposal by Northrop Page Communications to sell Morocco a $200-million electronic "integrated intrusion detection system," which was eventually installed along the wall built by the FAR around its northwestern enclave in Western Sahara in 1980–82 (*Washington Star,* October 15, 1978).

The Carter administration's curbs on arms sales were therefore quite limited. By the end of 1979, they had been lifted entirely. The fall of the shah of Iran that year was a severe jolt to Washington, and it prompted President Carter to strengthen security ties with traditional U.S. allies in the Third World. At the same time, there was growing concern in Washington that Hassan could end up suffering the same fate as the shah. After its victory over Mauritania, Polisario had taken the offensive against the FAR, scoring a string of impressive successes in 1979. Within Morocco, economic conditions were deteriorating, sparking off a major wave of strikes in 1979, for the first time since the start of the war. The national unity and social peace evident in the early stages of the conflict seemed to be breaking down, and an alarmist CIA report, leaked to the media in October 1979, suggested that King Hassan would "lose control of events, probably in the space of a year, and perhaps even his throne" (ABC Television, October 28, 1979). On October 16, 1979, the Policy Review Committee of the National Security Council advised President Carter to drop the restrictions on arms sales to Morocco. Carter concurred, and on January 24, 1979, his assistant secretary of state for Near Eastern and South Asian affairs, Harold Saunders, testified in Congress in support of plans to sell Morocco $232.5-million worth of aircraft—F–5s, Broncos, and helicopters. "We believe an outright victory over Morocco by Morocco's adversaries would constitute a serious setback to major U.S. interests," he argued. "First and foremost, such a development would destabilize the region in general, and the political equilibrium in Morocco in particular. Beyond that, the United States cannot turn a blind eye to the fact that Morocco has historically been a good friend and indeed, in a practical sense, an ally" (U.S. House of Representatives 1980).

A few liberal Democrats, notably Stephen Solarz, the chairman of the House of Representatives' Subcommittee on Africa, and Andrew Young, argued vigorously against the dropping of the short-lived arms sale restrictions. Writing in *Foreign Affairs,* just before the decision was announced, Solarz (1979–80, 295–296) argued that a change in the arms sale policy would damage relations with Algeria and encourage the Soviet bloc countries "to become involved in a conflict from which they have thus far abstained." Above all, Solarz questioned whether increasing arms sales to Morocco would help keep King Hassan on his throne. "By encouraging the King to maintain the illusion that a military victory is possible, we are much more likely to prolong the war than to shorten it," he suggested. "And with Morocco spending a million dollars a day on a war it cannot win the King will be less able to deal with the festering problems within Morocco itself." Solarz argued that "the sale of offensive American arms may do more ultimately to undermine the monarchy than to shore it up." Such views were shared by Young, who asked rhetorically in February 1980: "If Hassan is our friend, why do we aid in erecting a scaffold of weaponry upon which he can only hang himself?" (*International Herald Tribune,* February 20, 1980). These arguments cut little ice with the administration, however. The aircraft sale went ahead, and the total value of FMS agreements with Morocco rose to a record $274.4 million in FY1980.

While Solarz believed that the lifting of the arms sale restrictions would encourage King Hassan to reject compromise and strive for an impossible military victory, the administration acknowledged that Morocco could not win an outright military victory and claimed that increased support from the United States would enable King Hassan to negotiate from a position of strength. "The comprehensive purpose of the President's decision on arms sales to Morocco," explained Saunders, "is to help that country's efforts to defend itself while at the same time nurturing and encouraging a psychological climate in the region conducive to negotiations. Our efforts to strengthen Morocco militarily go hand-in-hand with our efforts to encourage both sides to come to the negotiating table" (U.S. House of Representatives 1980, 2–3). The idea was to signal to Polisario and Algeria that the United States would not permit Morocco to be driven out of Western Sahara. Such signals, the Carter administration hoped, would encourage a "psychological climate" in Polisario's ranks, or at least in Algiers, conducive to hammering out a settlement on terms acceptable to King Hassan. The Polisario leaders' "public posture remains uncompromising," Saunders noted, "but we hope and expect that as the prospects on the battlefield increasingly demonstrate the impossibility of their imposing a military solution, they will draw the necessary conclusions" (U.S. House of Representatives 1980, 4). However, when, for the first time in the course of the war, the U.S. government made formal contact with Polisario by sending a State Department official, Edmund Hool, to its camps near Tindouf in southwestern Algeria in December 1980, the Saharawi nationalists remained as resolute as ever. Hool's proposal that the Polisario settle for a form of Western Saharan autonomy was dismissed as "impossible." Only independence was acceptable (Radio Algiers, December 11, 1980).

The Reagan Plan for Morocco

When he took office in January 1981, President Reagan reinforced the pro-Moroccan tilt in U.S. Western Saharan policy that had already become evident in the last year of the Carter administration. "Morocco is important to broad American interests and occupies a pivotal strategic area," the deputy assistant secretary in the State Department's Bureau of Near Eastern and South Asian Affairs, Morris Draper, told Congress in March 1981. "We intend to maintain and reinforce our historically close relationship with reliability and consistency as our watchwords" (U.S. House of Representatives 1981, 3). This was in line with "the prevailing view of this administration that America's allies and close associates should expect understanding and reliable support." As Draper put it, "it would not be in the spirit of this administration's policy if support for America's traditional and historic friends—to meet reasonable and legitimate needs—were to be withheld or made conditional other than under extraordinary circumstances" (U.S. House of Representatives 1981, 5). Ironically, these "reasonable and legitimate needs" were construed as including arms to wage war in a territory where Morocco's claim to sovereignty was still not formally recognized by Washington.

Within two days of taking office, the Reagan administration had approved a major new arms sale to Morocco (108 M60 tanks worth $182 million) and authorized delivery of the F–5 and Bronco aircraft promised by the Carter administration a year earlier. However, the FAR suffered a serious reverse in October 1981, when Polisario decimated a Moroccan garrison at Guelta Zemmour, near the Mauritanian border, and shot down five Moroccan aircraft in the space of ten days. King Hassan claimed that Polisario had gained access to ramp-launched Sam–6 missiles, and he turned to the United States for increased military aid. General Vernon Walters, then President Reagan's roving ambassador, flew to Rabat to reassure King Hassan on October 29. On November 5, Francis "Bing" West, the assistant secretary of defense for international security affairs, toured Western Sahara in a Moroccan helicopter to assess the FAR's needs on the spot. "The United States is a true friend of Morocco" and "will do its best to be helpful in every way," promised the U.S. ambassador to Morocco, Joseph Verner Reed, the same day. "Count on us; we are with you" (*Le Monde,* November 8–9, 1981). The following December, a team of thirty U.S. instructors began training Moroccan pilots in antimissile tactics, and in the spring of 1982 another team, twenty-five strong, arrived in Morocco to train élite troops in counterinsurgency tactics—a consequence, it seemed, of Francis West's reported criticisms of the passivity of the Moroccan forces in the Sahara, who remained in purely defensive positions, leaving the initiative to the guerrillas.

The military axis between Morocco and the United States was consolidated when Haig visited Marrakesh in February 1982 to discuss transit rights for the RDF. In return, Haig offered a substantial increase in U.S. military sales credits. A Joint Military Commission was established, and held its first meeting in Fez in April, with no less than eighty U.S. officials in attendance, among them eight generals, an assistant secretary of state, and two assistant secretaries of defense. The commission established six working groups, responsible for overseeing access and transit rights, intelligence gathering, military training, mapping, military equipment (including the FMS program), and joint exercises—the first of which was held the following November, when more than 800 U.S. marines landed on the Moroccan coast near Al-Hoceima. On April 20, 1982, the State Department announced plans to more than treble credits to finance FMS sales to Morocco, from $30 million in FY1982 to $100 million in FY1983, and to increase the number of Moroccan military personnel training in the United States from 168 to 514. The same month, the administration announced that it planned to sell 381 Maverick air-to-ground missiles to Morocco for $28 million and that it had authorized the delivery of eighteen Bell helicopters manufactured under license in Italy. In July 1982 it transpired that the United States had been delivering antipersonnel cluster bombs to Morocco—and by 1984 journalists visiting Western Sahara with Polisario forces were reporting widespread evidence of their use. Meanwhile, in March 1983, Howard Wolpe, Solarz's successor as chairman of the House of Representatives' Subcommittee on Africa, claimed to have evidence that the Reagan administration had provided the Moroccan forces in the Sahara with airborne radar and "technical assistance in locating Polisario bases and tracing Polisario movements."[6]

The Reagan administration even broke off the contact established with Polisario by the State Department in the last year of the Carter administration, while, by contrast, it arranged visits to the Moroccan-held areas of Western Sahara, including military installations there, by high-ranking U.S. officials, including Ambassador Jeane Kirkpatrick in September 1983.

The increased military aid to Morocco (see Table 14–1), the increased U.S. training for the FAR, the May 1982 military agreement on transit facilities for the RDF, the new joint military commission, the joint U.S–Moroccan military exercises, the halting of contacts with Polisario, and the well-publicized visits to the Moroccan positions in Western Sahara—all these were elements of what Ambassador Joseph Verner Reed called the "Reagan Plan for Morocco." His "mandate," he told an American journalist visiting Rabat in January 1983, was "to illustrate to our friends around the globe that the Reagan Administration wanted to single out Morocco as the primary example of how America supported a proven ally and friend" (New York Times, February 1, 1983).

The Contradictions of U.S. Policy

After more than nine years of war in Western Sahara, the United States still claims to be neutral in the conflict and it officially supports a referendum, as urged by the OAU, to enable the Western Saharan population to determine its future. It still does not recognize Morocco's claims to sovereignty in the territory. Yet, since the start of the war, there has been massive U.S. military aid for one side in this conflict—the side whose claim to sovereignty has not been recognized and which originally entered the territory in 1975–76 by virtue of a pact with the former colonial power which, by all available evidence, went against the wishes of the Western Saharans and gave them no chance to vote on their future. Between fiscal years 1975 and 1984, U.S. military support for Morocco comprised $880 million in FMS agreements, $352 million in credits and $55 million in grants to finance these military sales, $84 million in licensed commercial arms exports, and $10 million in the provision of training. Only in 1978–79, in the middle of Carter's presidency, was there a brief and partial curtailment of this support. Since the start of the war, the role of the United States in arming and training the Moroccan forces has only been matched by France, which has about 250 military advisers and technicians in Morocco and has provided the Moroccan forces with such weaponry as Mirage F–1 aircraft, Alpha-Jets, armored vehicles, and Gazelle and Puma helicopters.

6. Opening remarks at hearing held by the House of Representatives' Subcommittee on Africa, March 15, 1983.

TABLE 14–1 U.S. Arms Sales and Military Aid to Morocco
(in millions of dollars, for fiscal years)

	1975–84[a]	1982	1983	1984 (estimated)	1985 (projected)
Foreign Military Sales (FMS)					
Agreements	$880.0	$14.0	$67.7	$80.0	$100.0
Credits	352.2	30.0	75.0	26.8	10.0
Military Aid (MAP) Grants	55.0	—	25.0	30.0	40.0
Military Training Aid (IMET)	10.4	1.1	1.3	1.5	1.7
Licensed Commercial Arms Exports	83.6	5.0	5.0[b]	5.5	5.5

[a] Actual for 1975–83, estimates for 1984.
[b] Estimate.

A joint Franco-American decision to halt the flow of arms to Morocco would leave King Hassan with little option but to accept the OAU's calls for talks with Polisario and proceed with a referendum. By the same token, however, the high level of U.S. and French arms deliveries appears to have encouraged the king to believe that he can soldier on in the Sahara without having to talk to Polisario or allow a genuine, internationally supervised plebiscite of the Saharan population. Indeed, the purpose of the Reagan administration's arms supply policy was, in the words of one Pentagon official, to "beef up the confidence of the king and restore the military equilibrium," so that Morocco could sustain the war (Interview 1982). The ultimate objective, presumably, was to signal to Algeria that it was backing an unwinnable cause and would do better to ditch the guerrillas.

By increasing the flow of sophisticated, powerful weaponry to Morocco since 1979, the United States has undoubtedly helped King Hassan shore up the FAR's position in the Sahara. To date, however, neither Polisario nor Algeria have shown any inclination to accept a settlement that falls short of genuine self-determination. For Polisario to do so would amount to abandoning all hope of achieving its fundamental goal of national independence. In Algeria's case, a decision to settle for less than self-determination would, at the very least, be embarrassing diplomatically after years of successful lobbying on the Saharawi nationalists' behalf, notably in the United Nations and the OAU. In fact, Algeria stepped up its support for Polisario, following King Hassan's refusal to honor the OAU's June 1983 resolution calling for direct talks with Polisario. This contributed to King Hassan's decision to sign a unity pact with Libya (the Treaty of Oujda) on August 13, 1984, but in so doing the king infuriated Algeria, prompting President Chadli Bendjedid to escalate support for Polisario still further.[7]

7. The Treaty of Oujda had been preceded by a year-long honeymoon between Libya and Morocco, originally motivated by the two states' mutual interest in stopping aid for their "backyard" enemies, in Western Sahara and Chad. King Hassan had been considering sending aid to President Habré of Chad in June 1984, when Colonel Qadhafi signaled his interest in rapprochement with Morocco. Both states also had a common interest in allying against Algeria, which had excluded them from the Maghrebi Treaty of Fraternity and Concord, signed by Algeria and Tunisia in March 1983 and extended to Mauritania in December 1983. Algeria had made Libyan accession to the treaty conditional on Libya dropping its claim to parts of southeastern Algeria (a claim analogous to its claim to Chad's Aouzou Strip), and had likewise told Morocco that it would not be eligible until it held talks with Polisario to settle the Saharan conflict. Libya hoped also to break out of its isolation in the Arab world (there was rapprochement with Saudi Arabia too in 1983), while Morocco hoped that its alliance with Libya would open the door to cheap Libyan oil, Libyan finance, and jobs for unemployed Moroccans in the labor-hungry Jamahiriya. Libya halted its military aid to Polisario in mid–1983. However, this was more of a moral than a material setback for Polisario. Libya has always been a second-order actor in the Saharan conflict, because of its distance. Algeria can easily make up for any shortfall in Libyan arms supplies to the Saharawi guerrillas. Indeed, the Treaty of Oujda seems to have put Morocco in a worse position in the Sahara, for, by nurturing an alliance with Libya, which has no direct leverage over Polisario, King Hassan has enraged Algeria, which does.

Moreover, the FAR's success in establishing a military equilibrium, or stalemate, is not a decisive setback for the guerrilla forces. Neither Algeria nor Polisario has ever anticipated winning an outright military victory. Very few, if any, guerrilla wars have been won in purely military terms. Indeed, Algeria's own independence war in 1954–62 was successful despite a significant weakening of the Algerian National Liberation Front's guerrilla forces in the last phase of their struggle; the French ultimately pulled out of Algeria for political reasons. The Western Saharan conflict is a classic example of a war of attrition. The guerrillas do not have to break through Morocco's defensive walls and seize El-Ayoun to achieve their objectives. They simply have to remain a permanent threat to the FAR. In so doing, they force King Hassan to keep a huge number of troops (over 100,000 by 1984) and a vast arsenal of weaponry in the Sahara, at a cost, in financial terms, which Morocco can ill afford. Eventually, Polisario hopes, economic factors will force King Hassan to come to terms or will lead to his downfall at the hands of the army.

The drain of resources into the war effort, which has been estimated to cost some $2 million a day, has indeed been a worrying problem for the king and his government. It has compounded an economic crisis which would be difficult enough to resolve without the added burden of a war to finance. This crisis is the combined result of the war; the rise in the price of oil, of which Morocco is a major importer; the country's chronic inability to grow sufficient food, even in nondrought years; the world recession and the prolonged slump in demand for Morocco's main export, phosphates; the increasingly protectionist barriers facing Moroccan exports to the EEC; and an accumulated burden of foreign debt, which by the end of 1984 totaled $13 billion, the equivalent of the country's entire gross national product. Merchandise exports ($2.4 billion in 1983) only just cover half of the cost of imports ($4.2 billion), while annual debt service charges have risen above $1 billion.

To satisfy the IMF and other foreign creditors, the Moroccan government has had to impose harsh austerity measures, in the hope of reducing the deficits in public finances and the balance of payments. However, these measures have worsened the lot of Morocco's poor. Fifty-six percent of Moroccans live below what the World Bank regards as an absolute poverty line. In the cities, where almost half of the population of 22 million now lives, at least 2 million live in sprawling slums and shantytowns. Unemployment is rife, and, since 1981, the government has repeatedly raised the prices of basic foods and other essentials in an attempt to reduce the budgetary burden of its subsidy fund, the Caisse de Compensation. On two occasions, price rises have resulted in violent rioting. In June 1981, at least 600 people died when the army quelled riots in the country's largest city, Casablanca. More recently, in January 1984, about 100 were killed and many hundreds jailed when troops broke up riots in several northern Moroccan cities and in Marrakesh.

Spontaneous and leaderless, such outbursts by the urban poor could not, in and of themselves, bring about King Hassan's downfall. Nor could any of

Morocco's political parties, which have very narrow clientèles and have proved unwilling or powerless to take advantage of the discontent revealed by the 1981 and 1984 riots. However, the degradation of economic and social conditions, amidst glaring social inequalities, has encouraged the spread of Islamic fundamentalism and other radical creeds. Most important of all, it could eventually spur the armed forces to move against the king. The FAR's political ambitions first surfaced in 1971 and 1972, when the king narrowly escaped death in two coup attempts, and there were rumors of another failed coup plot when the FAR's most senior officer, General Ahmed Dlimi, died in mysterious circumstances in Marrakesh in January 1983.

Thus, one of the ironies of U.S. policy on the Sahara is that, by enabling King Hassan to sustain his war, it is indirectly helping to worsen his country's economic difficulties, to exacerbate the social tensions in his kingdom, and to undermine his regime's political stability—the very opposite of Washington's objectives. By contrast, Polisario, whose forces appear to have suffered relatively few losses, and Algeria, which is economically much stronger than Morocco, can afford to sit out this long war. The American embrace itself has its costs for King Hassan, as the United States is widely regarded in Morocco as Israel's main prop and there is a long tradition of nationalist opposition to the presence of U.S. military facilities, going back to the days of the Strategic Air Command bases. The military axis with Washington tends to undermine the plausibility of the king's claims to champion the cause of Moroccan nationalism, "the ideological underpinnings of his Saharan policy" (Wright 1983, 179).[8]

However, withdrawal from the Sahara would be just as risky for the king as fighting on there. This is not so much because withdrawal would horrify his patriotic countrymen—although it would bring howls of protest from ultra-nationalist groups like the Istiqlal Party, which led Morocco's independence movement in 1944–56, or the Socialist Union of Popular Forces (USFP). The real problem is that a retreat from the Sahara, after more than eight years of grueling and costly war, for a cause elevated to the status of a national crusade, would humiliate the king before his own people. It would destroy his prestige and credibility. Moreover, although it would create better conditions in which to tackle the country's economic and social problems, it would not resolve them immediately. Finally, withdrawal from the Sahara would see the return northward of a humiliated and bitter army—with the perfect pretext (national disaster) to legitimate its seizing power. For these reasons, King Hassan has not dared to risk a volte-face in his Saharan policy. Instead, he has battled on in the Sahara, in the hope—so far a vain one—that Algeria will

---

8. It is noteworthy in this respect that the Moroccan government went to great pains to prevent the true purpose of the May 1982 U.S.–Moroccan military agreement (the provision of facilities to the RDF) becoming known in Morocco and claimed instead that it was designed to defend Morocco's "territorial integrity" (Wright 1983, 179).

one day prove accommodating. In Washington, policymakers have, by and large, concluded that there is not much else he can do. However, there have been some, notably Democrats in the House of Representatives' Subcommittee on Africa, who have judged that the king runs greater risks by persevering with his military option than by opting for a diplomatic solution based on self-determination.[9] They have periodically called for a reduction in U.S. military aid to Morocco, in the hope of prodding the king onto the diplomatic path—in what they believe are his own better interests and those of the West. However, all that is really clear is that King Hassan faces major risks whatever he does. Which course of action would be the more risky is almost impossible to predict.

REFERENCES

ABC Television. 1979. October 28.
Africa News (Durham, N.C.). 1979. November 2.
Defense Monitor (Washington, D.C.). 1976. Vol. 5, no. 2. February.
El País (Madrid). 1978. Testimony in the Cortes, March 13, 1978.
Franck, Thomas M. 1976. "The Stealing of the Sahara." *American Journal of International Law* 70, no. 4 (October):694–721.
Hassan II, King. 1975. *Discours de S M Hassan II: La Lutte pour le parachèvement de l'integrité territoriale.* Rabat: Ministère d'Etat Chargé de l'Information.
Hodges, Tony. 1984. *Western Sahara: The Roots of a Desert War.* Westport, Conn.: Lawrence Hill.
International Court of Justice. 1975. *Western Sahara, Advisory Opinion of 16 October 1975.* The Hague.
International Herald Tribune. 1980. February 20.
Interview. 1982. Author's interview at the Pentagon, May 20.
Le Monde (Paris). 1981. November 8–9.
New York Times. May 23, 1976; February 1, 1983.
Polisario Front (Algiers). 1978. *20 Mai.* No. 51 (November):10–17.
Radio Algiers. 1980. December 11.
Report of the United Nations Visiting Mission to Spanish Sahara. 1975. *General Assembly Official Records,* 30th Session, Supplement 23, UN Document A/10023/Rev. 1.
Solarz, Stephen J. 1979–80. "Arms for Morocco?" *Foreign Affairs* 58, no. 2 (Winter): 278–299.

9. At hearings on Western Sahara held by the House of Representatives' Subcommittee on Africa on March 15, 1983, for example, Congressman Howard Wolpe argued: "King Hassan faces a 'no-win' situation. If the war continues, as it has for over seven years, Morocco's defenses will be sapped, its fragile economy drained, and its moderate regime weakened. If there is an internationally acceptable political solution based on self-determination, Morocco could be forced to give up its claim to the territory, a claim on which the regime has staked much of its prestige. On balance, I believe that U.S. interests in both Morocco and the region require that we encourage King Hassan to take the diplomatic road which contains less risk of bringing about a weakened friend or a radical successor regime."

U.S. House of Representatives. 1977. *The Question of Self-Determination in Western Sahara.* Hearings before the Subcommittee on International Organizations and on Africa of the Committee on International Relations, House of Representatives, 95th Congress, 1st Session, October 12. Washington, D.C.: U.S. Government Printing Office.

————. 1978. *Foreign Assistance and Related Agencies Appropriations for 1978.* Hearings before a Subcommittee of the Committee on Appropriations, House of Representatives, 95th Congress, 1st Session, Part I. Washington, D.C.: U.S. Government Printing Office.

————. 1980. *Proposed Arms Sales to Morocco.* Hearings before the Subcommittees on International Security and Scientific Affairs and on Africa of the Committee on Foreign Affairs, 96th Congress, 2nd Session, January 24 and 29. Washington, D.C.: U.S. Government Printing Office.

————. 1981. *Arms Sales in North Africa and the Conflict in the Western Sahara: An Assessment of U.S. Policy.* Hearing before the Subcommittee on International Security and Scientific Affairs of the Committee on Foreign Affairs, 97th Congress, 1st Session, March 25, 1981. Washington, D.C.: U.S. Government Printing Office.

————. 1983. *Review of U.S. Policy Toward the Conflict in the Western Sahara.* Hearing before the Subcommittee on International Security and Scientific Affairs and the Subcommittee on Africa, House of Representatives, 98th Congress, 1st Session, March 15. Washington, D.C: U.S. Government Printing Office.

Veliotes, Nicholas A. 1977. *The Question of Self-Determination in Western Sahara.* Hearings before the Subcommittees on International Organizations and on Africa of the Committee on International Relations, House of Representatives, 95th Congress, October 12, 1977. Washington, D.C.: U.S. Government Printing Office.

Ware, Lewis B. 1975. *Decolonization and the Global Alliance in the Arab Maghrib: The Case of Spanish Sahara.* Montgomery, Alabama: Air University Institute for Professional Development.

Washington Star. 1978. October 15.

Wright, Claudia. 1983. "Journey to Marrakesh: U.S.–Moroccan Security Relations." *International Security* 7, no. 4 (Spring):163–179.

PART IV

Regionalism versus Globalism

Except for one brief interlude at the beginning of the Carter administration, U.S. foreign policy toward Africa has been molded by the view that the continent is a no-man's-land in the struggle for influence and/or control between West and East. This global concern has been the crucial determinant of American foreign policy interests in Africa, matching that of the Soviet Union.

This dominant strand in Washington's African policy is well illustrated by an anecdote told by Ambassador Averell Harriman in the early days of Lyndon Johnson's administration.[1] It will be recalled that at the beginning of the Kennedy administration a new priority was given to Africa when Chester Bowles, G. Mennen "Soapy" Williams, and G. Wayne Fredericks were put in charge of that side of policy at the State Department. However, one of Johnson's earliest decisions was to downgrade White House interest in Africa and to focus major attention on developments in Southeast Asia. In appointing Harriman to the State Department as undersecretary of state for economic affairs, the president gave him two major responsibilities—to advise on relations with the USSR and to oversee African policy. But, as Harriman tells it, the only communications he ever received from the White House on Africa were regular weekly calls from Johnson in which he rasped out the same question: "Tell me, Av, what is happening in that offshore island in—what's the goddam name of that place?" Its name was Zanzibar, and after the revolution there in 1964, it seemed (at least to Washington) that the USSR and China might succeed in turning the island into "another Cuba" from which to threaten the Indian Ocean littoral states. Abeid Karume and Mohammed Babu were still names to conjure with, and Julius Nyerere was thought to be too weak to handle the situation in his "offshore island"!

While this anecdotal evidence reflects the "Cuban syndrome" in American foreign policy (which has so unnecessarily complicated the negotiations over a Namibian settlement), its larger importance is the clear way in which it illustrates major U.S. preoccupations with those areas in Africa regarded as being most vulnerable to communist initiatives. This focus of interest has shifted successively from Nasser's Egypt, Nkrumah's Ghana, Sekou Touré's Guinea, Modeibo Keita's Mali, and Lumumba's Congo in the 1960s, to Sudan at the time of Numeiri's military coup in 1970, and subsequently to Somalia, Angola, Mozambique, Ethiopia, and lastly, to Libya. A parallel interest has been taken in those governments identified as being firmly anticommunist and, for that reason alone, deserving of special economic and military support: Morocco, Tunisia, Kenya, Ivory Coast, Zaire under Mobutu, Egypt under Sadat and Mubarak, Sudan under a "converted" Numeiri, and Somalia after the expulsion of the Russians.

This is not to say that other considerations—economic interests, human rights (thanks mainly to the Carter administration), and wider democratic

1. This anecdote was related to the author in a personal conversation.

concerns—have had no input at all into policymaking; but the central thrust of American policy in Africa (indeed, in the whole of the Third World) has been containment, the prevention of the expansion of Soviet influence. This global strategic approach is pursued through bilateral relations as well as on a regional basis; but the regional approach has always been dictated by tactical and practical considerations.

The question whether it is possible, or desirable, for foreign policymakers to adopt a purely regional approach to Africa is largely irrelevant, or purely theoretical, in a period when the central element in an essentially bipartisan American foreign policy has been an overriding concern with the global power struggle. To gloss over this outstanding characteristic of international politics in our time is to take a holiday from the world of political realities in which foreign policymaking is conducted.

The West's global strategy is essentially defensive in the sense that it is not primarily concerned with expanding its area of power, influence, or control, but with preserving so far as possible the position which Western powers, collectively, once held worldwide. With the balance of power already established in Europe, the rivalry for influence and/or control lies mainly in that vast spread of global territory loosely identified as the Third World.

The nations of the Third World have their own collective and separate interests. The overall interest of the great majority is to avoid, so far as possible, being dragged into the struggle between the world powers (expressed through the aspiration of nonalignment), and to achieve a more equitable international economic order. Both these dominant interests must be catered to in the foreign policies pursued by the rival world powers. There is no tidy formula for a global strategy that will accommodate the needs and interests of all Third World countries, especially since these often conflict with each other and, even more, with the rival interests of the major powers. Nevertheless, it is both possible and desirable for an effective American cum Western foreign policy to treat the Third World as a single political region in terms of its members' overarching aspirations and inspirations, e.g., through the North-South dialogue, or by pursuing the guidelines set out by the Brandt Commission.

However, a global approach to foreign policymaking demands, in practice, that it should be implemented within a regional framework. This is exemplified by the North Atlantic Treaty Organization (NATO) and the European Economic Community (EEC) on the side of the Western powers, and by the Warsaw Pact and COMECON on the side of the Eastern European communist nations. Seen in this perspective, globalism and regionalism are complementary; they become adversarial only when a regional approach to policymaking is advanced as an alternative to a global approach. Such an alternative approach would require that, if necessary, the interests of a particular region should be accepted as being more important than the American interest, even in those cases where this could involve taking policy decisions which, on the face of it, might seem disadvantageous to America's global interests. With the present state of world power relations, any idea that a regional approach should replace a global approach is unlikely to carry much weight in the contemporary decision-making process. Indeed, it was precisely for this reason that after the overthrow of the shah in Iran, the advocates of a regional approach to policymaking were eclipsed in the closing stages of the Carter administration.

The case in favor of adopting a regional approach as the guiding principle in foreign policymaking is that, in the long run, it is a more realistic way of promoting regional harmony and stability, thereby serving the wider interests of establishing a more peaceful world order and so directly serving the true interests of the United States. Such an approach has, at different times, been an important determinant of Washington's policy in Latin America. However, even in this exceptional area, that policy has been abandoned by the Reagan administration and the tendencies associated with U.N. Ambassador Jeane Kirkpatrick have overridden the more traditional attitudes of the State Department.

A major question confronting foreign policymakers is how to define the limits of a region. Does it, for example, make any sense to treat Africa as a political region simply because of its continental congruity? Certainly, Africans themselves insist on their continent being considered as a single political entity, as exemplified by the creation and survival of the Organization of African Unity (OAU). This concept is kept alive by a number of key issues (such as the removal of all vestiges of alien, white minority rule), which provide a unifying continental force, and which foreign policymakers cannot ignore. It is unrealistic, for example, to formulate a policy stance toward South Africa without considering its effects on the rest of the continent. Similar considerations arise in other conflict areas in the continent: the Horn of Africa, the Maghreb, and, in a slightly different context, the whole of Arab North Africa. However, even if there is some basis for treating Africa as a single region, it is nevertheless important to consider whether it constitutes a region on its own, or whether it is in fact only a subregion in view of the close ties which exist between the Middle East and African Arabs, and because the security interests of non-Arab Africans in the Red Sea area and the Indian Ocean are closely tied to developments in the Arab world. Such considerations would point to Africa and the Middle East constituting a single political region.

Most Western foreign offices choose to deal with this problem of overlapping "regions" by maintaining a Department for the Middle (or Near) East and North Africa. While such arrangements make some sense in the context of Middle East politics, it often results in confusion and difficulties because such departments are staffed by Arabists not trained to think about the nature of Afro-Arab relations. Nor can the problem inherent in the Afro-Arab connection be dealt with simply by detaching any part of Africa and attaching it to the Middle East for the convenience of regional policy planning. It is sometimes argued that Egypt belongs more properly to the Arab world than to Africa; but if you were to relocate Egypt in the Middle East region, what do you then do about its close ally, Sudan—or its keen enemy, Libya? The latter, after all, carries as much of a commitment to Arab and Islamic causes as does Egypt and, even more than Egypt, it is deeply involved in African causes—all the way from Chad and Ethiopia to Uganda and Lesotho.

The problems raised by adopting a regional approach, however one chooses to define it, are amply illustrated by what happened when the Carter administration was suddenly faced with the need to reshape American foreign policy to take account of the new situation created by the overthrow of the shah of Iran. The problems that had to be faced were *both* regional and global, and the actions proposed reflected both these considerations: how to prevent the USSR from exploiting the new situation and thus improving its world power position at the expense of the West; and how to strengthen the regional security and morale of the Arab Gulf states (especially Saudi Arabia), Egypt, and several of the Red Sea and Indian Ocean littoral states. One of the major decisions was to establish the RDF, which necessitated finding military facilities, not just in the Middle East region, but also in the Red Sea and Indian Ocean. This policy also called for strengthening the American and NATO naval presence in the area and the rapid completion of the military base at Diego Garcia. Thus, the Iran crisis had to be addressed by going way beyond the region of the Middle East into Africa and the Near East. Moreover, the steps taken to ensure the effectiveness of the RDF elicited countermoves from African, Arab, and East Asian countries opposed to what they saw as the buildup of an American military presence. Their opposition naturally had the backing of the Soviet Union.

This episode illustrates two fallacies: that foreign policymakers can define the limits of any region; and that it is possible to take a "regional approach" to a major crisis—such as that posed by the overthrow of the shah of Iran, or by the developing, ineluctable crisis in southern Africa. Since, by definition, a major international crisis is one which threatens to upset the existing balance of power to the disadvantage of either of the major powers, the only credible approach is a global one. This raises policy implications beyond merely looking at the nature of the *perceived* threat to the *conceived* American interest, but also requires consideration of the global fallout of any proposed course of action to deal with, or to limit, any such threat. But the first requirement is to determine whether the perceived threat is indeed a real threat to American interests in terms of producing a real change in the world balance of power, and not just a change in local or regional balances of power—as, for example, in the case of the war over Western Sahara.

Finally, it is necessary to address the issue of the economic dimension of foreign policymaking. Few would still choose to argue in this time of world economic crisis that it is possible to divorce economic from foreign policy. Even though Cancun was a failure and the North-South dialogue has made no progress to date, the fact is that these parleys took place in an international framework, which makes my immediate point. But the larger question is whether anybody seriously supposes that this great contemporary politico-economic crisis can be tackled in any way other than through a global approach. While it may be possible to alleviate some of Africa's problems through a regional approach, e.g., drought relief for the Sahel or backing for the Southern African Development Co-ordinating Conference (SADCC), it is hard to conceive that anything short of a global approach can possibly provide answers to the great economic divide between the developed and developing nations.

To sum up, I would argue in favor of two propositions:

1. That a regional approach to policymaking is justified, or possible, only in cases where neither major power feels threatened by, or sees any major advantage in, a changing political situation.

2. That the definition of a "region" cannot be either exact or static; however one chooses to define a region, it almost invariably overlaps with other regions which, in turn, overlap with further regions.

COLIN LEGUM

15

The Dangers of Globalism

HOWARD E. WOLPE

The validity of the globalism versus regionalism dichotomy as it is so frequently presented requires critical examination. Obviously Africa is involved in the world, as is the world in Africa. One simply cannot approach solutions to the problems in Africa without some reference to their global context, any more than one can approach these problems without some reference to African indigenous forces. However, this effort at academic even-handedness may be ill advised. The globalist side of the globalism-regionalism dichotomy holds particularly destructive implications for American policy toward Africa. My goal here is not to try to be academically comprehensive, but to highlight what I regard as the greater dangers of the globalist point of view.

Globalism has a long tradition in U.S. policy toward Africa under both Democratic and Republican administrations. The globalist point of view sees Africa's importance as arising from its influence on the military and political balance between the United States and the Soviet Union. It defines American interests fundamentally as resisting the spread of communism; its thrust is essentially anticommunist or, more specifically, anti-Soviet. It sees developments in Africa as primarily the consequence of ideological conflict and of the East-West rivalry. There is a constant interpretation of African political phenomena in terms of the role played by the United States and the Soviet Union behind the scenes. From the globalist perspective, our primary objectives in Africa must be to help build anti-Soviet support wherever we can; to establish warm relationships with friendly pro-American regimes, and even dissident movements; to pursue punitive initiatives toward pro-Soviet governments; to intervene in regional conflicts in favor of American friends and against Soviet-supported forces.

There is a "liberal globalist" view that is somewhat more sophisticated than the one I have just outlined. It insists that the best way to fight the cold war in Africa and to eliminate the opportunities for the spread of Soviet influence is to support economic and social reform, and in the case of southern Africa, black majority rule. However, an approach to Africa from any kind of globalist perspective tends toward a quite conservative definition of American interests. In a battle with the forces of evil it is best to rely on the most anticommunist, i.e., conservative forces, and on the devil you know as opposed to the devil you don't know. And when one fears Armageddon, one worries about the strategies of war, possible Soviet designs on mineral resources in Africa, naval movements to cut off sea routes, and so on. Africa's importance, then, emerges almost exclusively in terms of its significance in the cold war arena.

Clearly, on most issues the Reagan administration reflects the globalist perspective in its more conservative tendency. Thus, in testimony before the Senate Foreign Relations Committee, Assistant Secretary for African Affairs Chester A. Crocker, whose views on Africa are often more sophisticated than those of others in the administration, emphasized that "American interests include such obvious material and strategic interests as access to vital minerals and the importance of maintaining partnership with friendly nations flanking the transportation lanes to the Persian Gulf." He further stated that "we remain equally determined to prevent Soviet, Libyan, and Cuban adversaries from taking advantage of Africa's current weaknesses to pursue strategies of destabilization."

Perhaps the leading example and consequence of conservative globalism in recent years has been the Reagan administration's "constructive engagement" policy, which is predicated upon the assumed need to create a regional security relationship with South Africa against communist expansion in southern Africa. This, together with domestic policy considerations, has led the administration to link the question of the removal of Cuban troops from Angola with the issue of Namibian independence. It has resulted in greater trade and warmer diplomatic relations with the South African regime, and even in American promises to help end South Africa's pariah status in the world.

The Reagan administration has pursued characteristically globalist objectives in Angola, with continued nonrecognition of the Angolan government and through early statements giving legitimacy to the Savimbi insurgency; in the Horn, with increased military aid to Somalia and a continuing low level of representation in Ethiopia, although there are some recent signs of a broader diplomatic approach being taken in that region; in the Western Sahara, with a dramatic increase in U.S. military aid for counterinsurgency activity by Morocco. The globalist perspective has also characterized the Reagan administration's approach to Zaire, where congressional admonitions that the United States reduce its military assistance to the Mobutu regime and try to diminish American identification with that regime have been largely disregarded.

This same globalist orientation is revealed very dramatically in the change in emphasis and priorities in the Reagan administration's latest budgetary proposals. Between the last Carter budget of Fiscal Year (FY) 1981 and the proposals for FY1983 and FY1984, military aid to sub-Saharan Africa (excluding Morocco and Tunisia) has risen successively from 15 percent to 26 and 21 percent of the total; security-oriented economic support fund aid has risen from 30 percent to 36 and 43 percent; and development aid has fallen from 55 percent to 38 and 36 percent. If one takes into account Public Law 480 assistance in Africa, one finds that food aid provided under it has fallen from 37 percent to 20 and 18 percent of projected total assistance. The data on Morocco and Tunisia are just as dramatic in demonstrating the massive infusion of military aid and the relative diminution in the emphasis on economic assistance.

The liberal globalist posture, which takes into account to a much greater extent the regional realities as Africanist scholars understand them, is far more valid. Conservative globalist policies are counterproductive even in terms of their own objectives. Conflict and racial change are inevitable in southern Africa as long as the system of apartheid persists and as long as South Africa continues its illegal occupation of Namibia. American association with South Africa, therefore, will simply enhance Soviet-Cuban opportunities in the region, both with respect to SWAPO and with respect to South African dissidents. Diplomatic rejection of radical Soviet-aided regimes serves only to strengthen Soviet-Cuban influence over them, whether in Ethiopia or Angola. American reluctance to demand legitimizing social, economic, and political reforms or peaceful behavior by friendly, unstable regimes such as Zaire, Somalia, or Morocco creates a growing risk of political instability within those countries and eventual Soviet cooptation of opposition groups or regional rivals.

But even the liberal globalist viewpoint has significant limitations. While it does tend to moderate the implicit racism and paternalism that runs through the more conservative posture, it does not abandon such attitudes entirely. As African issues are debated with the Congress or the media, the often implicit assumption that African states are easily manipulated by outside forces is quite striking. Both liberal and conservative globalists appear to justify American involvement in Africa on the grounds that African states and African leaders do not have the capacity to make appropriate judgments on their own initiative. I am constantly impressed by the failure of American policy to accept the authenticity of African nationalist aspirations. Not surprisingly, the enduring racial attitudes, stereotypes, and myths of our society do inform American policy toward Africa or American journalistic treatment of that continent.

While the liberal globalist view may be seen as an advance beyond the conservative globalist posture taken by the Reagan administration, it is still very limited. For one thing, it leads to an almost entirely reactive policy. The United States is still shaping its approach to the African continent on the basis of a focus on the Soviet Union, and not on American and African interests more sharply and accurately defined. Its constant engagement in counterproductive initiatives causes African states to see it as concerned with Africa only in the context of the cold war conflict. The United States thereby loses much of its credibility as it approaches the continent.

Second, globalism in any form creates a self-fulfilling prophecy. This is strikingly revealed in the argument of Assistant Secretary of State Crocker that southern Africa represents the battleground of world political interests "for the simple reason that this region is likely to become one of the hot spots of East-West tension." There is nothing intrinsic to southern Africa that requires that region to become a hot spot of East-West tension. What would happen, for example, if the United States and the Soviet Union both supported national liberation movements in southern Africa? What is there about the region that compels us to assume that American and Soviet interests are in conflict? It is only because the administration makes this assumption that it feels the need to react to every Soviet initiative in the region. And every reaction produces a counterreaction. It is in this manner that both the United States and the Soviet Union tend to create a self-fulfilling prophecy of East-West conflict.

This pattern is not irreversible. It is possible to approach the African continent in a very different way that would be far more responsive to American as well as African interests. The focus on the cold war causes Americans, even the liberal globalists, to miss the real issues of African economic development and political integration. These are the fundamental problems in Africa, and for America. This is because the principal threat to American economic and political interests in Africa arises from what is happening within the African states themselves. Very seldom does the challenge to regime stability in Africa arise from external military threat or ideological conflict. Gerald Bender has reminded us that in its historical involvement in Angola, the United States was allied with China and North Korea in supporting two of the factions that were battling the Soviet-backed, and ultimately victorious, People's Movement for the Liberation of Angola (MPLA). In its ignorance of the far more significant ethnic and personal divisions among Angolans upon which the warring factions were based, the United States continued to blithely insist that there was critical ideological content to the internal Angolan struggle.

Another danger flowing from the globalist approach is that the United States becomes susceptible to manipulation by power contenders within the African states themselves. The same is true of the Soviet Union. The Somalis and the Ethiopians have both demonstrated enormous flexibility in terms of their alliances. Of equal relevance is the case of Zaire, where the anticommunist posture of the regime has led the United States to extend virtually

indiscriminate support to one of the most corrupt and repressive governments on the continent. In this instance, as in others, it is often difficult
to discern who is the manipulator and who the manipulated. American
interests, I submit, are hardly well served by this kind of knee-jerk
anticommunism.

It is time for the United States to move away from the negative, reactive
character of globalism, in either its liberal or its conservative mode, and move
toward a positive definition of American interests in Africa. From my perspective, the social structure and the history of African revolt against foreign
control pretty well foreclose the emergence of Soviet satellites in Africa that
threaten American interests. Even Angola and Ethiopia, where Cuban troops
are present in large numbers, have pursued policies that, in some significant
respects, are quite independent of the Soviet Union or Cuba. Thus, despite
the presence of 20,000 Cuban troops and 1,000 East German and Soviet advisers, Angola has consistently reached out for the normalization of its relationship with the United States and has sought to attract American private
investment. In testimony to its pragmatism, when Angola entered into negotiations with the American oil companies, its Marxist government hired as its
consultant Arthur D. Little of Boston, Massachusetts!

The Ethiopian case is similarily instructive. The government's approach to
land reform, for example, has departed dramatically from the approach the
Soviets have advocated. Likewise, Ethiopia spurned Cuban mediation of the
Eritrean conflict and has resisted Soviet encouragement to transfer power
from the military to the civilian workers' party. While a significant measure of
Soviet influence exists in both of these countries, reflected in votes in the
United Nations and also in their domestic policies, the notion that somehow
these countries are pursuing a policy that is totally subservient to the Soviet
Union or to Cuba is, I think, clearly belied by the facts. I would also argue that
a more adroit American approach toward those countries could well lessen
their dependence upon the Soviet Union and Cuba. In any event, it is clear that
Marxist states in Africa have taken a wide variety of forms and have become
increasingly pragmatic and non-ideological in their domestic policies and in
their relationships to the West.

One more globalist shibboleth needs to be addressed, namely, the fear of a
procommunist African cutoff of strategic minerals to the West. Such fears
ignore the substantial dependence of African states on Western economic
networks and institutions. Simply put, countries like Zaire and South Africa
would risk economic disaster by boycotting the West. Even the so-called radical Marxist leaders within southern Africa and elsewhere have insisted upon
the maintenance of trading and business relationships with the West. Indeed,
no African government has ever denied oil or strategic minerals to the West.
Even communist-aided dissident groups have refrained from destructive attacks on the mineral supply infrastructure they hope to inherit: during the

civil wars in Zimbabwe, Angola, and Zaire, those structures were left intact. That is not to say Western nations ought not plan for possible emergencies by coordinating stockpiling and sharing arrangements. It needs to be emphasized, however, that the disruption of strategic minerals supply is far more likely to result from civil and political unrest arising from internal factors than from Soviet or other external intervention.

I want to advance, in conclusion, three propositions that would, in my view, represent a far more effective guide for American policy toward Africa than the traditional globalist position. First, the United States has a need to prevent cold war competition in Africa from inflaming superpower tensions. If Brzezinski's statement that SALT was lost in the sands of the Ogaden is true, it indicates that developments in Africa can have an important negative impact on the prospects for world peace and the prevention of major superpower confrontation. Not solely to prevent communism or to preclude the entry of the Soviet Union, but to further world peace, America should promote diplomatic solutions to regional conflicts in places like the Western Sahara and the explosive Horn. To avoid the injection of cold war tensions, it should be seeking constructive, harmonious relations with all of the nations in the key regions of the continent. Particularly useful would be a revival of the attempt early in the Carter administration to reach regional arms-export control agreements with the Soviets directed at the African continent.

Second, the United States needs to take more systematic account of the extensive interdependencies that link it with Africa. Its policy agenda must move from the cold war tradition to the reality of interdependence with the Third World. For example, 40 percent of American exports today flow to the developing world. Exports specifically to Africa total over $4 billion annually and support 160,000 American jobs. In the not very distant past Africa supplied us with up to 40 percent of our oil imports and more than half of a number of critical strategic minerals. African cooperation is critical to the successful resolution of such international environmental, economic, and security issues as the law of the sea and the prevention of nuclear proliferation. Americans need to understand, as well, that it is not Soviet expansion, but African economic decay, disorder, and continued racial domination in South Africa which jeopardize U.S. economic, environmental, and political interests on the African continent. Henry Kissinger's nightmare of an embittered, estranged, disorderly Third World reacting to Western indifference is a real one. American policy toward Africa should include constructive approaches to North-South commodities problems and needed African economic policy reforms. It should address the issue of continued white domination in South Africa and should do so in a way that is quite different from the approach taken by the Reagan administration.

Finally, the United States must continue to stand consistently for human rights. It must reject the proposition that the advocacy of human rights, on

the one hand, and American national self-interest, on the other, are somehow incompatible. It cannot be indifferent to its own values in world affairs
without losing something of those values. A strong human rights posture in
Africa, I would argue, is totally consistent with American national self-
interest properly understood. Yes, there can be immediate, short-term economic or political risk associated with such an approach. But I would argue
that the long-term costs of close American identification with corrupt, repressive regimes of the Mobutu variety are far greater. Likewise, in the southern African region, American failure to understand that it is South Africa that
is the principal source of instability in that region and America's apparent
willingness to enter into a new accommodation with apartheid, will in the
long term actually exacerbate the potential for violent revolutionary conflict.
"Constructive engagement" has done little more than reinforce the intransi-
gence of the present South African regime; domestic repression has substantially increased, as has South African aggression against its neighbors; and
the South African political establishment now has the view that it can hold on
without any real costs or risks in terms of the American—South African relationship. What is at issue, then, in the human rights debate is not a conflict
between realism and idealism; the issue, rather, is whether the United States
will pursue policies calculated to advance its short-term or its long-term national interests.

16

Africa from a Globalist Perspective

PETER DUIGNAN

As a great power with global interests, the United States needs to have access to and influences within Africa. Soviet interests are also global (Grechko 1974). U.S. policies in Africa are therefore best viewed from a global, not just a regional perspective.

The United States wants to retain influence with Africa's governments (47) and its peoples (over 450 million), and it wants equal opportunities with other nations to bid for Africa's resources, and to invest and trade with its people. The United States and its allies need—and will increasingly need—the minerals of Africa. Finally, the United States also needs to utilize the passageways, ports, and airfields of the continent, and to protect its vessels in the sea-lanes around Africa. The route around that continent is of vital importance to the West: 70 percent of Europe's oil and 90 percent of its strategic minerals are shipped around the Cape of Good Hope. Soviet naval power now has the potential to threaten Western supply lines in that area as well as in the Persian Gulf region.

U.S. economic interests in the continent are not great: about 12 percent of its imports come from Africa, about 7.6 percent of its exports, and only 4 percent of its foreign investments go there. Still, even if Americans do not need Africa's markets or investment opportunities, they need its minerals and oil. In any case, the United States will be drawn into African affairs by virtue of Soviet interests in the region.

For most of Africa, conflict situations abound. The Soviets know how to use tensions for their benefit—and of these tensions there are all too many—troubles occasioned by rapid urbanization, unemployment, governmental instability, ethnic conflicts, poverty, rising oil prices for some, falling oil prices for others, and a general slump in the price of other raw materials and Africa's products. African nations face other difficulties: large foreign debts, protectionism and trade restrictions, declining foreign aid, and rising populations. The World Bank's survey, *Accelerated Development in Sub-Saharan Africa: An Agenda for Action* (1981), noted other major problems—corruption; inefficiency; national lassitude; excessive government control, ownership, and spending; and the neglect of agriculture. The picture is not uniformly bleak. Nigeria, with great statesmanship, has overcome the ravages of the civil war. Some countries, such as the Ivory Coast and Botswana, have considerable economic achievements to their credit. But overall, the picture remains bleak. Although the Soviet Union and its clients can benefit from such widespread difficulties, they have not caused—or helped alleviate—the economic difficulties. But they have encouraged liberation fronts and intervened in Ethiopia and Angola, and this has created civil wars and refugee problems.

Africa's chronic instability, its numerous civil wars and liberation struggles, the presence of valuable resources, and strategic locations suggest continued opportunities in the 1980s for great power interventions. In fact, the cold war has never ended in Africa. Detente (or peaceful coexistence) only applied to Europe, where it promised peace between nation-states, but not peace in the Third World, where the ongoing struggle between the competing social systems of capitalism and communism continues.

We have seen increased Soviet activity in Africa since 1974 when the Portuguese empire in Africa collapsed. The Soviets learned that proxy wars pay off; the whole of southern Africa was destabilized. As the Nigerian scholar Oye Ogunbadejo (1979) has noted, the "USSR's policy choices for the 1980s will no longer by restricted to the defensive, reactive sphere; they are likely to allow for greater initiative and assertion—with the Soviet Union increasingly becoming a truly global superpower, as opposed to what previously looked . . . like a regional superpower. Moscow would be able to flex its muscles, if it wanted to do so, much more than hitherto." The Soviets are now able to project their power anywhere in the world because of their new air and naval forces, and because they can use their allies and clients as surrogates under the guise of "proletarian internationalism." Soviet interests are global; therefore, U.S. interests must be global also.

The United States has never had an overall strategy or conceptual approach to Africa and its problems. It has generally sought a regional orientation, but time and again has been forced into global views—usually because of the fear of increased Soviet influence. But it has not been consistent, nor has it fully implemented either globalist or regionalist strategies. If the United States were fully committed to a global strategy in Africa, it should, for example, be supporting the Somalis more and encouraging guerrilla warfare among the dissident Ethiopian ethnic communities to force the breakup of the Amharic Empire as well as to push the Soviets and Cubans out. Instead, it restrains the Somalis and fails to aid the Eritreans, Gallans, or Tigreans out of concern for regional peace.

Historically, the United States has tacitly accepted the right of self-determination of African nationalism so long as Soviet support was only indirect and masked behind "fronts." The United States wanted a free Africa, but not one dominated by or beholden to communism. When Soviet-Cuban influence became direct and massive, that is, in Angola (1975) and Ethiopia (1976), the United States still hesitated to take a globalist view. The Reagan administration deserves credit for taking a new course when it introduced a globalist perspective in southern African affairs by calling for the removal of Cuban troops.

Many of the problems of the United States in Africa stem from Soviet involvement in "wars of liberation," and in Soviet attempts to keep avowedly Marxist regimes in power. African nationalists and governments have turned to the Soviet Union for arms, training, and financial assistance when the West refused such aid. As a result, the Soviet Union in varying degrees influences movements like the South West Africa People's Organization (SWAPO) in Namibia, the African National Congress (ANC) in South Africa, the Popular Movement for the Liberation of Angola (MPLA), and the Front for the Liberation of Mozambique (FRELIMO).

For example, the MPLA has been dominated by the Soviets and Portuguese communists since at least 1959. The groundwork was laid in 1955 when the Communist Party of Angola was formed and an underground organized. Later the Communists joined with other groups to form the MPLA. Not until 1959 was the popular front set up—the African Revolutionary Front for National Independence of Portuguese Colonies. A series of incidents caused a police crackdown; the front was established in Conakry and training for the war of national liberation began.

Both MPLA in Angola and FRELIMO in Mozambique thus had been formed with the aid of communist cadres who had provided the leadership core for these liberation movements. In 1977 both MPLA and FRELIMO transformed themselves from a movement, or front, into Marxist-Leninist vanguard parties, dedicated to the pursuit of "scientific socialism," to "democratic centralism," to the creation of socialist societies and of a "new man." Sustained by a large Cuban military force, MPLA faithfully supported the Soviet Union's foreign policy. FRELIMO in Mozambique, having attained and held on to power without Cuban proxies, was not as dependent on Moscow as MPLA; nevertheless FRELIMO likewise considered the Warsaw Pact countries as Mozambique's national allies—a line not surprising, given the close relations that had long existed between FRELIMO, the MPLA, the Communist Party of the Soviet Union (CPSU), and also the pro-Soviet Portuguese Communist Party (PCP). FRELIMO and the MPLA in turn also formed part of a wider African party alliance that included SWAPO in Namibia, and the ANC in South Africa. SWAPO guerrillas operated from bases in southern

Angola against Namibia; the ANC used bases in Mozambique against South Africa. Both made far-reaching claims as regards the assumed effectiveness of their respective incursions.[1]

The ANC by 1959 became for all intents and purposes a front organization of the South African Communist Party. Communist cadres continue to operate within the framework of the ANC. And white liberals such as Colin Legum and Donald Wood are refused membership in the ANC—only white communists are admitted.[2]

In return for political and financial support from the Soviet bloc, the ANC-SACP alliance followed every twist and turn of Soviet policy. On most issues *Sechaba* (the organ of the ANC) or *The African Communist* (the organ of the SACP) in no wise differed from *Pravda*.

The ANC is totally enmeshed in a complex network of pro-Soviet front organizations. To illustrate: Moses Mabhida, an ANC executive member and a vice-president of the South African Congress of Trade Unions (SACTU), a small, communist-dominated body, thus served as deputy member of the communist-dominated World Federation of Trade Unions (WFTU). Mark Williams-Shope, secretary-general of SACTU, was a full member of the WFTU. Brian Bunting, a member of the South African Communist Party's central committee, was a member of the communist-dominated International Organisation of Journalists (IOJ) and a *Tass* correspondent in London. Ruth Mompati, leader of the ANC's women's section, was a member of the pro-Soviet Women's International Democratic Federation (WIDF); Josiah Jele, member of the ANC executive, worked for the secretariat of the Soviet-dominated World Peace Council (WPC). Oliver Reginald Tambo, president-general of the ANC, also served as president-general of the WPC. Vella Pillay, a member of the SACP, served as vice-chairman of the anti-apartheid movement in London. The ANC sent out broadcasts through the Zambian, Tanzanian, and Angolan radio corporations. It published a number of journals, including *Sechaba*, printed in East Germany, ideologically aligned to *The African Communist*, which was published in London.

Soviet Imperialism

Africans must contend with the increasing influence of the Soviet Union. The Soviets have made their presence felt through their dealings with established non-Marxist governments, through pressures exerted by orthodox communist parties (which are mostly weak and ineffectual), and through lib-

1. Communist journals (*Tass, New Times, International Affairs, World Marxist Review*) are the best sources for documenting the development of fronts and the transformation of fronts into Marxist-Leninist vanguard parties. See for example, *International Affairs (1961)*. See also *Yearbook on International Communist Affairs (1970–)*.

2. Interview with Colin Legum, London, November 1, 1984. See also *The African Communist* (1978, 113–115) for communist participation in the liberation movement.

eration movements—originally designed as fronts, and including some non-communist elements—dedicated to bringing about "national democratic revolutions" as stepping stones on the way to socialism. After the revolution, according to communist theoreticians, these fronts should be gradually transformed into Marxist-Leninist "vanguard parties" dedicated to the pursuit of scientific socialism, operated through "democratic" centralism, and joined in a global struggle to bring about the world revolution under Soviet leadership.

The new Soviet imperialism, as we have seen, has been sustained in Africa by the deployment of Cuban troops assisted by Soviet and East German advisers. Early in 1984 the total number of Cubans in Africa exceeded 40,000, nearly one-quarter of Cuba's armed forces. The Organization of African Unity (OAU) has been in no position to deal with this new threat, any more than its members could cope with the supposed white menace in South Africa. The Soviet offensive is supported by a combination of diplomacy and military force. Not only is the Soviet fleet impressively strong, but the Soviet air force can transport large numbers of troops complete with heavy equipment over thousands of miles. Soviet efforts also benefit from an international army of well-wishers (not necessarily communist) who applaud any move that weakens the West. As communist theoreticians see it, the new form of "proletarian internationalism" involved in military intervention would shift the international "correlation of forces" in favor of the Soviet camp and help it to strategically and economically disrupt the strength of "imperialism."

The pursuit of revolution in Africa requires the transformation of progressive movements and fronts into disciplined cadre parties. This process began in Angola, Mozambique, South Yemen, and the People's Republic of the Congo; it is now under way in Ethiopia. The new parties are expected to accept Marxism-Leninism, perhaps as gradually as the Mongolian and Cuban ruling parties did earlier. At the same time, the new Marxist-Leninist states would "cement their solidarity" with the Soviet bloc.

Soviet political infiltration goes with its commercial, cultural, and, above all, its military expansion. It seems clear that Soviet strategists are looking for control over global "choke points," that is, places where maritime routes converge. Many American liberals are skeptical of this interpretation, but it makes sense from the Soviet standpoint. Why should the Soviets want to control the Horn of Africa if not for strategic reasons? Why support revolutionaries in Ethiopia and South Yemen when these countries have no valuable minerals and their foreign trade is insignificant? Why endanger detente by supporting revolution as far afield as South Africa and Afghanistan? The answer is clear: for strategic as well as ideological purposes.

The Soviets will therefore continue to combine the politics of subversion with a drive for strategic advantage. Fortunately, they face major problems in Africa. Given the diversity of the continent's ethnic composition and the relative weakness of the industrial proletariat in all African countries outside South Africa, the communists cannot succeed there as readily as their theoreticians assume. They also face other obstacles. These include the persistence of tribal modes of production in many parts of the continent, the dissension and lack of disciplined cadres within the new Marxist-Leninist ruling parties, and the inability of these parties to deal with the economic disasters engendered by domestic terror, wars, and civil strife. Above all, foreign intruders of whatever political conviction must cope with the extent and diversity of Africa; no single formula can cope with the problems of this entire continent (Henriksen 1981).

Trouble Spots

U.S. policies in Africa face their greatest difficulties in northwest Africa, the Horn of Africa, and southern Africa.[3] In these areas the United States should take a globalist approach, not a regional one.

Northwest Africa. Morocco has been fighting a secessionist group called Polisario (Popular Front for the Liberation of Sequiet el Hamra and Río de Oro) since 1975 when the Spanish withdrew from their Saharan colony. The Polisario is a Marxist group supported by Algeria and Libya and armed through them by the Soviet Union. For the present the Moroccans appear to have contained the war by building a mammoth dirt wall to keep the Polisario out.

The king's throne, however, is by no means secure. King Hassan is a traditionalist who depends on a religious and military élite; in effect, though, he governs alone. He tries to do too much by himself and is afraid to share power. According to the former U.S. ambassador to Morocco Richard Parker, the society is split between Arabic- and Berber-speakers, and the army is dominated by the Berbers. Hassan, or at least the royal family, is criticized for corruption, inefficiency, and ostentatious living, while 60 percent of the population remains in the backward sector of the economy. But the monarchy also has distinct assets, including the advantage of past association with the anticolonial cause. Hassan is a more skillful ruler than the erstwhile shah of Iran, and his foreign policy—aiming at the incorporation of what used to be Spanish Sahara—is popular.

It is in the U.S. interest that monarchical rule of a moderate nature should continue to prevail and that a friendly power should control the Strait of Gibraltar. The United States has used Moroccan territory for air bases and communications; it may need to do so again. An unstable or unfriendly Morocco could hurt the interests of Israel, Egypt, and Zaire. Moroccan troops have twice saved Mobutu of Zaire from losing the cobalt- and copper-rich Shaba Province. Five thousand troops keep Zaire in the Western camp. Morocco has been a moderate voice in Middle Eastern politics, and Hassan's support is necessary for U.S. efforts to make the peace treaty between Israel and Egypt,

---

3. For detailed analyses of these areas see Gann and Duignan (1981a) *passim.*

and ideally the surrounding Arab states, work. With these points in mind, it is difficult to justify the Carter administration's selling helicopters to President Qadhafi of Libya while refusing such hardware to King Hassan. U.S. support for Hassan can partially counter Libya's massive build-up of Soviet arms, which threatens its neighbors and NATO's control of the Mediterranean, and hopefully bring peace to the area.

The Horn of Africa.   The Horn of Africa is strategically important, dominating as it does the major maritime route through the Red Sea and the Suez Canal. Included in its area are the states of Djibouti, Somalia, and Ethiopia—the last being the most important of the three. U.S. interests here are both regional—it wants peace in the area—and global—it wants the Soviets and Cubans out.

Ethiopia is one of the most ancient and most populous (30 million) African states; militarily, it is more powerful than all of its African neighbors combined. Until 1974 it was subject to the rule of the Emperor Haile Selassie, but he was overthrown by a radical military coup. The Derg committed itself to a socialist system and terrorized the population. In 1977, Somalia attacked the Ethiopians in the Ogaden, a region the Somalis long claimed. Soviet air lifts and Cuban troops saved the day and pushed the Somalis back. Guerrilla warfare, however, continues in other parts of the state—in Eritrea and in the south, and even in the Ogaden.

Somalia had fallen under Soviet influence after General Mohammed Siad Barre staged a coup in 1969. The Soviets built up the Somali armed forces, and constructed a modern port and airfield at Berbera. When the Somalis invaded Ogaden in 1977, the Soviets had to choose between the Somalis and the Ethiopians. By electing to support the Ethiopians, the Soviets lost Berbera but gained assets and influence in a more strategically important state.

By 1985, the Ethiopian revolutionaries had failed to rebuild their empire. In some outlying areas such as Tigré, the military junta's writ did not run at all; wide stretches had been reduced to anarchy or to precarious forms of local independence. Starvation threatened the entire country in 1984. The army formed the country's main unifying force. Nevertheless, the growth of the Soviet's power in the Horn of Africa has far-reaching military implications. They and the Derg may not control the Ethiopian hinterland in its entirety, but their naval buildup in the Red Sea and the Persian Gulf is accelerating. Soviet pilots have tested flight routes from the gulf to Libya and Malta; Soviet aircraft operate from Aden and Massawa, where the Soviets have established a major air base. Soviet naval units use facilities at Aden, at Socotra off South Yemen, and at Massawa, where their presence forms a continuing threat to the vital Western oil route.

This expansion of Soviet power has placed the United States in a dilemma. Americans have no conceivable interest in encouraging a socialist Greater Somalia whose claims threaten both Ethiopia and Kenya. U.S. interests are best served by promoting peace and stability in Africa, an objective that cannot be attained if existing colonial boundaries are challenged. During the 1980s, the United States should supply sufficient arms to Somalia to prevent Ethiopia from expanding its territory at Somalia's expense. Somalia, however, must be persuaded to give up its former hopes for a Greater Somalia. On the other hand, it could be given grazing and watering rights in the Ogaden.

The United States should no longer permit itself to be driven onto the ideological defensive by the communists, their proxies, and the humanitarian "conscience vote." Instead, the United States should speak with a stronger voice. Ethiopian rule has been brutal. The United States should protest against the bloody Ethiopian repression of the Somalis in the Ogaden, and also against the repression of youth and minorities, such as the Falasha who are now being decimated.[4] The United States should likewise help the Galla and the Eritreans, thus placing additional strain on Ethiopia while helping to improve American-Arab relations. Ethiopian claims to Eritrea are comparatively recent; they have neither ethnic nor religious foundation.

Above all, the United States can derive no advantage from strengthening the Soviet Union's hold on the southern shores of the Red Sea. Until such time as Ethiopia adopts a friendlier policy, the United States should encourage rebellious ethnic groups within the Ethiopian empire. Perhaps Ethiopia should be rebuilt as a multi-ethnic confederation that would grant full rights to the Muslims and pagans who, between them, outnumber the Amhara ruling group. As a long-term objective, the United States should seek the withdrawal of Cuban troops and Soviet advisers from the Horn of Africa. The permanent neutralization of the Horn would be in the interest of the West. Neutralization, hopefully, would enable Ethiopia and Somalia to decrease the swollen military budgets that consume a large share of their respective gross national products. Furthermore, it would end the threat to the stability of the Sudan and Kenya that is fed by Somali ambition and Eritrean refugees. Primarily, neutralization would deny the Soviet Union one of the strategic prizes of Africa.

Zaire. Given Zaire's enormous potential wealth, its strategic position in the heart of Africa, and the current absence of an effective alternative to Mobutu's authority, the United States has little choice but to support Mobutu no matter how poor his record. There is at present no evidence that any of his opponents would be less corrupt or inefficient. Zaire is a major producer of two strategically important minerals, copper and cobalt; the latter is especially valuable to the United States for its use in superalloys for the aerospace, electronic, and machine-tool industries. There are at present no adequate

4. See annual issues of *Africa Contemporary Record* (London) since 1978. The 1980–81 survey refers to 10,000 to 40,000 political prisoners still held in Ethiopian prisons, and hundreds of thousands of youths on collectivized farms. For persecution of the Falasha see *Keesing's Contemporary Archives,* January 4, 1980:30019; September 10, 1982: 31687–31688.

substitutes or alternative sources of supply, and Zaire provides 50 percent of the West's production of cobalt.[5] The 1980s will see the West increasingly dependent on such strategic minerals. It is not in the American interest to promote the break-up of Zaire through the spread of anarchy. By diplomacy and security aid, the United States must ensure the country's stability. It should therefore continue, however reluctantly, to back Mobutu, hoping that a patient policy of persuasion, along with foreign experts to run his government and businesses, may improve somewhat the performance of his regime. The United States, with Belgian and French aid, should retrain the Zairian army and police, and should educate a new class of efficient administrators to reestablish administrative control in the provinces. The transportation system must be rebuilt and the peasants guaranteed security so that agricultural production can be restored.

Zaire is nevertheless unlikely to emerge from the mire unless it adopts a more decentralized form of government. Given the erosion of Kinshasa's control over the outlying provinces, the inefficiency of the central civil service, and the indiscipline of the army, Kinshasa would only be recognizing reality if it restructured its constitutional relationship with the provinces in general. A decentralized structure would probably enable Zaire to face the problems of the future with more success than a centralized state run as a despotism.

Angola-Mozambique. With the MPLA's victory in 1975, Angola moved into the international limelight. American academics have since kept calling for U.S. recognition of the Marxist-Leninist regime at Luanda and have been joined in their campaign by liberal politicians who considered such recognition justified by both self-interest and equity. To my mind, it is not in the American interest, or in the interest of the Angolan people, to recognize the MPLA government. For the present, the MPLA is an anti-Western group that looks to the CPSU as a model. According to its own statements, the MPLA is not simply a radical African nationalist group, as many claim in academia and even in reports by U.S. government agencies such as the Agency for International Development (AID). In 1977 the MPLA became a Marxist-Leninist vanguard party dedicated to the pursuit of "scientific socialism" and world revolution. The MPLA does not seek to pursue a neutralist foreign policy; it firmly sides with what it calls the socialist camp in the global struggle against the forces of world capitalism.

The party operates as a self-styled "vanguard of the proletariat," uniting workers, peasants, and intellectuals in a country overwhelmingly dependent on traditional farming. It believes in the Leninist principle of "democratic

5. While the West gets 52 percent of its cobalt from Zaire and Zambia, the United States must import 98 percent of its cobalt and Zaire is its principal supplier. The 1978 incursion of Katangans from Angola caused cobalt rationing in the United States and shot cobalt prices up by more than 400 percent.

centralism" and looks to the transformation of Angola into a socialist state. Its influence is weak among dissident ethnic groups such as the Bakongo in the north and the Ovimbundu in the south. By 1979, about half of the Central Committee were military professionals.

As mentioned earlier, in 1983 over 40,000 Cubans were still deployed in Africa—roughly one-quarter of Cuba's armed forces. This proportion is higher than the corresponding proportion of Americans in Southeast Asia at the height of the Vietnam War. Without Soviet and Cuban assistance, the MPLA would have a far more precarious existence. Without American for-bearance toward Cuba, Castro would not have dared to deploy so large a portion of his forces overseas.

Admittedly the MPLA permits Gulf Oil to operate on Angolan soil, but this is only common sense since a substantial portion of Angola's revenue is drawn from Gulf Oil's operations. Similarly, the Soviet Union and its allies have consistently asked for and received Western credits, and infusions of technology and managerial expertise. That does not mean that they are not communist governments or that they would not, in time of international ten-sion, stop selling oil to the West. The Soviet Union itself, moreover, considers these commercial relations as instruments in the international class struggle that they intend to win. Going beyond Lenin's predictions, capitalists now compete among themselves for the privilege of selling on easy credit terms the very rope by which they will be hanged.

In terms of international morality and civil rights, Angola's record has been deplorable. It is a police state complete with East German- and Russian-trained secret police and re-education centers. There is widespread political and religious persecution; whites have fled or have been forced to leave.[6] The MPLA is a minority party that rules through terror and Cuban troops; it represents only about one-third of the people. The other two-thirds are repre-sented by the not very active National Front for the Liberation of Angola (FNLA) and the União Nacional para a Independencia Total de Angola (UNITA), which holds large parts of the country. Freedom of speech and of the press and the right to vote—the same freedoms that the United States sought to establish in Zimbabwe through international embargo—are absent in Angola.

There is as yet no sign of improvement. Food shortages are everywhere; the Benguela Railway has not operated since 1975 because of guerrilla activi-ties; and exports have dwindled, except for oil from Cabinda. Angola has joined the long list of countries whose bright hopes in a revolution have been dispelled by postrevolutionary reality. The United States should not recog-nize the MPLA as the legal government of Angola; it should arm and train the FNLA and UNITA to force the MPLA to form a coalition government; and it

6. See various reports of Amnesty International, especially *People's Republic of Angola:* (1982). See also *Angola, A Country Study* (1979, 110–111).

should encourage the Cubans, East Germans, and Soviets to return to their respective homelands.

While FRELIMO, which controls Mozambique, has maintained somewhat more independence from the Soviet Union than has the MPLA, it is still a self-proclaimed Marxist-Leninist party (1983) and is an admitted member (as is the MPLA) of the international Marxist-Leninist movement. The United States should encourage FRELIMO to move out of the Soviet camp, to refuse all facility or base rights to the Soviets, and to practice a form of detente with South Africa.

Southern Africa.   As the richest, most developed part of Africa, southern Africa is of major strategic importance to the United States (Gann and Duignan, 1981b). The countries of southern Africa (South Africa, Namibia, Botswana, Swaziland, Lesotho, Zimbabwe, Zambia, and Mozambique) are welded into a state system dominated economically, politically, and militarily by South Africa. United States policy in southern Africa has been ambivalent and inconsistent, alternating between support for black nationalism and cooperation with South Africa.

In spite of the vital U.S. interests in South Africa, the United States has hesitated to promote these interests via an alliance with South Africa. The costs were seen as too high in terms of keeping on the good side of black nationalists and world opinion. Fundamentally, the United States has been, and is, committed to forcing reform on South Africa (ending apartheid as well as gaining independence for Namibia). The Carter administration initially pushed human rights issues in order to win black support against white rule in South Africa, but then muted its criticism when it realized it needed Pretoria's cooperation if peaceful settlements were to come to Rhodesia (Zimbabwe) and Namibia.

When President Reagan came into power in 1980, the State Department argued for further concessions to South Africa in order to get that country to end the stalemate in Namibia. A new policy of "constructive engagement" was announced that had both regional and global ramifications: it sought peace in southern Africa and it sought to get the Cubans out of Angola. Constructive engagement, according to an administration spokesman (Lyman 1981) appearing before the Subcommittee on Africa of the House of Representatives in 1981, has as its objectives: (1) fostering movement toward a system of government by consent of the governed and away from the racial policy of apartheid and political disenfranchisement of blacks; (2) maintaining continued access to strategic minerals that the United States and OECD countries are dependent on South Africa for; (3) assuring the strategic security of the Cape sea-route through which pass vital U.S. oil and mineral supplies from the Middle East and South Africa; and (4) preserving regional security in southern Africa against the Soviet-Cuban threat.

There are five components to the U.S. approach to the southern African region: first, internationally recognized independence for Namibia; second, internationally supported programs of economic development in all the developing countries of the region; third, negotiations to get the withdrawal of Cuban troops from Angola; fourth, detente between South Africa and the other states of the region; and fifth, peaceful evolutionary change in South Africa away from apartheid and toward a system of government based on consent of the governed.

The United States has also been negotiating bilaterally with South Africa on Namibian independence. The major new element in the negotiations is the requirement of withdrawal of Cuban forces from Angola. The United States believes this is necessary to get South Africa to give up Namibia and then to start constructive changes within South Africa itself away from apartheid. This reflects the new global outlook of the Reagan administration which sees Cuba as an integral part of the Soviet drive for world dominance.

President Reagan has indicated that his administration regards apartheid as repugnant to basic U.S. values, but that as long as South Africa appears to be attempting to move away from its racist system of government, the United States should be helpful and encouraging. Constructive engagement therefore is dependent on reform within South Africa and the attainment of internationally recognized independence for Namibia.

For this reason, after three years of Reagan's presidency constructive engagement was in trouble. Politically, the Reagan administration would not have been able to continue its policy in the face of severe African hostility without something to show for it. It appeared that constructive engagement had worked no better than President Carter's human rights approach. Namibia was no nearer independence than it was before Reagan took office. The Reagan administration appeared to have reassessed some of its former assumptions; constructive engagement had come under criticism within the State Department; pronouncements resembled more those of the Carter era than initial statements made at the beginning of the Reagan presidency. (The State Department, for example, welcomed Oliver Tambo, head of the pro-Soviet ANC in 1982, whilst denying a visa, even as a private citizen traveling on a South African passport, to Patrick Mphephu, a black anticommunist who heads one of South Africa's so-called black homelands.) But the new policy shift did not lessen the hostility of Reagan's African and domestic critics.

In South Africa, in spite of some constitutional reforms and new openings to Indians and Coloureds, there had been no new legislation to lessen discrimination since 1980. Furthermore, South Africa had increasingly militarized its relations with all its neighbors and attacked these countries with impunity and excessive force in the past two years. The United States was witnessing the Israelization of southern Africa.

African leaders have increasingly condemned U.S. efforts on the grounds that these were ineffective or constituted a form of closet collaboration with Pretoria. Yet, their alternative plans promise no solution either. The sad truth is that external pressure has failed and will continue to fail to produce reform until the internal conditions for change develop in South Africa. Only Pretoria can help the United States to continué its policy of constructive engagement by making bold domestic reforms, by cooperating on Namibian independence, and by stopping attacks on its neighbors. If this is not done, then we will see a new U.S. policy. The United States will probably distance itself, perhaps even disengage itself, from South Africa, or it will return to diplomatic harangues and increased sanctions.

In February and March of 1984, constructive engagement scored an impressive diplomatic victory. The United States, acting as an honest broker, got South Africa to negotiate first with Angola and then with Mozambique to end attacks on these beleaguered countries. The Accord of Nkomati (March 16, 1984) was the first nonaggression agreement between South Africa and any of its neighbors. Under its terms South Africa promised not to attack Mozambique and not to support the Mozambique National Resistance Movement (MNR); in return Mozambique promised to no longer make its territory available to the ANC for raids against South Africa. The Angolan agreement called for South Africa to withdraw from Angola and the Cubans to be sent home. Angola was also to prevent SWAPO from raiding into Namibia. On the face of it, U.S. diplomacy and South Africa have won a major victory but only time will tell if peace can continue between South Africa and its neighbors.

Still the Reagan administration did not hesitate to criticize South Africa for the preventive detention of black labor leaders in December of 1984 after strikes and rioting broke out. Constructive engagement continues therefore to call for quiet diplomatic pressure to bring about significant reforms in South Africa.

The international campaign against South Africa thus has developed great pressures for change. It has helped awaken black consciousness and has revived the liberation struggle. There is no evidence that the anti-apartheid movement will lessen its pressure in the future to isolate South Africa and to reduce the amount of assistance South Africa receives. While the abolitionists cannot force significant changes or defeat South Africa—only internal subversion and external assaults can do that—they can isolate South Africa, deny it goods and services, and thus raise the costs of continuing the apartheid system.

An unreformed South Africa will never again command the friendly respect which it enjoyed in the United States when Smuts was at the helm in Pretoria. The U.S. commitment to racial equality and to human rights is now too strong to embrace apartheid. South African whites will have to make more significant reforms than the recent constitutional changes establishing parliaments for Indians and Coloureds, and share power with blacks before the American people will accept an alliance, and this is true no matter how important the Cape route is, how much the West needs South Africa's strategic minerals, or how strong the Soviet-Cuban presence becomes. Neither South Africa's anticommunism nor its value as a military base during wartime will prove sufficient to overcome hatred of apartheid during a time of peace.

The United States and Africa Today and Tomorrow

The West cannot prevent Soviet aggressiveness, but an attempt to contain it should be made. The West's best option is to shore up key states, assisting them to develop economically and to govern themselves. For the second half of the 1980s, however, the picture looks gloomy and full of violence—ethnic, regional, and ideological—that will further draw in rival foreign powers. Indeed, World War III might conceivably begin in Africa. The Afro-Marxist and the military dictatorships will probably be economically worse off by 1990 than they were in 1980. The condition of the masses in many states in all likelihood will deteriorate steadily.

What of the future? The United States has been overly inclined to shape its foreign policy in Africa to meet the approval of the so-called Third World— the uncommitted nations of Asia and Africa that are supposed to hold the future world balance of power in their hands. This point of view neglects the military realities of power and looks on the present struggle for world supremacy as an ideological beauty competition between East and West, a competition in which the panel of judges is made up of Asians and Africans. Countries are indeed influenced by ideas, but economic and strategic factors play an even larger part in world affairs. It is doubtful how far the West would be justified in subordinating its interests to the real or imagined demands of neutralists. It is in fact only the strength of the West, and nothing but its strength, that has made it possible up to the present time for Afro-Asian countries to afford the luxury of neutralism. Once the West weakens, the fate of the new countries themselves is imperiled.

No simple rule of thumb will suffice for U.S. foreign policy in Africa as a whole. There are many African countries, and the United States accordingly needs many different African policies. It needs flexibility, realism, and avoidance of the view that American policy must somehow always be ideologically acceptable to others. Political and economic warfare against South Africa will not liberalize the republic or improve the lot of its black people. The United States should seek to cooperate with a reform-minded Pretoria insofar as collaboration is in American strategic interest. In Namibia the West should seek to support moderate forms of government rather than aid its declared enemies. Similarly, the United States should consider recognition of Angola only after all foreign troops—Cuban and East German—and Soviet military experts have left. This would force the MPLA to form a coalition government with the two guerrilla organizations that now oppose it from the bush. Such a withdrawal should be a necessary condition for U.S. recognition.

In a more general sense, the United States must become more realistic in the conduct of its African affairs, and be sufficiently firm to make it clear to African governments that certain policies they advocate are not in the best interests of the West. The United States will have to take sides on "issues"; not simply always back blacks against whites, or radicals against conservatives (Gann and Duignan 1981b).

The West has yet to evolve a coherent policy toward African development and security problems. The United States needs to focus its aid to shape events in countries that receive it; the United States should also directly aid countries rather than funnel funds through international bodies. Arms and security programs should be instruments of our diplomacy in Africa. The Reagan administration has wisely revived its military assistance program.

The United States therefore must reinvigorate its African policy by devoting more aid and military assistance to Africa (Crocker and Lewis 1979). The United States should denounce Soviet-Cuban involvement in Africa for the instability it has caused, respond positively to requests for security assistance when the states requesting it act in accordance with mutual local and American interests, and praise the French for maintaining regional security and do likewise. The United States must point out to African nations that it would be mutually beneficial to discourage Soviet domination and to develop policies that would promote peace and economic development.[7]

The Military Value of Southern Africa

Angolan and Mozambican bases would benefit the Soviets from the standpoint of financial economy. The Soviet admiralty would find it much cheaper to support a fleet of submarines from a nearby fixed base, furnished with ample stocks, machine shops, and dry-dock facilities, than from a distant home base. Access to an advanced base increases the "time on station," hence the effectiveness, of a submarine on patrol. Lower costs are an important feature in planning during peacetime, when Soviet strategists are well aware of the way in which military expenditures depress their sagging economy. In either a cold war or a hot war, overseas bases make possible faster turnaround and greater efficiency in rearming, restocking, and repairing ships; they can also serve as air bases to facilitate fleet reconnaissance and communications.

In the event of total war, facilities in Angola and Mozambique would increase the operational range of Soviet missile-carrying submarines. Soviet ships have mapped out the ocean floor and the currents of the Indian Ocean to

---

7. For an opposing view of these matters see Bowman (1982, 159–192).

learn where their submarines can hide from antisubmarine forces, and are doing similar work in the South Atlantic. They have learned, for example, that sonar detection may be ineffective under certain hydrographic conditions in the Indian Ocean. Submarines concealed in these areas would form a potent strategic threat.

The new Soviet 4,000-mile missile aboard a Soviet submarine operating from Angola would introduce new strategic possibilities. A missile capable of striking the United States from a submarine operating in the Indian Ocean has not yet been developed, but it is technically feasible. U.S. planners would be better able to counteract these and similar threats if they had access to South African harbors and to the excellent naval base at Simonstown, as well as to the vast complex of South African airfields and industrial and repair facilities.[8]

Bases in South Africa would supply the West with permanent facilities from which American ships and aircraft could operate. Ships and crews would not have to be shuttled from the United States or from Europe to the Indian Ocean, and from Atlantic to Indian Ocean ports, if South Africa's ample supply and repair facilities were made available. U.S. naval forces would save on fuel and resupply requirements as well as on man-hours and ship-hours lost in transit. Crews could be changed periodically through the use of aircraft. The U.S. strategic position in the Indian Ocean and the South Atlantic would be strengthened. Surveillance and defense of the Cape routes would be vastly facilitated. The United States could rely on an extensive industrial and military infrastructure and on substantial local forces.

The advantages of South African cooperation are now denied to the West because of internal and external policy. No black African government is willing or able to provide the kind of facilities that South Africa could furnish to the Western alliance in the South Atlantic and the Indian Ocean. The question then remains: Will the cost of military self-denial exceed the price?

REFERENCES

The African Communist. 1978. Vol. 72: 113–115.

Angola, A Country Study. 1979. Foreign Area Studies. Pp. 110–111. Washington, D.C.: The American University.

Bowman, Larry W. 1982. "The Strategic Importance of South Africa to the United States: An Appraisal and Policy Analysis." African Affairs. Journal of the Royal African Society 81, no. 323 (April):159–192.

Crocker, Chester A., and William H. Lewis. 1979. "Missing Opportunities in Africa." Foreign Policy 35 (Summer): 142–161.

Gann, L. H., and Peter Duignan. 1978. South Africa: War, Revolution or Peace. Stanford, Calif.: Hoover Institution Press.

8. See Gann and Duignan (1978), Chapter 2, on the strategic importance of the region.

_____. 1981a. *Africa South of the Sahara: The Challenge to Western Security.* Stanford, Calif.: Hoover Institution Press.

_____. 1981b. *Why South Africa Will Survive.* New York: St. Martin's Press.

Grechko, Marshall A. A. 1974. "The Leading Role of the CPSU in Building the Army of a Developed Socialist Society." *Voprosy Istorii KPSS* no. 5 (May 1974), as translated in USA/FN Soviet press translations nos. 74–77 (31), July.

Henriksen, Thomas H., ed. 1981. *Communist Powers and Sub-Saharan Africa.* Stanford, Calif.: Hoover Institution Press.

International Affairs. 1961. March. Pp. 116ff. Moscow.

Keesings Contemporary Archives. January 4, 1980: 30019; September 10, 1982: 31687–31688.

Lyman, Princeton. 1981. U.S. Congress, House Foreign Affairs Committee Hearings. H381–60.3. *U.S. Corporate Activities in South Africa.* Testimony before the Subcommittee on International Economic Policy and Trade and the Subcommittee on Africa (October 15): 87–117.

Ogunbadejo, Oye. 1979. "Soviet Policies in Africa." Research Paper. Ife, Nigeria: University of Ife.

People's Republic of Angola. 1982. *Background Briefing on Amnesty International's Concerns.* December. London.

Yearbook on International Communist Affairs. 1970–. Annual. Stanford, Calif.

17

France and Crisis Areas in Africa

EDMOND JOUVE

The geopolitical significance of Africa is undeniable. The Maghreb constitutes a bridge linking Africa to Europe. The Mediterranean is an intersection between east-west and north-south axes. Northeast Africa links the continent to the Middle East and the Indian Ocean, a gateway whose importance vastly increased with the opening of the Suez Canal in 1869. Today, however, large oil tankers sail around the Cape, which has become a link between the Middle East and Western Europe and America, and the Indian Ocean and its numerous small islands have acquired strategic importance.

Despite Africa's geopolitical significance and vast resources, it remains the least developed of all continents. During the past decade, the average annual growth in the GNP in the Third World was between 2.5 and 2.7 percent, whereas for African countries, it was less than 1 percent. Between 1970 and 1976, Africa's external debt tripled to $24.5 billion. Unemployment constantly increased. Colonialism provides a partial explanation for this situation; yet twenty years after independence the major problems persist. The vulnerability of the African countries is reflected in the formidable crises they confront from Western Sahara to the Horn of Africa and the Indian Ocean, and from Zaire to southern Africa; not a single region is free of a crisis (Jouve 1979, 397ff).

At the same time the continent lacks mechanisms for crisis containment or resolution. Thus, the conflict between Chad and Libya led to a proposal in 1979 to form a pan-African defense force by the Organization of African Unity (OAU) at its meeting in Monrovia, Liberia. Accepted in principle, the protocol was never concluded. It could not have been otherwise, given the existence of numerous defense pacts with Western countries. Indeed, Africa hardly controls its own destiny. Historically the closed reserve of European colonial powers, control or influence over its affairs is now hotly disputed by the two superpowers.

The Soviet Union has never abandoned its interest in Africa, displaying patience and determination in pursuit of its objectives. In 1978, thirty-six of the forty-eight members of the OAU had concluded commercial agreements with the Soviet Union. Of these, thirty-two had signed economic and technical cooperation agreements. The Soviet Union assisted in the construction of 450 industrial and other plants. In a declaration in June 1978, Moscow justified the Soviet presence: "The Soviet government's attitude toward Africa is totally unambiguous. In developing countries as elsewhere, we are with the forces supporting national independence, social progress and democracy, and we behave as friends and comrades in the struggle." Regions of Soviet concentration are Africa's Mediterranean, Atlantic, and Indian Ocean coastlines. Hence, the Soviet defense pacts with Angola, Mozambique, and Ethiopia. For the USSR crises are pretexts for gaining footholds in Africa; yet once these are established, it has problems consolidating its influence (Carrère d'Encausse 1982, 13). Ideology does not suffice (Laïdi 1980, 9; and 1982, 82ff). As a result, developing countries turn toward the United States, the other superpower.

The U.S. attitude toward Africa has been indecisive. The Congolese civil war of the early 1960s precipitated its first involvement. Thereafter, until Angola's independence in 1975, little interest was shown. After that time senior American officials (Henry Kissinger, Andrew Young, and more recently, Chester Crocker) have made frequent visits. A series of defense pacts has been concluded, and recent official statements affirm the American intention to be a major actor on the African political scene (Laïdi 1982, 82).

French interests are obviously affected by the policies and activities of the two superpowers. Africa is absolutely essential to the French economy. It remains France's major source of raw materials. France imports 40 percent of its phosphates from Morocco and 39 percent from Senegal and Togo, 63 percent of its cobalt from Zaire and 37 percent from Morocco, 16 percent of its iron ore from Mauritania, and 91 percent of its manganese from Gabon and South Africa. French interests are also dominant in manufacturing industries in Francophone countries. For example, in agribusiness their control ranges from 100 percent in the Congo to 72 percent in Gabon; in textiles from 82.4 percent in Senegal to 60 percent in the Congo; and in chemical and petrochemical industries, from 100 percent in the Central African Republic to 73.5 percent in Senegal and 60 percent in Gabon. Africa will furnish an increasingly greater percentage of France's needs in hydrocarbons. Globally, France's balance of payments is determined by its economic relations with the African continent. Thus, France has had critical stakes in Africa, which help to explain the temptations to which de Gaulle and Valéry Giscard d'Estaing often succumbed (*La Politique africaine du Général de Gaulle* 1980).

Given the centrality of Africa for French interests, what has been the French position on Africa and its crises since the Left under Mitterrand gained power in France? After an initial period of reassessment, the status quo seems to have prevailed. After a honeymoon of open idealism, realism and a globalist perspective appear to have gained the upper hand.

Idealism or Realism?

Before coming to power, the Socialists had vigorously criticized "Giscardian mercantilism" (*Les Socialistes* ... 1977, 80), exemplified by Giscard's apparently comfortable relationship with the emperor of the former Central African Empire. The importance of French economic relations with the latter, particularly in cotton and tobacco, forest reserves, and uranium, explained Giscard's "Dear Relative" salutation to Emperor Bokassa during the former's first presidential trip to Africa. Amin's Uganda also had cordial relations with the French government. And when Francisco Macias Nguema fell from power in Equatorial Guinea, France was the only Common Market country maintaining an embassy there. Before Mitterrand's accession to the presidency in 1981, it was widely believed that such situations were bound to change; however, *raison d'état* has meant that little change has occurred.

These were the contradictions which finally led Jean-Pierre Cot, minister of cooperation and development, to resign from the government on December 9, 1982. Idealism had given way to realism, ethical principles to economic necessity.

Idealism has been a constant factor in French politics. Like de Gaulle, most French people believe their country to be as pure "as a madonna on a cathedral fresco," and less a "cold monster" than other nations (Hoffmann 1982). Its behavior, they feel, must conform to certain exemplary ethical principles. Such an attitude allows little room for hypocrisy or indulgence. France must speak out if necessary, particularly when human rights are trampled upon. The Franco-Mexican declaration of August 28, 1981, falls into this context. However, in Latin America, as in Africa, peoples must find within themselves the force to resist tyranny. Consequently, one need not foment artificial danger zones, for example, by instigating coups d'état. As Jean-Pierre Cot (1982) declared:

> It is not the duty of France to wage revolutionary struggles on behalf of other peoples. Such is not at all our intention. In this respect, I would say that we risk deceiving others, sometimes, in certain countries—in Central Africa (and it was hoped that we would do the contrary of what had previously been done). No, we will not do it. We will respect States as they exist and situations as they are. When a people lacks the energy to fight its own battles, it cannot hope to find this energy abroad. I have a somewhat "Maoist" vision of the situation.

On the human rights issue, France has traditionally shown a most sensitive concern. One of the first actions of the present government was to participate in the International Conference on Sanctions against South Africa, held in Paris on May 20–27, 1981. The French government was represented by

Claude Cheysson, minister of external affairs, and Jean-Pierre Cot. The Paris Declaration highlighted "the explosive situation in southern Africa" and the violations of human and national rights perpetrated by South Africa (*Déclaration de Paris* 1981). It declared that such violations represent not merely a threat, but an obvious breach of international peace and security. Hence the conference condemned South Africa's policy and "criminal action," and worked out a program of sanctions aimed at forcing South Africa to "abandon its racist apartheid policy and to end its illegal occupation of Namibia."

As soon as he became president, François Mitterrand outlined the framework for a French policy on Namibia. On November 3, 1981, before the Eighth Conference of Heads of State of France and Africa, he declared:

> Among the conflicts currently threatening Africa, one of the most important concerns the independence of Namibia. After consulting traditional friends, France has accepted their request that it remain a member of the Group of Five [the Western Contact Group]. It thus intends to fulfill its mission as prescribed by the United Nations, whose Resolution 435 it wholeheartedly approved. Our efforts are now making progress and we consider that our membership in this group is not a pretext for endless negotiations and that a timetable must be fixed. (*Documents d'actualité internationale* 1981)

The French president further considered it "necessary to achieve Namibia's independence in 1982." Although such hope was obviously not fulfilled, further initiatives were taken within the Contact Group of Five (the United States, France, Great Britain, West Germany, and Canada), whose foreign ministers met on two occasions in 1982 at which they reaffirmed their goal of contributing to a solution of the Namibian problem within the scope of Resolution 435, according to which the Namibian people should exercise their right to self-determination. This imperative was reaffirmed again in the Final Communiqué of the Eighth Conference of Heads of State of France and Africa, on October 9, 1982, which stated that "Namibia must necessarily attain independence in 1983" (*Documents d'actualité internationale* 1982).

President Mitterrand linked the independence of Namibia to a rejection of the apartheid system. And on October 10 he added colorfully that "France is like a draft horse, not worn out by continuous effort, but it would like to be relieved of the burden, because usually such an effort involves team work" (*Le Monde*, October 12, 1982).

The right of peoples to self-determination undergirds this policy, and clarifies other elements of French politics. In humorous fashion, Mitterrand recalled that "the right of peoples to determine their destiny reminds one of a phrase in a French comedy, 'it is like a cream pie': something that we repeat endlessly with the result that the words almost lose their meaning. And yet, there is no greater truism in the modern world." In any case, France wants this principle to inspire the search for a solution to the problem of the Western

Sahara. According to Mitterrand (November 3, 1981), France should intervene "on the basis of the right of self-determination of the populations concerned," should support the efforts of the OAU, and should throw its weight behind "on-going attempts in the hope that they may reach a rapid conclusion." This position has frequently been reaffirmed. The president declared on October 8: "We know why the OAU summit failed, but it is not our duty to do otherwise than give our opinion. It must be clearly understood that it is within the OAU . . . that the path to be followed will be outlined. And in the final analysis, it is up to the people themselves to determine their destiny." On October 10, in Brazzaville, he clarified his position: "I favor the right of self-determination within the context of the transfer of sovereignty from the colonial state to that of independence." And he further underlined that this affair was "wickedly complicated" (*Documents d'actualité internationale* 1981). During his official visit to Morocco, from January 27 to 29, 1983, Mitterrand restated France's position: there must be an honest poll under the control of the competent authorities (*Le Monde,* January 28, 1983).

Mitterrand has repeatedly reiterated his attitude in favor of human rights: "Each time I visit a country, I always keep this urgent issue in mind without, however, attempting to give any lessons on political morality" (*Le Monde,* January 28, 1983). The French government also finds itself in an embarrassing position where human rights are concerned in Zaire. Recently, there were numerous accusations of systematic violations of the most basic rights: arbitrary arrests, torture, prolonged detention without trial, and trials conducted without elementary respect for the rights of the defense (Jouve 1983, 258). Yet despite all this, harsh economic necessities have, in the end, determined the policy of silence by the French government.

France and Economic Necessities

Economic considerations have led France to pursue commercial relations with states whose policies have hardly favored the protection of human rights. Such happens to be the case with South Africa. Thus on January 21, 1983, in an assessment of his ministry's action, Jean-Pierre Cot (1983) recalled this problem, pointing out that France was associated with South Africa by virtue of a number of economic agreements regarding supplies of raw materials. Furthermore, France counted on selling certain of its technological data on the South African market. In such a context, France could not "retreat overnight from such a fruitful partnership even if it obviously stands in contradiction to France's stated political goals, namely solidarity with the Third World and especially with Africa."

France maintains equally privileged relations with Zaire, one of the continent's giants, ruled by Marshal Mobutu Sese Seko. Since 1975 Zaire has faced major economic difficulties. By 1982, the interest on the national debt (over

$5 billion) had absorbed 26 percent of the national budget. France's role has consisted in helping Mobutu avoid bankruptcy. Early in his seven-year mandate (August 1975), Valéry Giscard d'Estaing made an official state visit to Zaire. France subsequently played a prominent role in the international rescue of the Mobutu regime during the two invasions of Shaba Province. In the first (April 1977), French transport planes airlifted Moroccan soldiers and vehicles to Shaba. The president stressed that "no French soldiers are currently engaged and none will be in Zaire. This is an operation of assistance and cooperation for transport between Morocco and Zaire. In so doing, we have intended to give two signals, namely, of solidarity and security" (Jouve 1981, 88). In the second (May 1978), France intervened in a salvage operation with elements of the Foreign Legion. They were critical in recapturing for Zaire the mining center of Kolwezi, then under seige by the invading forces of General Nathanael M'Bumba from Angola.

Since May 10, 1981, the basic premises of French military support of Zaire have not been questioned. France continues to supply arms to Zaire: Mirage jets, Alouette III helicopters, armored cars, and other military hardware. Moreover, under the terms of a military agreement signed on May 22, 1974, Paris has provided to Kinshasa technical military personnel for service with the armed forces of Zaire. During 1982 they instructed parachutists, trained Mirage pilots, and armored division troops, and gave basic training at the armed forces school. Major contracts have been signed in the telecommunications field and for projects for the installation of urban facilities and port construction as well as airport and administrative equipment. France also participates in the extraction of copper and cobalt deposits and in the development of the world's greatest reserve of hydroelectric power (Inga I and II, in Lower Zaire). By the end of Giscard's seven-year term, France was Zaire's third most important commercial partner, after Belgium and the United States, which together control Zaire's major mineral assets.

Under Mitterrand, Franco-Zairian relations have thus continued as before. The Eighth Conference of Heads of State of France and Africa, originally scheduled for Kinshasa, finally took place in Paris in May 1981; but the ninth was held in Kinshasa upon Marshal Mobutu's invitation. One of the sixteen points of the Final Communiqué considered security problems in Africa and recalled that participating members had "emphasized the importance of security as an element of peace, stability, and development. It further emphasized the urgent necessity of reducing tension in the world, especially in Africa, and called for the implementing of measures capable of inspiring confidence in international relations" (Documents d'actualité internationale 1983).

These statements implied certain commitments by France, particularly that of maintaining what Mitterrand termed an "Allied agreement," according to which:

France will scrupulously respect this engagement, all her engagements, on the very difficult principle of aid to security; I am speaking of aid to the independence and security of the African countries that have agreements with us. We will respect these engagements, as long as aid is not confused with meddling in the internal affairs of independent states. Our guidelines are good will, open dialogue and mutual respect. (*Documents d'actualité internationale* 1982)

These engagements entailed considerable credits granted by French military cooperation; the continued stationing of French troops in Djibouti, Senegal, Ivory Coast, Gabon, and the Central African Republic; special attention to the Horn of Africa (forty ships sail through the Mozambique channel every day); and the signing of a treaty with Djibouti on June 27, 1977, incorporating defense, military, and technical assistance. Finally, the initial role in East-West competition of the Republic of South Africa ("guardian of the route around the Cape") is acknowledged (Cornevin 1982, 110).

But Africa is not alone. Neither Africa nor France has the power to avoid engagement with world problems. France's president admits that "wherever we look we observe that the major powers, as well as others, cannot resist the temptation to advance their global interests, whatever the price to be paid" (*Documents d'actualité internationale* 1982). In Africa as elsewhere, and especially in African crisis areas, France has had to reconsider the problems she must resolve within a globalist or world perspective.

Regionalism or Globalism?

The *mondialisme* of Giscard d'Estaing had been strongly criticized by the Left opposition. Here again, however, the realities were quickly perceived. Partisans of globalism were on the scene; others aspired to reactivate France's universalist tradition. It was also believed that the privileged role reserved for Africa should not lead France to ignore the rest of the Third World: Asia, the Arab world, and Latin America. Yet, it was also realized that Africa was a high-stakes gamble for the major powers. In November 1981 Mitterrand revealed his anxiety to the African heads of state present in Paris. And in Niamey, on May 20, 1982, he reiterated this concern: "You wish to prevent Africa from becoming the arena of foreign rivalries and contradictions. We have the same attitude and this explains France's participation in Africa's efforts."

Concern over East-West relations must not, Mitterrand observed, obscure the need for continued North-South dialogue. In Abidjan in May 1982 he stated that "the complex East-West relations, which bear particularly on the competition between the super powers and the world division of their dominant interests, must not prevent us from considering North-South problems." Mitterrand restated this on May 22, noting that aside from conflicts regarded as merely local or regional affairs, the prospect is one which "facilitates the forceful return of typically East-West conflicts, the latter being substituted day by day for North-South problems" (*Documents d'actualité internationale* 1982). Despite this tendency, North-South relations retained a significant autonomy, and France had become the champion of the North-South dialogue. In Mexico on October 20, 1981, Mitterrand declared that "East-West antagonism cannot explain the freedom struggles of 'the wretched of the earth' any more than it can resolve them." He recalled that "it was in Mexico that the first juridical bases of a New International Economic Order were laid" (*Le Monde,* October 22, 1982). At the Cancun Conference, France became the spokesman for the world's outcasts.

Institutionally this is reflected in the new responsibilities of the minister of cooperation, to whom report aid and cooperation missions in twenty-five African states (Benin, Burundi, Cameroon, Central African Republic, Congo, Comoros, Ivory Coast, Djibouti, Gabon, Burkina Faso, Mauritius, Madagascar, Mali, Mauritania, Niger, Ruanda, Senegal, Seychelles, Chad, Togo, Zaire, Cape Verde, Guinea Bissau, Sao Tome/Principe, and Equatorial Guinea). The minister must be consulted on all matters concerning cooperation and development in sub-Saharan countries; he leads international negotiations on development issues.

The fact that Mitterrand waited several months to make his first trip to Africa (in May 1982) provoked some anxiety over the apparent neglect of Africa by the new government. One prominent editorialist (Diallo 1982, 37) used the shock title "Africa does not count," deploring "the systematic boycott of Africa by Claude Cheysson, minister of external affairs," and commenting: "It is with some bitterness, perhaps even irritation that sub-Saharan capitals refer to the quarantine practiced by the French foreign minister. People talk about a 'deliberate oversight,' a 'lack of consideration,' and even of 'contempt,' given the fact that Cheysson has already visited all the other areas of the world." The editorialist further added, "The truth of the matter is that, even though he made a stopover in Ethiopia on January 1st, Claude Cheysson has no time to waste on Africa, quite simply because this area of the world does not rank on the international chess board. Africa represents, at least for the time being, neither a major strategic force, nor a military power, nor a comfortable petrodollar mattress. When a region does not symbolize one of these three factors, it does not count, even in the opinion of a French socialist minister."

But Africa was not to be so easily forgotten. Major commitments existed under the Lomé Convention, and in May 1982 France had to help salvage the system. The OAU itself entered a period of crisis. Africa still commanded much attention, but inevitably observers began viewing the continent through the warped perspective of the East-West conflict.

France and the East-West Confrontation

Africa is certainly affected by the East-West conflict, with the continent's crises serving as vectors (Lemarchand 1983, 24). France's policy in the region has suffered some setbacks, including occasional clashes with U.S. African policy. Giscard "the African," by the grace of the Trilateral Commission and with American blessing, behaved as though he were the West's trustee, or policeman, in Africa. Principal actors have since changed, but the obstacles remain. The limited results obtained by the Contact Group in Namibia simply reflect the fact that Washington links Namibia's independence with the withdrawal of Cuban troops from Angola. On August 29, 1981, Chester A. Crocker openly admitted that the American diplomatic position regarded the Namibian and Angolan conflicts as closely linked, and that progress toward a peaceful settlement in Namibia would be facilitated by the withdrawal of Cuban forces from Angola (USA-Document 1981). On May 9, 1982, in Eureka, Illinois, President Reagan made similar observations.

Another crisis area of great power concern is the Western Sahara. Early in the crisis, Paris came to Mauritania's rescue, opening a military school in Atar in 1977. Arms and military advisers were dispatched, and convoys were increased after October 1977 in order to "protect French citizens." Yet over the years French policy toward the Western Sahara has fluctuated, being not a little influenced by the evolution of U.S. policy in that area.

The United States has developed a deepening engagement toward Morocco in the conflict. As one U.S. spokesman put it: "America's natural interests are best served, not only in North Africa, but generally by the aid granted to our trusted ally, Morocco" (*Sahara info* 1981). Along with Egypt, Oman, Kenya, and Somalia, Morocco has become an essential link in the Reagan administration's African strategy. Its location in the northern tier of Africa makes Morocco a choice outpost for developing U.S. influence in the Middle East. It is all the more crucial in view of the vulnerability of Washington's other Mediterranean allies. The United States must therefore prove its intention to directly influence events in Northwest Africa, especially around the Strait of Gibraltar, so vital to its Sixth Fleet.

The American military presence in Morocco, of course, is not recent. Prior to the latter's independence, France had placed five bases at the disposal of the American Strategic Air Command which were used until finally closed down in 1963. Subsequently, the United States relinquished its naval facilities in Kenitra. However, there has since been a gradual return. In October 1979, President Carter decided to lift the embargo on arms sales to Morocco for the Saharan war. On his arrival in the White House, Reagan welcomed closer ties between the United States and Morocco, a position reciprocated by Rabat. The Moroccan government sought assistance in order to "face the threat posed by the introduction of Sam–6 missiles in the war" (Hodges 1980).

There followed an acceleration of the pace of the implementation of what some observers call the "Washington-Rabat axis." Commencing in March 1981, the United States sold Morocco tanks and aircraft. On a visit to Morocco in February 1982 Alexander Haig deplored the fact that the Polisario acted as a Libyan and Soviet tool. King Hassan's visit to the United States three months later was followed by a U.S.–Morocco military agreement signed on May 27, 1982, according to which the Rapid Deployment Force (RDF) obtained transit facilities at certain Moroccan bases. In exchange, military aid to Morocco was increased and joint naval maneuvers were held in mid-November 1982.

Mitterrand's visit to Morocco in January 1983 was undoubtedly a response to a concern over America's growing influence in the region. France manifestly considers this influence to be disproportionate to its interests (*Le Monde*, January 28, 1983). With important commercial interests and 265 military advisers in Morocco, France could not remain inactive in the face of these American initiatives (*Sahara info* 1981). After an initial friendly gesture toward Polisario, France abstained in the November 1982 United Nations vote concerning the granting of independence to the peoples of the Western Sahara.

France also suffered setbacks as a result of Soviet policy in Africa. On October 8, 1976, Angola signed a twenty-year treaty of friendly cooperation with the Soviet Union which made available naval and airport facilities and provided for the presence of 2,700 Soviet troops, in addition to 19,000 Cubans (*Annuaire . . .* 1982, 62). Implementation of the two Lomé conventions has been negatively affected by Soviet influence in Africa. Sixty-three African, Caribbean, and Pacific (ACP) countries signed the Second Convention, but some, including Angola and Mozambique, have not done so. Ethiopia, however, has signed the conventions and is an ACP member, despite being within the Soviet sphere of influence, and despite having 11,000 Cuban troops, 1,200 military advisers and technicians from Warsaw Pact countries, and a South Yemen unit serving on its soil, as well as nineteen Soviet warships benefiting from its facilities (*Annuaire . . .* 1982, 75; Bressand 1981, 40). Moreover, between 1962 and 1981, the United States granted to Ethiopia economic aid worth $344 million, plus $244 million in military assistance; the Ethiopian case reveals the singularly complex nature of interests in this area of Africa produced by the East-West confrontation.

France is merely one among many actors on the diplomatic scene, even in French-speaking countries. Thus in 1975 among foreign diplomatic missions in Africa, the United States maintained 64, West Germany 62, Great Britain 51, the Soviet Union 52, China 48, and France 67 (Kontchou Kouomegni 1977, 39). France therefore faces serious competition. Due essentially to historic, linguistic, and cultural reasons, however, France holds some assets that are unavailable to the United States and the Soviet Union. Even if it often has fewer financial resources than the two superpowers, France still holds a privileged position with many African states.

A Soviet observer (Kouriavtsev 1982) states the problem in the following terms:

> It seems on the whole that the "Third Worldism" to which France links ambitious foreign policy objectives and the hope of occupying a privileged position among industrial states and developing nations—a position which confers on it the right to intervene on the international scene on behalf of young nations—must stand the test of time.

France possesses several assets for this role. In contrast to other nations it does not withdraw from its commitments. France is not only not reducing its aid to the Third World; it is increasing it—from 0.35 percent of the gross national product in 1981 to 0.52 percent in 1982, with a goal of 0.70 percent in 1988. Thus France's aid to the Third World amounts to $3 billion (two-thirds for bilateral aid and one-third for multilateral aid). The Ministry of Cooperation and Development controls about a third of the total. A significant portion of this is geared to cultural affairs, namely, to France's 13,000 technical specialists in Africa. The latter constitute its cultural strike force. On October 10, 1982, in Brazzaville, Mitterrand emphasized the "warmth and affection with which people of French-speaking states, having a similar training, feel immediately at ease whenever they get together" (*Documents d'actualité internationale* 1982). This Francophone nucleus has a certain magnetic attraction, as a result of which an increasing number of African states participate in Francophone conferences: thirty-four attended the Eighth Conference in Paris in November 1981, and thirty-six in Kinshasa in October 1982.

Africa is often perceived as a chessboard on which the big powers advance their pawns. Yet, is Africa merely a stalled continent, a mere battleground for foreign troops? No, it would be far too simplistic to take into account only external factors. In fact, internal factors are also deeply ingrained. The bureaucracy, corruption, violations of human rights, dictatorial one-party states, the pressure of national debts—all these factors overburden African peoples and become increasingly oppressive. At the same time, African peoples no longer intend to remain history's outcasts, history's forgotten victims in the contemporary world. They would like to put an end to underdevelopment. They want to eat, to be educated, and to have proper health care. They aspire to be nonaligned. Yet nothing can be taken for granted. The very chances of solving these problems seem to retreat day after day.

Such is the way of the world, built as it is on wars and conflicts, out of which emerge the assertion by a people of its right to existence and happiness. On receiving the Nobel Prize, a man (who was both French and American) invites us to remain calm despite the disorders besieging Africa. Saint-John Perse advises us (December 10, 1960):

History's worst upheavals are merely seasonal rhythms in a vaster cycle of continuity and renewal. And the Furies rushing across history's stage, their flame held aloft, light up but an instant of an unending theme. Ripening civilizations die not of an autumn's battles, but merely change. Inertia alone threatens.

REFERENCES

Annuaire de l'Afrique et du Moyen-Orient, 1982: Les forces armées dans le monde. 1982. Paris: Groupe "Jeune Afrique."

Bressand, Albert, ed. 1981. *Coopération ou guerre économique (RAMSES, 1981).* Paris: Editions Economica.

Carrère d'Encausse, Helène. 1982. "Préface," in Charles Bertram, ed. *La menace soviétique.* Paris: Berger-Levrault.

Cornevin, Marianne. 1982. *La République sud-africaine.* Paris: P.U.F.

Cot, Jean-Pierre. 1982. "Dialogue avec Jean-Pierre Cot" [interview of Sept. 9, 1981], p. 23 in *Université et développement solidaire.* Paris: Berger-Levrault et Institut international d'Etudes sociales.

———. 1983. Speech delivered at the Sorbonne, January 21, unpublished.

Déclaration de Paris sur des sanctions contre l'Afrique du Sud (et déclaration spéciale sur la Namibie), 27 mai 1981. 1981. Paris: Centre des Nations Unies contre l'apartheid.

Diallo, Siradiou. 1982. "L'Afrique noire ne compte pas." *Jeune Afrique* 1110 (14 avril).

Documents d'actualité internationale. 1981, 1982, and 1983. Paris: Secrétariat général du gouvernement.

Hodges, Tony. 1980. "La Stratégie américaine et le conflit du Sahara occidental." *Le Monde diplomatique,* janvier.

Hoffmann, Stanley. 1982. *Une Morale pour les monstres froids; Pour une morale des relations internationales.* Paris: Editions du Seuil.

Jouve, Edmond. 1979. *Relations internationales du Tiers Monde et droit des peuples.* Paris: Berger-Levrault, 2d ed.

———. 1981. "L'Afrique, enjeu mondial: Le rôle de la France," p. 88 in *La France contre l'Afrique.* Paris: F. Maspero.

———, ed. 1983. *Un Tribunal pour les peuples.* Paris: Editions Berger-Levrault.

———. 1984. *L'Organisation de l'Unité africaine.* Paris: Presses universitaires de France.

Kontchou Kouomegni, Augustin. 1977. *Le Système diplomatique africain.* Paris: A. Pedone.

Kouriavtsev, Andrei. 1982. "La France dans le monde: un an après." *Economie mondiale et relations internationales,* no. 11.

Laïdi, Zaki. 1980. "L'U.R.S.S. et l'Afrique. Fatalité de l'échec ou dynamique de la puissance?" *Revue africaine de stratégie,* juillet, août, septembre.

———. 1982. "Problèmes de consolidation de linfluence soviétique en Afrique." *Politique africaine,* septembre.

Lemarchand, René. 1983. "Quelles indépendances?" *Le mois en Afrique,* février-mars.

Le Monde. October 12 and 22, 1982; January 28, 1983.

La Politique africaine du Général de Gaulle (1958–1969). 1980. Paris: Pedone.

Sahara info. 1981. Septembre-décembre.

Les Socialistes et le Tiers Monde; Eléments pour une politique socialiste de relations avec le Tiers Monde. 1977. Paris: Editions Berger-Levrault.

USA-Document. 1981. Septembre.

18

Reflections on a Continent in Crisis

DAVID B. ABERNETHY

A few years ago Art Buchwald, a source not normally quoted in academic circles, wrote an essay entitled "The Crisis Crisis." Behind Buchwald's humorous prose lay a serious argument: that the world appears to be experiencing so many crises—each of them serious, apparently intractable, and causally linked to others—that we can all too readily experience a severe case of crisis overload, rendering us unable to cope with any one crisis because all of them seem to converge on us at once. African policymakers, and students of developments in that continent, are particularly vulnerable to the symptoms of crisis overload, for Africa is surely experiencing far more than its fair share of serious and interconnected problems. Analysts of contemporary African affairs bear the intellectual responsibility of affirming the magnitude, urgency, and complexity of the continent's crises. At the same time analysts bear the moral responsibility of considering how crisis overload may be avoided, or if possible surmounted, by policies which give priority to the resolution of certain crises before other ones are confronted.

In this essay, intended in part commentary on and in part as summary and critique of the preceding essays in this volume, I should like to pose several sets of questions.

First, how has the term *crisis* been defined and employed? Have other situations which could also be considered critical for Africa's future been neglected, at the possible cost of underestimating the overall severity of the continent's "crisis crisis"?

Second, what appear to be the characteristics of those political or military crisis situations in which non-African actors have been heavily involved?

Third, who have been the significant non-African actors in the crisis situations being examined? If other problems were considered, would the cast of characters based outside the continent look different?

Fourth, how should we analyze the interactions among African and non-African actors in the creation, evolution, and resolution of crises?

Finally, how are the African policies of major non-African actors—particularly the two superpowers—affected by their global perspectives and interests? Does a global perspective on the part of a superpower—in a literal sense, its worldview—produce policies which in regional (African) terms are seriously flawed?

Another Kind of Crisis

How has the term *crisis* generally been employed in this volume? The editors have provided a clear and quite specific definition: "a situation of acute tension and/or armed conflict generated and precipitated by local indigenous factors, interacting with external influences, which threaten to engage, or actually have engaged, the involvement of the United States and the Soviet Union either directly, or indirectly through their surrogates" (p. 1). The editors' definition, and the case studies presented in this volume, focus our attention on conflicts in the political and military arena where violence is extensively used and where the means of destruction cross national—and often continental—boundaries. Such conflicts are dramatic, the suffering they inflict is quite visible, and they call urgently for diplomatic attention as African and non-African governments alike must decide whether and how to take sides in a particular dispute.

My quarrel with this operational definition of *crisis* is not that it is incorrect but that it is incomplete. Insufficient attention has been paid to a crisis in the economic and ecological arena which is less manifestly dramatic and violent than wars, rebellions, and coups but that in all likelihood directly and harmfully affects the lives of many more Africans, throughout the continent, than the conflicts discussed in this volume. High and still-rising rates of population growth, deterioration of fragile ecosystems on which farmers and herders are utterly dependent, widespread drought, central government neglect and/or exploitation of the rural populace, the priority given by governments to maintaining a relatively expensive, consumption-oriented political and bureaucratic class, and limited demand for many of Africa's exports in a world still attempting to extricate itself from recession—all of these factors converge and interact in complex ways to produce what might be termed a *creeping catastrophe*. In order to stave off an even more precipitous and life-threatening economic decline, the continent has been spending increasingly large proportions of its scarce resources on imports of petroleum and staple foods and repayment of previous debts—all items that, however necessary from a short-term perspective, do not increase the productive capacity required over the long term to reduce debt dependency and move Africa toward self-sustaining economic development.

A brief recitation of economic statistics should suffice to demonstrate the magnitude of the economic crisis. The gross regional product of sub-Saharan Africa (not including South Africa) grew only 1.6 percent per year per capita from 1960 through 1979; low-income African countries, accounting for over half the region's population, grew at the even more marginal pace of 0.9 percent (World Bank 1981, 143). During the somewhat longer 1960–82 period, ten of thirty-eight countries in the region for which data are available experienced negative per capita growth rates; six grew between 0 and 0.9 percent, nine between 1 and 1.9 percent, eight between 2 and 2.9 percent, and only five at 3 percent and over (World Bank 1983, 218, 276). A continent the vast majority of whose people work hard to feed themselves is increasingly unable to sustain food self-sufficiency: between 1969 and 1971 and 1980 and 1982 per capita food production fell between 1 and 10 percent in seven African countries, between 11 and 20 percent in sixteen, and by over 20 percent in four (World Bank 1984, 228). A fall of 20 percent per capita for the region as a whole between 1960 and the early 1980s is not improbable. And the decline continues into the mid–1980s, with severe drought affecting virtually the entire region outside the areas of traditionally heavy rainfall along the West African coast and in the Zaire basin (*Africa Report* 1984). Ethiopia is the best-publicized but hardly the only country to experience in 1985 the horrors of mass starvation.

Even if an analyst wished to examine only political/military crises in Africa, it would not be wise to ignore the relationship of such crises to the alarmingly steady deterioration of the productive sectors of the economy in so many parts of the continent. Clearly, economic decline has the potential of exacerbating competition among groups, classes, and countries for scarce public sector resources, particularly when the cost of failure in this competition could well be large-scale loss of life among the losers. Equally clearly, political and military crises exacerbate the economic crisis by diverting government expenditure from the means of economic construction to the means of destruction, by creating large numbers of refugees who can no longer produce the food they need to survive, and by rendering it difficult if not impossible for political elites to carry out the shift of resources from urban areas to the rural sector that is necessary if national development is to have any chance of success. An urgent future agenda for scholars and policymakers is to examine the multiple linkages between the crises discussed in this volume, on the one hand, and the signs that the African continent may be confronting in years ahead the tragic specter of perennial and widespread famine, on the other.

Decolonization Patterns and Crises

What characteristics of Africa's political/military problems tend to transform these problems into crises that attract external intervention? One such characteristic is a decolonization process deviating in significant ways from what might be termed the *typical* pattern. In the typical case, a linguistically diverse group of Africans is subjected to formal colonial rule by a European power, which imposes clear boundaries around a territory that it considers legally under its jurisdiction. Eventually an indigenous movement arises which comes to dominate the politics of the colony and which assumes power at independence, either as a result of an electoral process certifying that the movement is more popular than its rivals or as a result of a violent struggle in which the movement demonstrates greater strength and staying power than the colonial regime or its own domestic competitors. However unwillingly, the new regime then accepts the existing, externally imposed boundaries as the least harmful of available territorial alternatives, and its efforts at nation-building are based on the premise that the nation-to-be consists of the inhabitants of the artificial entity created by outsiders during the colonial period. This broad description applies to the majority of African experiences with decolonization. The typical pattern has become normative as well, in that politically active Africans have tended to assume that decolonization should proceed in the fashion described.

Political/military crises are apt to erupt when a country deviates in important respects from this pattern. Several examples should suffice. In South Africa, the de facto rulers for over seventy years have been whites deeply rooted in the country, not a European power, and Afrikaner nation-building has come to entail denial of membership in the South African polity to the vast majority of the resident population that does not have a white skin. Majority rule is anathema to the South African government, except under conditions where whites constitute the majority because blacks have been relegated to pseudostates recognized by no one outside of Pretoria. Central government authorities the world over try to undercut fissiparous political tendencies in order to retain power; the South African government is unique in fostering fissiparous tendencies through its encouragement of ethnic Bantustans so that the white minority may retain power. South Africa is in many respects the ultimate deviant case.

South African (not European) rule of Namibia, and the efforts of the South African government to deny majority rule and to stress the separateness of Namibia's ethnic and racial groups rather than their potential national unity, clearly deviate again from the norm. The crisis in Angola is related to the failure of a single nationalist movement to dominate African politics; a tripartite civil war, each party aided by outside actors, in turn prevented a popular referendum from taking place that might have determined, as in so many other parts of the continent, who would assume political power at independence.

In the Horn of Africa, both Ethiopia and Somalia differ from the typical pattern described above. Except for a few years under fascist Italy, Ethiopia was able to resist European colonial designs, and the boundaries of the multiethnic empire developed largely under the indigenous leadership of Menelik II are not necessarily accepted as valid by non-Amharic groups currently fighting for autonomy from the central government in Addis Ababa. Eritrea, a former Italian colony, might normally have been expected to evolve toward independence following a referendum on the matter. Instead, the United Nations proposed a vague federation between Eritrea and Ethiopia, an arrangement abrogated in its turn in 1962 when Haile Selassie announced the administrative absorption of Eritrea into the Ethiopian state. This unilateral action set off a violent and protracted struggle for Eritrean independence that has eluded African diplomatic efforts to resolve it. Somalia, a much more ethnically homogeneous state than most others in Africa and one which defines a precolonial Somali identity as the basis for nationhood, does not accept the legitimacy of colonially imposed boundaries that prevent Somalis in neighboring Ethiopia, Kenya, and Djibouti from becoming citizens of a Greater Somalia. This stance sets it on a collision course with its neighbors, particularly Ethiopia—and on a collision course with a basic premise of the Organization of African Unity (OAU). Accordingly there are only limited prospects for early resolution of conflicts in the Horn over national identities and national boundaries.

In northwest Africa, the struggle for the Western Sahara is again founded on an atypical decolonization pattern. Spain, the colonial ruler, decamped in 1976 and effectively turned over control of the territory to Morocco and Mauritania on the basis of the Madrid Accords. A popular referendum posing the option of territorial independence, to which Spain had earlier pledged itself, was never held. Moreover, Morocco claimed the Western Sahara (as it had claimed Mauritania almost two decades earlier) on the basis of the enlarged territorial boundaries of a monarchical state that existed long before the European colonial era and that remained a sovereign entity even while a French protectorate. The ability of Morocco—as of Ethiopia—to retain precolonial political structures during and after relatively brief interludes of European colonial rule rendered the Moroccan claim to the Western Sahara quite unusual.

Paradoxically, the cooperation among independent African states that is seen as the precursor of eventual continental unity may depend on the uniform acceptance of externally imposed colonial boundaries and the uniform rejection of claims to build African nations on a more authentically African basis, such as ethnic homogeneity (Somalia) or the conquests of a precolonial indigenous state (Morocco).

As the above examples indicate, decolonization that deviates significantly from the typical pattern tends to produce intense conflict both within African countries and among them. Territories where majority rule has been stymied by white minorities experience increasingly militarized conflict, as groups within the suppressed majority attempt to gain the rights of citizenship and

political participation which African populations enjoyed in the great majority of countries when these countries attained political independence. Such
conflicts have the effect of unifying African opinion throughout the continent
in support of the liberation struggle, but the struggle assumes crisis proportions because of the high capacity and will of white minorities to retain power
and the high economic and strategic stake of the Western powers in the territories controlled by these racial minorities.

Territories without a white minority problem which decolonize without
the opportunity for a political or military movement to gain clear majority
support, whose transition to independence is blocked by their neighbors' designs on them, or whose borders are disputed by neighbors on precolonial
grounds are likely to experience severe political/military conflicts as well. In
these cases continental public opinion is often divided over the legitimacy of
the contending political and legal claims, and this division of opinion tends to
transform a regional (continental) conflict into an internationalized crisis because purely African mechanisms for settling the conflict are immobilized.
Non-African actors are tempted to intervene in national self-determination
struggles when the nature and the rights of the national "self" are themselves
a matter of uncertainty and dispute among independent African states.

External Actors

A third question: What non-African actors play a significant role in exacerbating, managing, or resolving African crises? A natural tendency for
Americans examining any area of the world is first to inquire how their own
country affects and is affected by events in that area. And since the United
States is a superpower locked in contention with another superpower, it is
also understandable that Americans ask what role the Soviet Union plays in
those international crises that have some bearing on the American national
interest. The essays in this volume have been consistent with these tendencies,
focusing largely on U.S. government policies and actions toward African crisis areas, with some attention given the Soviet Union as an actor in its own
right and as part of a superpower system, both of whose members are obsessively concerned with halting the advance of the other's penetrative institutions and political/economic ideologies.

But to dwell at such length on these two non-African actors, even when
one criticizes as regionally inappropriate the globalist perspectives of one or
both of them, is ironically to fall victim to the very East-West mentality one
decries. Professor Jouve's essay reminds Americans that France, among several other Western European countries, was not so long ago a dominant foreign power on the African continent. The ex-colonial European powers, by
virtue of the enormous and in many ways profoundly formative impact of
their colonial policies on patterns of twentieth-century African economic
growth, international trade, state formation, recruitment of indigenous lead-

ership, and linguistic and religious development, are from any historical per-spective far more important non-African actors than the two quite recently arrived superpowers. European powers are more influential in African poli-tics than they may appear, because they have at their disposal so many mecha-nisms of informal influence deriving from the colonial era. Cases in point are the conferences cited by Jouve at which the French president and his top ad-visers met privately and at length with the heads of state of Francophone African countries. The national interests pursued by the Western European powers are not, to be sure, identical with the interests of the superpowers to their west or east. At the same time, the ex-colonial powers are clearly a part of the West that finds itself pitted against the East. In this respect the presence of Western Europeans in Africa—whether as technicians, soldiers, teachers, policy advisers to governments, or private entrepreneurs—means that West-ern leverage on Africa is considerably greater than that of the Eastern bloc. While the United States worries about Cuban troops in Africa, the Soviet Union presumably worries about French troops in Africa and the potential they and their allies (e.g., Morocco) have for retaining the continent as a largely European sphere of influence.

The significance of any given external actor is determined by the kind of crisis one is examining. It makes eminent sense to focus on the superpowers if a crisis is defined in political/military terms and if both the Americans and the Soviets directly and openly support opposing parties, as in the Horn of Af-rica. It makes less sense to focus exclusively on the superpowers when a con-flict involves non-African countries closely linked to one superpower or the other but presumably acting in their own interests as well, as with the Cubans in Angola or the French in Francophone Africa. In the Congo crisis of 1960–63 the United Nations was an important diplomatic and military actor, and U.N. forces and election monitors might play a key supervisory role in Nami-bian decolonization elections if South Africa were to decide to terminate its illegal occupation of the territory. If the African crisis is defined in economic and ecological terms, East-West superpower rivalry becomes even less rele-vant, in part because the Eastern bloc plays a minimal role in rural develop-ment and food aid activities, in part because a whole set of nonstate actors becomes critically important: international financial institutions like the In-ternational Monetary Fund (IMF) and the World Bank; U.N.–related institu-tions like the Food and Agricultural Organization, the World Food Pro-gramme, the International Fund for Agricultural Development, and the High Commission for Refugees; and international and private voluntary agencies such as Care, Caritas, Church World Service, Oxfam, and Save the Children. The large number of African political/military crises, combined with the magnitude and geographical scope of the economic/ecological crisis, virtu-ally ensure the involvement in African affairs of a large and varied cast of non-African actors. Who is on stage at any given time will depend on which part of the complicated dramatic script is being enacted at the time.

Even if one chooses to examine only the United States, it may make greater sense to imagine this country as several actors rather than only one. The U.S. government consists of bureaucratic institutions with quite different and potentially competitive foreign policy goals: for example, the Departments of State (within which the objectives of the Agency for International Development [AID] do not always coincide with those of the Foreign Service diplomats), Agriculture, Commerce, Defense, Eximbank, the Peace Corps, and the CIA. The foreign policy of the executive branch may be at loggerheads with the foreign policy of some parts of the legislative branch; witness the constant skirmishes between Assistant Secretary of State Chester Crocker and the Democratic-controlled House Subcommittee on Africa over the moral and pragmatic value of "constructive engagement" with South Africa. In a relatively decentralized political system, state and local governments may affect our foreign relations, as when some states or localities decide to withdraw public pension funds from corporations or banks investing in South Africa.

Given the importance of the private sector in a capitalist political economy, it should not be surprising to learn that U.S.-based private profit and nonprofit institutions conduct their own foreign policies—and that these policies are not necessarily identical with those of the U.S. government. Examples include:

- Corporations. Gulf Oil has pressed for American diplomatic recognition of Angola, in ironic contrast to the official stance of the Reagan administration which, on grounds of protecting private enterprise from communism, opposes formal recognition of the Popular Movement for the Liberation of Angola (MPLA).
- Banks. New York bank executives have interacted more openly with leaders of the outlawed African National Congress of South Africa than have American diplomats.
- Small private agencies. Many such agencies have contracted with AID for research or development work.
- Foundations. The Rockefeller Foundation has actively supported African institution-building efforts in higher education and agricultural research.
- Universities. Land-grant colleges and universities have extensive research, training, and project-administering responsibilities in Africa through Title XII of the Foreign Assistance Act.
- Policy-oriented, nonprofit interest groups. These include, for example, the American Committee on Africa, Transafrica, Bread for the World, Washington Committee on Africa, and the Association of Concerned Africanist Scholars.
- Religious organizations active in proselytizing work and/or developmental and famine relief efforts. Some of these organizations refuse to accept

U.S. government funding, in order to exercise maximum autonomy in setting their own priorities and administering their own programs.

• Secular organizations active in development and famine relief work. This category includes, for example, Care, Oxfam, Africare, and Save the Children. Some of these organizations utilize P.L. 480 resources, while others prefer to depend solely on nongovernmental funding sources.

Even a quick glance at this quite cursory listing of the U.S.–based public and private sector institutions active in Africa indicates the difficulty of referring to the policy or impact of the United States on Africa. The more centralized the political and economic system of a non-African actor, the more readily one may generalize about its African policy and the impact of that policy on Africa. The more politically decentralized, economically privatized, and culturally plural the non-African country, the more cautious one must be in offering such generalizations. It is easier, therefore, to speak of the policy of the Soviet Union—or even the policy of France—than of the policy of the United States with respect to African crises.

Factors in the Internationalization of a Crisis

How might we describe the process by which a political/military crisis within a given African state becomes internationalized? It is helpful, I believe, to understand this process as involving two analytically separate but mutually reinforcing dynamics: (1) pressures from external actors to intervene in a country's domestic affairs, which I shall term *external push* factors; and (2) invitations to external intervention from within the country by groups engaged in conflict with each other, each group finding itself in need of external alliances and resources if it is to gain or hold power against its domestic adversaries. These I shall term *internal pull* factors. Either external push or internal pull factors might be sufficient to internationalize a domestic crisis. Taken together, they increase the likelihood of internationalization and often, unfortunately, reduce the chances of peaceful conflict resolution.

Clearly, external push factors are powerfully at work in the postcolonial era. Neighboring and nearby African states, non-African governments, private sector agencies, and international organizations may all possess the capacity and the will to intervene in domestic African affairs in pursuit of their own interests. The major non-African countries such as the United States, the Soviet Union, and the ex-colonial European states have a particularly marked capacity to penetrate, as it were, the political, administrative, economic, and cultural space of African countries. These external actors are large, relatively wealthy countries with high levels of military spending, impressive intelligence-gathering apparatuses, control over substantial flows of aid, trade, and investment, well-trained cadres available to provide technical assistance, and large and relatively efficient diplomatic missions. African countries, in sharp contrast, are small, poor, marked by artificial and permeable borders, vulnerable in the extreme to world economic trends over which they have minimal control, and lacking the numbers of skilled and experienced citizens needed to implement their ambitious plans for economic development. It is hardly surprising that African states should often find themselves unable effectively to resist the pressures for compliant behavior exerted by external actors.

Add to external penetrative capacity the will of outside actors to use their capacity—whether to promote their national interests, gain access to raw materials and markets, preempt advances by their ideological rivals, spread their language and culture, export their model of political development and economic modernization, or some mix of these powerful motives—and one has a truly formidable set of external push factors.

One should not ignore, however, the second, or internal pull, dimension to the internationalization of African crises. When one domestic group is competing with others for political power and for the economic resources which are expected to accompany political power, the stakes of winning and losing are extremely high, while the domestic resources at the group's disposal for winning this competition are quite limited. It is easy to understand why the leaders of a group are tempted—and indeed may consider it necessary for sheer survival—to appeal to sympathetic outside actors for the military equipment, training, and personnel, publicity, diplomatic recognition, economic assistance, and so on, that are needed. The fact that strong external actors wish to manipulate weak domestic actors for their own ends does not obviate the fact that weak domestic actors also wish to manipulate strong external actors for their own ends. The result is a process of mutual manipulation by unequally powerful parties.

The Angola crisis of 1975–76 is a case in which both external push and internal pull factors are clearly at work, and in a mutually reinforcing manner. Non-African actors like the United States (or rather the executive branch of the government—not, as it turned out, the Congress), the People's Republic of China, the Soviet Union, and Cuba, and regional actors like Zaire and South Africa, possessed the capacity and the will to intervene actively in the complicated internal struggle among contending Angolan forces seeking to replace the Portuguese and take command of an independent Angolan state. The contestants in the tripartite civil war between the MPLA, the National Front for the Liberation of Angola (FNLA), and the National Union for the Total Independence of Angola (UNITA) in turn actively solicited military and diplomatic support from sympathetic non-Angolan patrons, for each movement believed that it could not win power without such external assistance. That belief only grew more intense as each movement observed its opponents relying on foreign patrons; the more any one side internationalized its support base, the more the other side felt compelled to follow suit. A lively debate has ensued over which foreign country "started" the escalation of the Angolan decolonization conflict from a civil war to a highly charged ideological and geopolitical confrontation between the superpowers. Whichever position one chooses to take in this debate, it should not obscure the fact, on which both sides could agree, that once external push and internal pull factors converged on one side of the struggle for power in Angola, it was inevitable that the same convergence pattern would develop for the other side, by the kind of logic that impels international arms races.

Efforts to deal with Africa's economic/ecological crisis demonstrate the same pattern of external push reinforced by internal pull, even though the actors are quite different from the foregoing example of a political/military crisis. Non-African actors may wish for a variety of reasons to provide development assistance and sponsor famine relief programs in hard-hit African countries. At the same time African governments, confronted with huge demands upon the political system and with limited domestic resources to meet these demands, can readily conclude that heavy reliance on non-African resources is a necessary condition for coping with the crisis facing them. Even when an African government wishes to move toward self-sufficient, internally integrated development, reducing the extent of openness and vulnerability to the world economy, that very effort may entail increased external dependence. A case in point is the Lagos Plan of Action for Food, a well-publicized document produced by the 1980 Special Economic Summit of the OAU. The Lagos Plan of Action is widely regarded as a blueprint for African self-reliance, in contrast with the World Bank's 1981 report, *Accelerated Development in Sub-Saharan Africa,* which urges increased integration into the global economy. The plan does indeed call for continental food self-sufficiency by the year 2000. But who is to foot the bill for a program authors estimate will cost at minimum $21 billion (in 1979 prices) from 1980 through 1985? On this crucial point, the plan notes cautiously that "it would be desirable to aim at financing at least 50% of the investment requirements with domestic resources" (Legum 1981, C 22–25). The wealthy outside countries from whose clutches the Lagos planners wish to extricate Africa's "open" economy are the very ones whose vastly increased economic intervention is in effect demanded by the "radical" proponents of continental self-reliance.

In the Angolan illustration of the mutual reinforcement of external push and internal pull factors, the involvement of non-African actors only magnified and intensified the crisis. The effort of each outside actor to prevent its rival from supporting the winner of the civil war increased the flow of arms to the country and the ensuing pattern of death and destruction. For their part, the contending domestic movements lost whatever incentive they might have had to compromise with their rivals, because external support was contingent on their carrying on the violent struggle and because their rivals were seen as having betrayed the national cause by accepting aid from morally unacceptable foreigners (Cuba and the Soviet Union in the case of the MPLA, South

Africa in the case of UNITA). It is less clear whether external involvement in Africa's economic crisis will have the net effect of magnifying this crisis as well. To the extent, however, that foreign aid serves as a substitute for rather than a spur to national self-reliance, it could reinforce the pattern of dependent nondevelopment from which Africa is currently suffering. In either illustration, it should be clear that the non-African role in African crisis management is not necessarily a salutary one and that it has considerable potential for accentuating rather than resolving crisis situations.

A special complication during periods of intense superpower rivalry is that each superpower, anxious to contain its rival but equally anxious to avoid a direct confrontation in which it might not be able to prevail over that rival, seeks to exert international influence indirectly through client states which it supports in the expectation that they will "independently" advance the superpower's interests. Each superpower further assumes that its rival acts in the same indirect fashion and exercises ultimate control over the foreign policy of client states which serve as mere proxies or surrogates for their powerful patron. Thus the U.S. government perceives Cuban military activity in Angola and Nicaragua as the not-terribly-subtle means by which Soviet power is extended in southern Africa and Central America, and Libyan activity in Chad and the Sudan as the instrument of aggressive, destabilizing Soviet foreign policy. In a quite similar way, the Soviet Union probably perceives France, Belgium, Israel, South Africa, Morocco, and Mobutu's Zaire as surrogates for the African interests of the capitalist hegemon, the United States.

Reliance on client states, and suspicion that the other side relies on them even more heavily, may be helpful in avoiding the cataclysmic collision between the great nuclear powers that the whole world anticipates with such dread. Nonetheless, there are serious risks of miscalculation if a great power relies too heavily upon a surrogate strategy. The client may have the ability and will to use the patron for its own purposes—Israel's relationship with the United States is noteworthy in this respect. And a superpower may be tempted directly to challenge and humiliate the much weaker client of its rival even while defining the rival's client as simply the instrument of the rival's aggressive international designs.

Globalism and U.S. Goals

The effectiveness of any government's foreign policy depends on many factors beyond its control. But a government does have the power to set the objectives against which the effectiveness of its policy may be measured. Other things being equal, the more ambitious and territorially far-reaching the objectives, the greater the likelihood that a government's policy will be adjudged a failure in some important respect, or at least that a government will find itself trying to attain contradictory goals or behaving in specific instances in ways that can be said to undermine rather than enhance the broad national interest. An issue discussed extensively in this volume is the tension between the highly ambitious and literally global objectives of the United States—which, as defined with particular clarity by the Reagan administration, are to contain and if possible reduce the influence of the Soviet Union in world affairs—and the objectives of the United States in a particular part of the world, the African region. Does the global East-West orientation of decision-makers in Washington produce regional decisions that run counter, not simply to African interests, but also to the regional (and by extension the global) interests of the United States? If this is the case, what can be done to reduce the tension between American global and regional goals in a manner most consistent with what one defines as the interests of Africans? Such questions are vitally important. The answers to them are likely to be contentious, if only because people can have quite different understandings of the nature, and degree of compatibility, of American and African interests.

A starting point in attempting an answer is to note that the tension between global and regional objectives is by no means unique to the United States. Since both superpowers seem obsessed with countering each other's influence, there is no inherent reason why Soviet foreign policy interests in Africa could not also be harmed by their application to Africa of the same kind of East-West mentality that is so widely held, in mirror image, among the globalists of the Reagan administration. And since the Soviet Union, no less than the United States, has a strongly held, self-righteous sense of the value and exportability of its modernization model, Moscow is at least as likely as Washington to experience failure when its model proves far less exportable—and nominal Marxist-Leninist clients in the Third World far less reliable—than anticipated. Advocates of the messianic foreign policies of powerful states, whether in their capitalist or communist forms, are bound sooner or later to be disillusioned.[1]

Great powers, moreover, are not the only ones whose actions are strongly influenced by a global perspective. Weak states in the Third World, whose leaders define international politics in North-South terms and seek a New International Economic Order to rectify past and present economic inequalities among nations, are acting on the basis of a clearly defined worldview, even if the two points of the compass to which they refer are different from the two points apparently guiding the superpowers. Even a regional issue may be perceived by the regional contestants as involving issues of global import. Thus many Africans in South Africa and throughout the continent view the struggle for liberation in South Africa and Namibia in broad historical terms, as the last decisive attack on doctrines and practices of white racial superiority that informed the worldwide spread of European colonialism during the

---

1. See Feinberg (1983) for a comprehensive and well-written analysis of the reasons why the domestic and foreign policies of Third World countries cannot for long be controlled by either the United States or the Soviet Union.

past five centuries. South Africa, in this sense, is not a mere regional issue; apartheid is a deep affront to every person of color wherever that person lives, and to the extent that apartheid is supported by capitalist powers outside of Africa, the struggle against apartheid becomes a struggle against a global political/economic system that stands to gain from the officially enforced exploitation of black labor in this particular country. For their part, South African officials define their struggle to undermine African nationalism as part of a worldwide battle against a "total onslaught" directed from Moscow. It would be quite inaccurate, therefore, to imagine that only global powers have global perspectives, while small countries within geographic regions have only regional foreign policies. In fact, tensions between global and regional objectives are potentially present in the foreign policies of all the world's formally sovereign states.

If one confines oneself to the particular way in which the United States experiences a more general foreign policy dilemma, it is worthwhile to ask whether the issue is well posed as one of globalism versus regionalism. Globalism, after all, refers to one's primary unit of analysis, not to the stance one takes toward that unit. It is therefore possible to be a reactionary, conservative, liberal, or radical globalist, defining American global interests in quite different ways—for example, in North-South rather than East-West terms, or in terms that encompass, as it were, all four cardinal points. In this respect, the debate over American foreign policy is over what *kind* of globalism is appropriate for this country, not whether we ought or ought not to have a globalist foreign policy at all. In its turn, regionalism poses severe definitional and conceptual problems, as Colin Legum has demonstrated. What exactly is the "region" whose conflicts, resources, and interests Americans need to take into account when formulating foreign policy: the continent of Africa, its sub-Saharan portion, or a portion of the sub-Sahara such as "west" or "southern" Africa or the eastern Horn? Perhaps the region encompasses parts of Africa and parts of neighboring continents, as when strategists refer to the "arc of crisis" stretching from the Horn through the Middle East to southwest Asia. Legum convincingly argues that the concept of regionalism is situational: the nature and geographical scope of a crisis will determine the location and size of the area toward which a recognizable regional policy will apply.[2] Because crisis situations vary in their nature and scope, so will regions vary. And because one can never be sure in advance what the appropriate

2. Similar comments could be made about other world regions. Writing of the area now widely known as Southeast Asia, Milton Osborne (1983, 12) notes: "For the most part . . . neither the foreigners who worked in Southeast Asia before the Second World War, whether as scholars or otherwise, nor the indigenous inhabitants of the countries of Southeast Asia, thought about the region in general terms. The general tendency to do so came with the Second World War when, as a result of military circumstances, the concept of a Southeast Asian region began to take hold."

geographical unit of analysis will be for a particular crisis, regionalism cannot be touted as a viable foreign policy alternative to globalism.

These caveats, however necessary to avoid confusion when describing, analyzing, or prescribing American foreign policy, do not cause the foreign policy problems considered in this volume to disappear; rather, they simply call for a more precisely honed formulation of the American foreign policy dilemma. That formulation might read as follows: the United States, as a military superpower and as a wealthy state increasingly dependent for the maintenance of its high standard of living on access to raw materials and markets located in other countries, possesses an unusually high level of capacity and will to influence events throughout the world. Inevitably, therefore, its policymakers will consider the implications for its global power position of a policy developed toward any particular part (region) of the world. Given a rivalry with the Soviet Union that has a national security as well as an ideological dimension, American policymakers will inevitably consider the implications for the relative balance of American and Soviet power of a policy developed toward a particular region. There is no escaping globalist thinking of this sort; indeed, one might consider foreign policymakers in Washington (or in Moscow, for that matter) derelict in their duty if they did not go through such thinking exercises when deciding whether and how to act when confronted with a regional crisis.

The issue for the regional specialist is to determine whether a given American policy is consistent with America's regional goals and with the perceived interests of the governments and people in the region as well as with America's global interests as described above. Unless it can be shown that a policy favoring the goals of the United States in one region of the world would harm its interests in another region, a reasonable presumption is that the advancement of its regional goals is consistent with, and may even advance, its global interests. Regional goals may be and often are defined in positive terms—for example, fostering rapid, equitable, self-sustaining economic development, enhancing national self-determination, or affirming basic human rights—in contrast to the largely negative, containment-oriented rationale for global goals.

Given that global as well as regional goals will—and should be—considered when the United States formulates regional policy, the question arises whether the process of policy formulation should consider first the global and then the regional factor or whether regional objectives should be examined before global ones. Starting the process from a global perspective is likely to produce defective results for two reasons, in my judgment. First, globalists are generalists whose knowledge of a particular regional crisis is likely to be sketchy and derivative and whose application of general principles to a particular case can easily prove faulty and even counterproductive. Second, the largely negative, stop-the-Soviet-Union mentality of the globalists can by a kind of ideological Gresham's Law drive out the more positively phrased objectives of the regional specialists. The danger of starting the process of policy formulation from a regional perspective—namely, that regionalists lack knowledge of, or sensitivity to the "big picture" and will be unable to transcend their regional biases—is undoubtedly present. But it is more likely that the regional specialist will be aware of the big picture than that the global generalist will be aware of the complexities of the "little picture," and it is after all to the little picture that both individuals must direct their gaze. If the ideological Gresham's Law noted above does operate, it is preferable that objectives which the United States ought to support, as consistent with its own highest values, be considered first, before the more negative and emotionally more powerful objectives of countering the other superpower are brought into the discussion.

My objection to the Africa policy of the Reagan administration is not that it is globalist but that its globalism is of a type that inhibits and at times prevents realization of the positive goals for the African continent which it is in both the American and, as I perceive it, the African interest to support. Global considerations defined overwhelmingly in anti-Soviet terms take temporal and qualitative precedence over regional considerations that are normally defined in positive terms: support for economic development, national self-determination, and basic human rights. Ironically, the application to Africa of a reflexive anti-Soviet globalism gives a significant advantage to the Soviet Union, for it allows the Soviets to define the issues and take sides in regional conflict situations, determining in effect what our own policy, developed to counter theirs, will be. An American policy driven by determined opposition to whatever Moscow and its surrogates do and say can in this sense be "made in Moscow" fully as much as a policy that is reflexively pro-Soviet. Put differently, anti-Soviet globalism is not identical with pro-American globalism and may often be inconsistent with or even antithetical to pro-American regionalism. Thus, Washington's suspicion of the South West Africa People's Organization (SWAPO) and the ANC on grounds that they are Soviet- or Cuban-backed makes it difficult for us to see that they are, first and foremost, movements for African national liberation. If we paid closer attention to their domestic objectives and to their likely foreign policy behavior once in power, and defined them less in terms of their current external support system (itself largely a function of the absence of alternatives, as Western powers have proven unwilling to break with repressive minority-rule interests in South Africa), we might be able to develop a creative regional foreign policy that at the same time undercuts Soviet military assistance because such assistance is rendered unnecessary. A pro-American rather than a reflexively anti-Soviet policy could mean that we would occasionally find ourselves on the same side as the Soviet Union in a regional dispute. Such a result, far from proving that we adopted the wrong policy, might provide a rare instance in which superpower involvement in African affairs helped to resolve a dispute rather than exacerbate it.

Conclusions

At the outset of this essay I argued that analysts of the contemporary African scene have a moral obligation to supplement their analyses with proposals for creatively addressing the continent's "crisis crisis." The following guidelines, which are admittedly easier to state in the abstract than to apply to specific situations, and which derive from my own values and biases as well as from my analysis of the nature and causes of African crises, constitute an effort to meet this obligation. These proposals are addressed primarily to non-African government policymakers.

1. Given a large number and range of crises, priority should be given to the crisis in which (a) the largest number of people is suffering and dying, and (b) external intervention is least likely to intensify the problem. Africa's economic/ecological crisis places many more lives in jeopardy than its political/military crises; and it is less likely that externally funded famine relief and developmental activity would intensify the continent's economic problems, and more likely that external military and diplomatic support for the contestants in political/military conflicts would only render such conflicts more intractable. For these two reasons, the economic/ecological crisis should be given priority.

2. External responses to the economic/ecological crisis should as far as possible serve as a spur to African self-reliance rather than as a substitute for it. To the extent that self-reliance is aided by small-scale, inexpensive, grassroots efforts that minimize the diversion of scarce resources into donor and recipient bureaucracies, private voluntary agencies adopting this approach should be officially encouraged to expand their operations. Such an expansion might, of course, bring about the very bureaucratization of operations that the most effective peasant associations and private voluntary agencies have managed thus far to avoid. All parties should be acutely sensitive to the danger that rewards to organizations for past success in the development enterprise might become the unintended guarantors of subsequent failure.

3. External governmental actors should not hesitate to challenge official policies that exacerbate Africa's economic problems. It is unhelpful to debate whether outside governments or African governments are at fault here; a reasonable presumption is that *both* sets of governments bear some responsibility and that each should be pressured to act where its responsibility for problems can be identified. In the case of non-African governments, this means greater attention to measures increasing the volume and value of raw materials and manufactured goods imported from Africa; in the case of African governments, this means a range of policies (including price-setting for staple foods) that would improve domestic rural/urban terms of trade. African and non-African governments alike should devote much higher priority to family planning programs, in view of the potential of high and rising population growth rates literally to eat up modest output gains and to place fragile ecosystems at risk.

4. With respect to political/military crises, external push factors are so likely to accentuate conflicts within Africa featuring internal pull factors that any action limiting the interventionist role of non-African actors is likely to be beneficial. Since it is not feasible to expect self-restraint on the part of one external actor if its principal rival fails to practice comparable self-restraint, the key is to develop informal norms if not formal codes of mutual nonintervention. A function of the OAU might be to work quietly with the major powers to develop such norms or codes, and to appoint widely respected African political or intellectual leaders to examine and publicize instances in which non-Africans have violated them. The odds are against success in a venture of this sort—not least because Africans can apply so few sanctions against powerful outsiders who refuse to practice self-restraint. But the need for a concerted African effort to limit the external push factor is sufficiently urgent that the effort should be persistently made despite the obstacles in its way.

5. To the extent that a domestic or interstate crisis is due to a decolonization pattern deviating from the one typical of most African states, efforts by the OAU to identify the deviation and to make explicit the criteria of "proper" decolonization which are derivable from the typical pattern might help to clarify the issues at stake and provide a normative basis for crisis resolution. The OAU might be able to exert diplomatic pressure on non-African states militarily supporting an African regime that is unwilling, for instance, to permit or to accept the results of a pre-independence referendum in a neighboring territory formerly ruled by a European power. Such pressure could be applied against the United States in the case of Morocco's claims to the Western Sahara and against the Soviet Union in the case of Ethiopia's absorption of Eritrea.

6. To the extent that crises caused by the refusal of white minority groups to share political power are intensified and prolonged by flows of external economic resources to the minority-controlled public or private sector, these flows may be said actively to cause harm. A reduction in these flows until serious measures in the direction of majority rule are undertaken can be justified not as a matter of doing good but rather as a means of avoiding harm. A reasonable moral norm is that the responsibility to avoid doing harm takes precedence over the responsibility actively to do good. In this respect, a policy priority of Western governments, banks, and corporations should be to reduce trade, investment, and loan flows to South Africa. Willingness of the Pretoria regime to allow a pre-independence referendum in Namibia and to halt policies which in effect render South African blacks stateless could then lead to an increased flow of economic resources. This proposal is, of course, extremely difficult to implement, because so many public and private sector external actors are involved and because their short-term self-interest dictates maintenance of the political and economic status quo in South Africa.

7. Decisions by powerful non-African governments on whether and how to intervene in an African crisis will inevitably have to take into account factors specific to the country or countries in which the crisis is located and, at the other end of the scale, the non-African government's global concerns, interests, and strategies. The tendency of globalist analysis and prescription to override regionalist and country-specialist thinking suggests that whenever possible assessments of a crisis should commence at the country and then regional level and conclude with global considerations. A decision-making process that proceeds upward by induction from the particulars of a crisis is likely to produce fewer counterproductive results than a process proceeding downward by deduction from first principles.

As with the other guidelines, this one is difficult to implement, because global generalists tend to be located at the top of the foreign policy hierarchy, while regional and country specialists are apt to occupy less influential, middle-level positions. A bureaucratic hierarchy is eventually judged, however, by the quality of its policies. If adopted, this recommendation might improve the ability of external bureaucracies to cope effectively with African crises, to the benefit of non-Africans and Africans alike.

REFERENCES

Africa Report. 1984. July-August (issue on African drought).

Feinberg, Richard. 1983. *The Intemperate Zone: The Third World Challenge to U.S. Foreign Policy.* New York: Norton.

Legum, Colin, ed. 1981. "Plan of Action for Food," in *Africa Contemporary Record, 1980–81.* New York: Africana Publishing Company.

Osborne, Milton. 1983. *Southeast Asia: An Introductory History.* 2d ed. Sydney: George Allen and Unwin.

World Bank. 1981. *Accelerated Development in Sub-Saharan Africa: An Agenda for Action.* Washington, D.C.

———. 1984. *World Development Report.* Washington, D.C.

List of Acronyms

ACP	African, Caribbean, and Pacific countries
AID	[United States] Agency for International Development (also called USAID)
ANC	African National Congress
BET	Borku-Ennedi-Tibesti prefecture
CDR	Conseil Démocratique Revolutionnaire
CIA	[United States] Central Intelligence Agency
CNL	Comité National de Libération
COMECON	Council for Mutual Economic Assistance
CPSU	Communist Party of the Soviet Union
DTA	Democratic Turnhalle Alliance
EEC	European Economic Community
FAN	Forces Armées du Nord
FAP	Forces Armées Populaires
FAR	Forces Armées Royales
FLNC	National Front for the Liberation of the Congo
FMS	Foreign Military Sales
FNLA	National Front for the Liberation of Angola
FRELIMO	Front for the Liberation of Mozambique
Frolinat	Front de Libération National Tchadien
FY	Fiscal Year
GUNT	Transitional National Union Government
IMF	International Monetary Fund
IOJ	International Organization of Journalists
MDC	Multilateral Development Council
MNR	Resistencia Nacional Moçambicana (Mozambique National Resistance Movement)
MPC	Multi-Party Conference
MPLA	Popular Movement for the Liberation of Angola (Movimento Popular de Libertação de Angola)

341

NATO	North Atlantic Treaty Organization
NNF	Namibian National Front
OAU	Organization of African Unity
OECD	Organisation for Economic Co-operation and Development
PCP	Portuguese Communist Party
Polisario	Popular Front for the Liberation of Sequiet el Hamra and Río de Oro
RDF	[United States] Rapid Deployment Force
SACP	South African Communist Party
SACTU	South African Congress of Trade Unions
SACU	Southern African Customs Union
SADB	Southern African Development Bank
SADCC	Southern African Development Coordination Conference
SADR	Saharan Arab Democratic Republic
SMTF	Société Minière du Tenge-Fungurume
SNEC	[United States] Subnuclear Export Committee
SWANU	South West African National Union
SWAPO	South West Africa People's Organization
TPLF	Tigré People's Liberation Front
UNITA	National Union for the Total Independence of Angola (União Nacional para a Independencia Total de Angola)
UNT	Union Nationale Tchadienne
UPA	Union of Angolan Peoples
USAID	United States Agency for International Development (also called AID)
USFP	Socialist Union of Popular Forces
WFTU	World Federation of Trade Unions
WIDF	Women's International Democratic Federation
WIGMO	Western International Ground Maintenance Organization
WNLA	Witwatersrand Native Labor Association
WPC	World Peace Council
WSLF	Western Somali Liberation Front
ZANU	Zimbabwe African National Union
ZAPU	Zimbabwe African People's Union

The Contributors

DAVID B. ABERNETHY ("Reflections on a Continent in Crisis") is Professor of Political Science at Stanford University. Educated at Harvard and Oxford universities, he is the author of *The Political Dilemma of Popular Education: An African Case,* based on fieldwork in Nigeria, and of articles dealing with church and state in African education, the role of bureaucracy in African economic development, patterns of decolonization in southern Africa, and other subjects. He served as Visiting Lecturer at University College, Dar es Salaam, Tanzania, in 1968–69.

GERALD J. BENDER ("American Policy toward Angola: A History of Linkage") is professor in the School of International Relations at the University of Southern California. He is the author of *Angola Under the Portuguese: The Myth and the Reality,* and many articles on Angola, South Africa, and U.S. policy toward Africa. Educated at the University of Minnesota and the University of California, Los Angeles, he has taught at UCLA and UC San Diego. In 1971–74 he was Director of the Interdisciplinary Research Program on Angola, Mozambique, and Guinea-Bissau at UCLA. Since 1979 he has been an Associate Professor in the School of International Relations at the University of Southern California. In November 1985 he assumes the presidency of the African Studies Association.

JAMES S. COLEMAN ("Introduction") was Professor of Political Science and founding Director of International Studies and Overseas Programs at the University of California, Los Angeles. His publications include *Nigeria: Background to Nationalism*, *Politics of the Development Areas* (co-author and co-editor), and *Political Parties and National Integration in Tropical Africa* (co-author and co-editor). Educated at Brigham Young University and Harvard, he was a member of the Department of Political Science, UCLA, from 1953 to 1965 and 1978 to 1985. He was Rockefeller Foundation Representative in East Africa from 1967 to 1974 and in Zaire from 1972 to 1978. He was also a past president of the African Studies Association.

PETER DUIGNAN ("Africa from a Globalist Perspective") is Director of the African and Middle East Program, Curator of African Collections, and a Senior Fellow of the

Hoover Institution at Stanford University. Educated at the University of San Francisco (B.A.) and Stanford University (M.A. and Ph.D.), he began teaching at Stanford in 1955. His publications include *Colonialism in Africa,* 5 vols., and, as co-author with L. H. Gann, *African Proconsuls: European Governors in Africa, The Rulers of British Africa, 1870–1914, Africa South of the Sahara: The Challenge to Western Security,* and *The Middle East and North Africa: The Challenge to Western Security.*

WILLIAM J. FOLTZ ("United States Policy toward South Africa: Is One Possible?") is Professor of Political Science at Yale University and Director of the Yale Center for International and Area Studies. His publications include *From French West Africa to the Mali Federation, Nation-building* (co-editor), *Resolving Conflict in Africa,* and articles on international and communal conflict. He received his doctorate at Yale and served as Senior Fellow and Director of the Africa Project of the Council on Foreign Relations. He is Associate Director of the Southern Africa Research Program at Yale and has served in various teaching and research capacities at Makerere University College, the University of Cape Town, and Christian Michelsen's Institute in Bergen.

TONY HODGES ("At Odds with Self-Determination: The United States and Western Sahara") is currently Africa Editor at The Economist Intelligence Unit in London. A former analyst of African affairs at International Reporting Information Systems in Washington, D.C., he has written widely about Africa, specializing in the ex-Portuguese and ex-Spanish colonies. He is the author of *Western Sahara: The Roots of a Desert War* (1984), *Historical Dictionary of Western Sahara* (1982), and, with Colin Legum, *After Angola: The War Over Southern Africa* (1976). Educated at Oxford University, he conducted research on Western Sahara from 1978 to 1981 under a Ford Foundation grant.

ANNE FORRESTER HOLLOWAY ("Congressional Initiatives on South Africa") is Staff Director of the House Subcommittee on Africa, U.S. Congress. She was Legislative Assistant to Congressman Andrew Young 1975–77, Special Assistant to the U.S. Ambassador to the United Nations 1977–79, Ambassador to Mali in 1979–81, and Senior Research Fellow at the TransAfrica Forum 1981–82. Educated at Bennington College, Howard University, and Union Graduate School, she has taught at Howard University and the State University of New York at Buffalo. Her publications include a number of contributions to journals and anthologies.

ALLEN F. ISAACMAN ("Mozambique: Tugging at the Chains of Dependency") is Professor of History and Afro-American and African Studies at the University of Minnesota and taught Mozambican history at the Universidade Eduardo Mondlane of Maputo, Mozambique, from 1978 to 1980. His publications include *Mozambique: The Africanization of a European Institution: The Zambesi Prazos, 1750–1902; The Tradition of Resistance in Mozambique: Anti-Colonial Struggle in the Zambesi Valley, 1810–1921; A Luta Continua: Creating a New Society in Mozambique; Society, Economy and Politics in Southern Africa* (co-editor); and *Mozambique: From Colonialism to Revolution: 1900–1982,* with Barbara Isaacman. He was educated at City College of New York and the University of Wisconsin, and is currently Chair of the Joint SSRC-ACLS Africa Committee.

EDMOND JOUVE ("France and Crisis Areas in Africa") is Professor of Political Science at the University of Paris I (Panthéon-Sorbonne) and Director of the Centre d'Etudes et de Recherches sur le Désarmement. He was the cofounder of the *Annuaire du Tiers Monde*, the Association française pour l'etude du Tiers Monde (AFETI-MON), the Association française de recherches sur la paix (ARESPA), the Institut France-Tiers Monde, and the Institut international d'études diplomatiques (IN-EDIP). His publications include *Relations internationales du Tiers Monde et droit des peuples, Ordre ou désordre internationale?, Pour un droit des peuples* (co-editor), *Un tribunal pour les peuples* (editor), *Le Tiers Monde dans la vie internationale*, and *L'aide alimentaire fournie par la France et la CEE au Tiers Monde* (editor).

EDMOND J. KELLER ("United States Foreign Policy on the Horn of Africa: Policy-making with Blinders On") is Professor of Political Science an : Associate Dean of the Graduate Division of the University of California, Santa Barbara. Educated at Louisiana State University and the University of Wisconsin, Madison, he served as Research Associate at the Institute for Development Studies at the University of Nairobi in 1972–73 and at the Bureau of Educational Research in Nairobi in 1975; as Visiting Research Fellow with the U.N. Economic Commission for Africa in 1976–77; and as Professor of Political Science and member of the African Studies Faculty at Indiana University prior to his move to Santa Barbara in 1983. He is the author of *Education, Manpower and Development: The Impact of Educational Policy in Kenya, Revolutionary Ethiopia* (in progress), and many articles and reviews in professional journals.

COLIN LEGUM (Introduction to Part IV) is editor of the *Africa Contemporary Record* and joint editor of the *Middle East Contemporary Survey*. Until 1982 he was an associate editor of *The Observer,* London. He is the publisher of the weekly syndicated *Third World Reports*. His many published works include *Congo Disaster, The Western Crisis over South Africa, The Horn of Africa in Continuing Crisis, Crisis and Conflicts in the Middle East, The Changing Strategy from Iran to Afghanistan* (editor), and *Africa in the 1980's: A Continent in Crisis* (which has now been translated into Chinese).

RENÉ LEMARCHAND ("The Crisis in Chad") is Professor of Political Science at the University of Florida. He received his B.A. from Southwestern College in Memphis, Tennessee, and his M.A. and Ph.D. from the University of California, Los Angeles. He has written extensively on French-speaking Africa and is currently writing a book on Chad. His work on *Rwanda and Burundi* (1970) received the Herskovits Award from the African Studies Association (ASA) in 1971. He has served as Director of the African Studies Center at the University of Florida from 1963 to 1966, and more recently as a member of the Board of Directors of the ASA. He also served as a development consultant to Litton Industries, the World Bank, and USAID. He taught at the Ecole Nationale d'Administration (ENA) in Rabat in 1980, and at the University of Zimbabwe in 1983, and has lectured on behalf of the United States Information Agency in Gabon, Cameroon, Congo, Rwanda, Niger, Mali, and Senegal.

SAM C. NOLUTSHUNGU ("South African Policy and United States Options in Southern Africa"), is Lecturer in Government at the University of Manchester in England. He is the author of *South Africa: A Study of Ideology and Foreign Policy* and *Changing South Africa: Political Considerations.* He was born and raised in South Africa but completed his university education in Britain. He has held university appointments in Nigeria, Canada, and the United States.

NZONGOLA-NTALAJA ("United States Policy toward Zaire") is Professor of Political Economy in the African Studies and Research Program, Howard University. His publications include *Class Struggles and National Liberation in Africa: Essays on the Political Economy of Neocolonialism,* and numerous contributions to professional journals and symposium volumes. Educated at Davidson College, the University of Kentucky, and the University of Wisconsin, Madison, he has taught at the Free University of the Congo, the National University of Zaire in Lubumbashi, the University of Wisconsin at Madison, Atlanta University, and the University of Maiduguri, Nigeria.

DONALD K. PETTERSON ("Somalia and the United States, 1977–83: The New Relationship") is currently with the U.S. State Department in Washington, D.C. He was Ambassador to Somalia from 1978 to 1983, and Visiting Distinguished Scholar at the African Studies Center, University of California at Los Angeles, for a year prior to his present assignment. Educated at the University of California, Santa Barbara and Los Angeles, he has held foreign service posts in Mexico City, Zanzibar, Lagos, Freetown, and Pretoria; served on the Policy Planning Staff of the U.S. State Department 1975–77; as Director of South African Affairs 1977–78; and as Deputy Assistant Secretary of State 1978.

ROBERT M. PRICE ("Creating New Political Realities: Pretoria's Drive for Regional Hegemony") is Associate Professor of Political Science at the University of California, Berkeley. He is the author of *Society and Bureaucracy in Contemporary Ghana, U.S. Foreign Policy in Sub-Saharan Africa: National Interest and Global Strategy,* and numerous contributions to professional journals and symposium volumes. He was educated at Harpur College and University of California, Berkeley.

ROBERT I. ROTBERG ("Namibia and the Crisis of Constructive Engagement") is Professor of Political Science and History at the Massachusetts Institute of Technology, and Editor of the *Journal of Interdisciplinary History.* His publications include *Namibia: Political and Economic Prospects, Suffer the Future: Policy Choices of Southern Africa,* and other books and articles on African politics and history. He was educated at Oberlin, Princeton, and Oxford, taught at Harvard, and is leader of a special study group at the Center for International Affairs at Harvard.

BEREKET H. SELASSIE ("The American Dilemma on the Horn") is Professor of Law and Politics at Howard and Georgetown universities. He is the author of *The Executive in African Governments, Conflict and Intervention in the Horn of Africa, Behind the War in Eritrea,* and many articles in professional journals. Educated at the Universities of London and Hull, he was a founding member and first Chairman of the Eritrean Relief Association (ERA), former Attorney General of Ethiopia, Mayor of Harar, Ethiopia, and Vice-Minister of the Interior.

RICHARD L. SKLAR ("Introduction") is Professor of Political Science at the University of California, Los Angeles, and recent past president of the African Studies Association. His publications include *Nigerian Political Parties: Power in an Emergent African Nation, Corporate Power in an African State: The Political Impact of Multinational Mining Companies in Zambia,* and numerous contributions to symposium volumes and professional journals. He was educated at the Universities of Utah and Princeton, and has taught at Brandeis University, the University of Ibadan, the University of Zambia, and the State University of New York at Stony Brook.

HOWARD E. WOLPE ("The Dangers of Globalism") has been a congressman from Michigan since 1978. Currently he is the Chairman of the Subcommittee on Africa of the House Foreign Affairs Committee. His publications include *Nigeria: Modernization and the Politics of Communalism* (co-author and co-editor) and *Urban Politics in Nigeria: A Study of Port Harcourt,* as well as articles in professional journals. Educated at Reed College and the Massachusetts Institute of Technology, he taught political science at Western Michigan University. From 1973 to 1976 he was a member of the Michigan State Legislature, and from 1977 to 1978 he was Regional Representative to U.S. Senator Donald Riegle of Michigan.

CRAWFORD YOUNG ("The Zairian Crisis and American Foreign Policy") is Professor of Political Science at the University of Wisconsin, Madison, and is currently a Fellow at the Woodrow Wilson International Center for Scholars at the Smithsonian Institution in Washington, D.C. He is also a recent past president of the African Studies Association. His publications include *Politics in the Congo, The Politics of Cultural Pluralism, Cooperatives and Development* (as co-author), and *Ideology and Development in Africa.* He received his doctorate at Harvard. He served as Chair of the African Studies Program 1964–68, Associate Dean of the Graduate School 1968–71, and Chair of the Department of Political Science 1969–72 at the University of Wisconsin, Madison. In 1965–66 he was Visiting Professor at Makerere University College, and from 1973–75 he was Dean of the Social Science Faculty at the National University of Zaire.

Index

81–82, 93, 301; 1966–80 armed
struggle in, 14, 139–140; chromium
and nickel produced by, 33; British
policy toward, 51, 56; Zimbabwe-
Mozambique oil pipeline, 60; as
African Front Line state, 117; and
SADCC, 140; independence,
140–141; exports through Mozambican vs. South African ports, 140,

143–144; and MNR destruction,
143–144; troops sent to Mozambique,
148; dependence on the West, 289.
See also Rhodesia
Zimbabwe African National Union
   (ZANU), 70, 139
Zoabstad, 141
Zouar, 242n, 247

PUBLICATIONS

PUBLICATIONS OF THE AFRICAN STUDIES CENTER, UCLA

DeWilde, John (ed.), *Agriculture, Marketing and Pricing in Sub-Saharan Africa* (Joint publication of the Crossroads Press and African Studies Center, 1984).

Kalb, Marion, and Jamie Monson (eds.), *Women as Food Producers: A Development Perspective* (Joint publication of the Crossroads Press, the African Studies Center, and the Overseas Education Fund, 1985).

Siegel, Eric R. (ed.), *A Bibliography for the Study of African Politics*, Volume III (Joint publication of the Crossroads Press and African Studies Center, 1983).

Yoder, Stanley P. (ed.), *African Healing Systems* (Crossroads Press, with UCLA African Studies Center and the Charles R. Drew Post-Graduate Medical School, 1983).

PUBLICATIONS OF THE CENTER FOR INTERNATIONAL AND STRATEGIC AFFAIRS, UCLA

Brito, Dagobert L., Michael D. Intriligator, and Adele E. Wick (eds.), *Strategies for Managing Nuclear Proliferation: Economic and Political Issues* (Lexington: Lexington Books, 1983).

Brodie, Bernard, Michael D. Intriligator, and Roman Kolkowicz (eds.), *National Security and International Stability* (Cambridge, Mass.: Oelgeschlager, Gunn, and Hain, 1983).

Jabber, Paul, *Not by War Alone: Security and Arms Control in the Middle East* (Berkeley: University of California Press, 1981).

Jones, Rodney, Cesare Merlini, Joseph Pilat, and William Potter (eds.) *The Nuclear Suppliers and Nonproliferation: Dilemmas and Policy Choices* (Lexington, Mass.: Lexington Books, 1985).

Kolkowicz, Roman, and Andrzej Korbonski (eds.), *Soldiers, Peasants, and Bureaucrats* (Winchester, Mass.: Allen & Unwin, 1982).

Kolkowicz, Roman, and Neil Joeck (eds.), *Arms Control and International Security* (Boulder, Colo.: Westview Press, 1984).

Luciani, Giacomo (ed.), *The Mediterranean Region: Economic Interdependence and the Future of Society* (London and Canberra: Croom Helm; New York: St. Martin's Press, 1984).

Potter, William C., *Nuclear Power and Nonproliferation: An Interdisciplinary Perspective* (Cambridge, Mass.: Oelgeschlager, Gunn, and Hain, 1982).

Potter, William C. (ed.), *Verification and Arms Control* (Lexington, Mass.: Lexington Books, 1985).

Potter, William C. (ed.), *Verification and SALT* (Boulder, Colo.: Westview Press, 1980).

Ramberg, Bennett, *Destruction of Nuclear Energy Facilities in War: The Problem and Implications* (Lexington, Mass.: Lexington Books, 1980); revised and reissued as *Nuclear Power Plants as Weapons for the Enemy: An Unrecognized Military Peril* (Berkeley: University of California Press, 1984).

Ramberg, Bennett, *Global Nuclear Energy Risks: The Search for Preventive Medicine* (Boulder, Colo.: Westview Press, 1984).

Spiegel, Steven L. (ed.), *The Middle East and the Western Alliance* (London: Allen & Unwin, 1982).

Thomas, Raju G. C. (ed.), *The Great Power Triangle and Asian Security* (Lexington, Mass.: Lexington Books, 1983).

Tschirgi, R. D., *The Politics of Indecision: Origins and Implications of American Involvement with the Palestine Problem* (New York: Praeger, 1983).

Valenta, Jiri, and William Potter (eds.), *Soviet Decisionmaking for National Security* (Winchester, Mass.: Allen & Unwin, 1984).